ATLAS OF
GLOBAL STRATEGY

ATLAS OF GLOBAL STRATEGY

Lawrence Freedman

Facts On File Publications
New York

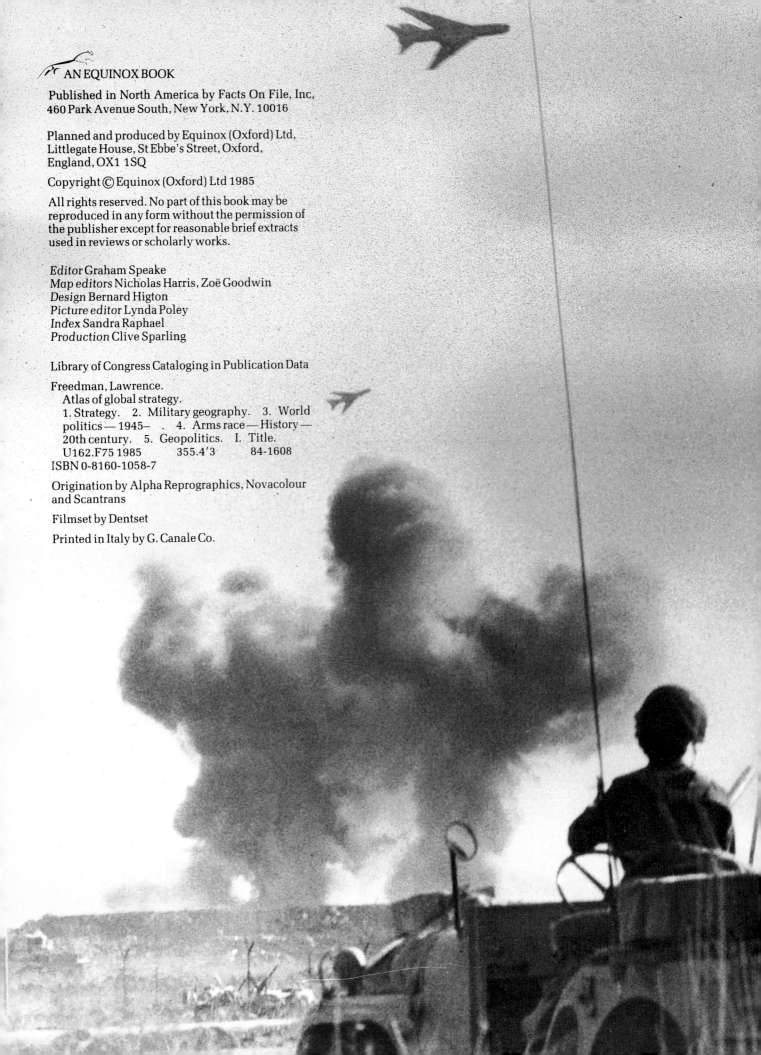

AN EQUINOX BOOK

Published in North America by Facts On File, Inc,
460 Park Avenue South, New York, N.Y. 10016

Planned and produced by Equinox (Oxford) Ltd,
Littlegate House, St Ebbe's Street, Oxford,
England, OX1 1SQ

Editor Graham Speake
Map editors Nicholas Harris, Zoë Goodwin
Design Bernard Higton
Picture editor Lynda Poley
Index Sandra Raphael
Production Clive Sparling

Library of Congress Cataloging in Publication Data

Freedman, Lawrence.
  Atlas of global strategy.
  1. Strategy. 2. Military geography. 3. World
  politics — 1945— . 4. Arms race — History —
  20th century. 5. Geopolitics. I. Title.
    U162.F75 1985   355.4'3   84-1608
  ISBN 0-8160-1058-7

Origination by Alpha Reprographics, Novacolour
and Scantrans

Filmset by Dentset

Printed in Italy by G. Canale Co.

CONTENTS

Featured Topics

CHRONOLOGY: MAJOR EVENTS SINCE 1945

1945

May	War in Europe ends
June	United Nations Organization formed
August	Hiroshima and Nagasaki destroyed: Pacific War ends
November	Nuremberg trials begin US, Britain and Canada offer atomic information to the UN

1946

March	Soviet troops withdraw from Manchuria
June	Baruch Plan proposed at the first meeting of the UN Atomic Energy Commission
July	Bikini Atoll tests, the first peacetime atomic weapons tests

1947

January	Failure of the Marshall mission to China
March	Truman doctrine of support of "free peoples"; financial aid to Greece and Turkey
June	Marshall Plan for economic recovery in Europe proposed
August	Independence and partition of India

1948

February	Communist coup d'état in Czechoslovakia
March	Brussels Treaty signed by Britain, France, the Netherlands, Belgium and Luxembourg
April	Cease-fire in Kashmir between India and Pakistan
May	State of Israel established; attacked by Arab forces
June	Berlin blockade begins Yugoslavia withdraws from the Soviet bloc
November	Truman reelected US president

1949

April	Armistice between Israel and Arabs 12 nations sign North Atlantic Treaty
May	Berlin blockade ends
September	Soviet Union explodes its first atomic bomb and ends the US nuclear monopoly Federal Republic of Germany established
December	Chinese Nationalists withdraw to Formosa and Communists take control of mainland

1950

January	US decides to build hydrogen bomb
June	North Korea invades the South
September	US divisions land at Inchon
November	Chinese launch counteroffensive against UN forces across Yalu river

1951

April	European Coal and Steel Community established
October	Greece and Turkey join NATO

1952

May	Proposed establishment of the European Defence Community
September	Establishment of SEATO
October	Britain explodes the first atomic bomb State of Emergency declared in Kenya
November	Eisenhower elected US president First thermonuclear bomb exploded by the US

1953

March	Death of Stalin
July	Final armistice declared in Korea at Panmunjon
August	Soviet Union explodes a thermonuclear bomb

1954

January	US announces massive retaliation policy
March	French garrison at Dien Bien Phu attacked
May	Dien Bien Phu falls First Geneva Conference starts
August	France refuses to join European Defence Committee US 7th Fleet committed to the defense of Formosa
September	ANZUS pact formed
September–December	Chinese bombard Quemoy and Matsu
October	West Germany admitted to NATO and permitted to rearm French troops leave North Vietnam
November	Fighting breaks out in Algeria

1955

April	US agrees to share information on nuclear weapons with NATO countries EOKA campaign starts in Cyprus
May	Establishment of Warsaw Pact Four-power occupation of Austria concluded
September	Egyptian arms deal with Czechoslovakia
November	Baghdad Pact formed

1956

February	20th congress of USSR: start of destalinization
June	Polish workers' revolt suppressed by Soviet troops
July	Nasser announces nationalization of Suez Canal
October	Soviet suppression of Hungarian uprising Israel invades Sinai
November	Eisenhower reelected US president British and French paratroops land at Port Said on Suez Canal
December	Britain and France withdraw from Suez Canal; Israel from Sinai

1957

March	Rome Treaty establishes EEC
May	Britain explodes its first thermonuclear bomb
August	Malaysian independence
October	Sputnik satellite launched by USSR Sino–Soviet nuclear agreement

1958

March	Khrushchev seizes absolute control in the USSR
June	De Gaulle returns to power in France
August	Quemoy and Matsu blockaded
December	Batista overthrown in Cuba: Fidel Castro assumes power

1959

March	Independence agreed for Cyprus: EOKA campaign ends
June	USSR rescinds Sino–Soviet nuclear agreement
August	Baghdad Pact becomes CENTO
September	Khrushchev visits the US
October	CENTO formed
December	First *Polaris* submarine commissioned by US

1960

February	France explodes its first nuclear device
May	U-2 spy plane shot down over the Soviet Union: abortive East–West summit in Moscow
July	Soviet experts recalled from China
November	Kennedy elected US president
December	US offers a multilateral nuclear force to Europe Civil war in Laos

1961

April	Abortive Bay of Pigs invasion First manned space flight by Soviet Union
May	First US manned space flight Cease-fire in Laos
July	Second Berlin crisis
August	Berlin Wall built
December	India occupies Goa

1962

February	Britain announces forces to be stationed in Aden
March	Cease-fire to Algerian War signed at Évian
October	Cuban missile crisis Khrushchev reveals Sino–Soviet split
November	Sino–Indian War
December	Nassau summit between Prime Minister Macmillan of Britain and President Kennedy

1963

January	France formally rejects multilateral nuclear force
April	US–Soviet "hotline" established
July	Nuclear Test Ban Treaty signed
October	US and USSR renounce weapons in space at the UN
November	President Kennedy assassinated, and is replaced by Lyndon Johnson Coup against Diem in South Vietnam

1964

August	Gulf of Tonkin resolution passed in Congress
October	China explodes its first nuclear device Khrushchev deposed and replaced by a collective leadership
November	President Johnson reelected US president

1965

February	US commits troops to Vietnam; bombing of North begins
August	Indo–Pakistan war over Kashmir
October	Pro-Communist coup in Indonesia

1966

January	Indo–Pakistan cease-fire Chinese cultural revolution begins
March	France withdraws from the military command structure of NATO
April	US forces land in Dominican Republic
August	Peace agreement between Malaysia and Indonesia

1967

June	Six-Day War between Israel and Arabs China explodes its first thermonuclear device
November	British troops leave Aden
December	NATO adopts the doctrine of "Flexible Response"

1968

January	Tet Offensive in Vietnam Britain announces its decision to withdraw forces from all bases east of Suez by 1971
August	Soviet, East German, Polish and Hungarian forces invade Czechoslovakia
September	Albania leaves Warsaw Pact
November	Richard Nixon elected US president

1969

March	Undeclared combat between Soviet and Chinese troops in Manchuria
July	Announcement of the Nixon (Guam) doctrine
November	Nuclear Non-Proliferation Treaty signed US and Soviet SALT delegates meet US renounces biological warfare and the first use of chemical weapons
December	Soviet–German talks in Moscow

1970

January	Soviet Union opens a military relationship with Egypt
May	US and South Vietnamese troops enter Cambodia
August	Soviet–West German Non-Aggression Treaty
December	Normalization of relations between West Germany and Poland

1971

February	Treaty to denuclearize the seabed signed
May	Mansfield Amendment on withdrawal of US troops from Europe defeated in Congress
June	Pentagon papers published
July	Nixon accepts an invitation to visit China
September	US–Soviet Nuclear Accident Agreement
December	Indo–Pakistan war; state of Bangladesh proclaimed

1972

February	Nixon visits China
May	Nixon visits Moscow SALT I signed including the Treaty on the Limitation of Antiballistic Missiles and the Interim Agreement on the Limitation of Strategic Offensive Weapons
June	Second round of SALT agreements signed including the Agreement on the Prevention of Nuclear War
October	Egypt asks for the removal of Soviet advisers
November	Nixon reelected US president
December	East and West Germany recognize each other's sovereignty

1973

January	Vietnam cease-fire agreement signed Denmark, Eire and Britain join EEC
June	Soviet leader Brezhnev visits the US
September	Geneva Conference on Security and Cooperation in Europe opens in Helsinki
October	Vienna talks on mutual balanced force reductions open Fourth Arab–Israeli War
November	Congress votes to limit the presidential authority to commit US troops overseas
December	World oil prices quadruple

1974

April	Coup d'état in Portugal
May	India explodes a nuclear device
July	Coup in Cyprus: Turkey invades
August	Nixon resigns and Gerald Ford becomes US president

1975

April	Fall of Saigon (Vietnam) and Phnom Penh (Cambodia)
June	Suez Canal reopens
August	Helsinki agreements on CSCE signed
October	Cuban troops arrive in Angola

1976

September	Death of Mao Zedong
November	Jimmy Carter elected US president

1977

September	US and USSR agree to abide by SALT I after its expiry

December	Soviet Union deploys SS-20s in Europe

1978

May	UN Special Session on Disarmament
December	Vietnam invades Cambodia US normalizes relations with China

1979

January	Shah leaves Iran Tanzanian troops enter Uganda
February	China invades Vietnam
June	SALT II treaty signed
July	Somoza regime in Nicaragua overthrown
September	CENTO dissolved
November	US embassy seized in Tehran, 63 hostages taken
December	Soviet invasion of Afghanistan NATO announces its intention to deploy 572 cruise and *Pershing* missiles Ceasefire plan agreed in Rhodesia

1980

January	US Senate suspends SALT II debate
May	Tito dies in Yugoslavia
August	Gdansk agreement, formation of Solidarity in Poland
September	Iraq attacks Iran
November	Ronald Reagan elected US president

1981

November	INF talks open in Geneva
December	Martial law declared in Poland

1982

April	Argentine forces occupy Falkland Islands Israeli troops enter Lebanon
June	START talks open in Geneva British forces retake Falkland Islands
November	Brezhnev dies and is replaced by President Andropov
December	Martial law lifted in Poland

1983

March	President Reagan announces the Strategic Defense Initiative
September	Soviet Union shoots down a South Korean airliner over its airspace
October	US troops and soldiers from other Caribbean countries occupy Grenada
November	First cruise missiles arrive in Europe; Soviet negotiators leave the INF talks
December	Soviet negotiators leave the START talks

1984

February	Andropov dies and is replaced by President Chernenko
November	Reagan reelected US president

1985

March	Chernenko dies and is replaced by President Gorbachov

PREFACE

Preparation for war has long been, and continues to be, a prime concern of governments of the industrialized countries. It takes up a large slice of their national budgets, occupies much of their manpower and scientific resources and informs a good part of their diplomacy.

It is now four decades since the major powers last fought for their survival. There is no reason to believe that they will feel obliged to do so again in the foreseeable future. Yet, simply because such challenges are few and far between, there is anxiety that when they come nations should not be caught unprepared. Furthermore, the major powers have regularly found reason to employ armed forces to shape events beyond their borders where they have felt their interests to be in some way involved. Meanwhile many powers below the first rank have taken part in bitter and bloody struggles, fighting for the highest stakes, and sometimes taking on the major powers in wars that the latter might describe as being only "limited."

So in order to understand contemporary international affairs we cannot ignore war. It is a subject which inevitably and properly arouses strong, and often contradictory, feelings. It is one of the critical agents of historical change; yet it is a messy and unsatisfactory way of settling disputes among nations. It provides opportunities for heroism, ingenuity and a sense of common purpose; but it also offers opportunities for cruelty and invariably creates enormous suffering and misery. Thinking about the nature and consequences of warfare can be unbearably depressing; yet its decisive moments are often full of drama and frankly exciting.

Such feelings make it difficult to get the measure of war in the modern world. To some it remains a vital testing ground for nations and an unavoidable feature of an imperfect world; to others it is a disease, transmitted by those with a perverse interest in its spread. In recent years the introduction of particular nuclear weapons into NATO's arsenal, questions relating to the Soviet Union's long-term intentions with regard to the West and the suspected recklessness of American foreign policy have stimulated intense debate. In these circumstances it is not surprising that much that is written on the subject is bound up with these debates and reflects their passions — or else takes refuge in mere description, providing facts, figures and pictures without much attempt at analysis.

This book offers some explanations for the character of contemporary conflict and military strategy, without advocacy and in a reasoned and dispassionate manner. This approach does not reflect an indifference to the wider moral and political issues raised by any discussion of war, but a firm belief that concern is best served by understanding. The most sincere and deeply held convictions sometimes turn out on close examination to depend on erroneous assumptions.

In the following pages a number of common assumptions will be subjected to critical examination, as we move from a general discussion of the character of conflict in the modern world and the basic trends that influence it to a more detailed discussion of nuclear and conventional strategy, considering some of the most important crises and wars of recent decades, before concluding with a chapter on the prospects for making the world safer and less belligerent.

This is not a straightforward reference work, although it is hoped that the information contained in these pages will be found to be useful and authoritative. The maps serve to illustrate and expand the points made in the text. This involves more than simply demonstrating the distribution of armed forces or the incidence of conflicts or providing a guided tour to the world's troublespots.

Although the text is mine, the book as a whole is very much a team effort and what quality it has is very much due to the professionalism of Equinox. Particular thanks are due to Nicholas Harris for the effort and imagination he has put into the design of the maps and to Graham Speake for his encouragement and guidance. Thanks are due also to Lynda Poley for finding the pictures, to Bernard Higton for the design and to Ian Anthony for help with some of the research.

Lawrence Freedman
March 1985

INTRODUCTION

An understanding of the consequences of a third world war has made the great powers extremely wary of such a conflict. Global strategy is increasingly concerned with containing the consequences of decolonization as much as the pursuit of superpower rivalry. Geopolitical theories overestimate the importance of the geographical dimension and, along with many other concepts of global strategy, underestimate local political factors.

The arrival of the United States as a superpower as seen by Salvador Dali in 1943 in *Geopoliticus Child Watching the Birth of a New Man.*

To describe the two great conflicts that have rocked our planet this century as "world wars" is apt. Few regions could feel untouched by the reverberations of the fighting, even when not directly involved themselves. The fighting itself ranged far and wide. World War II began in Europe and was concluded in the Pacific. All the great powers took part. Even those who tried to distance themselves from the fighting were dragged in. Fighting took place in deserts, jungles and snowy wastes; it overwhelmed famous capitals and rural outposts alike.

When we talk of a "third world war" the presumption is that, should any of the major powers, and particularly the two superpowers, come to blows in the future, everyone else will soon become engulfed in a global conflagration that might make the previous world wars seem minor by comparison. The innocent and the guilty will all suffer. If nuclear weapons are used on any significant scale, then, scientists now warn, the smoke from the burning forests and cities could blot out the sun's rays and bring about a "nuclear winter" that would devastate the ecology of the northern hemisphere (and much of the southern).

Even without such a catastrophe, the range and mobility of modern weapons and the global interests of the superpowers will ensure that a clash involving the two in one part of the world will soon spread. In the scenarios for the "next war," it is often the support of rival factions in some Middle Eastern conflict that serves as the trigger. From the Middle East the crisis moves to Europe — probably with West Berlin as the focal point — and then moves on to Cuba. The spread of the conflict is governed by the global spread of superpower interests. The talk of the world now being a "global village" encourages the notion that a tremor in one area will soon be felt throughout the globe.

An *Atlas of Global Strategy* might be expected to deal with the preparations for such a conflict and the military measures that might be likely to govern its course. In fact the argument of this book is that an understanding of the consequences of a third world war has made the great powers extremely wary of getting themselves involved in such a conflict. Despite the powerful and sometimes alarming rhetoric deployed in the speeches and declarations of political leaders, as they seek to reassure their allies, warn their adversaries and compete for influence among the uncommitted, in practice the major powers have been very careful not to allow the differences between them to get out of hand. Even the employment of military means against lesser powers is proving to be difficult. This is a result of the rapid increase in the number of independent sovereign states, many now in possession of advanced military capabilities, and the development of complex

The American experience in Vietnam serves as a warning of the difficulties that can face superpowers when they get involved in fierce regional conflicts.
Here a US T-28 trainer drops a phosphorus bomb on a village in the Central Highlands.

strategy is thus increasingly about the containment of local conflicts rather than their exploitation.

There are contrary trends, to which attention will be drawn in this book. The intention is not to encourage complacency about the rationality of the major powers in the presence of the arsenals of mass destruction, nor to mock the foolishness of those minor powers that still seek to redress their grievances or fulfill their ambitions through violent means. The intention is to do no more than convey a sense of the complexity of international conflict, and to question many of the easy assumptions that so often serve as a substitute for critical analysis when it comes to discussing strategic issues in this confusing, perplexing and dangerous world of ours.

Strategy and geopolitics

By "strategy" we are referring to the use of military means to achieve political ends. The stress on politics as the source of the objectives of strategy indicates that we are not talking about indulging in military activities for their own sake. Political objectives might range from the suppression of an insurrection to defense against predatory neighbors to imperialist conquests. The readiness to use or threaten violence in pursuit of these objectives reflects an acknowledgment of the limits to more peaceful forms of persuasion. But it does not preclude more civilized methods of settling disputes. President Theodore Roosevelt's dictum concerning the wisdom of talking softly and carrying a big stick indicates the experienced statesman's awareness of the value of keeping a military sanction in the background when conducting some of the more difficult diplomatic conversations.

"Military means" refers to much more than the actual employment of troops in warfare. It can also mean their use for purposes such as deterrence, intimidation and even reassurance of anxious neighbors that intentions are quite honorable. The actual disposal and maneuver of armed forces in combat are referred to as tactics. The distinction between tactics and strategy is one of level and degree, for the two merge into one another. The tactics employed in a particular engagement have to be judged alongside the overall demands of the campaign; the planning for the campaign has to take account of the tactical possibilities.

Even before we examine such factors as religious, ethnic and ideological differences

international relationships that cut across the simple model of a clash between the competing ideologies of capitalism and socialism. More than is often supposed, conflicts erupt for reasons peculiar to the locality and without any prompting from a superpower, and then subside with the effects confined to the belligerents or at least their close neighbors. The external powers which try to intervene often find that they are serving local interests rather than the other way around. Global

"The only secure border for Russians is one with Russians on the other side"

we can learn something of a country's security problems by considering its geographic position. A landlocked country may feel more at risk than one whose potential enemies are all at the other end of a large stretch of water. But a nation dependent on external sources for supplies of vital raw materials has to worry about distant nations, should they be suspected of having the means and the motive to interrupt those supplies. And then the more it is necessary to think of distant military operations, the more it is necessary to worry about setting up overseas bases and gaining access to ports. The security of the ports and bases tends to drive policy. In this way a sense of vulnerability which may or may not represent a genuine threat can be created, and a demand for a substantial overseas military presence generated.

The landlocked have their own problems. Are they likely to be threatened on more than one front? The desire to head off wars on two fronts, or at least to ensure that they are fought in the most favorable circumstances, has shaped much of German and Russian defense and foreign policy this century. What has to be on the other side of the border for it to be secure? A czarist foreign minister once answered that question by suggesting that the only secure border for Russians was one with Russians on the other side. This is the sort of logic that can lead to a continual expansion of territory for honestly defensive reasons. It helps to explain why the Soviet Union is so keen to hold on to its East European satellites and why it is now in Afghanistan, and in another context it helps to account for the current shape of the state of Israel.

In these various ways potential enmity can be defined, not simply by ideological or religious differences or even disputes over raw materials and particular pieces of land, but simply by a geographical position. Thus Britain's traditional approach to the balance of power in Europe was that it would be intolerable if any single country was able to dominate the continent, as it would then be able to employ the massed resources of the continent to challenge Britain. This basic principle has led it to oppose the expansionism of Napoleonic France, the Kaiser's and Hitler's Germany and Soviet Russia. It has increasingly found it necessary to draw on the United States to achieve this objective. In the first two world wars of this century it took a number of years before the United States recognized that its interests were

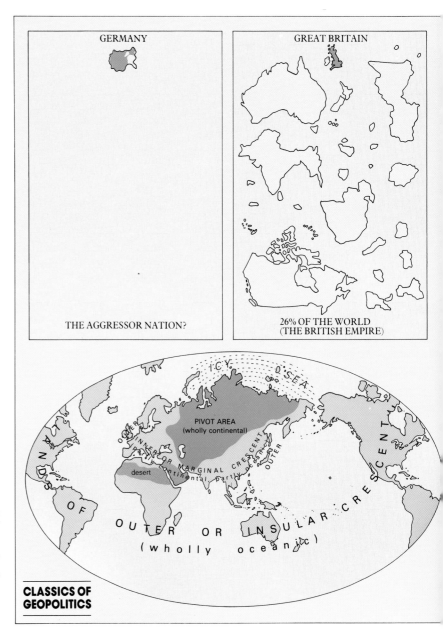

GERMANY

THE AGGRESSOR NATION?

GREAT BRITAIN

26% OF THE WORLD
(THE BRITISH EMPIRE)

PIVOT AREA
(wholly continental)

desert

ICY   SEA

MARGINAL   CRESCENT

OUTER   OR   INSULAR   CRESCENT

(wholly   oceanic)

CLASSICS OF GEOPOLITICS

bound up with the balance of power in Europe. The formation of the North Atlantic Treaty Organization (NATO) reflected the belief that the Soviet challenge was so formidable that there should be no doubt about American commitment to contain it.

In the first half of this century a school of geopolitics developed which sought to identify profound tendencies in international politics by studying their geographical setting. Less charitable definitions — for example, "a creature of militarism and a tool of war" — reflect the use made of geopolitics by the Nazis in order to justify their expansionist activities. This association, however, is unfortunate because the Nazis were not very good geopoliticians (or they would never have invaded Russia in 1941), but the theory

Geopolitics lives on in the domino theory and the arc of crisis

◀ These two maps, first published in 1942 by the American Robert Strausz-Hupé, challenge the conventional image of Britain as the beleaguered power by contrasting the territory of the British empire with that of Germany. In practice, size is irrelevant to the definition of aggression.

◀ Below, Halford Mackinder's world view of 1919. In the competition for influence the advantages were with the continental states and in particular those occupying the pivot area, the then newly created USSR.

▼ The sort of map that gave geopolitics a bad name. Gustav Fochler-Hauke, an associate of Haushofer, identifies the German-speaking areas of Europe in 1937.

can still serve as a source of insights on the character of international politics.

The founder of modern geopolitics was the British geographer Halford Mackinder, who first set out his ideas in 1904 and continued to develop them over the next four decades. Mackinder identified Eurasia as the "world-island," with its heartland (initially known as the "pivot" area) inaccessible to seapower (because of the impassability of the polar regions). This heartland is virtually equivalent to Russia, which gives his assessment, that control of the heartland would be the key to the control of the world-island and eventually the world itself, a slightly ominous ring. He saw the relationship between Germany and Russia as being central to the control of the world island, and the basic message behind much of his writing was a warning of the consequences for the British empire, should these two get together.

Challenging the land powers were the sea powers of the "outer crescent" (Britain, the United States, Japan). The contest was over the countries of the "inner crescent" which were adjacent both to the sea and to the heartland, and which later geopoliticians dubbed the "rimlands." Mackinder suspected that the land powers would win this contest because of the growing advantages enjoyed by land transport over sea transport. In this he took issue with those theorists such as the American Admiral Mahan who had argued that command of the sea allowed for command of much else because of the control it afforded over the world's communications. Once in control of the rimlands, the heartland powers would be able to challenge the powers of the outer crescent. They would remain invulnerable to direct land attack but could now be challenged on their own terms for command of the sea.

This sort of theorizing can be challenged on a number of counts. Land communications across and within the heartland have never been so well developed as to allow it to become the center of gravity of international politics for the reasons adduced by Mackinder. The rimland powers, and in particular those of Western and Central Europe, by virtue not only of their internal communications but also of the economic resources at their disposal, have been able to resist the heartland powers (though latterly only with help from the outer crescent). More seriously, these theories were influenced by the recent experience of imperialism in which the great powers enhanced their international standing by accumulating

territory. This underestimated the problems of overextension resulting from the need to secure individual territories against internal and external challenges.

Geopolitics came to be discredited because of its misuse by those, such as the German Haushofer, who used it to argue for territorial conquest for the greater glory of the state. This abuse allowed the more valuable and modest features of geopolitics to be forgotten. However, certain forms of geopolitical reasoning are still popular. One example is the "domino theory" which was used to justify American policy in Indochina. The assumption was that, once one country fell to Communist insurgency, then its neighbors would succumb, until a whole row of countries collapsed like dominoes.

It has been applied, though not with the same confidence, in other parts of the world. For example, in the mid-1970s, just after Turkey's invasion of Cyprus, which put it at loggerheads with Greece, and the Portuguese revolution, when Communist parties appeared to be gaining strength in Italy, Spain and France, there was much concern in NATO over the state of its southern flanks. This tended to be illustrated by maps with red arrows swirling around the Mediterranean. Within a few years, as Portugal sorted itself out and Communists failed to make headway, the concern subsided. This illustrates the danger of ignoring the distinctive causes and features of a series of related developments because of superficial similarities. Similar to this is the notion of an "arc of crisis" that came into vogue in the early 1980s and referred to the series of points of upheaval and tension from North Africa around to southwest Asia. This arc of crisis was uncomfortably close to the sources and routes of Western oil supplies, leading to the question of whether this proximity was wholly coincidental.

The fact that Laos and Kampuchea fell to North Vietnam after it had gained control of the South has been taken to give some limited validity to the domino theory. Clearly the effects of a war reverberate through a locality and are difficult to contain: refugees pour over borders; insurgents take short cuts through supposedly neutral territory which obliges their opponents to try to cut off their routes. Neighbors have to take a view about which side to support and, if they back a loser, they may well have to suffer the consequences. If a new power center is established in a region, then the weaker must take account.

Maps can lie

However, even a well-practiced aggressor will not automatically find a new neighbor an attractive victim or within his capacity to take over. Laos and Kampuchea would not have fallen into Vietnamese hands if they had not already been unstable. And while the original domino theory posited China as the first domino, subsequent events made clear that there was and remains little love lost between the Chinese and Vietnamese. In the case of another anticipated victim of the domino effect — Indonesia — the Communists, who had looked like consolidating their position, were turned upon and massacred in 1965 and failed to derive any benefit from the eventual North Vietnamese victory.

Like other geopolitical theories this over-estimated the importance of the geographical dimension, suggesting almost that the destinies of countries are determined by their location. Relations among states are governed by much more than the extent of their physical proximity or the existence of physical barriers such as seas and mountain ranges. The way the populations of these countries organize themselves, the resources available and their ability to exploit them, the nature of their beliefs, fears and aspirations still provide the basic raw material of international politics.

Moreover the view of the world provided by a map can be profoundly misleading. Most people in the West are familiar with the traditional Mercator projection of the world which has a simple north–south orientation and puts either North America or Great Britain at its center. This map has provided some of our basic political categories. Thus we identify the two great power blocs in terms of "East" and "West" (though where does Japan fit in?). We use the terms "north" and "south" to reflect the fact that by and large the states of the northern hemisphere are more industrialized and wealthier than those of the southern.

Though a useful source of political shorthand, the Anglo-Saxon view of the world that this projection encourages can lead to a lack of appreciation of how things might look from other parts of the world. It obscures the fact that the two extremities actually meet, and artificially exaggerates the distances between the land masses found at the top and the bottom of the map. It can even mislead North Americans by increasing their sense of isolation. If Americans look over the North Pole rather than across the oceans, they find the Soviet Union rather close at hand (this is in fact the route

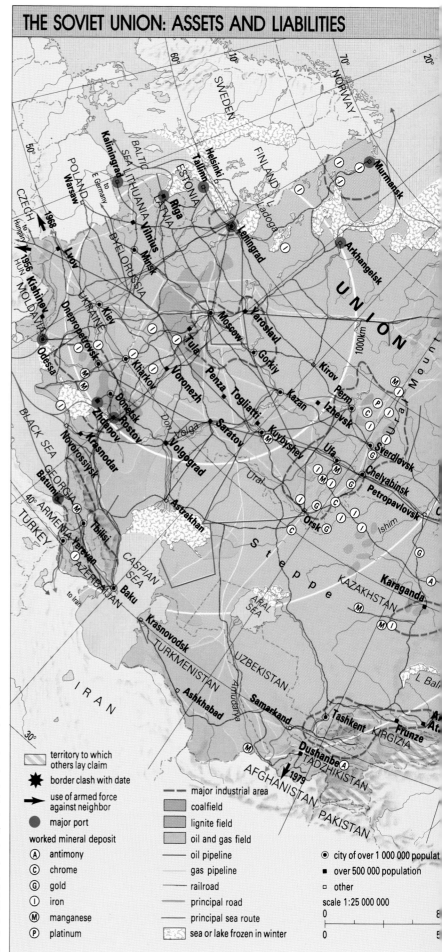

THE SOVIET UNION: ASSETS AND LIABILITIES

territory to which others lay claim

★ border clash with date

➤ use of armed force against neighbor

● major port

worked mineral deposit

Ⓐ antimony

Ⓒ chrome

Ⓖ gold

Ⓘ iron

Ⓜ manganese

Ⓟ platinum

--- major industrial area

coalfield

lignite field

oil and gas field

— oil pipeline

— gas pipeline

— railroad

— principal road

— principal sea route

sea or lake frozen in winter

◉ city of over 1 000 000 populat

■ over 500 000 population

□ other

scale 1:25 000 000

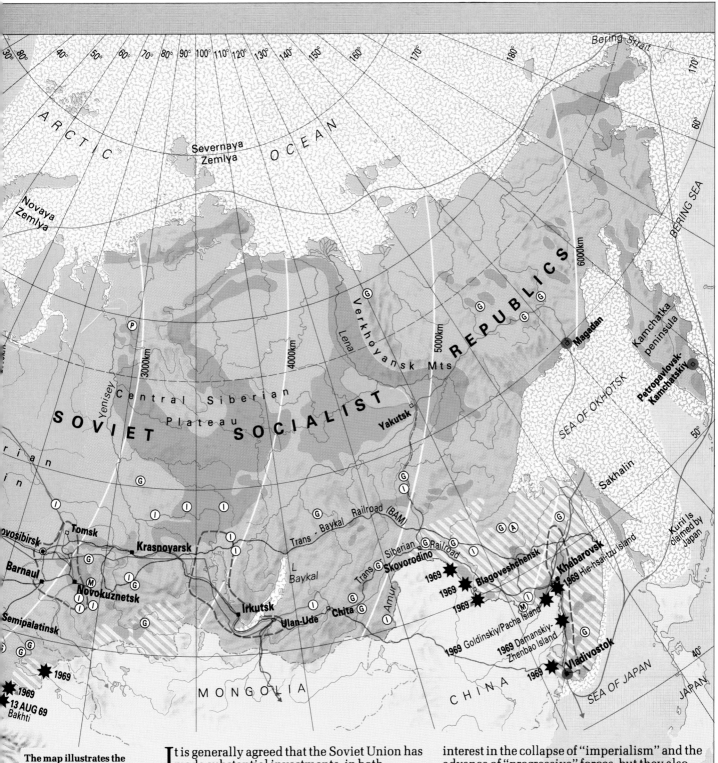

The map illustrates the source of some of the Soviet Union's security worries: its long land boundaries, many of them contested; the growing dependence for fuel and raw materials on the eastern part of the country while the bulk of the population and industry is to be found west of the Urals; the poor internal and external lines of communication.

It is generally agreed that the Soviet Union has made substantial investments, in both conventional and nuclear military capabilities, so that in some areas it rivals and even exceeds those of the United States. It is also known that the military establishment plays an influential role in Soviet society, creaming off the most talented scientists and running the most efficient industries; and that the Soviet leadership has not been averse to using military means to solve foreign-policy problems.

The concern of many is that this powerful military instrument has been developed to serve the revolutionary ideology of Marxism-Leninism. Soviet authorites do not deny their

interest in the collapse of "imperialism" and the advance of "progressive" forces, but they also insist that the necessary historical change will occur without their help. Certainly, if the objective is to spread Communism, the success rate has not been impressive.

A recognition of Soviet weakness does not resolve the debate in the West. Those most concerned about the "threat" tend to argue that the Soviet leaders might be tempted to engage in military adventures in order to distract attention from internal problems and secure the borders, while the more relaxed suggest that a sustained effort to reform an ailing economy requires a calm international environment.

MAPS AND WAR

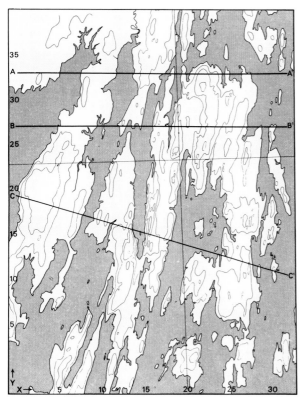

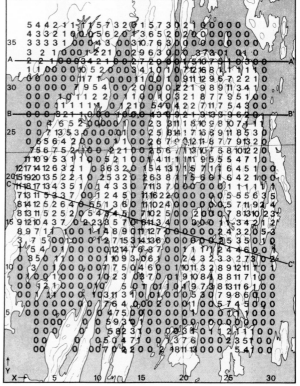

MISSILE TRANSPORTERS

12 GUIDELINE MISSILES

HEAVY EQUIPMENT

5 MISSILE DOLLIES

20 LONG CYLINDRICAL T

SILE TR

OPEN STORAGE

In most images of war, not far beyond the sound and fury of battle itself are maps: maps pinned up in front of attentive officers receiving their eve-of-battle briefing; maps dominating the operations room at headquarters as counters are moved to chart the course of the battle; maps illustrating the subsequent attempts to explain why and how one side emerged victorious. For the general commanding his forces in the field maps serve as his basic tool, helping him assess his situation, define his options and identify the obstacles that lie ahead. It was written of Napoleon that "through all countries, for the whole duration of his life, the map follows him, pierced with colored pins, illuminated at night by 20 or 30 candles, and a pair of compasses lying on it. This is the altar before which he offers up prayers. It is the real home of the man who has no home."

It is now possible for a missile to travel thousands of kilometers and land within meters of its target. Without accurate maps the sophisticated guidance mechanisms in the nose cone would be virtually useless because they would have nothing to aim at. Standard Soviet maps are known to have contained *deliberate* inaccuracies in order to confuse those bent on occupying or damaging their country.

The rules of war-gaming

```
7 3 0 2 1 0 0 0 0 0
5 2 0 2 0 0 0 0 0 0
6 3 0 0 0 0 0 0 0 0
3 0 0 0 37 3 0 1  0 1 0
0 0 0 1 5 10 7 5 1 0 3 0 0
0 1 0 7 12 16 8 1 1 1 1 0
0 1 0 9 11 12 9 6 7 2 2 1 0
0 0 2 2 1 9 8 9 11 3 4 1 0
1 0 3 2 1 8 7 7 9 5 1 0 0
4 0 4 2 2 7 11 7 5 4 3 0 0
3 0 9 2 1 9 13 8 9 6 2 0 1
3 3 11 1 8 10 9 8 10 7 1 1 1
5 8 14 17 16 8 9 11 8 5 3 0
6 7 9 0 12 11 8 7 7 9 13 2 0
5 6 7 11 13 10 7 6 8 10 12 2 0
4 11 1 111 9 5 5 5 4 7 1 0
4 13 11 5 7 11 6 4 5 1 0 0
3 8 11 5 6 0 1 6 4 2 1 0 0
3 7 0 0 0 0 0 1 1 1 1 1
5 22 0 0 0 0 0 5 5 5 6 3 5
0 24 0 0 0 0 0 5 7 11 9 2 4
2 5 0 0 2 0 0 7 8 13 10 2 3
3 4 0 0 3 0 0 11 3 4 2 1 2
7 0 0 0 0 0 2 4 3 2 0 5 3
6 0 0 0 0 0 2 5 3 5 0 1 0
7 0 0 1 1 1 2 4 4 6 0 0 1
1 0 0 2 4 3 2 3 3 2 7 3 0 2
0 0 1 10 11 3 2 8 9 12 11 1 0 1
0 0 1 9 10 8 1 8 8 11 7 1 0 0
0 1 10 1 9 7 3 8 13 11 6 1 0 0
1 0 0 0 5 3 0 7 9 8 6 0 0 0
2 0 0 0 1 0 0 5 7 4 5 0 0 0
0 0 0 0 1 0 0 0 1 1 1 0 0 0
0 0 0 0 0 0 0 0 0 0 0 0 0 0
0 0 0 3 1 0 1 1 2 1 1 1 0 0
0 1 3 7 6 0 0 0 2 3 5 1 0 0
2 1 8 11 13 0 0 0    5 4 1 0 0
```

▲ **By using terrain contour matching (TERCOM) radar in its nose cone, a cruise missile is able to check the layout of the ground below against the information that is taken from satellite photographs, digitized and stored in the computer (see p.104). The means by which a map can be turned into numbers is shown above. This enables the ground-hugging missiles to reach their destination without crashing into some unexpected obstacle en route. However, the information must be updated regularly. Otherwise, there is a risk of being caught by some new construction or even something as basic as the blanket of snow characteristic of the Russian winter.**

◀ **During the Cuban missile crisis of October 1962 American U-2 aircraft took photographs identifying the location of the new missile sites and showing the construction in progress (see p.108). Rather than keep these to themselves, the Americans released them to gain maximum public support for their position.**

by which intercontinental ballistic missiles would travel to their targets).

These limitations need to be borne in mind when viewing many attempts to illustrate strategic phenomena by reference to maps. They encourage an Olympian view of the world whereby we look down and are able to detect broad trends and linkages that would not be readily apparent from any other vantage point, and the rather less conventional projections in this book are an attempt to provide such new perspectives. But though valuable, this macroscopic view can never be wholly free from bias and cannot give due weight to the perceptions and feelings of those on the ground. What matters in the end is that the people who take the critical decisions of war and peace appreciate the position of their countries in the scheme of things and the character of the threats and opportunities that they face.

The game of strategy

Games are another source of simplistic metaphor for describing international politics and should be used with the same degree of caution as maps. The image of international strategy as some sort of grand game played for the highest stakes is deeply rooted. For example, the approaches of the two superpowers have been compared by noting the predilections of the Americans for poker, demanding steady nerves and a capacity for bluff, and of the Russians for chess, with the emphasis on cool, long-term calculations. There are board games that enjoy considerable popular appeal in which the players compete for chunks of the world, accumulating or losing substantial military forces, advancing or withdrawing them, forging or abandoning alliances, until someone has conquered the globe. Even those in reality responsible for defense and foreign policies attempt to anticipate the problems that might be faced in a crisis or check the functioning of command and control procedures by "war-gaming."

Needless to say, one cannot expect such games to match reality. By definition, games are only practicable if they are simplified to exclude complicating factors which are difficult to accommodate in the play, however crucial they might turn out to be in actual conflict. It is also normal in games played for fun and profit for the rules to be known and understood beforehand and agreed by the players, and not made up in ad hoc fashion once play has begun in earnest. This is not the case with games played for survival.

Rules are not wholly absent from international conflict. Both sides often recognize that the cost to themselves might be minimized if there were tacit understandings not to bomb civilian targets and to allow each other's economies to continue functioning. There are formal agreements on such matters as the treatment of prisoners or the extension of conflict into third-party countries. Even in peacetime there are conventions for avoiding unnecessary provocations, such as promoting dissension within the other's alliance and guiding the management of crises. However, the maintenance of rules during the course of a bitter conflict is less easy. What sort of challenges can one side mount against the fundamental interests of the other? What methods may be legitimately employed? How do we know when one side has "won"?

It is a very rare conflict in which both sides agree to play by the same rules for the duration. When one side is in danger of losing, it is likely to attempt to change the rules. (We tend to call this "escalation.") Equally the ability to impose rules that suit your strengths on a conflict is the first step to victory, and so the initial stages of a conflict will, as likely as not, take the form of a competition to set advantageous rules. Field Marshal Bernard Montgomery, Britain's most renowned 20th-century general, made this point in explaining why it is difficult to treat warfare as a game: "Strategy is often likened to a game of chess; no, quite different! In chess, you make your plans and opening moves, get your pieces in balance, and then say, 'Check' and whatever you shall do I shall checkmate you in three moves; so you may as well throw your hand in now, whereupon your opponent concedes victory. Not so in warfare! When you say 'Check', your opponent may reply 'No, you are quite mistaken. This is where the fighting is going to begin.'"

Montgomery was talking about the tactical level — when two armies are joined in battle. But the point holds for the grander strategic level at which national leaders are having to calculate the costs and benefits of fighting on or giving up. Over the past two centuries the institution of war has been transformed from a relatively contained activity into something which knows no natural limits of time, space or sheer destructiveness because ways continue to be found of avoiding checkmate.

The simplest sort of war would be one in which two regular armies maneuver around each other until they meet in a decisive

THE VIEW FROM MOSCOW

NICARAGUA

Havana

CUBA

PUERTO RICO
(US)

U S A

C A N A D A

Greenland
(Denmark)

ICELAND

Svalbard
(Norway)

A T L A N T I C   O C E A N

2500km

NORWAY

PORTUGAL

SPAIN   FRANCE

BENELUX   DEN

UK

W
GER

E
GER

CZ

POLAND

(several)

U · S

⊙ MOSCOW

ITALY

HUN

ROM

GREECE   BULG

LIBYA

Latakia

TURKEY

SYRIA

ISRAEL   IRAQ

IRAN

AFGHANISTAN

EGYPT

PAKISTAN

I N D

CONGO

Dahlak Island

Luanda

S YEMEN

ETHIOPIA

Aden

Socotra
(S Yemen)

ANGOLA

SOMALIA

SEYCHELLES

MOZAMBIQUE

Diego Suarez

SOUTH AFRICA

Beira

Maputo

MADAGASCAR

I N D I A N   O

friends of the USSR

Warsaw Pact

others — by treaty of friendship

adversaries of the USSR

Soviet facilities

forward air base

naval anchorage

A high-risk business

It has been suggested that the Soviet Union is the only country surrounded by hostile Communist powers. It certainly has little reason to feel comfortable with its neighbors. The main preoccupation is with Europe. Here at least it has established a buffer against the West, but it cannot be confident of the enduring loyalty of the states which make up the buffer. To the east, there is the other Communist giant and erstwhile ally, China, which has now turned into an awkward opponent. More recently instability has started to develop on its southern border, with substantial forces committed to Afghanistan.

encounter, the result of which fixes the terms on which the dispute which brought the two parties to blows in the first place is settled. But with conscription it was possible to revive an army even after it had been disastrously defeated in battle. Industrial production could ensure that equipment and ammunition were replaced rapidly. The railroads would make it possible for these extra men and materials to be transported to the front to carry on the war.

If all this made it difficult to achieve a result on the battlefield, then by sea and air it might be possible to shift forces so as to attack the enemy from another direction, or mount a blockade of his ports to starve him out, or bombard his cities to pound him into submission. And if all that failed, there was always the hope that your scientist might come up with some ingenious new weapon that might just turn the tide. In World War I they came up with tanks, fighting aircraft and poisoned gas; in World War II, with missiles and the atom bombs.

Wars, therefore, particularly between the major industrial powers, became contests of production and technology as well as of fighting skills. At risk were not only the nation's fighting men but the civilian population as well, and, ultimately, in the nuclear age, the very survival of the society and the civilization of which it was a part. Nuclear weapons represent the logical conclusion of this trend, but the implications were evident well before their arrival on the scene.

All these factors provide powerful arguments against getting involved in war — certainly with a nation or group of nations of equivalent strength. By the time the attrition had taken its toll and the other's strength was sapped, the victor too would be exhausted. The stakes had to be very high before any country would risk such a strain. It took a ruthless and evil adversary to persuade democratic nations to go to war again in 1939 while the memories of the slaughter of 1914–18 were still fresh.

Other factors evident in the modern world are making it difficult to take on opponents that are on the surface far less capable. In the popular board games which allow the players to set off on campaigns of global conquest they are allowed to trample over territory at will, with determined obstruction provided by their main opponent, but no resistance offered by either the terrain or its occupants. Up until 1945 this would not have been wholly unrealistic in that most parts of the world were in the possession of the likely

Today the stakes are even higher

belligerents. But with decolonization there has been a vast increase in the number of independent states unwilling to be trampled over and increasingly able to resist any such violation of their territory. This development has turned out to be as important for the shape of contemporary conflict as nuclear weapons. It has made the international environment less and less conducive to the exercise of military power as it has been traditionally understood.

Imagine a chessboard on which individual squares refuse bishops a base or deny knights overflying rights or suddenly disappear from view because of an internal disorder. Or imagine a game in which the following things happen: in the midst of your opening gambit half of your pawns declare that they have had agonizing reappraisals and are no longer committed to battle; as soon as you capture the opponent's castles, or even his queen, he receives a new supply from an external source; once a piece is committed to a certain square, it gets stuck and becomes almost impossible to withdraw; as soon as a checkmate is in sight, the opponent's king is suddenly surrounded by the pieces of a completely new player. And lastly imagine an end game in which you are battling against not only your opponent but a

referee insisting that it would be best for all concerned if a stalemate could be arranged as soon as possible, irrespective of the positions of the pieces on the board.

Obviously such a board and such a game would require a rewriting of the textbooks. The grandmaster's art would have to be extended. Moves would be devised dependent on the minimal number of squares at any given time. Individual squares would be judged with reference to their own distinctive characteristics and not just by their relationship to those occupied by the opponent's pieces. Effort would be put into keeping individual pieces loyal and committed and even subverting those of the other side, and into designing new pieces to catch the opponent unawares. A reliable supplier of replacement pieces would be required. It would be very helpful to find some way of ingratiating oneself with, or even obtaining some influence over, the referee. A game played according to these rules — or lack of rules — would either become very confusing or, as likely, very defensive. The inclination would be to hold on to what one had, moving out only with the greatest caution. Because it would be so hard to plan ahead, high-risk offensives or unfamiliar squares would need to be avoided.

▲ The opening of the Great War of 1914-18 was marked by the hurried movement forward of large armies using the railroads. Here German troops en route to the front wave to the cameras.

Where major powers fear to tread

▼ The fragility of alliances. Smiles from Mao Zedong of China and Nikita Khrushchev of the Soviet Union in July 1957, their last meeting before relations began to deteriorate. Below, more uncertain smiles as West German President Heinrich Lübke attempts a reconciliation between US President Lyndon Johnson and President Charles de Gaulle of France at the funeral of West German Chancellor Konrad Adenauer in April 1967. The previous year de Gaulle had taken France out of NATO's Integrated Military Command. In the long run the Sino–Soviet split proved to be deeper and more damaging than that between France and its allies.

If we compare our fantasy chess game with the contemporary strategic environment, there are clear similarities. The incidence and course of wars are conditioned by the cohesion of alliances, the pattern of the arms trade, the acquisition of overseas bases, the degree of interest shown by third parties, including the United Nations, and the internal stability of the warring parties. All of these factors are harder to organize in advance of a conflict than they were. To fight a war successfully therefore requires considerable political skills as well as old-fashioned military attributes and is still heavily dependent on the behavior and attitudes of other countries which are both highly uncertain and difficult to control.

As we shall see in the following pages, the recognition of these factors has made the great powers more and more disinclined to become directly involved in major military actions. This has clearly not extended to ruling out such actions altogether; nor has it stopped an increasing number of second- and third-order powers stepping in where the first-order prefer not to tread. The diffu-

sion of military and political strength, which has made it difficult for the major powers to act with a confident superiority in many parts of the world, has also made it possible for the lesser powers to seek to settle their own regional conflicts by force of arms.

The growing difficulty that the major powers have experienced in establishing their authority beyond their own borders through force of arms has had a number of significant effects on international politics. First and foremost it has impeded the putting together and keeping together of large power blocs. The most dramatic evidence of this was the inability of the old colonial powers to hold on to their empires. The attempts to suppress national liberation movements were costly in economic, military and political terms for the metropolitan countries, and in all cases ultimately futile.

Nor has it proved to be much easier to put together new coalitions or alliances. The United States has been able to keep its main postwar alliances intact — with Canada, Western Europe, Japan, Australia and New Zealand — but the secondary alliances in both Central and Southeast Asia collapsed, and countries whose friendship was considered vital have turned against the United States. The most important of these was Iran.

The Soviet Union has fared even worse. In Eastern Europe it lost control of Yugoslavia early on in the cold war. The Yugoslav leader, Marshal Tito, had achieved power by his own efforts and with popular support rather than on the back of the Red Army. In 1961 Albania detached itself from the Warsaw Pact as a reflection of intense insularity; and Romania has played an extremely independent role in the Pact, while remaining formally a member. More seriously, there have been rebellions or substantial divergences from orthodoxy in East Germany, Hungary, Czechoslovakia and Poland, two of which required major military interventions to suppress. Only Bulgaria has consistently followed Moscow's guidance. Outside Europe the Soviet Union has had even less success in building up a powerful coalition. In the early 1960s the international Communist movement was riven by the split between the Russians and the Chinese — the result of a combination of differences over ideology, foreign policy and geography (they have a common border of 7250 kilometers (4500 miles), much of it disputed). The problem here was more than the loss of an ally: it was also the acquisition of an enemy of uncertain stability and close proximity.

Economic sanctions are of limited value

◄ President Jimmy Carter poses with the shah of Iran in November 1977. Two years later the shah was overthrown.

► This map shows why many people believe that the natural condition of the United States is isolationist. The Atlantic was seen as a welcome divide from the decadent and disputatious Europe from which many Americans had fled. Only in the New World itself did it feel obliged to take an active interest in foreign affairs — and this continues with its persistent involvement in

Central America and the Caribbean. However, despite the distances, the United States has found it difficult to neglect global politics. It was drawn into the two world wars of this century, and after 1945 it concluded that it had little choice but to play an active international role.

THE VIEW FROM WASHINGTON

Less significant but by no means trivial, given the Soviet investment, was the break with Egypt in 1972 which was made absolute in 1974. On the other side of the ledger there have been a number of acquisitions — Cuba, Vietnam, Ethiopia, Afghanistan — but what is striking about all of these countries is their poverty and the amount of subsidy that has been required to keep them viable.

The second consequence of the limitations on the application of military power has been a growing reliance on other forms of power. Many of those in the West who have drawn attention to the limits of military power as a political instrument in the modern world have suggested that alternative forms of leverage could be found in economic power or control over key resources. After the debacle of Vietnam the United States began to sample the alternative forms of pressure. These included uranium and food supplies, technology transfer and financial holdings, and even sporting links.

While less costly in human life, in other respects these forms of pressure are as difficult to use as military force. At least soldiers are prepared to be the servants of foreign policy and train in that role. This is not the case with farmers, sportsmen, bankers and traders. They are not organized to exert leverage and often complain bitterly when they are asked to do so. The lack of prior preparation is likely to result in even more unforeseen practical problems than normally afflict military operations and a lack of agreed procedures for securing the cooperation of allies. The cost of their employment as forms of international pressure may be the long-term politicization of what had hitherto been purely commercial transactions or cultural exchanges. This can be seen with the Soviet boycott of the 1984 Los Angeles Olympic Games after the American boycott of the 1980 Moscow games which had served as the main Western sanction after the Soviet invasion of Afghanistan. (Of

Vishakhapatnam

SINGAPORE

THAILAND

KAMPUCHEA

LAOS

VIETNAM

CHIN

Hong Kong

MON

Clark
TAIWAN

Subic Bay

PHILIPPINES

Okinawa
(Jap)

N KOREA

S KOREA

(several)

JAPAN

Agena, Apra Harbor

Guam (US)

Yokosuka

PACIFIC

Marshall Is (US)

Midway I (US

AUSTRALIA
(AND NEW ZEALAND)

Johnston I

Pearl Harbor

OCEAN

American Samoa (US)

INDIAN OCEAN

ATLANTIC OCEAN

15 000km

12 500km

10 000km

7500km

5000km

2500km

• Réunion I (Fr)

⚓ SEYCHELLES

Diego Garcia (UK)
⚓ ✈

⚓ **Trincomalee**

Masirah ⚓
Muscat
Sib ⚓
Salalah ⚓
Berbera ⚓
OMAN

Mogadishu ⚓
SOMALIA
Mombasa ⚓
KENYA

MOZAMBIQUE

ETHIOPIA

D I A
PAKISTAN
AFGHANISTAN
IRAN
BAHRAIN
Manamah
SAUDI ARABIA
Dhahran ⚓

SOUTH
AFRICA

ANGOLA

CONGO

Simonstown ⚓

IRAQ
SYRIA ISRAEL
EGYPT
Incirlik ✈
TURKEY
Crete

⚓ **Ras Banas**
Suda Bay ⚓✈
Hellenikon ✈
LIBYA

USSR

BULG GREECE
(ROM) ALB
HUN ITALY
CZ
POLAND
E.GER W
GER
DEN BENELUX FRANCE
(several) UK SPAIN
NORWAY
Torrejón ✈
Zaragoza ✈

Gaeta, Naples ⚓✈
Comiso ✈
La Maddalena ⚓
Aviano ✈
MOROCCO
PORTUGAL
Rota ⚓✈

Ascension I (UK)
⚓✈

Holy Loch ⚓

Svalbard
(Norway)
ICELAND
Keflavik ⚓✈
Azores (Port)
Lajes ✈

Thule ✈
Greenland
(Denmark)
Sondrestrøm ✈

Goose ✈

⚓ **Adak**
Alaska
(US)

⚓ **Unalaska**

CANADA

⚓ BERMUDA

◉ *WASHINGTON*

USA

PUERTO
RICO
(US)
Roosevelt Roads ⚓✈

DOM REP
Ramey ✈
HAITI
CUBA
Guantanàmo Bay ⚓

B R A Z I L
VENEZUELA
COLOMBIA

PARAGUAY

BOLIVIA
URUGUAY

PERU
ARGENTINA

CHILE

Howard ✈
HONDURAS
GUATEMALA NIC
MEXICO EL PANAMA
SALVADOR COSTA RICA
ECUADOR

friends of the USA

	NATO and ANZUS
	others
	Rio Pact co-signatories

| | adversaries of the USA |

US facilities

✈ forward air base
⚓ forward naval base
⚓ naval anchorage

23

Characteristics of the superpowers: how similar are they?

course, the politicization of sport goes back to well before 1980.) The history of oil embargoes and economic sanctions suggests that they can have a short-term "shock effect" but are limited as a long-term means of forcing a change of policy out of the victims. They are often employed more as a means of signaling displeasure in the absence of more effective forms of pressure.

Most attention has been given to control over vital resources — food, fuels such as oil and uraniums and critical non-fuel minerals — as the cause of a shift in the structure of international power. Oil became an important form of political currency in the 1970s because the suppliers seemed ready and able to turn it on and off at will, and it was also a source of immense wealth. It has to be said, however, that because trade in these commodities serves the interests of suppliers as well as recipients, they are only willing to disrupt it in extreme circumstances and so cannot use it politically as a matter of course without losing markets. Thus the power deriving from reserves of these vital resources has been less than many imagined. It is only when a country has a monopoly or can organize a cartel (and even with oil this proved to be temporary) that it can be used with any confidence as a source of international influence. Certainly attempts to form new power blocs based on these alternative sources of influence have proved to be less than durable. More durable have been groupings based on a sense of common grievance — such as the Group of 77 which organizes common policies for the developing nations — but even here consensus can usually be found only at a rather general level. Groupings of disparate states soon find that, when it comes to the specifics, what holds them together is rather more tenuous than what pulls them apart. The result is therefore not that a new international order based on economic or resource power has come about to displace one based on military power, but that a rather confusing mixture has developed.

This theme of the diffusion of power and its influence on the shape of contemporary warfare is one that will be explored in the following chapters. Rather than international conflict being seen as something essentially conducted between the two great power blocs led by the United States and the Soviet Union, a picture will emerge of paralysis at the superpower level that is both partly the result of, and partly responsible for, increasing turbulence beneath this level.

Before moving on to examine the development of this confused international system it is worth making one point about the role of the superpowers. In lumping the two together there is a suggestion that they play similar roles in international affairs. Of course they do share the characteristics of immense military — and especially nuclear — capabilities and global reach. They both cover a large land area and have comparable populations — in the order of 230 million. They are both rich in natural resources and not dramatically dependent on international trade for their economic well-being. But there the similarity ends.

First it is not wholly irrelevant that one has a liberal democratic and the other a totalitarian form of government, and that one feels more or less comfortable with the world as it is and the other at least claims to desire radical changes. The United States is one of the powerhouses of the international economy and its currency plays a central role in the financing of international trade. It has a large development aid program and it plays a leading part in the organization and policy-making of most major international bodies. The Soviet Union is on the periphery of the international economy, does not have a large aid program and is often irrelevant to the conduct of much of the world's business. Furthermore the United States is a maritime power while the Soviet Union is a continental one.

If we look at the maps showing the views from Moscow and Washington, what is striking is that for the Soviet Union hostile countries and ideologies are very close at hand, to be found most of the way around its vast periphery. The United States, on the other hand, is distant from its likely enemies and the world's troublespots. The only exception to this is its "backyard" of Central America — but in terms of a direct threat to the United States this remains somewhat limited.

The corollary of this, however, is that its very proximity to sources of trouble puts the Soviet Union in a better position to send forces to deal with the trouble. It always has reserves close at hand. For the United States military intervention is much more difficult to organize on an opportunistic basis. It requires overseas bases and elaborate logistical planning. In the story of postwar international politics which the following pages will attempt to tell the significance of these differences should become very apparent.

THE CHANGING INTERNATIONAL ORDER

Origins of the cold war: a perverse sort of stability. NATO and the Warsaw Pact come into being. First steps in détente serve to ratify the status quo. Superpower rivalry in the third world leads to exaggerated fears. Dependence of the West on raw materials from the third world and even the power of oil are overestimated. Power in the modern world has become more diffuse.

The "big three" — Stalin, Truman and Churchill — meet at Potsdam in July 1945 after Germany's defeat to decide on the shape of postwar Europe.

The United States and the Soviet Union concluded World War II in quite different states. The United States had fought the war almost effortlessly — committing forces to two separate theaters of operations and supplying equipment to its major allies without any evident sign of strain. Indeed its economy grew rapidly during the war years to the extent that, by the time that it was concluded, the United States accounted for some 50 percent of the total world GNP. Apart from the initial assault on Pearl Harbor, American territory had not been harmed and so the population had been able to carry on daily life free from the perils of either air raids or occupation — from which few in Europe escaped, and the scars of which remain to this day. The question of invasion by foreign armies never arose. Casualties were not heavy. Its forces suffered severe losses only after the Normandy landings in 1944. Losses of up to a million men had been anticipated, should it have proved necessary to occupy the Japanese mainland, but the enemy surrendered before the invasion could be mounted, prompted in part by the atomic bombs. The development of these bombs provided yet another illustration of America's scientific and technical prowess. For the moment America shared with Britain leadership of the Western world, but the latter had used up its resources in two world wars and the days of the empire on which its international standing rested were numbered. This was now the "American century."

1945: TWILIGHT OF IMPERIALISM

The world in 1945. The idea of the "superpowers" was developed in 1944 by an American author, who based it on the ability to deploy preponderant power wherever it was needed. He identified three: the Soviet Union, the United States and Great Britain. The Soviet Union expanded its area of control in the closing stages of the war as its troops liberated Eastern Europe, took over the allotted sector of Germany and seized islands from Japan. The United States became the dominant Pacific power and was soon vital to the political balance in Europe. Britain's status rested on its past achievement and its ability to hold on to its overseas possessions. As the latter proved to be impossible, very soon the "big three" had been reduced to the "big two."

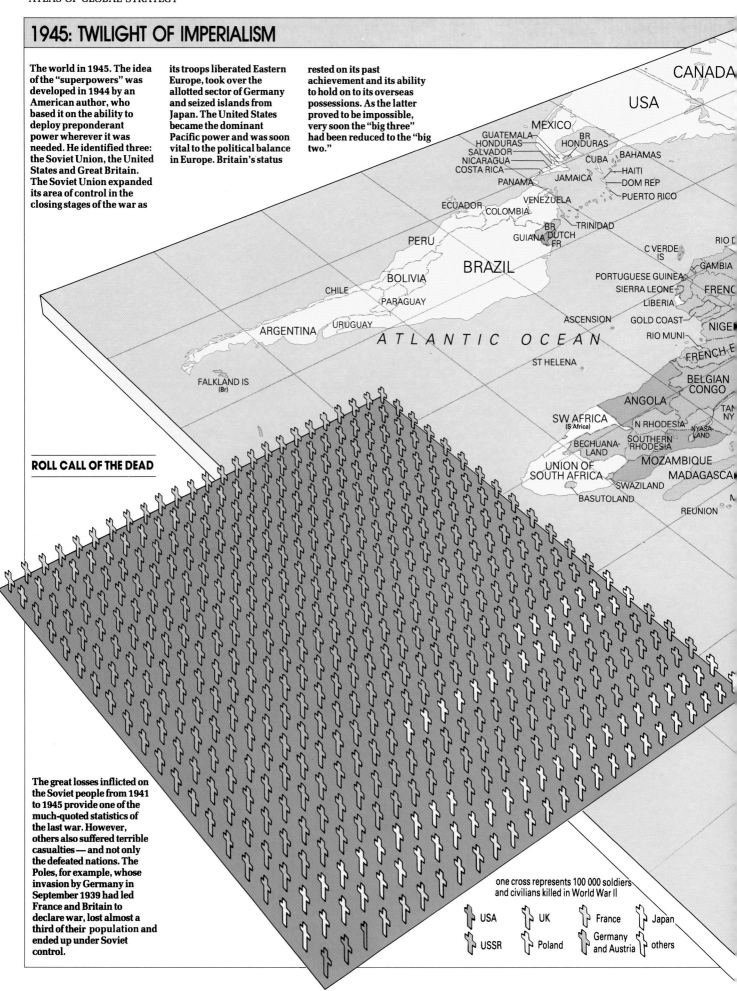

ROLL CALL OF THE DEAD

The great losses inflicted on the Soviet people from 1941 to 1945 provide one of the much-quoted statistics of the last war. However, others also suffered terrible casualties — and not only the defeated nations. The Poles, for example, whose invasion by Germany in September 1939 had led France and Britain to declare war, lost almost a third of their population and ended up under Soviet control.

one cross represents 100 000 soldiers and civilians killed in World War II

USA   UK   France   Japan
USSR   Poland   Germany and Austria   others

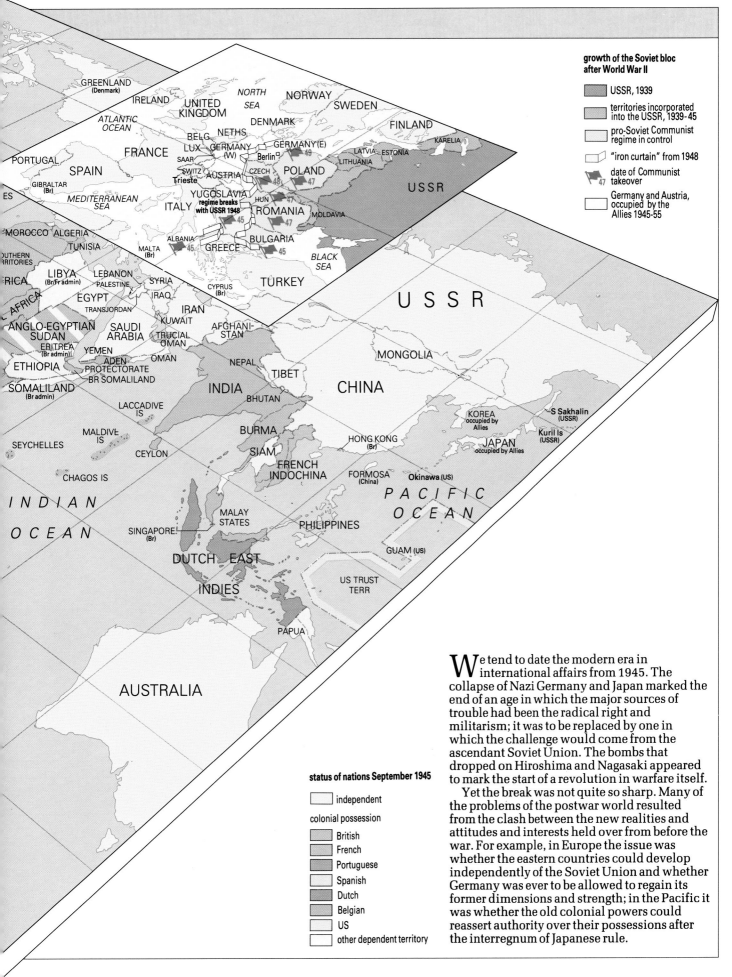

growth of the Soviet bloc after World War II

- USSR, 1939
- territories incorporated into the USSR, 1939-45
- pro-Soviet Communist regime in control
- "iron curtain" from 1948
- date of Communist takeover
- Germany and Austria, occupied by the Allies 1945-55

status of nations September 1945

- independent

colonial possession
- British
- French
- Portuguese
- Spanish
- Dutch
- Belgian
- US
- other dependent territory

We tend to date the modern era in international affairs from 1945. The collapse of Nazi Germany and Japan marked the end of an age in which the major sources of trouble had been the radical right and militarism; it was to be replaced by one in which the challenge would come from the ascendant Soviet Union. The bombs that dropped on Hiroshima and Nagasaki appeared to mark the start of a revolution in warfare itself.

Yet the break was not quite so sharp. Many of the problems of the postwar world resulted from the clash between the new realities and attitudes and interests held over from before the war. For example, in Europe the issue was whether the eastern countries could develop independently of the Soviet Union and whether Germany was ever to be allowed to regain its former dimensions and strength; in the Pacific it was whether the old colonial powers could reassert authority over their possessions after the interregnum of Japanese rule.

The cold war begins

The Soviet experience could not have been more different. The minimum estimate for Soviet losses during the war is 20 million dead — over 12 million of them civilian. Others put the figure as high as 24 million. This tragedy came to a society that had been rocked in the decades before the war by revolution, civil war, collectivization and purges. Hitler's armies had reached the outskirts of Moscow after occupying half of the country's agricultural and industrial capacity and were only expelled with an enormous effort. However, the war had also transformed the Soviet Union into a modern military power of the first order. The Soviet leader Stalin was now in a position to shape the postwar world in conjunction with his British and American allies. In particular, his troops were occupying large sections of territory contiguous with the borders of the Soviet Union. In the hard bargaining over the future of Europe Stalin's first priority was to keep these lands under his control, sealing off some well-trodden invasion routes and providing a buffer between the Soviet homeland and potential enemies. The Russians had no reason to expect assistance in this from the capitalist countries. At the end of World War I they had intervened rather ineffectually in the civil war in an effort to turn the tide against the Bolsheviks, and there was no reason to believe that their hostility to Communism had waned. Stalin was not one to rely on the goodwill of others. He was therefore wary of what he suspected to be Anglo-American attempts to undermine his buffer.

The West may have gained a new respect for Soviet strength during the war, but it remained suspicious of Communism. Having just fought a war against a totalitarian state, it was unwilling to connive at the imposition of something similar in Eastern Europe, especially when it had been the fate of one of the countries involved — Poland — that had prompted the British and French declaration of war in the first place. Furthermore the Americans disliked notions of "spheres of influence" dominated by great powers (this view also caused problems with Britain, France and other European allies seeking to reestablish their authority in their prewar colonies that had been occupied by the Japanese) and they wished to see more stress placed on the collective security arrangements embodied in the new United Nations.

The Russians lacked confidence in the United Nations, which was dominated by the friends and clients of the United States. They had only agreed to take part on the basis of being able to veto any decision which they did not like. But the more they sought to secure the East European buffer, the more the West saw this as an affront to democracy. Moreover there was no certainty as to where the buffer might stop. There were large and active Communist parties — all loyal to the Soviet Union — in France, Italy and Greece, the last of these involved in a civil war. Communist takeovers in these countries would completely shift the balance of power in Europe. But the measures chosen to thwart a Communist advance in Europe also threatened the quality of the Soviet buffer. For example, the injection of American economic aid to stimulate postwar recovery was seen in Moscow as encouraging the revival of a Germany hostile to the Soviet Union. Thus began the cold war.

While the Western powers objected to the Soviet imposition of a Communist system in Eastern Europe, there was not much that they could do about it. Equally, once the Western powers had resolved not to permit further Communist gains in Europe (under the name of the policy of "containment"), there was not a lot that the Soviet Union could do about that. As neither side was at all interested in yet another war and each was mainly concerned with preventing the other from making inroads into its sphere of influence, the situation right from the start promised a perverse sort of stability.

This was not apparent at the time. The mutual suspicions encouraged the formation of alliances. In 1949 the North Atlantic Treaty was signed. This soon acquired an associated military organization, but the basic purpose was simply to tie the United States into the affairs of Europe. The West European countries were aware that they could not cope with the Soviet Union on their own, especially in their state of postwar economic and political exhaustion, and were concered that the Americans' inclination would be to distance themselves once again from the quarrels of the "old world." The assumption was that, if the Kaiser or Hitler had known from the start that he would end up fighting the Americans, he would not have bothered to open hostilities at all. In response to the rearmament of West Germany in NATO the Soviet Union organized the Warsaw Pact which came into being in 1955.

The second reason why it was not immediately apparent that a rather stable system was under development was that the boun-

In June 1948 the Soviet Union blocked all road, rail and canal traffic into West Berlin (formed from the British, American and French sectors) in an effort to prevent its integration into the emerging West German state. Until September 1949 the 2·5 million people of West Berlin were kept supplied by an allied airlift. Here children wait for an American plane to land. Below, towards the end of the airlift, the millionth bag of coal arrives.

daries between the two sides were not clear-cut. At the conclusion of the war Germany was divided into four zones — British, French, American and Russian. The same arrangement was repeated on a smaller scale for the capital, Berlin, which was well inside the Soviet sector. As the cold war developed, the Western- and Soviet-controlled parts of Germany became integrated into their respective blocs, but this left West Berlin as a Western outpost in the middle of East Germany. In 1948 Britain and the United States mounted a massive airlift to break a blockade of West Berlin. The blockade was lifted but the issue was not resolved. Furthermore the West Germans refused to accept the permanence of the division of their country. It was not until the last Berlin crisis of 1961, when the Russians built a wall to prevent a flow of refugees escaping from East to West, that it became apparent that neither side was willing to take great risks to alter the status quo.

This was the last time that there appeared to be any sort of likelihood of the divisions of Europe resulting in war. In practice the severity and completeness of the divisions produced their own stability. Two distinct economic, political and military systems grew and developed apart from, and in rivalry with, each other. Within each bloc ideological homogeneity, economic interdependence, political conformity and military alliance have been maintained by a variety of fair means and foul. The two Soviet invasions that have breached the peace — against Hungary in 1956 and Czechoslovakia in 1968 — did not penetrate the iron curtain but were within the Socialist camp and were designed to put an end to radical departures from bloc norms. Equally the major diplomatic effort that brought all the European countries together in a joint assembly (in the 1975 Helsinki Conference on Security and Cooperation in Europe and subsequent follow-ons) was concerned with regularizing contact between the two blocs rather than agreeing the foundations for an alternative security system.

The system now is fortified by bureaucratic and political inertia, and it is by no means clear that an alternative security system would eliminate the need for

DISMANTLING THE EMPIRES

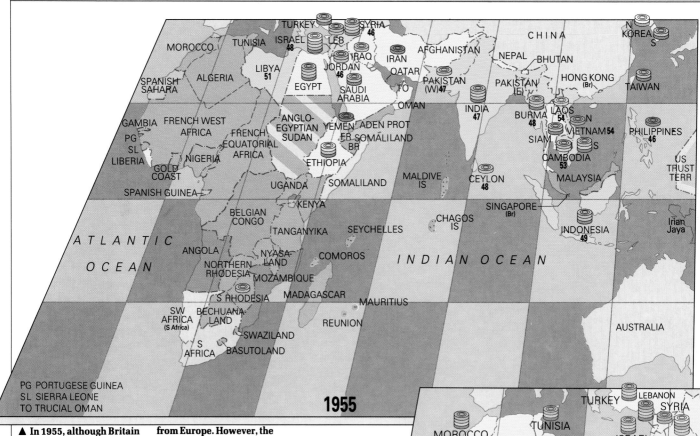

1955

PG PORTUGESE GUINEA
SL SIERRA LEONE
TO TRUCIAL OMAN

▲ In 1955, although Britain had left the Indian subcontinent and pulled out of Palestine, the French had relinquished their hold on Indochina and the Dutch had been forced out of Indonesia, much of the world was still controlled from Europe. However, the national liberation movements in Africa were beginning to get restive and the "winds of change" could already be felt.

For the first two decades after World War II one of the most potent political forces in the world was anticolonialism. The great colonial powers, and in particular Britain and France, found it difficult to hold on to overseas territories, especially in the face of a hostile local population and the strength of the idea of self-determination, which had arguably been one of the values for which the war had been fought. Certainly both superpowers, in quite different ways and for quite different reasons, included anticolonialism as part of their ideological makeup.

The end of the colonial era began when Britain granted independence to India in 1947, but it was some 30 years before the process neared completion, with the remaining colonies either nervous of the consequences of independence or just too small to survive as independent entities.

As the empires were dismantled, new alliances and supernational organizations appeared in their place (see below, p.46). Not all of these turned out to be as robust or as cohesive as those that they had replaced. The pattern of political relationships with the industrialized world is illustrated in these maps by reference to arms transfers.

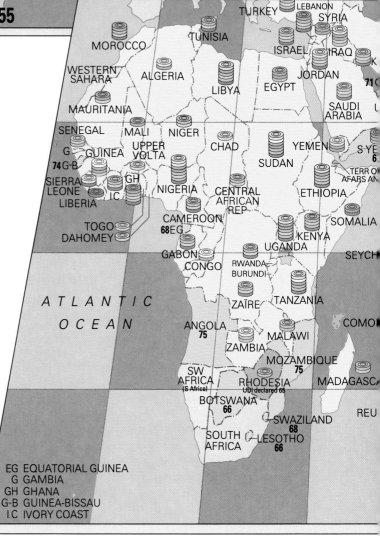

EG EQUATORIAL GUINEA
G GAMBIA
GH GHANA
G-B GUINEA-BISSAU
I.C IVORY COAST

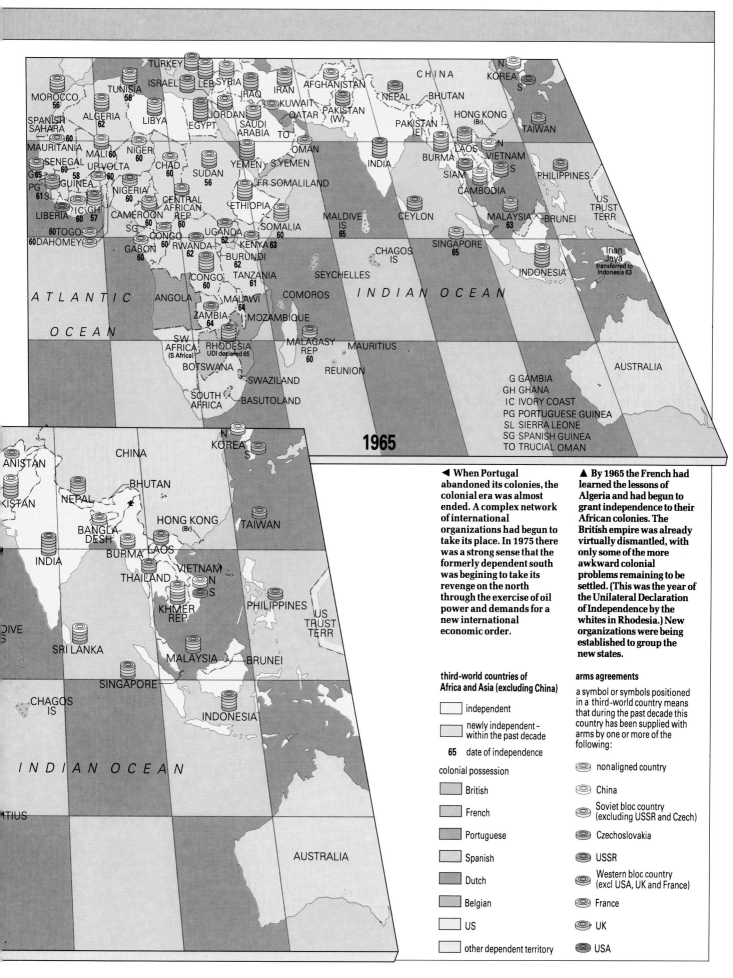

1965

G GAMBIA
GH GHANA
IC IVORY COAST
PG PORTUGUESE GUINEA
SL SIERRA LEONE
SG SPANISH GUINEA
TO TRUCIAL OMAN

◄ When Portugal abandoned its colonies, the colonial era was almost ended. A complex network of international organizations had begun to take its place. In 1975 there was a strong sense that the formerly dependent south was begining to take its revenge on the north through the exercise of oil power and demands for a new international economic order.

▲ By 1965 the French had learned the lessons of Algeria and had begun to grant independence to their African colonies. The British empire was already virtually dismantled, with only some of the more awkward colonial problems remaining to be settled. (This was the year of the Unilateral Declaration of Independence by the whites in Rhodesia.) New organizations were being established to group the new states.

third-world countries of Africa and Asia (excluding China)

☐ independent

☐ newly independent – within the past decade

65 date of independence

colonial possession

☐ British

☐ French

☐ Portuguese

☐ Spanish

☐ Dutch

☐ Belgian

☐ US

☐ other dependent territory

arms agreements

a symbol or symbols positioned in a third-world country means that during the past decade this country has been supplied with arms by one or more of the following:

⬤ nonaligned country

⬤ China

⬤ Soviet bloc country (excluding USSR and Czech)

⬤ Czechoslovakia

⬤ USSR

⬤ Western bloc country (excl USA, UK and France)

⬤ France

⬤ UK

⬤ USA

31

The pros and cons of détente

large standing armies. Old fears and, perhaps, ambitions would be resurrected while new dangers and opportunities would have to be recognized. The NATO–Warsaw Pact balance is familiar and manageable. Even the Soviet Union prefers it to having to cope with the power vacuum left after an American withdrawal, especially if this vacuum were to be filled by Germany.

The final reason why the antagonism has not turned out to be as dangerous as might have been expected is the fact that it rests upon a situation of military paralysis. Despite the presence of large and asymmetrical forces, no existing or foreseeable military advantages will permit either side to disregard the risks of nuclear war attendant on any conflict.

The question for the future is whether the sense of risk can cope with a resurgence of political turbulence in Europe. Many scenarios for World War III begin with unrest in Eastern Europe, of the sort that we have recently witnessed in Poland, getting out of hand. There is no doubt that the Soviet Union considers the maintenance of ideological orthodoxy and alliance loyalty to be absolutely vital and is willing to go to extreme lengths if these are under threat. NATO has in the past made it clear that it will not intervene in any internal Eastern-bloc disputes, at least not by military means, however much it may sympathize with dissident groups. Eastern Europe may provide the greatest source of anguish in the future, but it is not likely to be a source of anxiety about war unless the Soviet Union fails to be as efficient in its repression as it has been in the past.

Détente

By the late 1960s the stability of the system was recognized sufficiently for the two sides to seek to regularize matters. The key agreements in this process normalized relations between West Germany and the East and confirmed the existing position in Berlin with allowance for more contact between the two halves of the city. There were also attempts to regularize the military balance through arms control. There was some hope that this process of détente would lead to a steady improvement in relations. Instead of glowering at each other across two clearly marked and well-defended boundaries, the two blocs might become friends and trading partners.

However, the fact that the two sides were not on a collision course did not mean that

the differences between them were trivial. The two ways of life were quite different. This made the experience of détente rather confusing. Instead of fraternization there was, as often as not, friction as the two distinct systems ground against each other. An example of this was the human rights issue. The notion of the free movement of people and ideas represents a fundamental challenge to the Soviet bloc to which it cannot give way. Yet in the West there was an expectation that improvement in relations would be marked by improvements in the position of dissidents inside the Soviet Union. Such an expectation merely confirmed the suspicion of the KGB that the objective of the West was to use increased contact to subvert Soviet society.

Similarly with economic relations. The Western hope was that somehow the two sides would be drawn closer together, in a complex web of relationships, providing an extra stake in the preservation of peace. It was also suggested that a fat Russian was likely to be less belligerent than a thin one, though this observation has been disputed! The East saw the value of the contact in filling some of the gaps in its own economic structure — mainly its lack of advanced civilian technology. To the extent that the import of Western technology aids the Eastern economies there is less need for a diversion of resources from the military to the civilian sector or thoroughgoing economic reform. As things turned out, Western technology was not a panacea for the East. It proved difficult to transplant it into the Socialist economies, while the cost of buying it led a number of East European countries into debt, which in turn made them more rather than less reliant on the Soviet Union. In general, détente was used to strengthen the bloc system rather than to weaken it.

There were beneficiaries of détente: inhabitants of Berlin; ethnic Germans anxious to leave Poland or Jews keen to leave the Soviet Union; Western farmers and purveyors of high technology; Communist consumers. The closer one got to the East–West border, the more substantial these benefits appeared. Further away, especially in North America, they appeared slight. In particular there was disappointment that they had not fulfilled the high hopes of the early 1970s that something more positive might emerge than merely a ratification of the status quo or recognition of the dangers of nuclear war.

However, the main source of the problems which undermined détente, and with it

Few organizations posed more of a challenge to Soviet hegemony in Eastern Europe than the independent trade union Solidarity. By means of the threat of Socialism's traditional weapon, the general strike, against a Socialist government it was able to extract a series of concessions. Here Solidarity's leader, Lech Walesa, confers with colleagues as the movement gathers momentum at the Gdansk shipyards in October 1980. In December 1981 Solidarity was outlawed and martial law was imposed. The movement has been suppressed but by no means extinguished.

The United States provided the main international backing for the shah of Iran, in the belief that he would be able to look after Western interests in the vital Gulf region. When the Iranian people turned against the shah they also turned against the United States. When the United States admitted the deposed shah in November 1979 for medical treatment, revolutionary students took over the US embassy in Tehran with some 60 diplomatic hostages. After the abortive American attempt to rescue the hostages (see p.132) diplomatic and economic pressure eventually forced the Iranians to release them just as President Carter was leaving office in January 1981.

The battle for third-world hearts and minds

many of the associated negotiations such as those on arms control, was the persistence of conflict well away from Europe in the third world.

East–West relations and the third world

During the 1950s and 1960s, as the old colonies gained their independence, it was widely assumed that they would follow the Eastern or Western models of industrial development. Neither side admitted any role for neutrals. The United States in the 1950s put a lot of effort into trying to organize key third-world countries into alliances modeled on NATO lines. Those for Central Asia (CENTO) and Southeast Asia (SEATO) lasted until the 1970s. CENTO itself was the result of the failure of the Baghdad Pact, which had been established in 1955 by states bordering the Soviet Union — Iraq, Turkey, Iran and Pakistan — with the backing of the United States and Britain, and which had collapsed after the 1958 revolution in Iraq. The ANZUS Pact, with Australia and New Zealand, was naturally more resilient . However, even here, arguments over a ban on nuclear-armed or -powered US warships entering New Zealand harbors undermined it in 1985.

To the extent that the colonial powers resisted the liberation movements — for example, France in Indochina and Algeria — the Soviet Union enjoyed a clear start in engaging the sympathies of those seeking and achieving independence. The Americans hoped that their anticolonial record and economic dynamism would more than offset these Soviet advantages. It is of note that a 1960 book on economic growth in developing countries by Walt Rostow, who went on to advise Presidents Kennedy and Johnson on national security affairs, was subtitled *An Anti-Communist Manifesto*.

This rivalry for friends and influence in the third world was based on a misapprehension that the political and economic structures under development would in some way match those in either the first or second world. In practice the structures reflected local cultures, traditions and conditions as well as a desire to forge distinct identities.

Nevertheless, both the United States and the Soviet Union attempted to interpret conflicts in any region of the world essentially in East–West terms. The ostensible allegiance of particular factions to one or other of the superpowers would be used to determine their worth, whatever their local support or the relevance of their policies to local needs. In practice the superpowers

1985: THE POSTIMPERIAL WORLD

newly independent countries
of the Caribbean

1 ST CHRISTOPHER-NEVIS **83**

2 ANTIGUA AND BARBUDA **81**

3 DOMINICA **78**

4 ST LUCIA **79**

5 ST VINCENT **79**

6 GRENADA **74**

7 BAHAMAS **73**

Decolonization is now virtually complete. In 1984, for example, Britain agreed that Hong Kong should be incorporated into China after the lease runs out in 1997, and began tentative steps to discuss with Spain how the two countries' dispute over Gibraltar could be brought to an end. It should be noted that in both these cases the local populations have been less than enthusiastic concerning their prospective change in status.

The consequences of decolonization for the former colonies have been mixed. A number have been able to develop their economies and also robust political institutions (which do not always conform to the dictates of liberal democracy but may be in keeping with local conditions). For others the experience of independence has been harrowing, for they are too disadvantaged economically to be able to satisfy their people's demands for improved standards of living, and often as a result in a state of constant political turmoil. A number have been forced to turn to the former imperial power for assistance in the face of security threats that they have been unable to handle themselves. This has happened several times recently in Francophone Africa.

Few traces are left now of the empires or even of some of the institutions set up to replace them, such as the NATO-style alliances which the Americans attempted to establish around the periphery of what until the 1960s was known as the "Sino–Soviet bloc." New regional groupings, such as the Organization of African Unity, have been undermined by the persistence of local differences. See below, pp.46–47.

The lessons of Vietnam

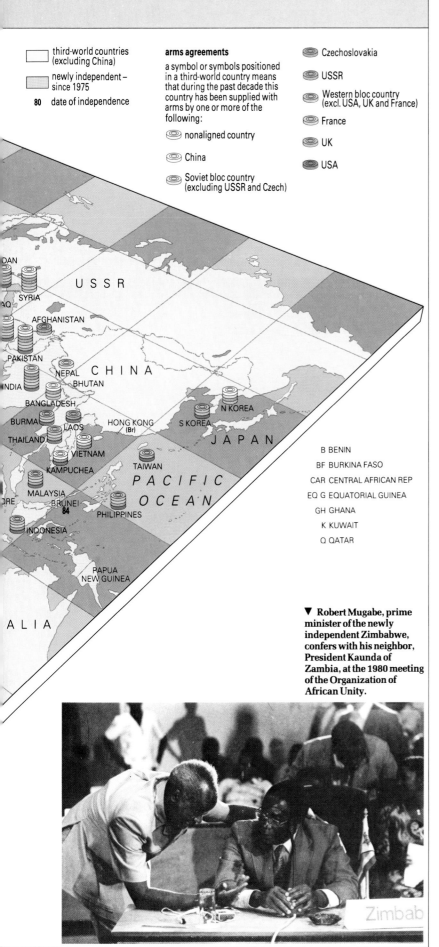

third-world countries (excluding China)

newly independent – since 1975

80 date of independence

arms agreements

a symbol or symbols positioned in a third-world country means that during the past decade this country has been supplied with arms by one or more of the following:

nonaligned country

China

Soviet bloc country (excluding USSR and Czech)

Czechoslovakia

USSR

Western bloc country (excl. USA, UK and France)

France

UK

USA

B BENIN
BF BURKINA FASO
CAR CENTRAL AFRICAN REP
EQ G EQUATORIAL GUINEA
GH GHANA
K KUWAIT
Q QATAR

▼ Robert Mugabe, prime minister of the newly independent Zimbabwe, confers with his neighbor, President Kaunda of Zambia, at the 1980 meeting of the Organization of African Unity.

found themselves being used by local politicians with little long-term interest in the East–West balance for their own purposes.

The more the United States chose to view challenges to any moderately pro-Western regime as inspired by either the Soviet Union or China, the more it was likely to get drawn in to deny a Communist victory. The Vietnam War, which eventually claimed the lives of some 46 000 Americans, will be considered in a later chapter. For the moment the relevance of this experience lies in its effect on American thinking as to the wisdom of direct military intervention as a means of promoting its interests.

The United States had appeared physically and temperamentally unsuited to protracted guerrilla campaigns in rural areas, preferring more open and decisive forms of fighting, and had been forced to recognize that these essentially political wars could not be waged by irredeemably unpopular regimes. Indeed, in the reaction to Vietnam, it came to be assumed that only corrupt and insensitive regimes would get themselves in the sort of mess where they needed outside assistance.

Unfortunately the Soviet Union had not learned the same "lessons of Vietnam." Its doctrine and ideologies teach it a respect for raw military power, while it lacks the alternative diplomatic instruments derived by the United States from its key role in the international economic system. Soviet overseas influence is to some extent dependent on conflict because the main resources on offer to would-be clients are military equipment and advice. There is little significant trade, spare foreign exchange or economic know-how to attract clients.

While the Americans were bogged down in Vietnam for much of the 1960s and early 1970s, the Soviet Union was investing in all forms of military power and in the ability to project this power throughout the globe. During the 1970s, as opportunities arose rather than as part of some grand design, it managed to get some return on this investment by airlifting Cubans or East Germans into strife-torn African countries (Angola, Ethiopia) or by assisting Vietnam in filling the vacuum left by the American collapse in Indochina.

The timing of this activity was doubly unfortunate. First to many in the United States it was in defiance of the spirit of détente. In fact the Kremlin had always made it clear that it did not expect "peaceful coexistence" (its phrase for détente) to pre-

35

A Soviet threat to the West's oil routes?

clude following the dictates of "proletarian internationalism" (support for national liberation movements). And it could also point to the fact that the first détente agreements had all been signed while the United States was still heavily involved in Vietnam. If this was followed by a period of US inactivity, it was not because of détente, but because the Americans were still licking their wounds after Vietnam.

However, Western alarm was based not only on the fact of the Russians boasting that this was being done close to areas of crucial importance to the Western economies. The West was becoming very conscious of its dependence on a number of third-world countries — notably the oil producers of the Middle East.

All this Soviet activity encouraged the view that the third world was now once again becoming the main area of confrontation between the two superpowers. One argument was that the very success of the West in containing Soviet expansionism in Europe had encouraged the Kremlin to search for alternative means of mounting its challenge. The dependence of the West on vital raw materials meant that they had to be concerned not only with the durability of the suppliers in the face of domestic upheaval or external predators, but also with the vulnerability of the commodities themselves as they were transported by sea where they might be intercepted in an effort to deprive the West of its essential supplies. One did not even have to presume an offensive intent. One CIA report of the mid-1970s suggested that the Soviet Union was about to move from a position as a net exporter of oil to being a net importer, and, given its lack of foreign exchange, might it not resort to rather unorthodox methods to secure access to the oil reserves of the Gulf?

Doubters were advised to look at a map. The movement of Soviet troops into Afghanistan brought them even closer to Iran, and put them in a position to exploit the turbulence in that major oil-producing state. By fomenting insurrection in Oman the Soviet Union hoped to gain a stranglehold on the vital Strait of Hormuz through which 40 percent of the West's oil must pass. It was already moving into a commanding position at the region's other major choke point at the exit from the Red Sea where the Russians were well in with the Marxist government of South Yemen (formerly the British colony of Aden) and had successfully courted the formerly pro-Western Ethiopia (albeit at the

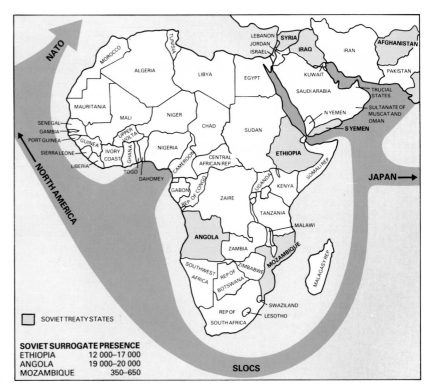

SOVIET TREATY STATES

SOVIET SURROGATE PRESENCE
ETHIOPIA   12 000–17 000
ANGOLA   19 000–20 000
MOZAMBIQUE   350–650

expense of relations with the formerly pro-Soviet Somalia). Look further down from the Horn of Africa to the south. Leftist governments had taken over the old Portuguese colonies of Mozambique and Angola, and the Russians expected to benefit from the overthrow of the white regime in Rhodesia (now Zimbabwe), the end of South African control over Namibia and even the eventual collapse of white rule in South Africa. Not only would this allow access to the West's strategic lines of communication (SLOCs), as the Pentagon has renamed the old trade routes, but they would then control the major reserves of some of the world's most vital non-fuel minerals.

This scenario has exercised a considerable influence on Western policy. After the Soviet invasion of Afghanistan and the downfall of the shah of Iran in 1979, the Americans stepped up preparations to intervene in the Gulf in an emergency, and President Carter warned that the United States had vital interests bound up in this region and would act accordingly, should these interests be threatened. Because matters which affected the functioning of the international economic system were at stake rather than the less tangible questions of ideological rivalry, and because there had been a series of developments that could be interpreted as clear moves and countermoves by the superpowers, it was understandable that the idea took root that the third world was now truly

THE SOVIET THREAT: SOUNDING THE ALARM

This map, taken from a presentation by the chairman of the American Joint Chiefs of Staff to Congress, provides a standard presentation of the vulnerability of Western strategic lines of communications (SLOCs) to interruption from states under the influence of the Soviet Union.

Soviet interventionism — a poor record

Cuban soldiers in Angola in 1976. The Cubans are generally viewed as being surrogates for a Soviet presence in Africa and they certainly could not have got to Angola and later Ethiopia, nor been properly equipped, without Soviet help. However, Fidel Castro of Cuba had his own reasons for wanting to take a more active role in third-world affairs. As a leading member of the nonaligned nations Cuba was certainly less objectionable to other African states than the Soviet Union and its involvement was less likely to trigger a US response. The American government wanted to respond to Cuban intervention, but this was disallowed by Congress.

turning into an area of superpower confrontation.

Such an interpretation does not stand up too well to close examination. As we shall see when we consider these areas in detail, it is difficult to explain the various Soviet moves as an attempt to "go for the Western jugular."

In no case has the Soviet Union taken over a country out of the blue. Either it, or more often its allies, has been invited in out of pique with the West or in return for services rendered (Cuba, Ethiopia, Vietnam, Yemen) or else it has moved to support a Soviet faction in trouble (Angola, Afghanistan). The stimulus has come from political developments within the countries concerned. In none of these cases was the Western position strong. Either colonialists had been expelled or pro-Western leaders had been overthrown as a result of a collapse in their domestic support. In Afghanistan there had always been a leaning towards the Soviet Union in foreign policy, though this has not been matched by an attempt at a Socialist domestic policy. Nor had the Soviet Union been able to take advantage of all the opportunities presented by a weakening of the Western position. It is not highly regarded in independent Zimbabwe, and the Soviet-backed Tudeh Party has been ruthlessly suppressed in post-shah Iran.

Nor have its interventions, or those of the Vietnamese and Cubans which it has supported, proved to be as decisive as might

have been expected. They have prevented their clients' defeat (which was as often as not the main purpose of the intervention), but in no case have they been able to secure an outright victory. The extent of Soviet control in Afghanistan remains limited by rebel activity. In Angola the anti-government UNITA guerrillas have recently been gaining ground. The Eritreans remain troublesome in Ethiopia, and the Khmer Rouge have yet to be suppressed in Kampuchea. Meanwhile, Soviet clients have a tendency to be extremely poor and in need of large subsidies which makes them something of a financial burden.

The Soviet Union's past record in holding on to clients is dismal, with China, Sudan, Somalia, Egypt and a number of smaller fry not only being lost but in a number of cases turning into implacable opponents. Three reasons for this stand out. First, a tendency towards colonial posturing which irritates local leaders who are proud of their independence. Second, an insensitivity to local issues which cut across the East–West divide, a failing often exhibited by the West. In particular the Kremlin has underestimated the offense caused to Islamic states by support of the Ethiopian government against the Eritrean separatists and against Somalia, and by the invasion of Afghanistan. Third, and perhaps most important, an inability to offer either a compelling model for economic growth or dynamic economic assistance.

We have noted that much of the concern in the West over Soviet activity has been based on the access being gained to key routes in the Gulf, Indian Ocean and the south Atlantic for the passage of oil and other key raw materials. This concern may have been exaggerated. Interference with oil supplies would be a *casus belli*. However, as a way to start a war it would be something of a lost opportunity. It would have no disarming effect, nor would it introduce immobility for some time. In the early stages of a conventional war the key sea routes would be across the Atlantic, with fresh men and materials being brought over to do battle in Central Europe. If the Russians were concentrating their naval capabilities on the Atlantic, then they would not have enough, as things stand at the moment, to impede the supply of oil as well. Even if they could, the immediate effect would be limited, especially if the West has maintained strategic stockpiles. Apart from anything else, if the Russians really wanted to prevent oil getting to the West, they could cut it off at source without

OIL POWER

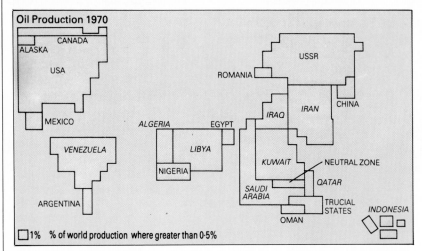

Oil Production 1970

1% % of world production where greater than 0·5%

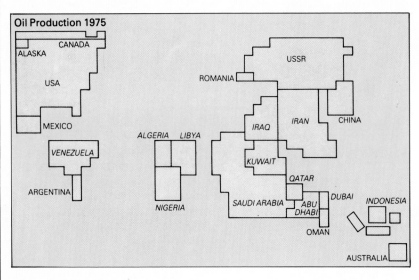

Oil Production 1975

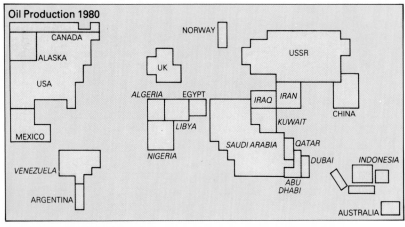

Oil Production 1980

One of the most influential developments in the 1970s was the growing power of the oil producers, especially those of the Middle East. The postwar economic growth in the industrialized world, based on cheap oil, was brought to an abrupt halt with the sudden rise in oil prices, while Arab producers sought to use their control over supply and surge of wealth to encourage a more anti-Israel stance in the West. But the extra cost of oil encouraged consumers to reduce their requirements and new producers to enter the market. By the early 1980s supply was exceeding demand, and the oil producers' power declined.

OIL TRADERS OF THE 1980S

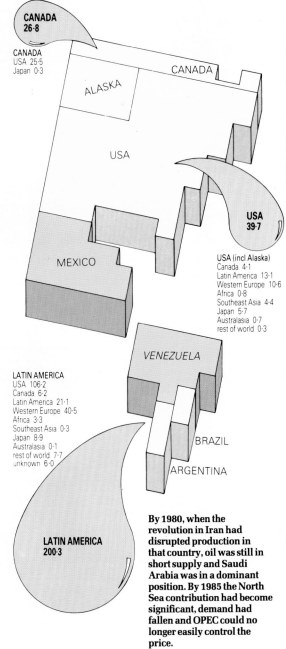

At the start of the 1970s the United States was still a net exporter of oil while Saudi Arabia had yet to exploit fully its large reserves. By 1975, with the United States no longer able to meet its own needs, Iran and Saudi Arabia were dominant. Revenues remained high, even if production was held down.

1% % of world production where greater than 0·5%

LIBYA member of OPEC

exports in million tonnes, with importing countries or regions listed 2·7

reserves/production (r/p) ratio remaining oil reserves at the end of any year divided by the production of that year gives number of years reserves would last if production continues at the same rate

50
30
15

CANADA 26·8
CANADA
USA 25·5
Japan 0·3

USA 39·7
USA (incl Alaska)
Canada 4·1
Latin America 13·1
Western Europe 10·6
Africa 0·8
Southeast Asia 4·4
Japan 5·7
Australasia 0·7
rest of world 0·3

LATIN AMERICA
USA 106·2
Canada 6·2
Latin America 21·1
Western Europe 40·5
Africa 3·3
Southeast Asia 0·3
Japan 8·9
Australasia 0·1
rest of world 7·7
unknown 6·0

LATIN AMERICA 200·3

By 1980, when the revolution in Iran had disrupted production in that country, oil was still in short supply and Saudi Arabia was in a dominant position. By 1985 the North Sea contribution had become significant, demand had fallen and OPEC could no longer easily control the price.

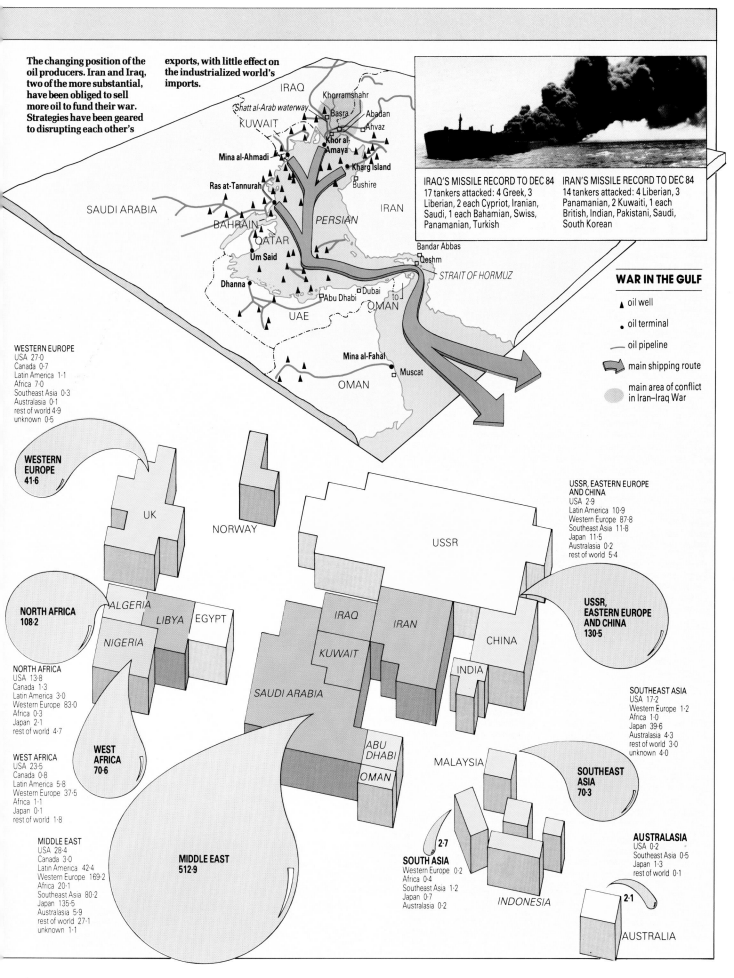

The changing position of the oil producers. Iran and Iraq, two of the more substantial, have been obliged to sell more oil to fund their war. Strategies have been geared to disrupting each other's exports, with little effect on the industrialized world's imports.

IRAQ'S MISSILE RECORD TO DEC 84
17 tankers attacked: 4 Greek, 3 Liberian, 2 each Cypriot, Iranian, Saudi, 1 each Bahamian, Swiss, Panamanian, Turkish

IRAN'S MISSILE RECORD TO DEC 84
14 tankers attacked: 4 Liberian, 3 Panamanian, 2 Kuwaiti, 1 each British, Indian, Pakistani, Saudi, South Korean

WAR IN THE GULF
▲ oil well
• oil terminal
— oil pipeline
⮑ main shipping route
main area of conflict in Iran–Iraq War

WESTERN EUROPE
USA 27·0
Canada 0·7
Latin America 1·1
Africa 7·0
Southeast Asia 0·3
Australasia 0·1
rest of world 4·9
unknown 0·5

WESTERN EUROPE 41·6

NORTH AFRICA
USA 13·8
Canada 1·3
Latin America 3·0
Western Europe 83·0
Africa 0·3
Japan 2·1
rest of world 4·7

NORTH AFRICA 108·2

WEST AFRICA
USA 23·5
Canada 0·8
Latin America 5·8
Western Europe 37·5
Africa 1·1
Japan 0·1
rest of world 1·8

WEST AFRICA 70·6

MIDDLE EAST
USA 28·4
Canada 3·0
Latin America 42·4
Western Europe 169·2
Africa 20·1
Southeast Asia 80·2
Japan 135·5
Australasia 5·9
rest of world 27·1
unknown 1·1

MIDDLE EAST 512·9

USSR, EASTERN EUROPE AND CHINA
USA 2·9
Latin America 10·9
Western Europe 87·8
Southeast Asia 11·8
Japan 11·5
Australasia 0·2
rest of world 5·4

USSR, EASTERN EUROPE AND CHINA 130·5

SOUTHEAST ASIA
USA 17·2
Western Europe 1·2
Africa 1·0
Japan 39·6
Australasia 4·3
rest of world 3·0
unknown 4·0

SOUTHEAST ASIA 70·3

SOUTH ASIA
Western Europe 0·2
Africa 0·4
Southeast Asia 1·2
Japan 0·7
Australasia 0·2

2·7

AUSTRALASIA
USA 0·2
Southeast Asia 0·5
Japan 1·3
rest of world 0·1

2·1

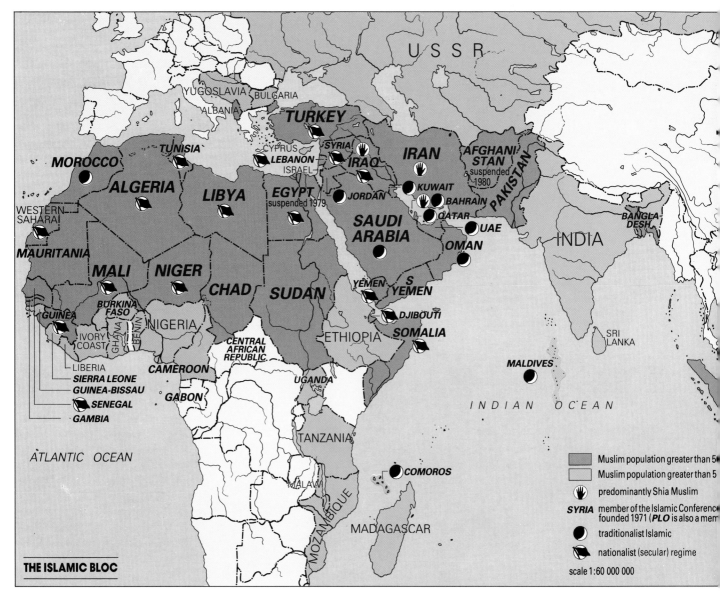

THE ISLAMIC BLOC

Muslim population greater than 5●
Muslim population greater than 5
predominantly Shia Muslim
SYRIA member of the Islamic Conferenc●
founded 1971 (*PLO* is also a mem
traditionalist Islamic
nationalist (secular) regime
scale 1:60 000 000

going to the considerable bother of doing so in transit. Their proximity to the Gulf makes this a serious possibility, but there is nothing new in this. It is not necessary for the Soviet Union to go through Afghanistan to threaten Iran. It shares a long border — which it crossed to occupy a substantial portion of northern Iran in 1945, only to withdraw later.

The question of Western vulnerabilities and Soviet objectives in the third world is important because the answer is relevant to the shaping of Western policy. The more gloomy interpretation of Soviet actions overtook the post-Vietnam mood of withdrawal from third-world conflicts and led to preparations for more active intervention, not only by the United States but also by Britain and France. The development of the new American Rapid Deployment Force (RDF), which will be examined more closely in the next chapter, serves as a symbol of a new commitment to take whatever action is necessary to defend American and more generally Western interests. But there remains an uncertainty, which those Gulf states that might be expected to benefit from American protection have not failed to pick up, as to whether the contingency in which the RDF might be employed would be one designed to contain Soviet aggression or to deal with a troublesome third-world country that has no links whatsoever with the Russians. In Central America there has been a vigorous debate as to whether the region's instability is Soviet-sponsored through Cuba and more recently Nicaragua, or whether it is the result of decades of poverty, corruption and repression.

Raw materials from the third world

Behind much of this argument is the assumption that the West is becoming more dependent on the third world for supplies of vital raw materials to an extent that can be exploited for dubious political ends — either those of the suppliers themselves or of a Soviet Union that might one day wish to

▼ A sharp illustration of the variety of forms of Islam as participants at the second Islamic summit at Lahore in 1974 kneel to pray. From the left, Hussain of Iraq, Bhutto of Pakistan,

Western dependence on the third world can be overestimated

Gaddafi of Libya, Faisal of Saudi Arabia and the shaikh of Kuwait.

interfere with supplies to its Western adversaries.

Like so many other simple guides to international conflict the raw materials thesis is inadequate in a number of respects. First it should be noted that, even when it can be shown that the West secures some vital commodity from third-world countries, this does not in itself constitute a vulnerability. For there to be true vulnerability, and for this to have an immediate and unavoidable impact on the functioning of the Western economies, the suppliers must be able to control the supply in all key respects. Even if this condition can be met, the supplier countries may be even more vulnerable to the disruption of the trading relationship than the recipients. Countries trading with the West, even if they are politically hostile, do so out of a sense of their own self-interest and cannot easily disrupt trade without doing immense harm to their own economies.

When it is pointed out that scrambles for raw materials led to wars in the past, it has to be remembered that the past conflicts were often not between a supplier and a recipient but between a number of countries anxious to gain control of reserves of key resources that were not under any power's effective control. This is decreasingly the case, though it is of note that a competition for access to new reserves is still the source of a substantial amount of international conflict.

The best example of this is the sea. During this century the idea of the "high seas" being under no national jurisdiction has been gradually undermined as coastal states began to make claims for territorial waters stretching beyond the traditional three nautical miles to at first a tentative 12 and then a more ambitious 200. Uncertainties as to the status of these claims led to a whole series of disputes about the key resources of fish and offshore minerals as well as the more traditional questions of freedom of navigation. The feeling generated by these matters was illustrated by the so-called "cod war" between Iceland and Britain. In April 1982, after eight years of intensive negotiations, the third United Nations Conference on the Law of the Sea (UNCLOS) set down a code which authorized 12-mile limits for coastal states and then a 200-mile exclusive economic zone in which they would control both mineral and fishing rights. However, one of the reasons why some of the key maritime states have yet to sign the new law is that many of the most interesting new resources

that the sea has to offer are well beyond the extended zones of the coastal states. As a result of new technologies — in the possession of the developed rather than the developing world — "manganese nodules" may be mined from the ocean floor. These nodules contain nickel, cobalt and copper as well as manganese. Those countries with companies in a position to extract these nodules are anxious to enjoy the benefits. Those already exporting the relevant minerals are anxious about future disruption of the market; there is a general disinclination to allow the more advanced countries to get all the benefits of this common resource. These concerns were reflected in the new code which a number of countries, including the United States, have refused to sign.

The Western dependence for primary products on the third world is not as great as is often supposed. For example, the Western world is self-sufficient in food. Rather than the developing countries exporting to the developed, the norm is the reverse. The United States is self-sufficient in many of the key non-fuel minerals, and Europe's supplies come as often from Canada, Australia and South Africa as from developing countries. There are very few individual countries, or cohesive groups of countries, which have sufficient market dominance in a particular mineral to be able to gain a significant economic or political benefit from this as OPEC has with oil. One exception may be cobalt in Zaïre (which is why there was so much interest in the unrest in Shaba province in the late 1970s). The major vulnerabilities of the West lie with that group of minerals — chromium, gold, manganese, platinum, vanadium and types of asbestos — which have been supplied almost exclusively by the Soviet Union and South Africa. The fear is not so much of the Soviet Union or even a new regime in South Africa cutting off supplies out of malevolence, but of the impact on mining in the event of any future convulsions in South Africa as a result of the black hostility to apartheid. Even here the question of vulnerability depends on the uses made of the particular minerals in, for example, specialist steels and the possibility of substitution of alternative minerals.

Oil is the obvious and most critical area of Western dependence on a collection of third-world countries. For much of the 1970s the oil factor almost overtook East–West relations as the dominant preoccupation of international statesmen. The Arab oil embargo imposed during the October 1973

STRATEGIC RESOURCES AND RESERVES

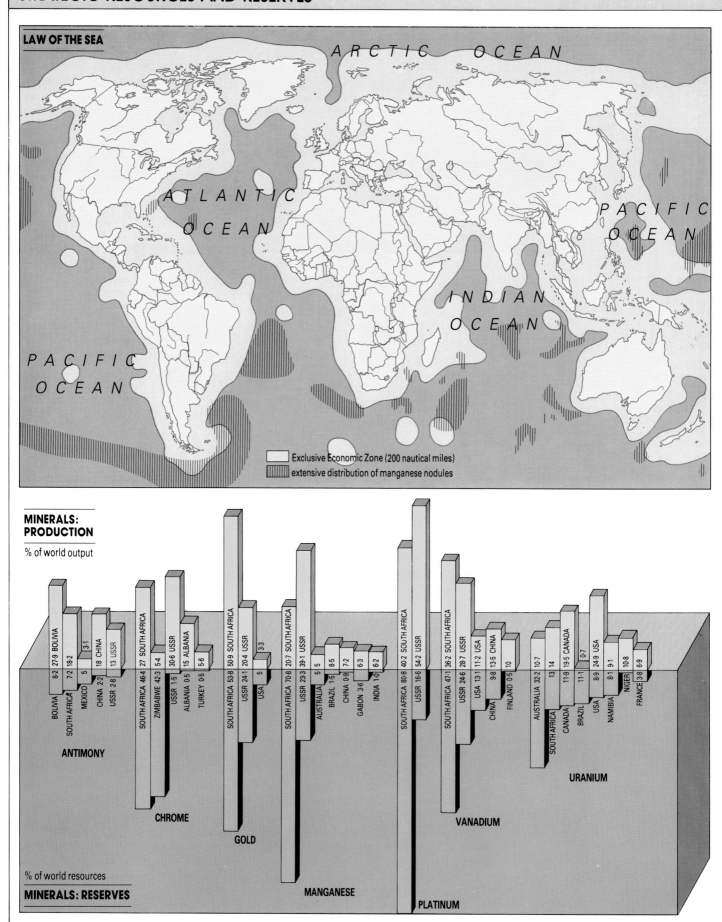

LAW OF THE SEA

ARCTIC OCEAN

ATLANTIC OCEAN

PACIFIC OCEAN

PACIFIC OCEAN

INDIAN OCEAN

☐ Exclusive Economic Zone (200 nautical miles)
▦ extensive distribution of manganese nodules

MINERALS: PRODUCTION

% of world output

ANTIMONY

BOLIVIA 8·2 27·9 BOLIVIA
SOUTH AFRICA 7·2 18·2
MEXICO 5 3·1
CHINA 2·2 18 CHINA
USSR 2·8 13 USSR

CHROME

SOUTH AFRICA 46·4 27 SOUTH AFRICA
ZIMBABWE 42·3 5·4
USSR 1·5 30·6 USSR
ALBANIA 0·5 15 ALBANIA
TURKEY 0·5 5·6

GOLD

SOUTH AFRICA 53·8 50·9 SOUTH AFRICA
USSR 24·1 20·4 USSR
USA 5 3·3

MANGANESE

SOUTH AFRICA 70·8 20·7 SOUTH AFRICA
USSR 23·3 39·1 USSR
AUSTRALIA 5 5
BRAZIL 1·5 8·5
CHINA 0·9 7·2
GABON 3·6 6·3
INDIA 1·0 6·2

PLATINUM

SOUTH AFRICA 80·8 40·2 SOUTH AFRICA
USSR 16·6 54·2 USSR

VANADIUM

SOUTH AFRICA 47·1 36·2 SOUTH AFRICA
USSR 24·6 28·7 USSR
USA 13·1 11·2 USA
CHINA 9·8 13·5 CHINA
FINLAND 0·5 10

URANIUM

AUSTRALIA 32·2 10·7
SOUTH AFRICA 13 14
CANADA 11·9 19·5 CANADA
BRAZIL 11·1 0·7
USA 8·9 24·9 USA
NAMIBIA 8·1 9·1
NIGER 10·8
FRANCE 3·8 6·9

% of world resources

MINERALS: RESERVES

*Recession drives down
the demand for oil*

▶ The "cod war" was a curious episode in which two allies, Britain and Iceland, engaged in skirmishes in the mid-1970s. It resulted from British support for trawlermen who wished to fish in traditional waters which the Icelanders intended to keep for themselves. Here the Icelandic gunboat *Thor* collides with the British frigate HMS *Andromeda* in early 1976.

◀ Modern methods of fishing and exploration for both fuel and non-fuel minerals have made states more conscious of the potential value of any adjacent seas. The desire to extend control over sea resources was a marked feature of the UN Conference on the Law of the Sea.

▼ One area of concern relates to those minerals which are important to Western industries (such as steel production) and of which South Africa (often along with the Soviet Union) is a dominant producer. The fear is that a political conflagration in South Africa could severely disrupt supplies.

There is a popular theory that a struggle for raw materials is the most likely cause of war between the great powers. This sort of consideration may have been of relevance in the last century: it is of only marginal importance now. By and large it is usually cheaper to import the vital raw materials on the open market than to go to war to gain access, especially as for many key minerals other industrialized states are the main suppliers.

MINERALS: EEC IMPORTS

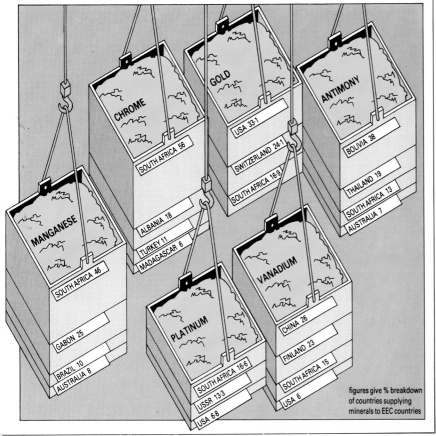

CHROME
SOUTH AFRICA 56
ALBANIA 18
TURKEY 11
MADAGASCAR 6

GOLD
USA 33·1
SWITZERLAND 24·1
SOUTH AFRICA 16·9

ANTIMONY
BOLIVIA 38
THAILAND 19
SOUTH AFRICA 13
AUSTRALIA 7

MANGANESE
SOUTH AFRICA 46
GABON 25
BRAZIL 10
AUSTRALIA 8

PLATINUM
SOUTH AFRICA 16·6
USSR 13·3
USA 6·8

VANADIUM
CHINA 26
FINLAND 23
SOUTH AFRICA 15
USA 6

figures give % breakdown of countries supplying minerals to EEC countries

Arab–Israeli War and the four-fold increase in oil prices from 1973 to 1974 brought home to the West that it could no longer ignore the economic and political interests of the major Arab oil producers. As the oil states grew richer and richer and the industrial countries were plunged into recession, the importance of the oil producers as markets for Western goods added to the sense of dependence on their goodwill. The forecasters warned that oil would continue to be in short supply throughout the 1980s.

The forecasters were wrong. The recession drove down demand for oil. High energy costs encouraged conservation and the development of alternative sources of energy such as coal and nuclear power. New oil reserves by and large controlled by countries outside OPEC (membership of which depends on oil being the major source of export earnings) were exploited and came on stream — in Alaska, Mexico and the North Sea. As supply problems were eased, the price began to come down. Those oil producers who had embarked on ambitious modernization programs on the assumption of continued oil wealth found it necessary to increase their production levels to compensate for falling prices and so added to the glut. OPEC was severely weakened. While supplies were short, it could agree on prices, but it lacked the cohesion to impose production quotas when supplies were plentiful.

Nothing illustrates the decline in the oil producers' position more clearly than the Iran–Iraq War. In the late 1970s a war between these two major producers, each of which was seeking to interrupt the other's oil production, with attacks on oil tankers and threats to cut off the Strait of Hormuz, would have sent the Western world, and especially the financial markets, into a flat spin. It was the worst that could happen. Yet now it has happened and the West has taken it all in its stride. The attacks on oil supplies were relevant only in the effect they had on the belligerents' economies.

Of course the oil market could change again as demand picks up and as the new reserves begin to dry up. One of the consequences of the recent glut has been that reserves have been depleted faster than might otherwise have been considered prudent. Nor is nuclear power being developed as an alternative as fast as was once expected. OPEC has not as yet fallen apart and may one day rise again. But for the moment its influence is on the wane.

Will the poor south rise up against the rich north?

A global class war?

By and large it is the third world that is dependent on the industrialized nations rather than the other way around. This is especially true for the poor and the hungry, which rely on Western aid to help them maintain even a minimal standard of living. It is important to note that not all countries that are still categorized as "third world" (which is a somewhat unsatisfactory category in the first place) are poor and hungry. A number, particularly in Asia, are industrializing fast and following Japan's example in carving out substantial markets in manufactured goods. Others have great economic potential which has yet to be realized either because of corruption and incompetence or else, as has been the case with a number in recent years, because they have been caught by unnaturally high interest rates. Such rates make the servicing of the debts that these nations took on in the 1970s to fund investment now almost impossibly burdensome — to the extent that the risk of a major default exercises the banking community.

An awareness of the gross inequities in the current international system, with the wealth divided up between relatively few industrialized countries while the rest struggle against economic odds stacked against them; a belief that the economic weakness of many third-world countries is a result of their past exploitation as colonies; a frustration with the failure of the wealthy countries to dispense even the recommended 0·7 percent of their GDP in economic aid, and an irritation with the political strings attached to this aid: these three factors have led many to expect a tide of radicalism to sweep the third world, similar to that expected by Marxists in individual countries as the more numerous oppressed mount a challenge to the ruling elite. On a global scale the poor south will demand a redistribution of international wealth from the rich north.

This global class struggle has yet to materialize. Many of the more disadvantaged third-world countries naturally blame the international economic system for their problems. Their attempts to organize themselves to do something about it have not produced much by way of results. The Group of 77, which now numbers many more than that number, is a collection of third-world countries that has held together through a shared feeling that the rules of the international game have been designed to favor the industrialized world. However, much of the cohesion has benefited from what American politicians call "log-rolling." The policy preferences of individual nations are aggregated together to satisfy everybody without resorting to hard and acrimonious bargaining to decide between these preferences. This behavior is easiest when there is little chance of proposals being implemented. In a different atmosphere, where the hard choices could not be avoided, the differences would become more evident. The group contains debtors and those building up financial reserves, those barely industrializing and those well along that road, oil producers and oil consumers. (Developing countries were especially hard hit by the rise in oil prices and had no reason to be impressed by the measures taken by the producers, in the name of third-world solidarity, to protect them.)

The means by which the Group of 77 achieved its consensus rendered its proposals somewhat unreal. Policies which directly oppose the interests of the industrialized world and the major international companies are unlikely to get very far. It is relatively easy to get their proposals adopted by international gatherings because the third world can always muster a majority, but this has not persuaded the industrialized world to transfer large-scale resources. The challenge is resolutionary rather than revolutionary.

The third world might have numbers on its side, but as the leaders of these countries are only too well aware, large populations do not count for much in the international arena — even with such gigantic populations as India's and China's. Large populations require feeding and the effort to do this tends to occupy much of the energies and spare cash of these countries. They are a drag rather than a spur to modernization. They strain administrative capabilities. This is made even worse when they are not homogeneous and they contain a number of disparate nationalities speaking a number of different languages. It has been a problem for many of the newly independent countries that their boundaries and internal composition reflect past colonial convenience rather than the basis for harmonious domestic politics.

It is therefore only when demands can be backed up by real muscle that a challenge can be mounted against the status quo. This muscle by and large resides with the major powers. The monopoly has been broken — most notably with oil — but the countries able to exercise this new power choose to do so with somewhat narrower ojectives than the overthrow of the established order.

WEALTH, NUMBERS AND DEFENSE SPENDING

A close examination of some of the most basic statistics of the countries of Asia reveals that the relationships between size, wealth and military power are less clear than one might expect. The top cartogram demonstrates the extent to which the wealthier countries (in per capita terms) are likely to be among the smaller. In the case of Asia this includes the fast-growing so-called NICs (newly industrializing countries) of the Far East and some of the smaller Gulf oil producers of the Near East. It is also interesting to note the small size of Saudi Arabia's population despite its landmass.

If population determined military power, then China and India, with numbers reaching into hundreds of millions, would sweep all others aside, while Indonesia would dominate Southeast Asia. If wealth was the determinant, then Japan would be the leader.

Not surprisingly it transpires that, while numbers and wealth are relevant, the most critical factor is security policy. As can be seen from the second cartogram, a number of states anxious to deter a neighbor from aggression (South Korea, Taiwan) or engaged in conflict (Iran, Iraq, Vietnam, Syria, Israel) have disproportionate military establishments. Again not surprisingly, in building up their strength countries draw on their area of comparative advantage, be it wealth or numbers. However, note the extent to which Israel's population is mobilized and, as a result of its war, Iraq's.

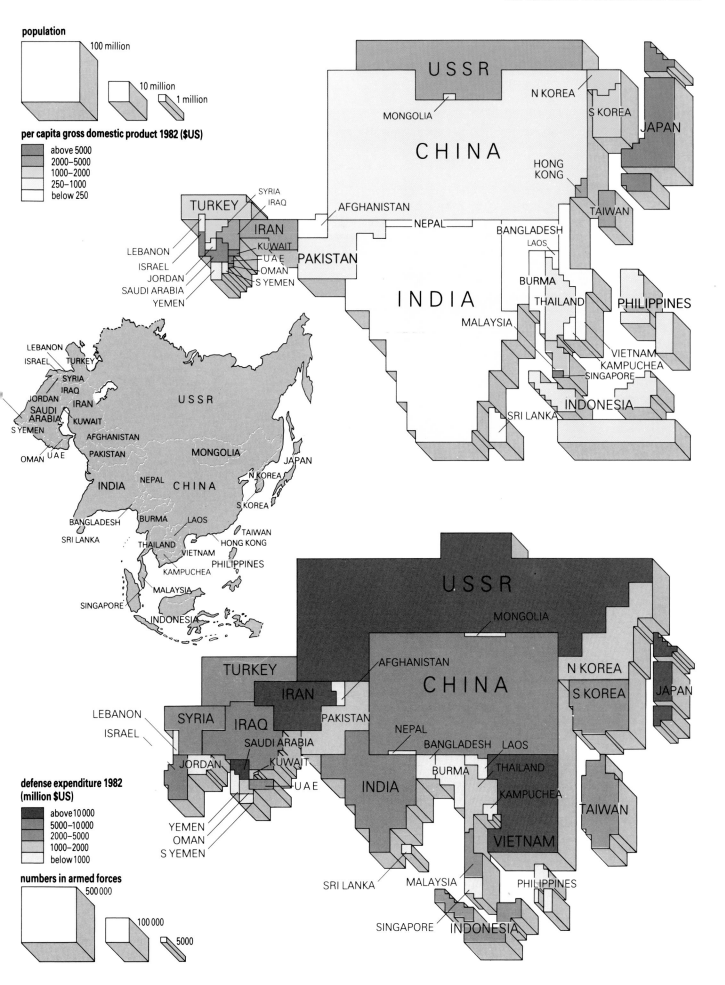

population

100 million

10 million

1 million

per capita gross domestic product 1982 ($US)

above 5000
2000–5000
1000–2000
250–1000
below 250

USSR

MONGOLIA

N KOREA

S KOREA

JAPAN

CHINA

HONG KONG

TAIWAN

TURKEY

SYRIA
IRAQ

AFGHANISTAN

NEPAL

BANGLADESH

IRAN

KUWAIT

LAOS

LEBANON

U A E

BURMA

ISRAEL
JORDAN
SAUDI ARABIA
YEMEN

OMAN
S YEMEN

PAKISTAN

INDIA

THAILAND

PHILIPPINES

MALAYSIA

VIETNAM
KAMPUCHEA
SINGAPORE

SRI LANKA

INDONESIA

LEBANON
ISRAEL
TURKEY
SYRIA
IRAQ
JORDAN
IRAN
SAUDI ARABIA
KUWAIT
S YEMEN
AFGHANISTAN
OMAN U A E
PAKISTAN

USSR

MONGOLIA

JAPAN

N KOREA

S KOREA

INDIA

NEPAL

CHINA

TAIWAN
HONG KONG

BANGLADESH

BURMA

LAOS

SRI LANKA

THAILAND

VIETNAM

PHILIPPINES

KAMPUCHEA

MALAYSIA

SINGAPORE

INDONESIA

USSR

MONGOLIA

AFGHANISTAN

CHINA

N KOREA

S KOREA

JAPAN

TURKEY

IRAN

PAKISTAN

NEPAL

SYRIA

IRAQ

BANGLADESH

LAOS

LEBANON

ISRAEL

SAUDI ARABIA

BURMA

THAILAND

JORDAN

KUWAIT

U A E

INDIA

KAMPUCHEA

TAIWAN

YEMEN
OMAN
S YEMEN

VIETNAM

defense expenditure 1982 (million $US)

above 10 000
5000–10 000
2000–5000
1000–2000
below 1000

SRI LANKA

MALAYSIA

PHILIPPINES

numbers in armed forces

500 000

100 000

5000

SINGAPORE

INDONESIA

45

INTERNATIONAL AFFILIATIONS

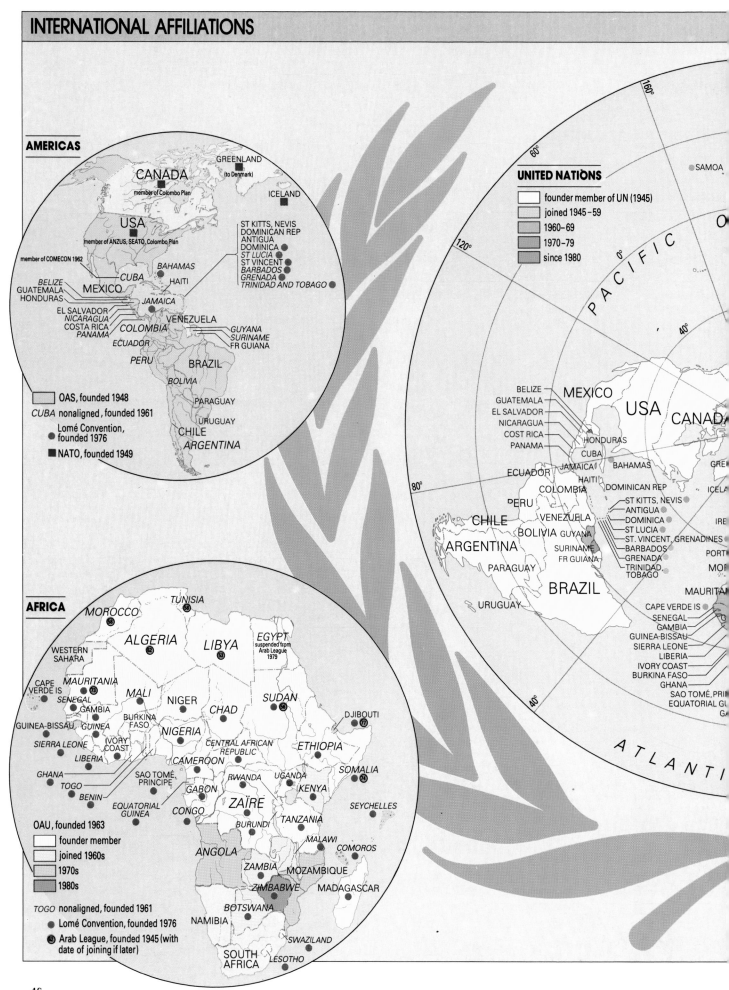

AMERICAS

GREENLAND
(to Denmark)

CANADA
member of Colombo Plan

ICELAND

USA
member of ANZUS, SEATO, Colombo Plan

member of COMECON 1962

ST KITTS, NEVIS
DOMINICAN REP
ANTIGUA
DOMINICA
ST LUCIA
ST VINCENT
BARBADOS
GRENADA
TRINIDAD AND TOBAGO

BAHAMAS
CUBA
HAITI

BELIZE
GUATEMALA
HONDURAS
MEXICO
JAMAICA

EL SALVADOR
NICARAGUA
COSTA RICA
PANAMA
VENEZUELA
COLOMBIA
ECUADOR

GUYANA
SURINAME
FR GUIANA

PERU
BRAZIL

BOLIVIA

PARAGUAY

URUGUAY

CHILE
ARGENTINA

OAS, founded 1948
CUBA nonaligned, founded 1961
● Lomé Convention, founded 1976
■ NATO, founded 1949

UNITED NATIONS

☐ founder member of UN (1945)
☐ joined 1945–59
☐ 1960–69
☐ 1970–79
☐ since 1980

SAMOA

PACIFIC O

BELIZE
GUATEMALA
EL SALVADOR
NICARAGUA
COST RICA
PANAMA
MEXICO
USA
CANADA
HONDURAS
CUBA
JAMAICA
BAHAMAS
GRE
HAITI
ICELA
DOMINICAN REP
ST KITTS, NEVIS
ANTIGUA
DOMINICA
ST LUCIA
ST. VINCENT, GRENADINES
BARBADOS
GRENADA
TRINIDAD, TOBAGO
IRE
PORT

ECUADOR
COLOMBIA
PERU
CHILE
BOLIVIA
ARGENTINA
VENEZUELA
GUYANA
SURINAME
FR GUIANA
BRAZIL
PARAGUAY
URUGUAY
MO

MAURITANIA
CAPE VERDE IS
SENEGAL
GAMBIA
GUINEA-BISSAU
SIERRA LEONE
LIBERIA
IVORY COAST
BURKINA FASO
GHANA
SAO TOMÉ, PRIN
EQUATORIAL GU
GA

ATLANTI

AFRICA

TUNISIA ⑤⑧
MOROCCO ⑤⑥
ALGERIA ⑤②
LIBYA ⑤③
EGYPT
suspended from
Arab League
1979

WESTERN
SAHARA

CAPE
VERDE IS ⑦③
MAURITANIA
SENEGAL
GAMBIA
MALI
NIGER
CHAD
SUDAN ⑤⑥
DJIBOUTI ⑦⑦

GUINEA-BISSAU
GUINEA
BURKINA
FASO
NIGERIA
CENTRAL AFRICAN
REPUBLIC
ETHIOPIA
SOMALIA ⑦④

SIERRA LEONE
*IVORY
COAST*
CAMEROON

GHANA
TOGO
BENIN
SAO TOMÉ,
PRINCIPE
GABON
EQUATORIAL
GUINEA
CONGO
ZAÏRE
RWANDA
UGANDA
KENYA

BURUNDI
TANZANIA
SEYCHELLES

MALAWI
COMOROS

ANGOLA
ZAMBIA
MOZAMBIQUE
MADAGASCAR

ZIMBABWE

NAMIBIA
BOTSWANA

SWAZILAND

SOUTH
AFRICA
LESOTHO

OAU, founded 1963
☐ founder member
☐ joined 1960s
☐ 1970s
☐ 1980s

TOGO nonaligned, founded 1961
● Lomé Convention, founded 1976
㉜ Arab League, founded 1945 (with
date of joining if later)

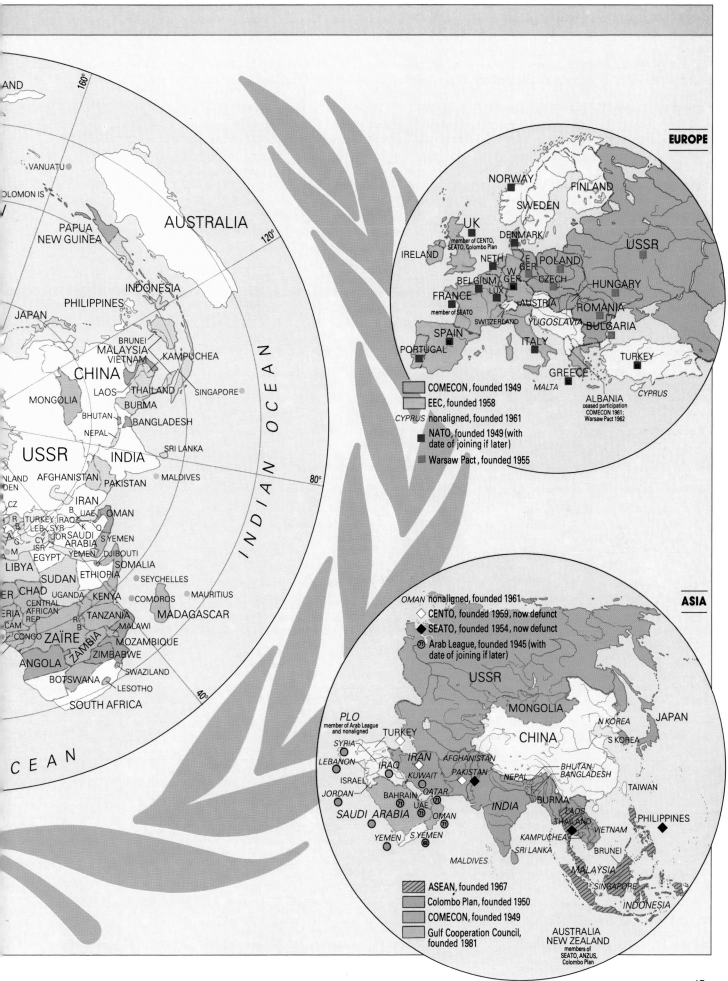

New alliances and new rivalries

The new international order

This does not mean that the old great powers can carry on as before. Decolonization may not have removed the old colonies from certain forms of economic dependence, but sovereignty does produce some power. There are votes to be cast in international organizations, such as the United Nations. When the two superpowers are in competition, a state willing to suggest that its allegiance is up for grabs can obtain significant benefits.

When the United Nations was formed in 1945, there were only 51 members, of which 20 were Latin American and hardly any were Asian or African. Forty years later the membership has more than trebled. Some states that are only barely viable as independent entities now cast votes in the General Assembly.

In 1961 at Belgrade a number of non-aligned countries came together to form a Nonaligned Movement to make clear their dissatisfaction at the paralysis produced by superpower deadlock and to ensure that alternative perspectives on international issues were pushed to the fore. It was formed by leaders of newly independent countries (such as Nehru of India and Nkrumah of Ghana) or those asserting their independence from one of the blocs (such as Tito of Yugoslavia) to provide an alternative to a polarized international system. In the late 1970s it began to be asked exactly how nonaligned the movement actually was, as Fidel Castro's Cuba moved into a leadership position and began to argue that the Soviet Union was really quite sympathetic to the views of the nonaligned and supportive of their interests. This argument was opposed vigorously at the time and did not in practice survive the Soviet invasion of Afghanistan.

The lasting effect of the movement has been to emphasize the unwillingness of the majority of countries to tie themselves too closely to one particular bloc. As a basis for a positive diplomacy, it has now been superseded by smaller groupings which can address local problems of real substance. Two of the major regional groupings — the Arab League and the Organization of American States — were established just after the war (1945 and 1948 respectively) and have been extended since. The influence and effectiveness of these groups depend very much on their internal cohesion, which means that the larger and more disparate their number, the weaker they tend to be, and on the nature of their regional problems. Thus the Organ-

ization of African Unity (which was established in the 1960s) can unite in abhorrence of apartheid, but many of its members have little choice but to respect South Africa's economic power; and in attempting to adjudicate in disputes among its members it is often forced to rely on rigid rules such as respect for all existing boundaries. Those states unwilling to respect these rules, or lacking confidence in the organization's ability to impose them, still tend to call on more powerful countries from outside the region to intervene on their behalf when they look like losing out in a particular conflict. The politics of the Organization of American States are very much bound up with relationships between the Central and South American countries and the United States, which in turn tend to get bound up with the ideological divisions of the continent, symbolized in the past by Cuba and more recently by Nicaragua.

The problem for these groupings is that the more success they have in pushing the major powers to the sidelines, the more traditional conflicts and rivalries reassert themselves — perhaps suppressed for decades in a common battle against the imperialists — or new rivalries begin to appear, as in economically troubled and politically confused parts of the world a struggle develops to shape the local balance of power.

The more successful regional groupings — and the more recent in origin — tend to be smaller still. Two examples are the Association of South East Asian Nations (ASEAN) formed in 1967, and the Gulf Cooperation Council in 1981. In general, however, international power beyond the major blocs does not so much reside in new groupings as in strong regional states.

The UN Security Council in action in June 1967 as it unanimously called on all parties to the Arab–Israeli War then under way to agree to an immediate cease-fire.

2

THE CHANGING PATTERN OF WARFARE

The great powers grow less inclined to police the world's conflicts — whether they be colonial wars marking the end of the imperial age, regime wars in countries undergoing major internal change, or straight interstate wars. Logistics govern the projection of military might and this has become a limiting factor for the major powers. This is especially true in the US, hence the Rapid Deployment Force. The growth of the conventional arms trade is supported by the major powers as an alternative to military intervention, to promote regional stability as well as commercial interests. As such it has had a mixed record. Membership of the nuclear club remains circumscribed.

Relations between the major powers have settled down to an underlying stability brought about by a recognition of the dangers associated with any confrontation. The significance of this development has been somewhat obscured by a high degree of antagonism, much of which results from uncertainties over what each side is really up to in the third world. In practice, and despite the popular image of global strategy as a game being played between the great powers, both East and West are finding it difficult to develop reliable and influential clients.

What is notable about so many recent conflicts is that they are either between countries without strong links to East or West or else they are "in the family." The Communist family is smaller than the Western, but relations within it are much more tempestuous. Thus the main victims of Soviet power have been Eastern European governments deviating from the straight and narrow, and an unreliable Marxist regime in Afghanistan. In Asia the Soviet Union, China, Vietnam and the Khmer Rouge are squabbling with each other, despite the fact that they are all notionally Marxist.

Most countries in the world are more attached to the West than to the East, especially when one includes the Latin American and Caribbean countries with close ties to the United States, the British Commonwealth and Francophone Africa, so the Western "extended family" is larger. In any disputes within this "extended family" the loyalties of those not directly involved may be severely tested. In these circumstances the strain is most acutely felt by the head of the family who normally feels obliged to assert his authority to reestablish more wholesome relationships. But as the members of this family become more interested in local problems and less confident that their superpower protector will come to their aid in a crisis, the more ties within the family become stretched and remote, with some members exhibiting disturbing signs of delinquency.

Naturally either superpower will fear that feuding in its own family will serve as a source of weakness in its dealings with the other superpower and its family. Thus the greater the sense of confrontation between the two superpowers, the more energetic their overall diplomacy. In an era of détente they might not see the need to get so involved. It is not altogether clear whether the opportunities for third-world countries to pursue their distinctive interests are greater in an era of confrontation or in one of détente. In the former they can play the superpowers off against each other, but also find them paying excessive attention to their affairs; in the latter they may be left more alone, but on the other hand they may find that their interests have been sold out by a superpower protector which has reached some sort of understanding with the other superpower. There is an Asian proverb: whether the elephants fight or make love, the grass gets trampled.

Family troubles

While the two superpowers might still put their relations with each other as the critical factor, determining all else in their international diplomacy, in practice their crisis diplomacy now has little to do with managing confrontations with each other. It is more about preventing clashes among friends, allies and close acquaintances getting out of control, or at least containing their impact on what should be the most positive side of their foreign policy. Thus in 1982 a Reagan administration, which had entered office identifying the Soviet Union as the source of all international conflict, found that its major foreign-policy headaches involved three of its staunchest allies — Begin's Israel, Galtieri's Argentina and Thatcher's Britain.

Nor can the current position be understood simply as new participants in an old game that is still played according to traditional rules. The country that has emerged as the world's most dynamic economic power — Japan — has held back from an assertive foreign policy, largely because of memories of the last time that it asserted itself on the international scene. Other countries which might have aspired to a more active world role have either overextended themselves, such as Iran, or been forced to recognize that they can make their influence felt most keenly by concentrating on their own region, such as Saudi Arabia, China and India.

The arrival over the past three decades of almost 100 extra sovereign states has undermined the old forms of power politics. The frustrations and resentments harbored by many of these newly independent states are often shared by other states which have been independent for some time but are still low down the international pecking order. But the differences among these states have undermined attempts to forge alternative power blocs able to mount a sustained challenge to the old order. The only serious challenge was mounted by the oil producers in the 1970s. International politics now feature a variety of regional disputes and rivalries which increasingly find expression in open conflict.

The reluctance of the superpowers to risk a devastating third world war is even more marked when the argument is in areas of peripheral interest. This is compounded by an awareness of the problems involved in intervening effectively in parts of the world well away from home territory to sort out other people's arguments, the nuances of which can only be dimly understood.

When the United Nations was formed, it was envisaged that the great powers, deriving

their authority from the new international body, would act almost as policemen, employing their irresistible military might against any aggressor who offended the new conventions of international behavior. The only time the UN was used in this way was in response to the North Korean invasion of the South in 1950. The Soviet Union had absented itself from the Security Council at the time, in a fit of pique over recent Western-sponsored resolutions, and so failed to cast its veto. The same mistake was never made again.

The major powers tend to describe their postwar interventions as "police actions," as if they were solely and in some disinterested

After 1945 Japan renounced war, the possession of war potential and the right of belligerency in Article 9 of its new constitution. However, it maintained the right to self-defense on which it decided to spend no more than 1 percent of GNP; but when GNP grows to the size of that of modern Japan, 1 percent can buy a considerable amount. The Americans have also been putting pressure on the Japanese to do more, particularly when it comes to protection of key sea routes. In this picture members of Japan's self-defense force (which now

numbers some 250 000) are on parade.

manner wishing to impose order in unruly parts of the world by dealing with the local troublemakers. Over time, the problems of intervention effectively discouraged intensive policing (certainly of a disinterested nature). As a result all sorts of local conflicts previously suppressed came bubbling up to the surface. The result is evident to anyone who keeps in touch with international news. Wars of one sort or another are common occurrences. They take a variety of forms from prolonged struggles against guerrilla groups seeking to overthrow the established authority to traditional encounters which might flare up suddenly and end almost as quickly after a decisive clash of arms.

The variety is so great that there are no agreed estimates of exactly how many violent conflicts that might be described as "wars" there have been since 1945. A reasonable estimate puts the figure at something approaching 150, with total casualties probably in the region of some 20 million. Statistics such as these cannot be precise and must be treated with care.

There are important arguments over what constitutes a war. Must a substantial number of casualties be involved to qualify? One academic work has suggested 1000 dead, but this seems extremely arbitrary. The Falklands conflict of 1982 would be borderline on this criterion. Some wars are characterized by

CONFLICT SINCE 1945

The observation that nuclear deterrence has helped to secure 40 years of peace and stability clearly applies only to Europe. In most other parts of the world (with the notable exception of Australasia) conflict has been rife. Wars have not become markedly less frequent or less violent. The main change has been in the decline in colonial wars and the rise of old-fashioned interstate wars in the third world. Wars have been caused more often by issues such as territorial boundaries and national self-determination than by a struggle for resources.

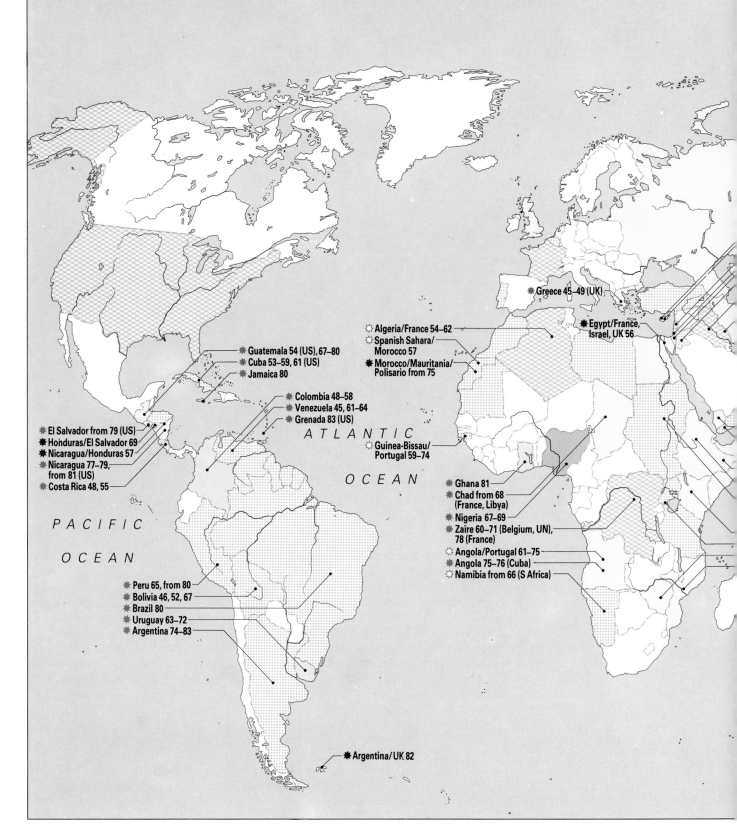

Greece 45–49 (UK)

Algeria/France 54–62
Spanish Sahara/Morocco 57
Morocco/Mauritania/Polisario from 75

Egypt/France, Israel, UK 56

Guatemala 54 (US), 67–80
Cuba 53–59, 61 (US)
Jamaica 80

Colombia 48–58
Venezuela 45, 61–64
Grenada 83 (US)

ATLANTIC

El Salvador from 79 (US)
Honduras/El Salvador 69
Nicaragua/Honduras 57
Nicaragua 77–79, from 81 (US)
Costa Rica 48, 55

OCEAN

Guinea-Bissau/Portugal 59–74

Ghana 81
Chad from 68 (France, Libya)
Nigeria 67–69
Zaire 60–71 (Belgium, UN), 78 (France)
Angola/Portugal 61–75
Angola 75–76 (Cuba)
Namibia from 66 (S Africa)

PACIFIC

OCEAN

Peru 65, from 80
Bolivia 46, 52, 67
Brazil 80
Uruguay 63–72
Argentina 74–83

Argentina/UK 82

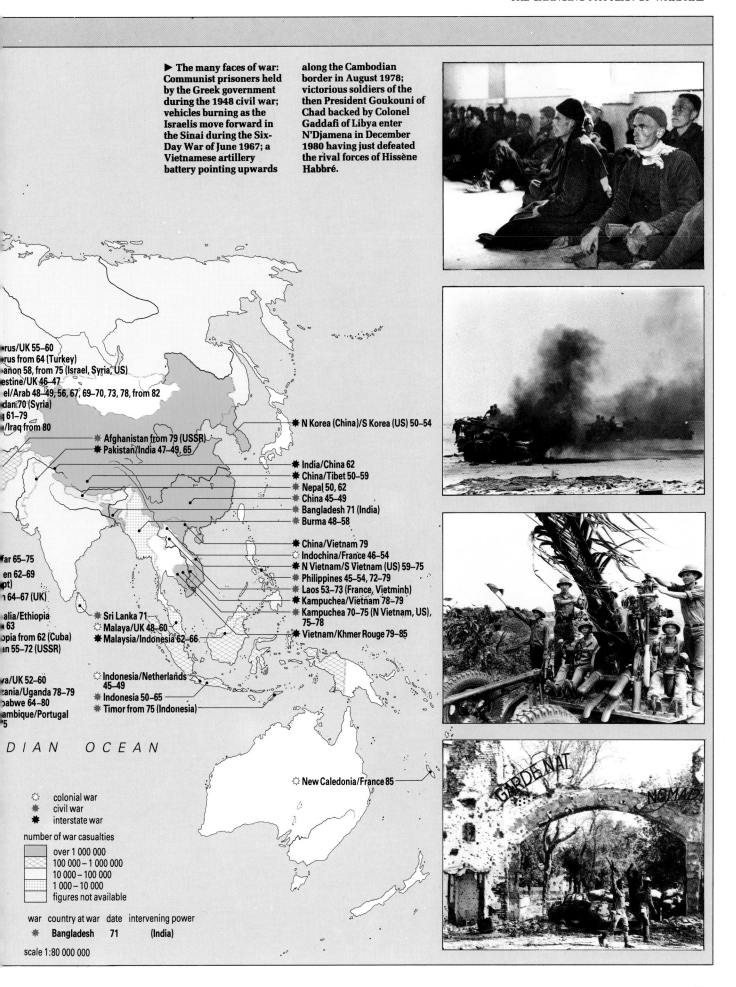

▶ The many faces of war: Communist prisoners held by the Greek government during the 1948 civil war; vehicles burning as the Israelis move forward in the Sinai during the Six-Day War of June 1967; a Vietnamese artillery battery pointing upwards along the Cambodian border in August 1978; victorious soldiers of the then President Goukouni of Chad backed by Colonel Gaddafi of Libya enter N'Djamena in December 1980 having just defeated the rival forces of Hissène Habbré.

rus/UK 55–60
rus from 64 (Turkey)
anon 58, from 75 (Israel, Syria, US)
estine/UK 46–47
el/Arab 48–49, 56, 67, 69–70, 73, 78, from 82
dan 70 (Syria)
61–79
/Iraq from 80

❉ Afghanistan from 79 (USSR)
✴ Pakistan/India 47–49, 65

✴ India/China 62
✴ China/Tibet 50–59
✴ Nepal 50, 62
✴ China 45–49
❉ Bangladesh 71 (India)
❉ Burma 48–58

✴ China/Vietnam 79
○ Indochina/France 46–54
✴ N Vietnam/S Vietnam (US) 59–75
❉ Philippines 45–54, 72–79
✴ Laos 53–73 (France, Vietminh)
✴ Kampuchea/Vietnam 78–79
✴ Kampuchea 70–75 (N Vietnam, US), 75–78
✴ Vietnam/Khmer Rouge 79–85

✴ N Korea (China)/S Korea (US) 50–54

ar 65–75
en 62–69
pt)
64–67 (UK)

alia/Ethiopia
63
opia from 62 (Cuba)
an 55–72 (USSR)

a/UK 52–60
ania/Uganda 78–79
abwe 64–80
ambique/Portugal
5

❉ Sri Lanka 71
○ Malaya/UK 48–60
✴ Malaysia/Indonesia 62–66

○ Indonesia/Netherlands 45–49
✴ Indonesia 50–65
✴ Timor from 75 (Indonesia)

DIAN OCEAN

○ New Caledonia/France 85

○ colonial war
✴ civil war
✴ interstate war

number of war casualties
█ over 1 000 000
▨ 100 000 – 1 000 000
☐ 10 000 – 100 000
▦ 1 000 – 10 000
☐ figures not available

war	country at war	date	intervening power
✴	Bangladesh	71	(India)

scale 1:80 000 000

Colonial wars are superseded by regime wars

such effective offensive thrusts that the victim gives up almost without a fight. Another problem is how to distinguish wars from riots and other civil disturbances or border incidents that may result in casualties but are contained in their effects. Does war have to be declared? If so, then there have hardly been any since 1945 because it has become the normal practice not to make a declaration.

Our concern will be with attempts to settle disputes by violent means with at least one side using regular armed forces. Rather than attempt statistical precision in categorizing wars, a more useful exercise might be to see to what extent it is possible to identify patterns in the types that have come to the fore at particular times since the end of the last global conflict.

Warfare since 1945

Stress has already been laid on the most important piece of negative evidence. The type of war most feared has not occurred. Apart from the Sino–Soviet clashes of 1969 (when China was just on the verge of becoming a nuclear power) there has been no actual fighting between nuclear powers. It is notable that, with few exceptions, wars since 1945 have taken place away from the territory of the industrialized world.

The most familiar conflict for much of the 1940s and 1950s was the colonial war, associated with the dismantling of the old European empires. The old colonial powers res-

isted the powerful demands from the subject peoples for control over their own destinies — the "winds of change" as they were described by British Prime Minister Harold Macmillan in 1960 — with varying degrees of conviction and effectiveness. At best they delayed independence, but in no case did they prevent it, and the more bitter the war the less sympathetic the post-independence regime was to the old colonial power.

The British fought a number of holding actions but were soon persuaded to bow to the inevitable. Many of their potential colonial wars were resolved while matters were still at the stage of police actions against illegal nationalist groups. The French, by contrast, fought two protracted conflicts in Indochina and Algeria, and then gave up exhausted, concentrating instead on ensuring that the ties with the old colonies were as close as possible. The empires were all being wound down by the mid-1960s, with the exception of Portugal's which stuck it out longer than the others. In 1974 the Caetano regime in Portugal was overthrown, partly as a result of the never-ending colonial wars. With Salazar went the Portuguese empire. Independence soon came to Guinea-Bissau, the Cape Verde Islands, Mozambique and Angola (though in the last case not without a bitter struggle between competing factions for control which has yet to be effectively concluded).

When Britain finally managed to hand over to a majority government in Zimbabwe in 1980, 15 years after the unilateral declaration of independence by a white-minority government, the colonial era had effectively come to an end. It is of note that the disputes which have bothered British policy makers since then have not been wars of liberation but the problems of dealing with the few surviving bits of empire whose occupants wish to remain British and are distrustful of neighbors with claims on the territory — Guatemala and Belize, Spain and Gibraltar, Argentina and the Falklands, China and Hong Kong.

With the passing of colonialism a different type of war came to the fore. New governments of slight experience and uncertain authority came to preside over countries whose make-up was often contested, both from within and from without, and whose people often savored expectations that were unlikely to be fulfilled. These instabilities led to a number of what we might call regime wars in that they were concerned with the political structure of the countries involved.

▲ The Union Jack comes down in Zimbabwe, formally Rhodesia, in April 1980. Britain was relieved at being able to disentangle itself from what had been its most awkward foreign-policy problem since 1965 when the white-controlled government unilaterally declared independence.

◀ Portuguese soldiers cheerfully keeping order after the popular army-led revolution of 1974 are applauded by civilians.

These afflict not only newly independent countries but can affect any country undergoing substantial internal change.

Regime wars can be divided into two types. First there are those which, in terms of commitments of regular forces, remain essentially civil wars — often prompted by secessionist or insurrectionary movements. There are plenty of examples of this sort of war from all continents — China in the 1940s, Cuba in the 1950s, Nigeria in the 1960s, Nicaragua in the 1970s. The second type are those where an external power intervenes directly on behalf of one side. Both Britain and France have felt obliged on a number of occasions to intervene with quite small forces to support regimes which they had helped implant to oversee independence. A responsibility for

the security of "first-generation" governments drove much of Britain's "East of Suez" policy until economic circumstances forced a disengagement in the late 1960s. These interventions varied from helping to quell army mutinies in East African countries to the Malayan emergency. French policy in Africa is still motivated by such considerations. The United States tended to stand rather aloof from the colonial wars but did get drawn into regime wars, often motivated by East–West considerations. Vietnam is the most important example.

The final type might be called interstate wars. These are comparatively old-fashioned affairs, involving clashes between regular forces, fought between undivided states, as a result of a clash of economic or political

Interstate wars are not surrogate East–West conflicts

interests. They may include attempts to interfere with another's internal affairs but are also likely to be related to regional power balances. For many years this tradition was kept going by the Indians and Pakistanis, and by the Arabs and Israelis, with the two sets of belligerents almost taking it in turns. The Indo–Pakistan wars were in 1947, 1965 and 1971; the Arab–Israeli in 1948, 1956, 1967 and 1973.

What is striking about the past decade is the greater frequency of this type of war. Over the past 10 years we have had wars pitting Vietnam (newly united after 30 years of civil war) against both Kampuchea and China, Israel against the PLO and the Syrians in the Lebanon, Ethiopia against Somalia, Iran against Iraq, Britain against Argentina. In addition, there have been a number of conflicts at the borderline between regime and interstate wars, such as the Soviet Union in Afghanistan, the United States in Grenada, the Tanzanians in Uganda, France in Chad and Zaïre, Cuba and South Africa in Angola and any number of countries mixing it in Central America. These and some of the conflicts mentioned earlier have great implications for the political structures of individual states, but much of their interest results from the effects that they have on local power balances.

These wars have not been proxy East–West conflicts. Even when they have appeared as such, local and regional factors provide better explanations for their origins. For example, in the fighting between Somalia and Ethiopia over the Ogaden region the two sides were backed by superpowers but the two belligerents swapped superpowers in the middle, indicating that they were acting for themselves rather than on behalf of some grand global cause. Even the Shaba guerrillas in Zaïre, who were portrayed as Communist-sponsored, have over the past couple of decades enjoyed a variety of sponsors from the extreme right as well as the extreme left. The only constant is their cause. The West may have rallied to support the Afghan rebels in the face of the Soviet occupation of their country, but these rebels were very similar in ideological make-up to the revolutionary leaders in next-door Iran who caused the Americans such trouble.

By the Hilton Hotel in Beirut in October 1975, Christian Phalangists face heavy fire from Islamic fighters in the battle for the streets of the Lebanese capital.

Superpower involvement in local conflicts

The influence of the superpowers

Where the superpowers have committed forces, it has been into neighboring countries — Afghanistan and Grenada. They have been acting more as regional than as global powers. Because of the persistence of regime wars in ex-colonies, Britain and France have actually made more commitments of forces — though usually on a much smaller scale than would be expected of a superpower. Otherwise, the major powers are spectators to most conflicts, or have at most a marginal involvement, however interested they may be in the outcome.

Nevertheless, when wars occur or seem imminent, the natural interest is in whether a major power will become involved and, if so, whether this will result in the flames of war being dampened or fanned into something that will burn with even more fury and danger. Will the trouble spot turn into a flash point? The natural reaction of the news media is to send correspondents not only to the scene of the actual or prospective fighting but to find out the views of Washington and Moscow.

The presumption is still that in the end the course of most wars will be shaped by the superpowers. They may not intervene themselves, but they might supply equipment or intelligence information to one of the belligerents. They might indicate their concern over what is going on by sending a carrier task force to the region or (as has increasingly been American practice) an airborne early-warning plane (AWACS) to keep an eye over what is going on. The Russians respond to most crises by launching a number of spy satellites to keep themselves fully informed. At the UN Security Council most attention will be focused on the activities of the permanent members.

All this activity may signify an interest in these conflicts and even substantial anxiety over their course. Often it represents an attempt to exert influence over events. But that does not mean to say that influence will in practice be exerted. These conflicts have not been instigated by the great powers. Those setting them in motion are aware that they may face pressure from larger powers and have taken this possibility into account in their calculations. As often as not it is those who find themselves fighting against their better judgment who look to outside sources for help. Countries who suspect themselves of being in the weakest position in a local conflict may well seek to gather outside support by giving the conflict an East–West dimension, however artificial. They might

warn Western powers that the East is on the verge of a great breakthrough. Sometimes powerful outsiders will succumb to such blandishments, but actually they are generally reluctant to do so if it looks as if the opposition really will be fully backed by another great power. When intervention does occur, the objective is normally to achieve little more than a return to the status quo ante before the friendly regimes, or at least the friendly policies, had been disturbed. There is far less willingness to underwrite more radical adventures.

Clients which have expected wholehearted backing from their superpower in some argument with the other superpower have often been bitterly disappointed. An important instance of this came in 1958 when China began to build up pressure on Taiwan, where the Nationalists had fled from the mainland after their defeat in the civil war in 1949. The offshore islands of Quemoy and Matsu, also occupied by the Nationalists, were bombarded from the mainland. The Americans moved in strongly on behalf of the Nationalists. The Russians were far more cautious on behalf of the Communists, pledging their support only if there were an attempt to launch an offensive against the mainland but not in support of a Communist attempt to reunite China by taking Taiwan. This added to the disenchantment in Beijing with the comrades in Moscow and encouraged the split which occurred a few years later between the two Communist giants. Ironically, just over two decades later, Moscow used

▶ The AWACS aircraft, able to provide excellent surveillance over a wide area, has become the modern equivalent of the gunboat. Unarmed, it is not as provocative as a gunboat, yet it enables America's allies and clients (in this case Saudi Arabia) to watch for untoward moves by their opponents.

▼ In 1958 the Communists on the Chinese mainland began to bombard Nationalist strongholds on the islands of Quemoy and Matsu in the Formosa Strait, partly in order to test the extent of Soviet support for themselves and American support for the enemy. They were disappointed on both counts. Here Nationalist soldiers in Quemoy are on alert for a Communist invasion.

ACTS OF TERROR

In October 1984 the Irish Republican Army came close to killing a large portion of the British government, including the prime minister, when a bomb exploded in the Grand Hotel, Brighton, at the end of the Conservative Party Conference. Five people were killed and two cabinet ministers were hurt.

One of the factors encouraging a sense of increasing international disorder is the frequency of terrorist attacks. One authority has identified almost 6500 international terrorist incidents from 1973 to 1982, resulting in over 11 000 casualties of which about a third were fatal. Those most at risk have been diplomats, with businessmen, soldiers and politicians coming next. Western Europe suffers more than any other region, followed by the Middle East and Latin America. However, it is United States citizens and property that are most at risk.

There is a long history of political groups seeking to make their views felt through acts of terror, on the presumption that rather than endure further attacks the authorities will comply with the group's demands. The methods involved are not necessarily sophisticated, at most reflecting trends in small arms and explosives. Rather it is modern communications and the complexity of our societies that have created more opportunities to wreak havoc. The terrorists (which is rarely the name that they choose for themselves) travel long distances in search of what they suspect to be their opponent's Achilles' heel. The appetite of the news media ensures that maximum publicity will be given to the most outrageous incidents — in the process drawing attention to the cause. Thus, the factional fights of the Middle East are fought out on the streets of Western capitals.

DIARY OF TERRORIST ACTIVITIES IN THE MIDDLE EAST 1970–72

The evidence of the table below suggests that the PLO used terrorist tactics to ensure that it was not excluded from any political settlement of problems in the Middle East. It was especially conscious of moves that might have led to Jordan taking decisions in negotiations on its behalf. It also demonstrates how terrorism can trigger a powerful counterreaction.

POLITICAL EVENTS

December 1969 US unveils Rogers Peace Plan: basically an Israeli return of territory occupied in 1967 in exchange for Arab recognition of Israeli territorial integrity.

25 June 1970 Rogers announces US peace initiative aimed at ending the "war of attrition" across the Suez Canal.

24 July Nasser accepts cease-fire proposal; Jordan and Israel follow suit.

7 August Cease-fire announced; tension increases within Arab world between the UAR and Jordan on one side, Syria, Iraq and the Palestinians on the other.

15 September Civil war breaks out in Jordan between Jordanian troops and Palestinians.
18 September Syrian intervention on behalf of PLO.
22 September Syrian troops withdraw; crisis ends with victory for Jordanian forces.
28 September Nasser dies; Sadat takes over.

December Rogers Peace Plan revived.

8 February 1971 UN envoy Gunnar Jarring asks Egypt and Israel for a public endorsement of UN Security Council Resolution 242.

January/February 1972 Israel attacks bases used by PLO guerrillas in south Lebanon as a retaliation for cross-border raids.

15 March King Hussein proposes a plan for the unification of Jordan, the West Bank area and the Gaza Strip into a single entity called the United Arab Kingdom.

April UN observer force increased in size.

June Israel launches the fiercest-ever air strikes in south Lebanon.

September Israeli air strikes extended into the Bekaa valley; further increase in the number of aircraft on each mission and the weight of bombs dropped.

24 October First evidence of an Israeli willingness to "fight fire with fire"; a series of letter bombs, all posted in Belgrade, arrives on the desks of PLO leaders in Lebanon, Egypt, Libya and Algeria.

8 December Mahmoud Hamshari, the PLO representative in Paris, is killed by a bomb in his telephone. Wael Zwaiter, Fatah representative in Rome, is shot outside his apartment.

TERRORIST EVENTS

February 1970 PFLP blow up a Swiss airliner in midair; 55 killed.
10 February Arab terrorist grenade attack kills one Israeli, wounds 11 other people at Munich airport.

22 July Palestinian commandos hijack a Greek passenger jet and demand release of seven guerrillas held in Greece.

6 September PFLP commandos hijack three airliners — two US, one Swiss — and fail to hijack a fourth. One plane flown to Cairo, two to Dawson's Field, Jordan.
7 September US plane blown up in Cairo.
9 September British plane hijacked and flown to Dawson's Field.
12 September All three planes at Dawson's Field blown up; all hostages released or rescued by Jordanian forces by 29 September.

6 November Two bombs in a Tel Aviv bus station kill one person.

28 November 1971 Jordanian prime minister shot dead in Cairo by PLO.

22 February 1972 PFLP hijack a German airliner to Aden; plane and passengers released after a $5 million ransom is paid.

April Black September/PFLP "Easter Commando" group is arrested in Israel before they can execute planned attacks on tourist hotels.

8 May Black September hijack a Sabena aircraft and force it down at Tel Aviv; Israeli paratroopers disguised as mechanics storm the plane; one passenger killed as well as two of the terrorists.
31 May Three Japanese kamikaze attackers working with the PFLP kill 23 people and wound 28 at Lod airport.

5 September Seven Black September terrorists take nine Israeli athletes hostage at the Olympic village in Munich; all the hostages, five terrorists and one policeman die in the ensuing gun battle.
9 September Over the next few days 50 letter bombs, all posted in Amsterdam, are discovered; followed by two more batches posted in Malaysia and India.

29 October Lufthansa plane hijacked by Black September terrorists in midair; the three surviving members of the Munich squad are released when the terrorists threaten to blow up the plane in midair.

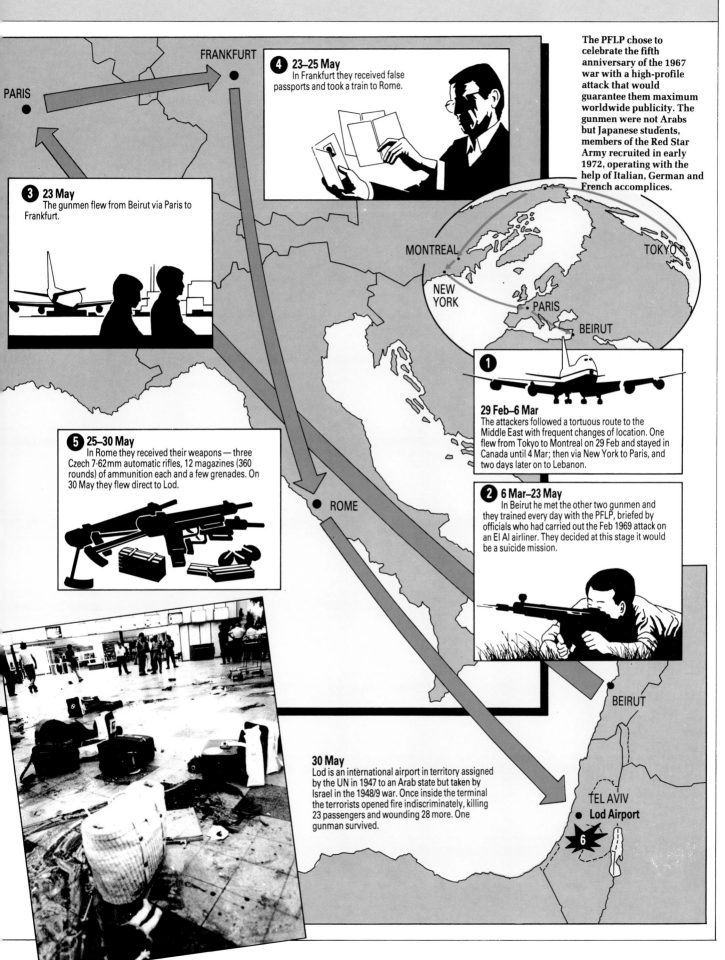

4 23–25 May
In Frankfurt they received false passports and took a train to Rome.

3 23 May
The gunmen flew from Beirut via Paris to Frankfurt.

The PFLP chose to celebrate the fifth anniversary of the 1967 war with a high-profile attack that would guarantee them maximum worldwide publicity. The gunmen were not Arabs but Japanese students, members of the Red Star Army recruited in early 1972, operating with the help of Italian, German and French accomplices.

1
29 Feb–6 Mar
The attackers followed a tortuous route to the Middle East with frequent changes of location. One flew from Tokyo to Montreal on 29 Feb and stayed in Canada until 4 Mar; then via New York to Paris, and two days later on to Lebanon.

5 25–30 May
In Rome they received their weapons — three Czech 7·62mm automatic rifles, 12 magazines (360 rounds) of ammunition each and a few grenades. On 30 May they flew direct to Lod.

2 6 Mar–23 May
In Beirut he met the other two gunmen and they trained every day with the PFLP, briefed by officials who had carried out the Feb 1969 attack on an El Al airliner. They decided at this stage it would be a suicide mission.

30 May
Lod is an international airport in territory assigned by the UN in 1947 to an Arab state but taken by Israel in the 1948/9 war. Once inside the terminal the terrorists opened fire indiscriminately, killing 23 passengers and wounding 28 more. One gunman survived.

6

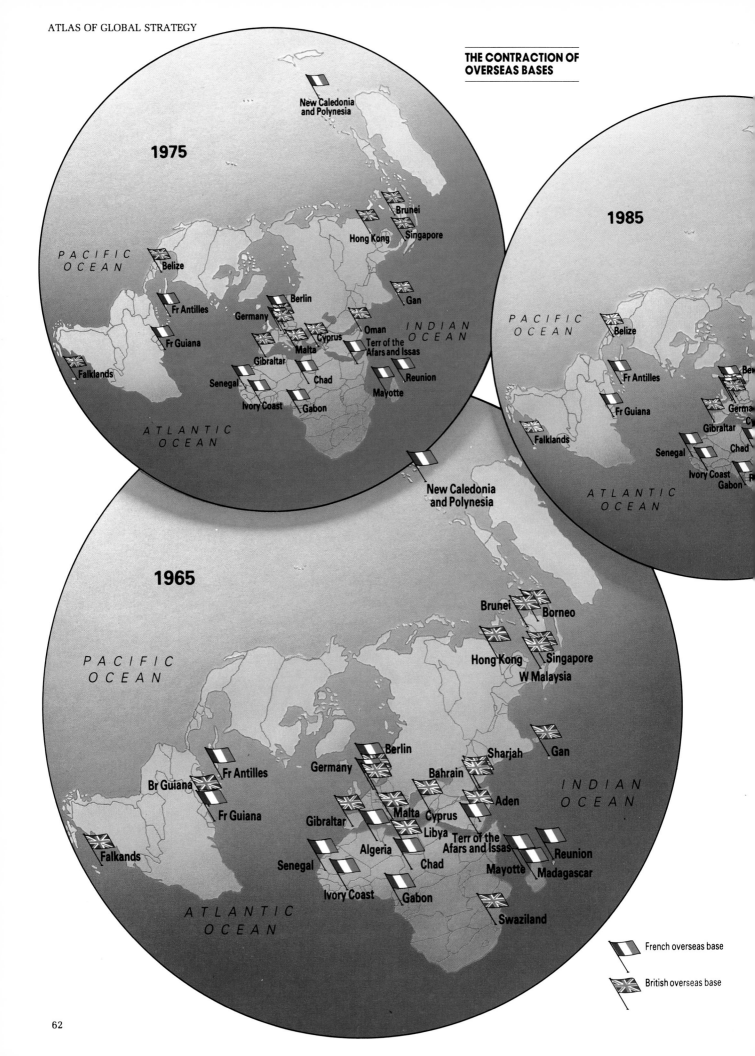

1975

New Caledonia
and Polynesia

*PACIFIC
OCEAN*

Belize

Brunei

Hong Kong

Singapore

Gan

*INDIAN
OCEAN*

Fr Antilles

Berlin

Germany

Fr Guiana

Cyprus

Malta

Oman

Terr of the
Afars and Issas

Falklands

Gibraltar

Senegal

Chad

Reunion

Ivory Coast

Gabon

Mayotte

*ATLANTIC
OCEAN*

1985

*PACIFIC
OCEAN*

Belize

Ber

Fr Antilles

Germa

Fr Guiana

Gibraltar

Cy

Falklands

Senegal

Chad

Ivory Coast

Gabon

R

*ATLANTIC
OCEAN*

New Caledonia
and Polynesia

1965

*PACIFIC
OCEAN*

Brunei

Borneo

Hong Kong

Singapore

W Malaysia

Gan

Berlin

Germany

Sharjah

Bahrain

*INDIAN
OCEAN*

Fr Antilles

Br Guiana

Aden

Fr Guiana

Gibraltar

Malta

Cyprus

Libya

Terr of the
Afars and Issas

Reunion

Falkands

Algeria

Chad

Mayotte

Madagascar

Senegal

Ivory Coast

Gabon

Swaziland

*ATLANTIC
OCEAN*

French overseas base

British overseas base

62

Superpower loyalties and client responses

Between 1965 and 1975 the number of British troops based outside the NATO area was cut by some 75 percent. A decade later the trend appeared to be partly reversed with 4000 troops based in the south Atlantic defending less than half that number of Falkland Islanders against a repetition of the Argentine invasion of 1982. However, the token British contribution of 100 men to the multinational force in Beirut in 1983-84 indicates the reluctance to return in numbers to a part of the world where Britain had once been the dominant military power.
The French, by contrast, have kept up a steady and consistent military capability in Francophone Africa, including a major base at Djibouti, and have maintained specialist forces with which they can intervene rapidly in areas of concern. This has enabled them to continue to exercise substantial influence among their former colonies.

equally cautious phrasing when expressing its support for Vietnam in its scrap with China.

Those countries which rely on others for their security inevitably become nervous when they consider the possibility of their protector having second thoughts when the latter appreciates the full implication of meeting its obligations. Anxieties of this sort have been exhibited by America's allies and clients at one time or another. This is especially so with the beneficiaries of nuclear guarantees made at a time of American superiority, which in an age of strategic parity are now surrounded by question marks. This does not mean that these allies or clients have many interesting alternatives to dependence on the United States, but where possible they are increasingly trying to limit their dependence, for example by maintaining an option to "go nuclear" themselves or by ensuring that their own conventional forces remain well stocked. Equally, the major powers have sought to reduce the degree of their commitments to others. Sometimes, as was the case with Britain in 1967 when it decided to withdraw from "East of Suez," this is done abruptly by concluding the commitments. More often it has been by enabling allies and clients to fight their own battles by providing the latest military hardware on relatively favorable terms. The implications of this will be discussed further below.

Countries contemplating involvement in a war must assume that they will not require the active cooperation of allies. Their wish is only to be left alone and that the victim may not be actively supported. Thus military action is predicated not only on calculations concerning the military balance between the two belligerents but on political assumptions concerning the attitudes and reactions of external powers and possibly of the internal capacity of the victim to withstand and respond to the initial assault. In 1971 India judged correctly that greater Pakistan could easily split into two (the eastern part becoming Bangladesh) and that probably neither China nor the United States would do much to rescue Pakistan. In 1973 President Sadat of Egypt also made correct assumptions concerning the impact of yet another Arab–Israeli war on US foreign policy, especially given its desire to improve relations with the anti-Soviet parts of the Arab world. In early 1979 China correctly judged that the Soviet Union would not come directly to Vietnam's aid if it suffered a punitive action as a result of its own invasion of Kampuchea. In 1980 Iraq

incorrectly judged that Iran's international isolation and internal disarray made it vulnerable to a quick assault.

It is when things go wrong and it becomes necessary to turn to an outside power at a moment of desperation that the outsider can exercise real influence. One of the most dramatic examples of this came with the October 1973 Arab–Israeli War. The American view was that, whereas it was vital that Israel should not be defeated, it would do no harm for it to be shocked into recognizing the need for some sort of agreement with its Arab neighbors. Also, if Egypt's President Sadat came out of the conflict with his reputation enhanced, then he would have the authority to enter into a constructive diplomacy. Israel was extremely dependent on the United States for supplies of equipment and ammunition, especially after the setbacks of the first few days. By slightly delaying the resupply effort the Americans ensured that the Israelis got their shock, but once the airlift of material began in earnest, the Israelis were able to turn the tide of the war. Towards the end the Israelis surrounded the Egyptian 3rd Army and were preparing to inflict a stunning blow. The Russians warned the Americans that they could not allow that to happen and were prepared to intervene to prevent it. The Americans for their part warned the Russians of the dangers of such intervention but also put pressure on the Israelis to hold back. This was resisted in Tel Aviv but, as Israeli Defense Minister Moshe Dayan explained to the Knesset (the Israeli parliament), in the end it was the Americans who paid for the shells.

This is a classic example of a superpower helping to determine the course of a conflict. Less than a decade later, however, there were two contrary examples when the United States found it extremely difficult to control its allies. In 1982 Argentina and Great Britain, which both enjoyed close relations with the United States, came to blows over the Falkland Islands. Secretary of State Alexander Haig attempted to use these good relations to arrange a settlement before the fighting began in earnest. Despite the fact that it was reasonably clear that in the absence of substantial concessions from the Argentine government the United States would be obliged to aid Britain, no concessions were forthcoming. Once the fighting was under way and Britain was close to victory, the Americans attempted to encourage Britain to leave the door open for serious negotiations over the disputed islands. In this they also failed. Later in the same year, Israel invaded Lebanon, osten-

Supplying the RDF

sibly to clear the southern border of terrorist groups which had been shelling Israeli settlements in Galilee. Emboldened by early success, it became more ambitious and decided to drive the Palestine Liberation Organization (PLO) right out of the Lebanon. The human cost of this drive and the added difficulties it created for American efforts to encourage moves towards an Arab–Israeli settlement were not welcomed in Washington. Nevertheless, little could be done to stop the Israelis.

The difference between these two examples and the first is the extent of dependence on the superpower. In the latter two cases the belligerents could keep fighting without the help of the United States.

Logistics

The importance of sufficient supplies to sustain an army in the field is often neglected by those who focus on the quantity and quality of forces in a country's inventory or the art of battle itself. If, as one American general put it, success in war depends on getting there "the fastest with the mostest," then the art of moving forces and keeping them supplied — of logistics — can be seen to be critical. General Wavell of Britain observed after World War II: "The more I see of war, the more I realize how it all depends on administration and transportation ... It takes little skill or imagination to see *where* you would like your army to be and *when*; it takes much knowledge and hard work to know where you can place your forces and whether you can maintain them there. A real knowledge of supply and movement factors must be the basis of every leader's plan; only then can he know how and when to take risks with those factors, and battles are won only by taking risks."

It is logistics that determine the speed with which an army can move, and therefore the art has developed along with modern forms of transportation. The link between the development of the railroads and the early stages of World War I has often been remarked upon. Our concern here is with the movement of forces, or supplies for forces already in place, over large distances in order to engage an enemy at the other end. The consumption rates of equipment and ammunition in a modern intensive war would be far higher than anything experienced in the past. In World War I some 65 tons of material were consumed each day by the armies in the field. By World War II the figure was 675 tons. It had risen to 1000 tons by Vietnam and to 2000 tons by the October 1973 war. Once a country

found itself in a real contest rather than a walkover, it could soon experience critical shortages in vital areas. By looking at this factor we can help to explain the difficulties facing major powers, not only in mounting substantial overseas operations of their own, but in supplying those of others already under way.

The sort of effort required can be illustrated by looking at American plans for a Rapid Deployment Force (RDF) able to intervene in a future Middle East crisis, especially one prompted by a Soviet offensive against Gulf states. The distances from the United States are 11 265 kilometers (7000 miles) by air and 12 875 kilometers (8000 miles) by sea (assuming the Suez Canal is open — 19 312 kilometers (12 000 miles) if it is not). Planning for the force was set in motion in 1980 as a result of the combined anxieties over increasing Soviet assertiveness and Western vulnerability to the disruption of oil supplies. In 1980 it would have taken two days to get a battalion to the Gulf and a month for a division of some 13 000 marines. There was no rapid sealift capability and the only bases of relevance

▲ **In September 1982 Christian militiamen massacred hundreds of Palestinians in the refugee camps of Sabra and Chatilah near Beirut, despite the close proximity of the Israeli army.**

How long would it take the Americans to reach the Gulf?

▲ Top, Prime Minister Begin of Israel and US President Jimmy Carter embrace after the signing of the peace agreement between Israel and Egypt at Camp David in 1979. President Sadat of Egypt looks on applauding.

Masirah) and Egypt (at Ras Banas), but rely largely on "near-term prepositioning ships," which have been loaded with supplies to support a marine brigade, and anchor them at Diego Garcia.

In the first two days of a crisis the United States would now hope to move elements of an airborne battalion and a brigade into the region to secure airfields, and to join up with that equipment stored or made available by the friendly states or steaming up from Diego Garcia on the prepositioned ships. Air cover would be provided by fighter aircraft moved to bases in Saudi and other Gulf states. Within two weeks the combat elements of a light division of some 16 000 men could have been unloaded. A month later from five to seven divisions could have been moved into the Gulf. By 1987, when extra air and sealift capability will be available, it is hoped to be able to have over two divisions available after 15 days, and five to seven after 30. There is much that could go wrong with such an operation. It depends on cooperation from a large number of states. A crisis elsewhere putting its own demands on airlift and sealift capabilities could dramatically reduce the movement of forces. There could still be problems with the reliability of individual aircraft or fuel shortages. There have been many doubts expressed about the efficiency of the command arrangements which at times have seemed more designed to allow every branch of the services their appropriate "piece of the action" rather than to permit a smooth operation.

Even if everything worked according to plan, there are doubts whether the forces would be sufficient. The Soviet Union (if that is the opponent) has advantages of proximity that will enable it to move forces more easily than the United States. On the other hand it has been pointed out that distances can be illusory. The Soviet Union shares a border with Iran, but its forces on that border are not maintained at a high state of readiness. They would have to be beefed up during a crisis, and that would provide warning that an offensive was in the offing. The overland route to what is suspected to be the most interesting part of Iran — the oilfields in the south — would involve traveling along 1930 kilometers (1200 miles) of awkward roads and traversing two mountain ranges. Simply dropping airborne troops around the oil wells would leave them without air cover unless the Russians have already managed to come to some arrangement with a local power, such as Syria, for the use of air bases. Given these

were Diego Garcia in the Indian Ocean 3200 kilometers (2000 miles) away and Incirlik in Turkey. To support the new force the United States moved to improve both airlift and sealift capabilities, including the masive C-5 cargo aircraft that can each (at a pinch) carry two 50-ton tanks and new roll-on/roll-off ships. Egypt and Morocco have agreed to the use of air bases for refueling, while there are "contingency access rights" for air bases and ports in Oman, Somalia and Kenya.

Because those countries in the region on whose behalf the RDF might be used were not altogether sure about America's motives, they were not willing to make available bases to the United States. It was one thing to promise to take on the Russians, but what if the same force was used to help Israel or gain control of Arab oil production? All that could be done was to transfer advanced equipment (including the AWACS early-warning and surveillance aircraft) to countries such as Saudi Arabia in the expectation that they would be made available to the United States in an emergency, negotiate storage for reserves with the more pro-Western Omanis (at

Military success depends on an understanding of the political context

difficulties, it would be an open question whether the Russians could reach their destination in the two weeks before the Americans could bring substantial forces to bear. It is argued that the important thing about the RDF is that it confronts the Soviet Union with a realistic prospect of a clash with the Americans if it did try to do anything untoward. Even if this clash took the form of a tiny advance force being completely overrun, there would be a risk that this could escalate into a nuclear confrontation. This risk should be sufficient to act as a deterrent.

A much more difficult prospect might be an intervention designed to bring stability to some regional dispute. The problem here is not of dispatching substantial forces in time to confront an equally or more powerful enemy but of getting bogged down in a politically chaotic situation. Schemes for taking over Saudi oil production, for example, in response to an unusually tight embargo or a leftist overthrow of the ruling family, run into the problem of the continued vulnerability of the occupying forces and the oil installations in question to terrorism and sabotage. Risks of this sort were brought home to the United States and some of its European allies in the multinational force that was based in the Lebanon in the aftermath of the Israeli invasion from 1982 to February 1984, when they left in something of a hurry. The political objective of providing a calming influence as the country's warring factions sorted out their differences became transformed into apparent military backing for one of the factions — except that the constraints under which the force had been inserted into the Lebanon rendered it incapable of playing a decisive military role. Instead it provided a provocation to, and a target for, the more fanatical members of other factions. In April 1983 47 lives were lost in a bomb explosion at the American Embassy in Beirut. Later that October 239 marines were killed when a bomb-laden truck was driven into their quarters. At the same time the French and the Israelis were learning the same uncomfortable lessons about maintaining regular forces in a hostile environment.

This experience brought home the more general lesson that is so often forgotten when military actions are planned as straightforward encounters between opposing forces: a failure to understand the political context is likely to result in military failure. The logistical problems that we have described and the consequences of an open-ended commitment remain powerful disincentives to entering

THE US RAPID DEPLOYMENT FORCE

After the Soviet invasion of Afghanistan in December 1979, President Carter warned the Soviet Union that the oil-producing Gulf was an area of vital interest to the United States and that any further Soviet trespass into it would meet with a firm response. The Rapid Deployment Force (RDF) was seen to be one means of underlining that message. Some in the Middle East suspected that this new capability for power projection might be used not only against the Soviet Union but also against any Arab state which took action contrary to US interests. With the continued strong support for Israel in Washington, even the more conservative anti-Soviet Arab countries do not assume that their interests necessarily coincide with those of the United States.

Getting American forces to a crisis spot in the Middle East would involve a substantial effort. One reason for this is that the countries that would be the supposed beneficiaries of the RDF have mixed feelings about its likely mission and so are not keen to have large and permanent US bases on their territory.

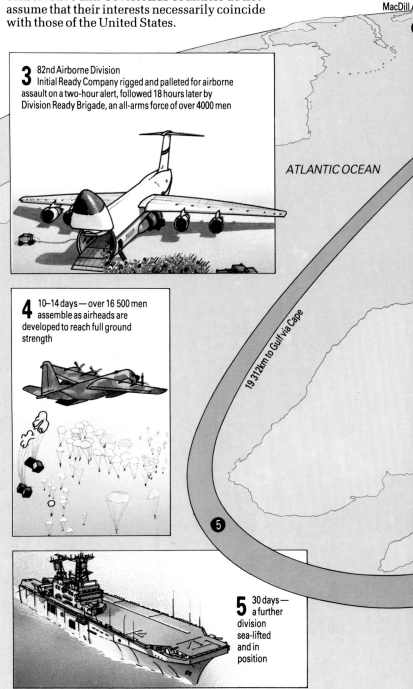

3 82nd Airborne Division
Initial Ready Company rigged and palleted for airborne assault on a two-hour alert, followed 18 hours later by Division Ready Brigade, an all-arms force of over 4000 men

4 10–14 days — over 16 500 men assemble as airheads are developed to reach full ground strength

5 30 days — a further division sea-lifted and in position

MacDill

ATLANTIC OCEAN

19 312km to Gulf via Cape

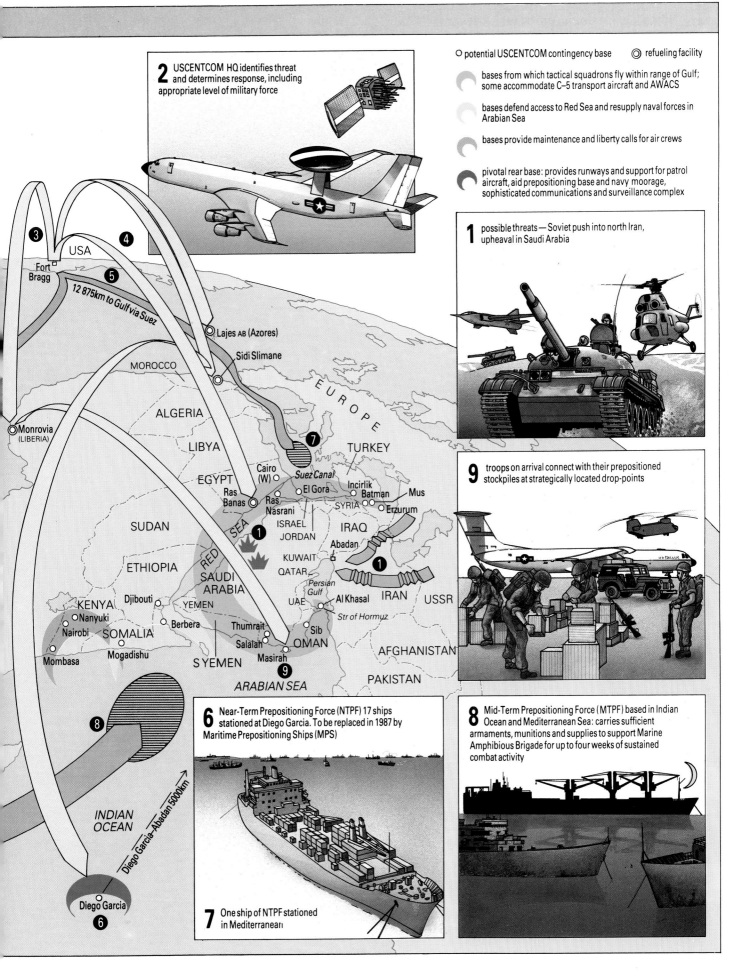

○ potential USCENTCOM contingency base   ◎ refueling facility

bases from which tactical squadrons fly within range of Gulf; some accommodate C–5 transport aircraft and AWACS

bases defend access to Red Sea and resupply naval forces in Arabian Sea

bases provide maintenance and liberty calls for air crews

pivotal rear base: provides runways and support for patrol aircraft, aid prepositioning base and navy moorage, sophisticated communications and surveillance complex

2 USCENTCOM HQ identifies threat and determines response, including appropriate level of military force

1 possible threats — Soviet push into north Iran, upheaval in Saudi Arabia

9 troops on arrival connect with their prepositioned stockpiles at strategically located drop-points

USA
Fort Bragg
12 875km to Gulf via Suez
Lajes AB (Azores)
Sidi Slimane
MOROCCO
Monrovia (LIBERIA)
ALGERIA
LIBYA
EGYPT
EUROPE
Cairo (W)
Suez Canal
Ras Banas
Ras Nasrani
El Gora
Incirlik
Batman
Mus
Erzurum
TURKEY
SYRIA
ISRAEL
JORDAN
IRAQ
Abadan
KUWAIT
QATAR
Persian Gulf
SUDAN
SAUDI ARABIA
RED SEA
ETHIOPIA
KENYA
Nanyuki
Nairobi
Mombasa
SOMALIA
Mogadishu
Djibouti
YEMEN
Berbera
S YEMEN
Thumrait
Salalah
Masirah
Sib
OMAN
ARABIAN SEA
UAE
Al Khasal
Str of Hormuz
IRAN
USSR
AFGHANISTAN
PAKISTAN
INDIAN OCEAN
Diego Garcia–Abadan 5000km
Diego Garcia

6 Near-Term Prepositioning Force (NTPF) 17 ships stationed at Diego Garcia. To be replaced in 1987 by Maritime Prepositioning Ships (MPS)

7 One ship of NTPF stationed in Mediterranean

8 Mid-Term Prepositioning Force (MTPF) based in Indian Ocean and Mediterranean Sea: carries sufficient armaments, munitions and supplies to support Marine Amphibious Brigade for up to four weeks of sustained combat activity

THE FALKLANDS CHAIN GANG

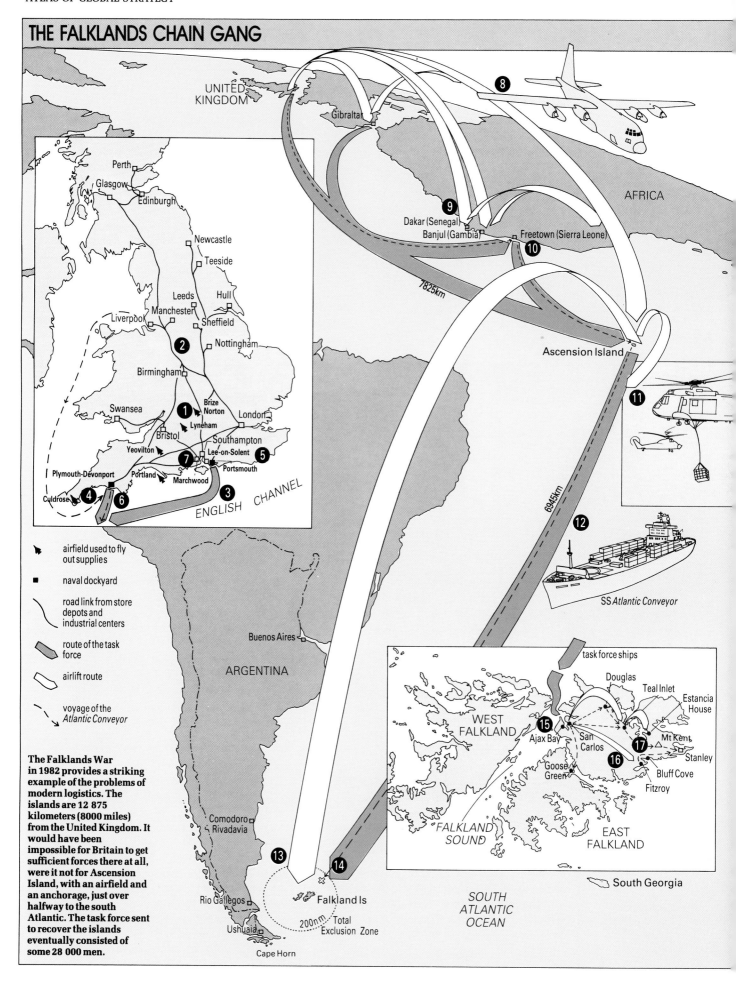

United Kingdom

Perth
Glasgow
Edinburgh
Newcastle
Teeside
Leeds
Hull
Liverpool
Manchester
Sheffield
Nottingham
Birmingham
Swansea
Brize Norton
London
Lyneham
Bristol
Southampton
Yeovilton
Lee-on-Solent
Plymouth-Devonport
Portland
Marchwood
Portsmouth
Culdrose

ENGLISH CHANNEL

airfield used to fly out supplies

naval dockyard

road link from store depots and industrial centers

route of the task force

airlift route

voyage of the *Atlantic Conveyor*

The Falklands War in 1982 provides a striking example of the problems of modern logistics. The islands are 12 875 kilometers (8000 miles) from the United Kingdom. It would have been impossible for Britain to get sufficient forces there at all, were it not for Ascension Island, with an airfield and an anchorage, just over halfway to the south Atlantic. The task force sent to recover the islands eventually consisted of some 28 000 men.

UNITED KINGDOM
Gibraltar
AFRICA
Dakar (Senegal)
Banjul (Gambia)
Freetown (Sierra Leone)
7825km
Ascension Island
6945km

SS *Atlantic Conveyor*

Buenos Aires
ARGENTINA
Comodoro Rivadavia
Rio Gallegos
Ushuaia
Cape Horn
Falkland Is
200nm Total Exclusion Zone

task force ships
WEST FALKLAND
Douglas
Teal Inlet
Estancia House
Ajax Bay
San Carlos
Mt Kent
Goose Green
Stanley
Bluff Cove
Fitzroy
FALKLAND SOUND
EAST FALKLAND
South Georgia
SOUTH ATLANTIC OCEAN

Costs of supplying the wars of others

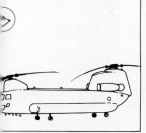

A. the Killer Satellite   B. Pershing II   C. MX Missile

D. Trident Submarine   E. SS-20   F. Car Bomb

"Guess which modern weapons system has killed the most people." A wry American comment on the destruction of the US marine quarters in Beirut in 1983 when a truckload of high explosives was driven into the building by a terrorist on a suicide mission.

into such commitments. Except where direct involvement cannot be avoided, the preference of the major powers remains one of supplying the wars of others rather than making them their own.

Not that supplying others is necessarily that straightforward. We have already drawn attention to the massive American resupply effort for Israel during the October 1973 war. On 12 October 1973, six days after Egyptian armed forces had crossed the Suez Canal, President Nixon ordered an immediate airlift to begin to aid Israel. The only airforce base available between the United States and Israel was in the Azores (Lajes AB). *Skyhawk* and *Phantom* aircraft were flown directly to Israel. New tanks, self-propelled guns, helicopters, anti-tank missiles, ammunition and aircraft spare parts had to be delivered by air for the sake of speed. From mid-October to mid-November in 566 separate flights some 22 400 tons of cargo were delivered. It took more fuel to supply the airlift than it did to support the entire Israeli airforce. It should be noted that most of the supplies arrived after verbal agreement had been reached on a cease-fire on 21 October (although the cease-fire was not actually signed until 11 November) and that over the following two months almost three times the quantity of supplies, as delivered by air, was delivered by sea in order to replenish the depleted Israeli forces. The Soviet Union delivered some 15 000 tons of material by air to its clients and

was also transporting material by sea. This sealift probably had more impact on the course of the war because of the shorter distances involved.

Mounting this operation certainly gave the Americans more leverage over the Israelis, but the Israelis had at best mixed feelings about their dependence on the United States being illustrated in such a dramatic manner. There were other foreign-policy costs. Many European allies had adopted a more pro-Arab stance and so refused support for the resupply operation, leading to bitter recriminations later on. An immediate consequence was an Arab oil embargo directed against the United States. If it was necessary to supply another's war, better, it would seem, to supply it in advance.

The arms trade
As the major powers have become more reluctant to get drawn into the chaotic politics of the third world, countries unsure about the degree of support they would get from an outside power in an emergency have increasingly sought to develop the means to look after themselves. For a variety of reasons the major powers have helped them to do this, thereby making it even more dangerous for themselves to venture into what are now becoming heavily armed parts of the world.

The growth of the arms trade has been well documented, but the full implications

have been neglected because of the tendency to treat this as a moral rather than a strategic issue. The suppliers have been castigated for their willingness to make profits through the sale of instruments of death and destruction to countries with far more pressing priorities for their scarce funds. The continued willingness of the recipients to buy modern armaments has been portrayed as a consequence of their susceptibility to the techniques of the arms salesmen or a misplaced sense of grandeur.

Operation Bright Star, conducted in late 1981 in Egypt, Oman, Somalia and the Sudan, tested the ability of US army, marine and airforce units in the RDF to get to soutwest Asia and fight together.

A buyer's market

manipulating its arms supplies. In practice the influence has been in the reverse direction. Cutting off arms supplies is not only commercially but also politically expensive, for the erstwhile recipient will be affronted. When President Carter attempted to link arms supplies to human rights violations, offending countries took their trade elsewhere. It is only in wartime, as we have noted, that the supplier has the upper hand. Otherwise it is a buyer's market. With more countries developing the means to produce — and export — sophisticated items of military equipment, it is becoming even more of a buyer's market. Rather than the arms trade serving as a means by which the north continues to assert its control over the south, it has been the means by which the south has gained military independence from the north. This is one of the main explanations for the change in the pattern of warfare that was described at the start of this chapter.

The arms trade reached its peak in the 1970s, but the origins can be detected in the 1960s. The economic and political costs of basing large military forces overseas led to friendly countries being encouraged to take on a greater responsibility for their own security, using local manpower and imported sophisticated equipment. President Nixon made this explicit in 1970. The other factor was the desire of Western countries to improve their balance of payments. An aggressive American sales policy in the mid-1960s helped to create a climate of fierce competition for large orders which the British and French felt obliged to meet.

In the aftermath of the four-fold rise in oil prices in 1973–74 the market took off. The industrialized nations were anxious to regain some of the petro-dollars that were flowing to the Middle East and arms sales seemed suited to this task. The "boom" of the 1970s can be attributed to OPEC states which accounted for some 75 percent of all sales. Iran led the rush. Between 1974 and 1975 the shah ordered 400 combat aircraft, 500 helicopters, 730 tanks, 18 warships and thousands of missiles. This profligacy was encouraged by the United States which hoped that the shah would act as a calming influence on the Gulf — and also remember his friends!

As the volume of trade grew, so did concern over its strategic implications. It was noted that modern arms sales involved much more than the transfer of available pieces of military equipment. The expansion of armed

Security considerations were seen to be only marginally relevant to the demand side of the equation. If they were relevant to the supply side, it was because the industrialized north still wished to exercise control over the notionally independent south by

Carter fails in his attempt to control the arms trade

forces put demands on the country's infrastructure. The trade came to involve barracks, air bases, hospitals, roads and training schemes as well as weaponry. The technology involved was extremely advanced and difficult to maintain. It therefore had to come complete with instructors and engineers and sometimes even operators to ensure that the investment would not be wasted. A Congressional report in the mid-1970s observed with concern that up to 15 000 civilian Americans might be working on defense contracts in Iran by the end of the decade. Might not they be held hostage in a future crisis or lead the United States into a more general commitment to Iranian regional policies than might be wise?

Iran eventually came to illustrate a different sort of problem. The close association with the West and the general distortion of the economy brought about by the shah's extravagant purchases contributed to the severe social and political pressures building up in the country. These finally exploded in 1979 with the overthrow of the shah and the arrival of an Islamic fundamentalist regime led by the Ayatollah Khomeini. Because the United States and Britain were seen as the shah's backers, the new regime considered them sworn enemies. Rather than long-term influence, enmity had been bought instead. Given the fluctuating condition of international politics, it is hard to guarantee that a supplier's armed forces will not find themselves facing an enemy equipped with the same kit — which they had purchased a few years earlier. This happened to Britain in the Falklands.

During the shah's reign it was very hard to deny him the weapons he wanted. There was big money involved and the suppliers were anxious to secure lucrative contracts. Moreover to deny a country weapons appears as a calculated insult, reflecting on the stability, trust and credit-worthiness or technical competence of the would-be recipient. When the client can influence the price of oil or is in the market for civilian goods or plays a critical role in regional politics, care is taken not to give offense.

President Carter tried in the late 1970s to introduce some order into the international arms market. He insisted that individual deals should be carefully scrutinized and that there should be no touting for business. He entered into discussions with other countries concerning the possibility of controlling the arms trade. Lastly, he promised that the United States would not be "the first

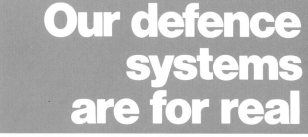

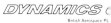

supplier to introduce into a region a newly developed advanced weapons system which would create a new or significantly higher combat capability."

His initiative was not successful. It was not popular with other suppliers, who generally welcomed the business and saw American restraint as an opportunity rather than an example. Nor was it popular with the potential clients who complained about imperialist attempts to deny them modern means of defense and keep them militarily backward. In general, arms transfers could not be isolated from the overall state of international relations. President Carter was reluctant to sell advanced weapons to Pakistan, but in the end the American hand was forced by the British and French sale of *Jaguar* aircraft to India, hints from Islamabad that, in the absence of a sufficient conventional capability, Pakistan might be forced to "go nuclear" and, most important of all, the Soviet invasion of Afghanistan which put Pakistan on the "front line."

There are now very few areas of the world — as can be seen from the map on p.74 — in which the more sophisticated missiles and aircraft would appear as novelties. Sometimes systems are being sold for export before

In many areas the market is now saturated

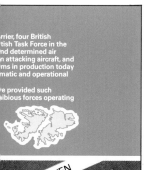

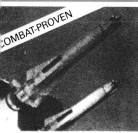

antic

Dart, the long-range ship-
ed area-defence system, denied the
the use of high-level reconnaissance
gh-level air attack. It imposed upon
aircraft the use of patterns of approach
ike which significantly increased their
ability to the close-range systems and
d these systems to account for large
rs of attacking aircraft.

Harrier missile integration programmes.

The regular advances in
military technology mean
that many items of
equipment have never been
tested in combat, and so
there are major
uncertainties about how
reliable, easy to operate and
damaging to targets they
will prove to be in practice.
As a result, when conflicts
involving relatively
sophisticated armed forces
occur (for example in the
Middle East), every detail of
the fighting is scrutinized in
immense detail, not only for
broad strategic and tactical
lessons but also for
evidence on the quality of
performance of the
equipment in use.

Above, one British firm
takes full advantage of the
fact that its products were
involved in the Falklands
War to attach the "combat-
proven" label, while, right,
the cartoonist Lurie offers
his own comment on this
tendency to use war as a
showroom for new
weapons, also drawing our
attention to the extent to
which the weapons in use
by both sides in this war
came from members of
NATO.

they reach the inventories of the home armed services. More serious for any attempt to control the trade is the extent to which a number of countries have made strenuous efforts to become self-sufficient in arms and have even moved on to become suppliers. (It should be noted, however, that self-sufficiency in military technology is normally a matter of degree: foreign components are often essential.)

In some cases the development of arms industries has been stimulated by the commercial prospects. More often it is a response to uncertainty over access to advanced weaponry in the future. South Africa, for example, has been the subject of a UN embargo. This has led it to develop its own defense industry to make up for its lack of access to the international market. Similarly Israel, having been let down by France in 1967, and very conscious of its dependence on the United States, has developed a diverse range of defense goods, some of which are proving to be profitable export items. South Korea and Taiwan have been moved by similar considerations. Over the past couple of years non-Communist countries other than the United States and the major Western European countries have increased their share of the market from under 8 percent to almost 20 percent.

Thus, by the time that it was recognized that there were risks attached to distributing advanced weapons to any country willing to pay (and not actually an enemy), there was little that could be done to control matters. Sales were a response to demand and not to pushy suppliers, and would continue so long as the demand was there.

Demand has in fact dampened down since the 1970s, but not as a result of more stringent international controls, let alone reduced anxieties over security. Since 1975, according to some of the more reliable estimates (in an area where all figures are highly suspect), some 116 nations — in what we loosely describe as the third world — have spent almost $250 billion on armaments. About a third of these have been from the US, a third from the Soviet Union, and the rest from a variety of other suppliers, with France and to a lesser extent Britain playing a significant role. Sales peaked around 1980, largely on the basis of contracts signed earlier in the 1970s, and there has since been a decline in the number of new contracts. The suppliers cannot afford to be free with easy-credit terms; the recipients have also found themselves short of cash. However, the basic reason may be that in many areas of the world the market is simply saturated.

THE ARMS TRADE

The arms trade combines commerce with high politics, in such a way that it is often quite unclear whether deals are being secured in order to make money or to influence local politics. In the first couple of decades after the war, the trade often involved the established military powers selling obsolete or surplus equipment at knockdown prices to clients in need of support. Increasingly, with more sophisticated systems in demand and the industrial countries competing for the large export orders, the commercial aspects have come to figure more prominently.

All attempts to provide an accurate description of the trade falter on the lack of reliable statistics. The large deals involving the high-technology combat aircraft get noticed, but little attention is given to the less spectacular but equally lucrative contracts involving, for example, the construction of new barracks or the training of a new air force. The amount of money being spent is often overstated as a result of advantageous credit terms. Other countries insist on secrecy because they do not want their potential adversaries to know what new weapons are being acquired.

▼ One way in which the diffusion of military power can be illustrated is by noting the spread of sophisticated systems such as modern combat aircraft to new parts of the world. Another is the development of indigenous arms industries within many countries which used to depend wholly on imports.

▶ The arrival of a new clientele for the arms trade after 1975 is shown by this map. But so is the extension of the competition.

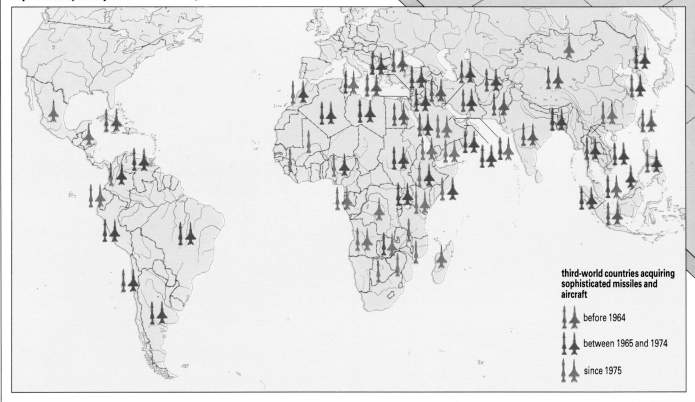

third-world countries acquiring sophisticated missiles and aircraft

before 1964

between 1965 and 1974

since 1975

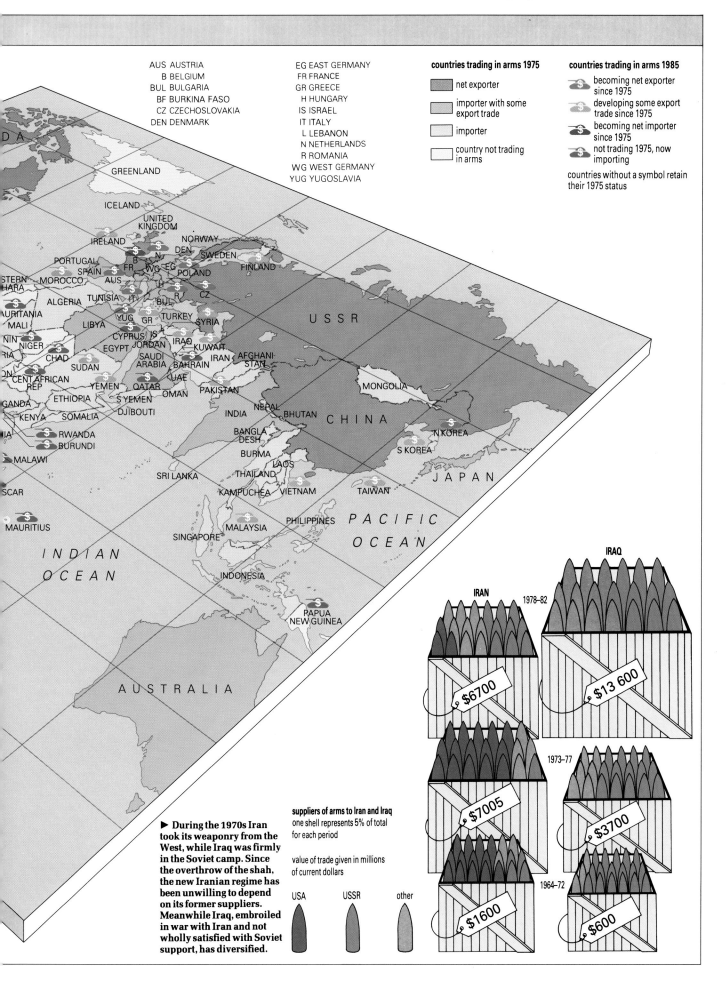

AUS AUSTRIA
B BELGIUM
BUL BULGARIA
BF BURKINA FASO
CZ CZECHOSLOVAKIA
DEN DENMARK

EG EAST GERMANY
FR FRANCE
GR GREECE
H HUNGARY
IS ISRAEL
IT ITALY
L LEBANON
N NETHERLANDS
R ROMANIA
WG WEST GERMANY
YUG YUGOSLAVIA

countries trading in arms 1975

net exporter

importer with some
export trade

importer

country not trading
in arms

countries trading in arms 1985

becoming net exporter
since 1975

developing some export
trade since 1975

becoming net importer
since 1975

not trading 1975, now
importing

countries without a symbol retain
their 1975 status

▶ During the 1970s Iran
took its weaponry from the
West, while Iraq was firmly
in the Soviet camp. Since
the overthrow of the shah,
the new Iranian regime has
been unwilling to depend
on its former suppliers.
Meanwhile Iraq, embroiled
in war with Iran and not
wholly satisfied with Soviet
support, has diversified.

suppliers of arms to Iran and Iraq
one shell represents 5% of total
for each period

value of trade given in millions
of current dollars

USA   USSR   other

IRAQ

IRAN   1978–82

$6700 $13 600

1973–77

$7005 $3700

1964–72

$1600 $600

There are still only five declared nuclear-weapon states

Nuclear proliferation

One area where there has been more success in controlling the spread of deadly weapons than might have been expected is in nuclear proliferation. There have been regular warnings since the late 1950s of an imminent nuclear epidemic which will lead in a matter of years to up to 20 states having nuclear arsenals. Yet we still have only five declared nuclear-weapon states. Nevertheless, if we look at the development of this issue, we can see it fitting into the general trend that we are describing of critical security issues devolving to particular regions.

The problem for those anxious to control the spread of nuclear weapons is that much of the relevant technology is spread with civilian nuclear technology. This is ironic, for the spread of civilian technology reflects an early hope that, if only states could be offered the benefits of the peaceful atom, they would stay well clear of the military atom. In 1953 President Eisenhower announced an "atoms for peace" program to make the civilian technology available to the non-Communist world. It was hoped to discourage countries from maintaining their own research capabilities and to encourage the adoption of technologies unsuited for military purposes and dependent on enriched uranium supplied by the United States. Nevertheless, the long-term consequence

was the development by many countries of indigenous capabilities that made them far less subject to American influence. A close association was seen between nuclear weapons and great-power status. For example, when Communist China replaced Nationalist Taiwan in the "China" slot on the UN Security Council in the early 1970s, it meant that the five permanent members were also the five nuclear powers. It is important to remember that up to the late 1960s the proliferation problem was largely seen to be confined to the industrialized states.

The Eisenhower administration sought to deflect the envy of its allies by allowing them access under "dual-key" arrangements to short-range nuclear systems. Most were satisfied with this arrangement. Britain was already developing a weapons capability, drawing on its wartime cooperation with the United States. West Germany had only been allowed to rearm on condition that it would not develop nuclear or chemical weapons. Italy decided against its own nuclear weapons and so did neutral Sweden. The real problem was France, attempting to regain its place as a major world power after the humiliations of the 1940s and 1950s. It began development of its own nuclear capabilities in the 1950s: during the next decade this became a major source of contention between the United States and France.

◄ A 1978 picture from within the Indian Bhabba atomic research center at Trombay, named for Homi Bhabba, the first chairman of India's Atomic Energy Commission. A reprocessing facility at Trombay enabled India to extract sufficient plutonium from its Cirus research reactor (which had been supplied without safeguards by the Canadians) for its "peaceful" nuclear explosion in 1974.

THE NUCLEAR CLUB

NUCLEAR TRADE

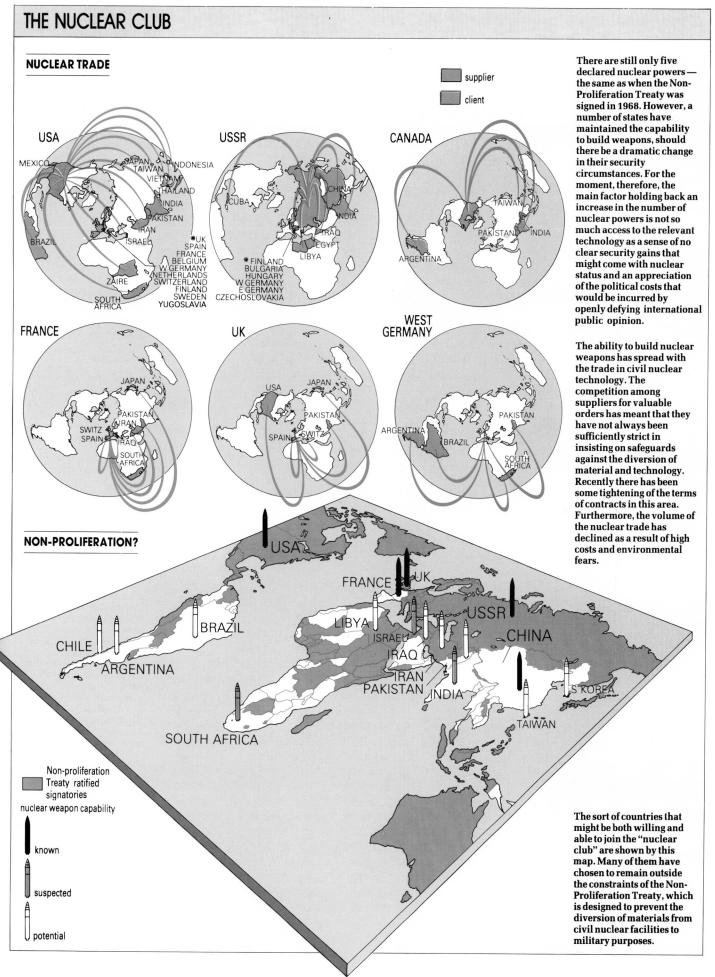

supplier
client

USA

MEXICO
JAPAN
TAIWAN
INDONESIA
VIETNAM
THAILAND
INDIA
PAKISTAN
IRAN
BRAZIL
ISRAEL
ZAIRE
SOUTH
AFRICA

*UK
SPAIN
FRANCE
BELGIUM
W GERMANY
NETHERLANDS
SWITZERLAND
FINLAND
SWEDEN
YUGOSLAVIA

USSR

CUBA
CHINA
INDIA
IRAQ
EGYPT
LIBYA

*FINLAND
BULGARIA
HUNGARY
W GERMANY
E GERMANY
CZECHOSLOVAKIA

CANADA

TAIWAN
PAKISTAN
INDIA
ARGENTINA

FRANCE

JAPAN
PAKISTAN
IRAN
SWITZ
SPAIN
IRAQ
SOUTH
AFRICA

UK

USA
JAPAN
PAKISTAN
SPAIN
SWITZ

WEST GERMANY

PAKISTAN
ARGENTINA
BRAZIL
SOUTH
AFRICA

NON-PROLIFERATION?

CHILE
ARGENTINA
BRAZIL
SOUTH AFRICA
USA
FRANCE
UK
LIBYA
ISRAEL
IRAQ
IRAN
PAKISTAN
INDIA
USSR
CHINA
S KOREA
TAIWAN

Non-proliferation
Treaty ratified
signatories

nuclear weapon capability

known

suspected

potential

There are still only five declared nuclear powers — the same as when the Non-Proliferation Treaty was signed in 1968. However, a number of states have maintained the capability to build weapons, should there be a dramatic change in their security circumstances. For the moment, therefore, the main factor holding back an increase in the number of nuclear powers is not so much access to the relevant technology as a sense of no clear security gains that might come with nuclear status and an appreciation of the political costs that would be incurred by openly defying international public opinion.

The ability to build nuclear weapons has spread with the trade in civil nuclear technology. The competition among suppliers for valuable orders has meant that they have not always been sufficiently strict in insisting on safeguards against the diversion of material and technology. Recently there has been some tightening of the terms of contracts in this area. Furthermore, the volume of the nuclear trade has declined as a result of high costs and environmental fears.

The sort of countries that might be both willing and able to join the "nuclear club" are shown by this map. Many of them have chosen to remain outside the constraints of the Non-Proliferation Treaty, which is designed to prevent the diversion of materials from civil nuclear facilities to military purposes.

There has not yet been a nuclear epidemic

The American view was that this sort of development would divert resources away from more urgent requirements such as conventional forces, would result in vulnerable and limited capabilities and would make decision-making in war extremely difficult. In return the French argued that allies were of doubtful reliability in the nuclear age and that the only really credible deterrent was that made by a country on its own behalf. Rather than bow to American pressure, France in 1966 left NATO's Integrated Military Command.

The Russians were facing similar problems with their allies. China wanted nuclear weapons to support its foreign-policy objectives. The Soviet Union considered the Chinese too reckless for such a trust. It refused to help and did its best to hinder the Chinese program, adding to the tension that led to the split between the two Communist states. The Chinese surprised and alarmed both superpowers by the speed of the move from their first atomic bomb test (1964) to the first hydrogen bomb test (1967). As they moved to an operational capability in the late 1960s, the Russians dropped dark hints that they might consider a preemptive attack, while the United States was prepared to spend billions of dollars on a limited antiballistic missile defense specifically designed against a Chinese ICBM threat anticipated for the early 1970s (which has yet to materialize, though an ICBM was tested in 1980).

In an effort to put pressure on both France and China and also to discourage others tempted to follow their example, the superpowers sponsored moves designed to inhibit nuclear proliferation. The Partial Test Ban Treaty of 1963 (to which 111 states have now acceded) banned atmospheric tests and so added to the difficulty of becoming a nuclear power. Underground tests are still permitted, and it is not absolutely necessary to test at all to develop weapons. In 1974 India exploded a device which it claimed was permissible because it was for peaceful applications only.

A more significant move was the Non-Proliferation Treaty (NPT) which came into force in 1970 and to which 115 states are now parties. It was a sort of bargain between the nuclear haves and the have-nots. In return for renouncing the nuclear option, the have-nots would be provided with the peaceful benefits of nuclear energy and the best efforts of the haves to achieve significant measures of arms control and disarmament.

In terms of freezing the status quo of 1970 at five nuclear powers the NPT can be said to have succeeded. However, it has come under increasing strain as the relevant technology has spread and the number of potential proliferators has grown to include many third-world countries. The NPT bargain has been put at risk by a desire to impose restrictions on the transfer of so-called "sensitive" nuclear technologies which are ostensibly civilian but invaluable in developing a military option, and by the failure of the nuclear haves to achieve much by way of arms control and disarmament. The NPT has been likened to a plea by drunkards for abstinence from others.

Most of those suspected of nuclear intentions — Israel, South Africa, India, Pakistan, Brazil, Argentina and Chile — have not acceded to the treaty. The best that could be hoped for was to ensure that "going nuclear" would not be facilitated by easy access to the necessary technology and would certainly incur substantial political costs.

The International Atomic Energy Agency (IAEA), based in Vienna, is responsible for ensuring through a process of systematic inspection that nothing untoward happens at civilian nuclear installations. This largely involves checking that no fissionable materials are secreted out of nuclear power stations.

A number of key facilities installed prior to the NPT are not subject to inspection. For example, reactors acquired by India and Israel (from Canada and France respectively) have been used to help them develop their nuclear option. Furthermore, a number of possible proliferators such as South Africa and Argentina have sophisticated nuclear industries of their own. A final source of concern is that the prospect of large export earnings might lead to offers of sensitive technologies and laxity in the imposition of safeguards.

After the oil price rises of 1973–74 nuclear power came to be seen as an attractive alternative source of energy to oil and a brisk business began in nuclear reactors. The trade began to move into the sensitive areas of uranium enrichment and fuel reprocessing. In 1974, not long after India's "peaceful" test, West Germany concluded a deal with Brazil involving these technologies. These two events together generated alarm that matters were getting out of control.

In the United States in particular there was a tendency to view proliferation as an epidemic to which almost any state might be susceptible and which was carried by an

France became an effective nuclear power in 1964 when its first *Mirage IV* bombers became operational. Since then France has added 18 land-based intermediate-range missiles that are subject to regular modernization, and is steadily increasing its missile-carrying submarine fleet. Five vessels have been built, a sixth is under construction and a seventh is planned. A new missile for these submarines — the *M-4* — is shortly to enter service. Each missile will carry up to six warheads.

France has been much more confident in the strength and the durability of nuclear deterrence than the other nuclear powers, and has been prepared to sacrifice the quality of its conventional forces in order to ensure a high-quality nuclear capability. In developing this capability it lacked the sort of assistance from the United States that was available to Britain. The French insist that any attack of whatever sort against French territory will meet with a firm nuclear response. While this threat may have credibility, a more difficult question for France is the extent to which it feels a responsibility to its allies or accepts that its security is bound up with the general state of affairs in Central Europe. It left NATO's Integrated Military Command in 1966 and is unlikely to return, but there have been increasing signs of cooperation with allies, especially West Germany.

The ambiguity in French doctrine was exemplified by the short-range nuclear missile, *Pluton* (opposite). Fired from French soil, this could only reach West Germany, which might make sense if it was designed to be a warning shot against Soviet forces moving towards France, but only at the expense of further devastation of West Germany. On the other hand, if it were moved to participate in NATO's forward battle, then this would contradict the emphatic link between France's nuclear force and the protection of France's territory.

Who's next?

unusually virulent form of technology. The cure was seen in extra restraint by the nuclear suppliers, especially when it came to the specialist technologies. This attitude was seen by many as unduly alarmist, patronizing and reneging on commitments to make available the peaceful benefits of nuclear power. (The more cynical saw it as an attempt to dampen down trade in an area where the comparative advantage resided with West European countries.) The main result of the American pressure was an agreement to write strict safeguards into contracts. The general problem also declined as nuclear power lost its allure and the trade in reactors declined dramatically.

However, on moving from the general to the specific, it soon became clear that a number of countries were not above suspicion when it came to their nuclear acquisitions. France, for example, with a reputation for not respecting international norms in this area, became involved in a series of deals involving South Korea, Pakistan and Iraq. A combination of American pressure and French second thoughts got the first two cancelled. Pakistan has since employed a variety of methods to stay abreast of advanced nuclear technology. Iraq refused to cancel. On 7 June 1981 Israel, as is its wont, took matters into its own hands by destroying the Iraqi reactor at Osiraq in an air raid.

The position that we have now reached is that a number of states have acquired or are close to acquiring a nuclear option, but have refrained from exercising it because of the political costs involved. But the option can be held in reserve as a hedge against a change in the security context. Even making known that the option exists can be a source of strategic advantage. Israel, for example, has used its putative nuclear capability to persuade the Americans to keep up stocks of conventional arms and to intimidate its Arab neighbors. In September 1977 considerable pressure was exerted on South Africa not to test a bomb in the Kalahari Desert after a Soviet warning that one was imminent. No test took place but South Africa's nuclear capability was confirmed.

A major aspect of security policy for any country will concern relations with the superpowers. Those already independent of the superpowers can confirm their status as regional powers by acquiring a nuclear status. Those currently dependent on a superpower but worried that they might be abandoned have every incentive to develop an option. This thought has influenced the Israelis, Pak-

istanis and to a lesser extent the South Koreans and Taiwanese.

Put this way, proliferation can be seen as a function of the tensions within the "Western family" described at the beginning of this chapter. States are unlikely to feel that going it alone would be preferable to US security guarantees, but if it looked as if those guarantees were to be withdrawn then they would have no choice. It is part of the general diffusion of international power. As the spread of conventional arms makes regional disputes more virulent and harder to control, the superpowers may wish to keep their distance from countries that have in the past looked to them for protection. The more they keep their distance, the more likely it is that some of these countries will develop their own nuclear capabilities — so adding to the superpower reluctance to get involved. Other countries may then feel obliged to respond with their own capability.

This sort of process has already started in Asia. China signaled its independence from the Soviet Union with its nuclear tests. India, which had fought a border war with China in 1962, developed its own option in response. After the Indian test of 1974, the Pakistanis made clear their determination to acquire a nuclear option (Prime Minister Bhutto said he would "eat grass" if necessary). Israel's nuclear capability has spurred the Arabs into action (with Colonel Gaddafi of Libya typically trying to buy a bomb on the open market). Despite the Osiraq raid, Iraq may be able to develop an "Arab bomb." Iran could not ignore such a development. And so on with Japan, Australia and Indonesia all watching carefully.

It is important not to exaggerate this trend. A military nuclear capability is still extremely difficult to achieve, with high scientific, financial and political costs. Even if weapons can be produced, it is by no means easy to find ways of delivering them to enemies in quantity. A new nuclear capability acts as a provocation to other states in the vicinity, with the risks of added tension, arms races and even preemption. It could lead to a break in relations with an otherwise well-disposed superpower. These are the sorts of reasons why the spread of military nuclear power has thus far been much less than anticipated. The increasing number of countries in a position to go nuclear, should they so desire, and the growing unruliness in the international system create a risk of the scales being tipped in favor of exercising the nuclear option in those countries.

THE NUCLEAR ARMS RACE

Modern developments dwarf the Hiroshima bomb, though neither side has come close to a decisive first-strike capability. The fear of a breakthrough has helped fuel an offense–defense duel. Submarines are the mainstay of second-strike capabilities, largely because of the vulnerability of land-based forces. Trident II combines ICBM accuracy with submarine invulnerability. Nuclear weapons play a crucial role in deterrence in Europe, but they also inhibit superpower assertiveness in international affairs.

The familiar mushroom cloud of a nuclear explosion, rising from a test by French forces on the Mururoa Atoll in 1983. Many Pacific countries have objected to these tests polluting their atmosphere, but France has not signed the 1963 Test Ban Treaty.

Nuclear weapons have dominated international politics since 1945. The destruction of the two Japanese cities of Hiroshima and Nagasaki warned of the horrendous prospects opened up by mankind's new-found ability to exploit atomic energy. The warning made its mark, reinforced regularly by leaps in the numbers, power and sophistication of nuclear weapons. Since August 1945, despite persistent international tension and periods of intense crisis, no nuclear weapons have been used in anger.

So far so good. But there is a natural worry that the success of nuclear deterrence will be only temporary. It is like hearing of an airline that has been operating for years without a serious accident. We are not sure whether to back the record or deduce from some law of averages that the airline must now be due for a serious disaster. This concern is accentuated by the thought that any mishap would be so devastating that it would be a miracle if any civilized society emerged from the ruins.

In this chapter we shall therefore consider the durability of nuclear deterrence. Is it the case, as many have been arguing in recent years, that a combination of technical innovations and new doctrines is unsettling the essential stability of the balance of terror? Can any nuclear balance withstand prolonged periods of tension or the sort of severe political turbulence that seems to have become so common around the globe? To answer these questions it is necessary to maintain a sense of perspective over some of the contemporary controversies. This requires an analysis of the development of the nuclear arsenals and their impact on world politics over the past four decades. Through an understanding of how we arrived at the current position we may be able to identify future sources of instability.

The race against Hitler creates the nuclear option

The start of the arms race

If there was a time when the phrase "nuclear arms race" was particularly appropriate it was in the early 1940s when American and British scientists felt that they were competing against comparable research into atom bombs in Nazi Germany. There was indeed a research project under way in Germany, but it lacked the high-level support and resources enjoyed in the allied countries. Apart from anything else the flight of so many top scientists from Germany and the occupied countries meant that the talent that should have been supporting one effort was in fact supporting the other.

By the time that the multi-million-dollar Manhattan Project had achieved the first successful test of an atom bomb in New Mexico in July 1945 Germany was beaten and it was clear that the "race" had been rather one-sided. Nevertheless, Japan was still fighting on and the American government was ready to use the new bomb to end the war. On 6 August 1945 the citizens of Hiroshima became the first victims of a nuclear attack. Three days later those of Nagasaki suffered the same fate. After another five days — on 14 August — Japan surrendered. This first use of the bomb has since attracted much criticism (see opposite). But the incontrovertible association between this use and the war's end immediately made the reputation of the new weapons. Furthermore, the growing hostility among the wartime allies provided a context in which there was keen interest in the atom bomb's future military potential. In the West it was seen as a valuable counter to the Soviet Union's advantage in conventional forces, especially in Europe — where the world war just ended had originated and where the unsettled political situation provided the likely trigger for any future war.

As we now know, through the efforts of their own scientists and with information passed on to them by spies in the American project, such as Klaus Fuchs, the Soviet Union was already well on the way to developing its own nuclear capability. The real nuclear arms race had begun! By 1949 the Russians had tested their own atom bomb. Partly in response the Americans moved on to the thermonuclear (fusion) bomb, and the Russians followed suit. By the early 1950s the Americans could mount a formidable nuclear threat against Soviet territory. It took until much later in the decade for the Russians to be able to threaten the continental United States by means of long-range

HIROSHIMA AND NAGASAKI

The first atomic bomb was dropped by a single American B-29 aircraft, *Enola Gay*, from the Tinian air base. The detonation was at 8.15 a.m. on 6 August 1945. By the end of the year some 140 000 people had died as a result of the explosion. The deaths of many since can be attributed to the long-term effects of the radioactivity. The second bomb was dropped on Nagasaki at 11.02 a.m. on 9 August 1945. This was the second choice on the target list: the first, Kokura, was saved by cloud cover. Some 70 000 died at Nagasaki.

The decision to atom-bomb these two cities has been much criticized. The American view at the time was of a Japan at the brink of defeat yet stubbornly refusing to surrender and indeed continuing to fight in the most ferocious manner possible. It was presumed that only a full-scale invasion of Japan — planned for November 1945 — would achieve the desired victory. However this would be enormously costly in the lives of allied servicemen.

The few in the American government making the decision did consider the possibility of demonstrating the power of the bomb to the Japanese without inflicting massive civilian damage. However, they decided against this because they were unsure just how impressive the bomb would be, because the Japanese might put American prisoners in the area of the detonation, and because a failure could be counterproductive in strengthening Japanese resolve. They do not seem to have taken seriously the possibility of not using the bomb at all. Too much blood had been spilled, too much frustration had built up and too many resources and expectations had been invested in the project for an opportunity to end the war quickly to be passed up. The surrender of Japan immediately after Nagasaki confirmed — to those responsible — the wisdom of this decision.

▶ The damage caused by the Nagasaki bomb was largely confined to the Urakami river district, with the rest of the city protected by a hill. Here a survivor tries to sustain life a few days after the explosion.

▲ The Sei Hospital was located directly beneath the epicenter of the blast. Its ruins are now known as the Atomic Bomb Dome and are located in the Hiroshima Peace Memorial Park.

Hiroshima is built on a delta at the mouth of the Ota river, which flows into the Seto Inland Sea from the northern mountains. The explosion occurred at the heart of this flat city; the damage extended in all directions.

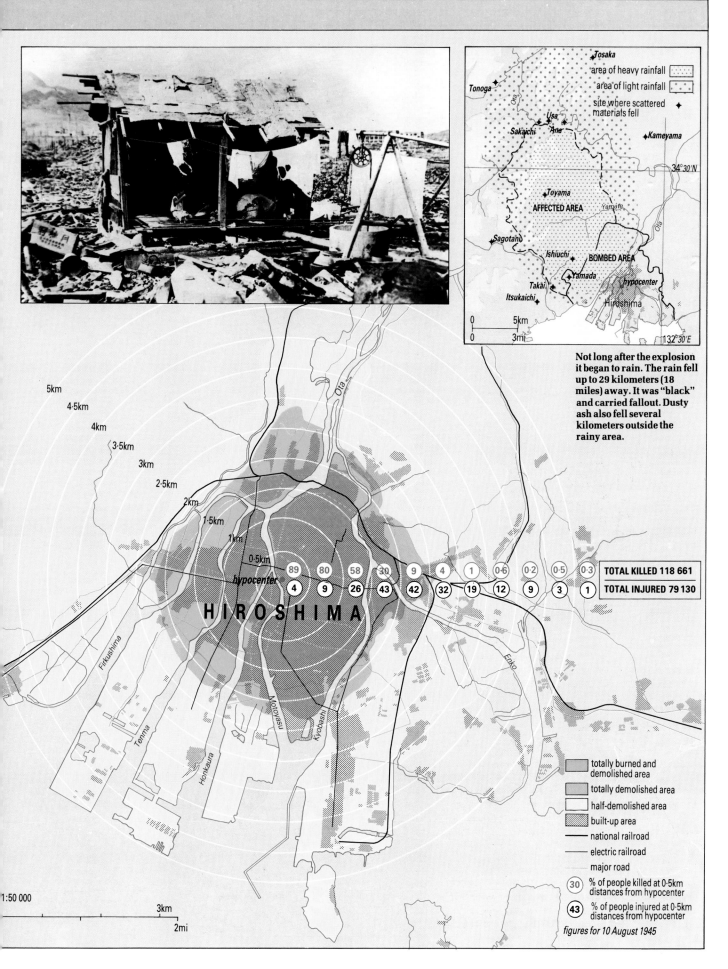

area of heavy rainfall
area of light rainfall
site where scattered materials fell

Tosaka
Tonoga
Usa
Sakaichi
Ana
Kameyama
34°30'N
Toyama
Yamate
AFFECTED AREA
Sagotani
Ishiuchi
BOMBED AREA
Yamada
hypocenter
Takai
Itsukaichi
Hiroshima

0   5km
0   3mi
132°30'E

Not long after the explosion it began to rain. The rain fell up to 29 kilometers (18 miles) away. It was "black" and carried fallout. Dusty ash also fell several kilometers outside the rainy area.

5km
4·5km
4km
3·5km
3km
2·5km
2km
1·5km
1km
0·5km
hypocenter

H I R O S H I M A

Furkushima
Tenma
Honkaura
Motoyasu
Kyobashi
Ota
Enko

89	80	58	30	9	4	1	0·6	0·2	0·5	0·3	
4	9	26	43	42	32	19	12	9	3	1	

TOTAL KILLED 118 661
TOTAL INJURED 79 130

totally burned and demolished area
totally demolished area
half-demolished area
built-up area
national railroad
electric railroad
major road
% of people killed at 0·5km distances from hypocenter
% of people injured at 0·5km distances from hypocenter
figures for 10 August 1945

1:50 000

3km
2mi

THE DEFEAT OF JAPAN

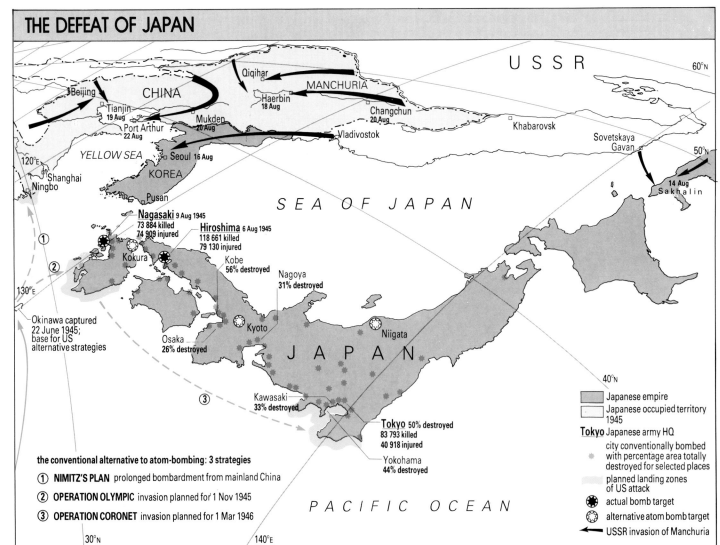

Nagasaki 9 Aug 1945
73 884 killed
74 909 injured

Hiroshima 6 Aug 1945
118 661 killed
79 130 injured

Kokura

Kobe
56% destroyed

Nagoya
31% destroyed

Kyoto

Niigata

Osaka
26% destroyed

J A P A N

Okinawa captured
22 June 1945;
base for US
alternative strategies

Kawasaki
33% destroyed

Tokyo 50% destroyed
83 793 killed
40 918 injured

Yokohama
44% destroyed

the conventional alternative to atom-bombing: 3 strategies

① NIMITZ'S PLAN prolonged bombardment from mainland China

② OPERATION OLYMPIC invasion planned for 1 Nov 1945

③ OPERATION CORONET invasion planned for 1 Mar 1946

PACIFIC OCEAN

Beijing CHINA
Tianjin 19 Aug
Port Arthur 22 Aug
Mukden 20 Aug
Qiqihar
MANCHURIA
Haerbin 18 Aug
Changchun 20 Aug
Vladivostok
Khabarovsk
U S S R
Sovetskaya Gavan
Sakhalin 14 Aug
YELLOW SEA
Seoul 16 Aug
KOREA
Pusan
Shanghai
Ningbo
SEA OF JAPAN

Legend:
- Japanese empire
- Japanese occupied territory 1945
- **Tokyo** Japanese army HQ
- * city conventionally bombed with percentage area totally destroyed for selected places
- planned landing zones of US attack
- ✵ actual bomb target
- ✵ alternative atom bomb target
- ← USSR invasion of Manchuria

It is now reasonably clear that Japan would have surrendered before the planned November invasion with or without the atom-bombing, although not necessarily before many more lives had been lost. It is often forgotten that the destruction of Hiroshima was not the only shock suffered by the Japanese leaders in early August. At the same time the Soviet Union declared war on Japan, so ending the last lingering hope that Moscow could serve as an intermediary in negotiating a conditional surrender in which the position of Emperor Hirohito would have been protected. This plus the atom-bombings persuaded the emperor himself to tilt the internal political balance in Tokyo in favor of an immediate surrender. So the atom-bombing may have been unnecessary. Of course, that does not mean that it was wholly unreasonable, given the situation as it appeared in Washington at the time.

The most critical, with the wisdom of hindsight, argue that if the bombing of the two cities was not required to end the war then the Americans had other purposes in mind. Two are normally suggested. The first, which is not supported by any evidence, is that those who had produced the bomb were very anxious to use the Japanese cities for experimental purposes — to see how well their new weapon really worked. The second charge is more

serious. The background to the concluding stages of World War II was the first stirrings in what later became known as the cold war. As the "Big Three" — America, Britain and Russia — consulted on the future of postwar Europe, substantial conflicts of interests arose and it was thought that this demonstration of a major Western advantage would give the Russians pause. As it turned out, the bomb was far less influential in the diplomatic battles over the shape of postwar Europe than troops on the ground in occupation of critical territory.

The closing stages of the last world war. Having for a brief period been master of the Pacific, Japan prepares for a last-ditch stand with only a committed army and no navy and little air force. Note the extent to which Japan had already suffered massive conventional bombing — some of it, including the fire bombing of Tokyo in March 1945, on a scale comparable to the atom-bombing of Hiroshima and Nagasaki. The conventional bombing did not stop to make way for the atom bombs and the USAF leadership tended to see the atom bomb as no more than a supplement to the established offensive.

Japan formally concedes defeat on board the US battleship *Missouri* in Tokyo Bay on 2 September 1945.

Russian device tested in 1961 was 3700 times as powerful as the Hiroshima bomb

bombers, though Western Europe was put at risk early on. Soon both sides were competing to deploy the first operational intercontinental ballistic missile, to be followed by submarine-launched missiles. Then came antiballistic missiles, and before long this effort was overtaken by the arrival of multiple warheads.

All this activity, with an apparently endless stream of technical innovations and a rapid growth in the size and the complexity of the nuclear arsenals of the two sides, created a strong sensation of arms-racing. The "nuclear arms race" has in fact become something of a cliché, which is why perhaps it needs to be examined with care. An arms race implies some sort of winning post, a point at which one side feels that it has achieved a sufficient lead to be able to turn aggressively on the other side. Or at least it suggests a desperate effort by each side to ensure that the other does not achieve such an advantage. There is certainly the assumption that this activity is closely related to the degree of political antagonism between the two sides, and that the acquisition of extra weapons both feeds on and fuels this tension.

There have been elements of all this in East–West relations over the past four decades, but it would be unwise to set too much store by the imagery. In its respective weapons decisions each side has not been simply responding to the stimuli provided by the other. There have been political, economic and technical factors at work too, in addition to variations in strategic doctrine. Moreover there is a degree of institutionalization in the development and production of new weapons that makes them in some ways independent of the broader political relationship. The most important question, however, concerns the objective of all this activity. Is there really a decisive strategic advantage available to either side? Or else, given the destructive power of a single nuclear warhead, is it really the case that there is now so much nuclear strength around on both sides that what might appear to be major surges in the arms race in fact make slight difference to the fundamental strategic position?

The arsenals
The explosions at Hiroshima and Nagasaki were equivalent to about 15 000 tons (15 kilotons or KT) of TNT. Explosions of this sort would now be put just above the tactical category, useful on the battlefield but insufficient for strategic purposes. Although a corruption of the true meaning of the term,

"strategic" is now taken to refer to attacks on major political, military and economic centers in the enemy homeland. Since the fission process of the atomic bombs was superseded in the early 1950s by the fusion process of the hydrogen bomb, explosive yields have reached the equivalent of 25 million tons (25 megatons or MT) of TNT in some of the larger Soviet missiles. The Russians in 1961 even tested a monster which yielded 56 megatons, although no rocket was ever built to carry such a powerful load. Most modern weapons have yields of between one and five megatons. When a number of warheads are delivered by a single missile their yields tend to be measured in hundreds of kilotons.

As an illustration of the extent to which the quantity of nuclear weapons has grown let us consider one of the new American *Ohio*-class ballistic-missile-carrying submarines (SSBNs). Each carries 24 *Trident-I* missiles. Each missile is MIRVed — that is to say it has multiple independently targetable re-entry vehicles. The eight on each *Trident-I* have yields of 100 kilotons so that one of these boats can attack 192 individual targets with warheads, each some six times more powerful than the bomb which destroyed Hiroshima. Each of these new submarines represents barely 1 percent of American strategic power (depending on how it is measured), and this still excludes American intermediate-range forces based in Europe. As a proportion of total nuclear weapons in the world it may barely represent 0·3 percent. At the end of the 1980s the Americans intend to introduce the even more powerful *Trident-II* missiles which will carry up to 14 warheads each. Britain also intends to introduce this weapon. Thus it is that capabilities which aroused such awe and apprehension in the 1940s now appear puny and almost insignificant.

However, the raw figures of nuclear capability can be misleading. Destructive effects do not grow in proportion to the number of targets, for the simple reason that after a while a nuclear attack would run out of targets. In some rather gruesome calculations made by the Systems Analysis Office of the Pentagon in the mid-1960s it was demonstrated that the actual effects of a large amount of megatonnage depended on the way that it was distributed. In an attack on the Soviet Union a law of diminishing returns would be at work in terms of the damage inflicted on Soviet society.

With both sides now possessing tens of thousands of warheads it is clear that there is

TARGET NEW YORK CITY

Some idea of the immediate effects of a nuclear explosion can be gauged from this representation of the impact of a one megaton air burst with its epicenter at the southern tip of Manhattan. The effects are unlikely to follow a standard pattern. Furthermore, no broad-brush treatment of the effects of nuclear weapons can convey the multitude of individual tragedies that it would create.

Nuclear explosions release energy in the form of blast, direct nuclear radiation, direct thermal radiation (most of which takes the form of visible light), pulses of electrical and magnetic energy and radioactive fallout. Of these, blast, which constitutes about 50 percent of the energy released, causes the most damage, taking the form of sudden changes in air pressure that can crush buildings or a high wind that will knock down people or objects in its path. Thermal radiation takes the form of a flash which will precede the blast by several seconds and can blind anyone observing it from a distance of many miles, cause severe burns and ignite combustible material over a wide area. Those exposed to intense ionizing radiation will either become extremely sick or die, depending on the dosage as well as their age and general health. For larger nuclear weapons ionizing radiation causes only a small proportion of casualties because of the more lethal blast and thermal radiation effects. The ultimate effects will depend on the total number of nuclear weapons used. One current fear is that the smoke and debris from burning cities and forests could blot out the sun's rays for a sufficient time to ruin the ecology of the northern hemisphere.

12km
Wind speed 55 kph (35 mph). Light damage to buildings. Branch damage to trees. Sporadic fires. People flash-blinded by reflected light. Severe 2nd-degree burns. Blistering of skin.

8km
Wind speed 150 kph (95 mph). Telephone lines blown down. 30 percent trees blown down. Grass and shrubs catch fire.

6½km Wind speed 260 kph (160 mph). Buildings severely damaged. Upholstery, canvas, clothing ignite. Possible long-term risk of people receiving lethal dose of radiation from fallout.

5km
Wind speed 470 kph (290 mph). Houses destroyed. Multistory buildings, bridges severely damaged. Main fire zone: aluminium window frames melt, car metal melts, wood and roofing felt ignite. Fatal burns. Charring of skin.

3km
Wind speed 760 kph (470 mph). Reinforced-concrete multistory buildings and bridges leveled. Factories leveled. Houses distributed by debris. Cars and trucks blown long distances. 90 percent trees blown down. Fire extinguished by general destruction of buildings. Unprotected people receive lethal dose of radiation. But people this close to explosion killed by blast and heat.

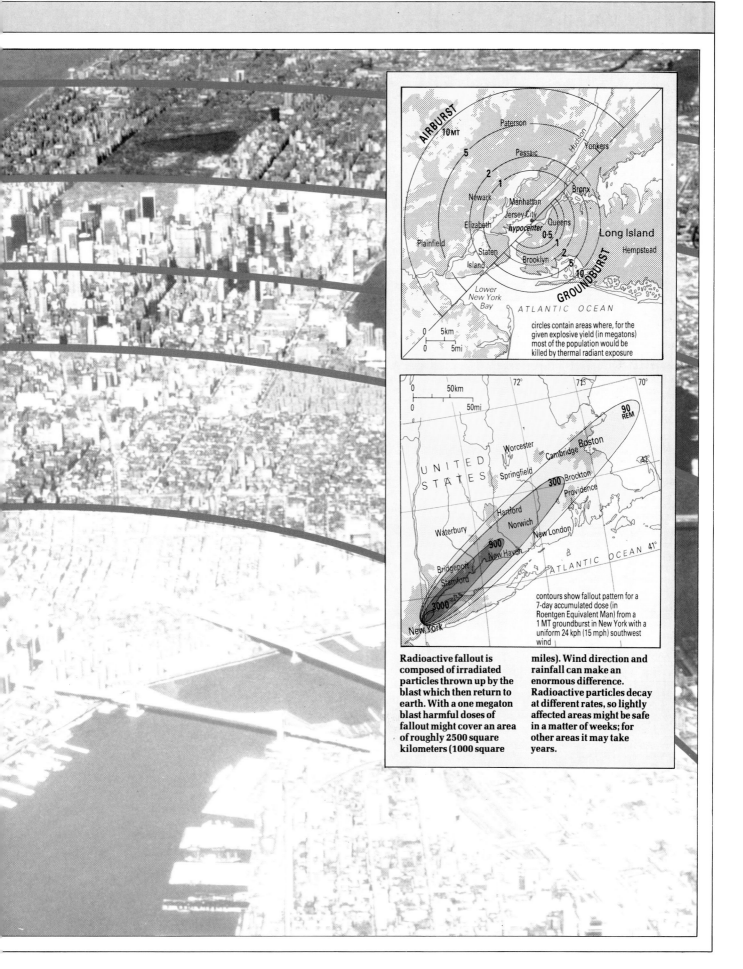

AIRBURST
10MT

Paterson

Passaic

5

2
1

Newark

Manhattan
Jersey City

Elizabeth

Queens

Plainfield

hypocenter

0·5

Staten
Island

1
2
5
10

Brooklyn

Lower
New York
Bay

Hudson

Yonkers

Bronx

Long Island

Hempstead

GROUNDBURST

ATLANTIC OCEAN

0   5km

0   5mi

circles contain areas where, for the
given explosive yield (in megatons)
most of the population would be
killed by thermal radiant exposure

0   50km

0   50mi

72°   71°   70°

90
REM

Worcester

Cambridge   Boston

42°

Springfield

300   Brockton

UNITED
STATES

Providence

Hartford

Waterbury

Norwich

900

New London

New Haven

41°

ATLANTIC OCEAN

Bridgeport
Stamford

3000

New York

contours show fallout pattern for a
7-day accumulated dose (in
Roentgen Equivalent Man) from a
1 MT groundburst in New York with a
uniform 24 kph (15 mph) southwest
wind

**Radioactive fallout is
composed of irradiated
particles thrown up by the
blast which then return to
earth. With a one megaton
blast harmful doses of
fallout might cover an area
of roughly 2500 square
kilometers (1000 square**
**miles). Wind direction and
rainfall can make an
enormous difference.
Radioactive particles decay
at different rates, so lightly
affected areas might be safe
in a matter of weeks; for
other areas it may take
years.**

Surplus capacity is seen as insurance against first-strike capability

substantial surplus capacity around. This is commonly referred to as "overkill" and is often accompanied by the observation that there seems little point in holding on to so much destructive capacity when it is possible to destroy the world so many times. How many times can the world be destroyed? But it is not as simple as that, because such comments assume that each side would be able to deliver all its megatonnage against the enemy. If one side was able to develop means of destroying large numbers of the enemy's weapons in a surprise attack or of intercepting them in the air before they reached their targets, then the enemy might well feel that it could no longer be certain of inflicting unacceptable levels of damage by way of retaliation and so would be at the other's mercy.

Mutual assured destruction
The ability to disarm the enemy of his capacity to retaliate through a surprise attack is known as a "first-strike capability." It should be noted that, given the horrendous consequences of even a few nuclear detonations, there would not be much point in launching a first strike unless there was a reasonable chance that it would be a total success. A partial success would invite retaliation from the enemy's remaining forces. A "second-strike capability" refers to the ability to maintain forces to inflict a devastating retaliation, even after absorbing a surprise first strike. In the 1960s the Americans attempted to define this precisely as an "assured-destruction capability" — the ability to destroy 20 to 35 percent of the Soviet population and 50 to 75 percent of industrial capacity. The condition in which both sides were in this position was described as "mutual assured destruction," often referred to by its unfortunate acronym MAD.

There is general agreement that if one side did achieve a first-strike capability then the nuclear relationship would be much less stable. There are those on both sides who question whether MAD is really equivalent to stability. They argue that it would be much better if their side was quite unconstrained by the other's nuclear capabilities. Initially the United States had a nuclear monopoly and naturally enough considered this situation to be preferable to one in which this advantage had been neutralized. As we shall see later, many of the problems in nuclear strategy result from the commitments to provide nuclear protection to others that were made by the United States at a time when it still

"BABY PLAY WITH NICE BALL?"

enjoyed a substantial superiority over the Soviet Union. However, as this superiority was lost, it was recognized that a different — but much more durable — stability might result.

As the Soviet Union caught up with the United States in the 1950s, Robert Oppenheimer, the leading scientist in America's early nuclear program, observed that the two superpowers were becoming like two scorpions in a bottle. If one attempted to kill the other he could expect to be killed himself. With each nuclear power capable of destroying the other it was felt that a system of mutual deterrence was being established, in which neither East nor West would dare to make the first move lest it prove to be suicidal. Winston Churchill was one of the first to recognize the importance of this new relationship. In one of his last speeches as prime minister in 1955 he suggested that the risk of nuclear destruction could well be a

Right from the start the arrival of the atom bomb was seen to give mankind an awesome choice between life and death. The cartoonist David Low does not appear wholly confident that the right choice will be made, either because of mankind's immaturity or because of apathy. But at least he recognizes that the atom that the scientist is offering has a positive as well as a negative potential.

A destabilizing breakthrough in defense seems unlikely in the foreseeable future

stabilizing factor because of the great caution that it would impose on both sides. "It may well be that we shall by a process of sublime irony have reached a stage in this story where safety will be the sturdy child of terror and the twin brother of annihilation."

All this assumed that neither side could develop a first-strike capability. So far, despite many gloomy predictions to the contrary, this assumption has turned out to be right. Nevertheless, there has been a persistent belief in the possibility of some technical breakthrough that would result in a decisive shift in the balance of advantage, allowing the successful power to rescue its nuclear strength from the constraints imposed on it by the nuclear strength of the adversary. Such a development would transform that superpower relationship. It would even be possible to think of a victor in a nuclear war.

Offense and defense
Such a breakthrough would require the ability either to defend against an enemy nuclear attack or to destroy his nuclear forces in a surprise attack, or, most likely, a combination of the two. It has been the prospect of advances in either of these areas, rather than simply a competitive accumulation of megatons and weapons systems, that has determined the character of the nuclear arms race. It can be described as an offense–defense duel, a stream of technical innovations in which each countered the impact of the one before. The hope was for a decisive, if transient, superiority; the fear was of a moment of terrifying vulnerability. What is remarkable is that despite these powerful motivations both sides have failed to achieve such dramatic breakthroughs.

Defensive measures tend to be described as either "passive" or "active." Passive measures are generally known as civil defense. Although societies can be provided with a certain amount of protection, there is really very little that can be done against a determined adversary. The best that can be hoped for is to preserve an administrative apparatus, basic services and a modicum of law and order in the aftermath of an attack.

Active measures involve defenses against both aircraft and missiles. The possibilities against aircraft were demonstrated during World War II with the combination of radar to warn of and help track the incoming raid and fighter aircraft to intercept it. The development of surface-to-air missiles put attacking aircraft in even greater danger, forcing a search for greater speed and altitude as well

as measures to confuse the enemy's radar. This particular duel remains finely balanced as can be seen from the relative performances of air defenses in the successive Arab–Israeli wars (see below, pp.128–29).

The move to missiles for offensive purposes threatened to pose insuperable problems to the defense because of their sheer speed. The need was for a system that could spot incoming missiles early on and then track them with sufficient accuracy for them to be caught by interceptor missiles. The actual interception presented less of a problem than the timely identification of the targets and the prediction of their routes. Even when these problems seemed close to solution in the 1960s, involving radars and data-processing systems of immense sophistication, the potential achievement was thwarted by advances in offensive technology — maneuverability, decoys, chaff and, most important of all, multiple warheads.

By the end of the 1960s the programs for developing effective ballistic-missile defenses had run out of steam in both the United States and the Soviet Union. In May 1972 they agreed in one of the most important arms-control settlements to limit their deployments of antiballistic missiles. Neither reached even the permitted levels. The Americans scrapped their newly completed *Safeguard* system and the Soviet Union was left with only 64 launchers protecting Moscow, and this number was later reduced to 32.

This does not mean that interest has evaporated in the possibility of a future breakthrough in missile defense. Both powers have maintained active research programs. In March 1983 President Reagan lauched a drive to examine the feasibility of a space-based defense system, probably involving forms of directed energy. Although this is now being actively researched, it is extremely difficult to see how energy could be generated in sufficient quantities from a space-based system, or how the problems of covering large expanses of space, tracking and identifying individual objects, and overcoming a number of possible (and cheaper) countermeasures are to be overcome. Nevertheless the attraction of a near-perfect defense commands great enthusiasm and will stimulate research for some time to come. In the unlikely event that this research is successful it will take until the next century for it to be turned into some sort of operational system — by which time the offense problem itself might well have changed.

If a first strike could not depend on

THE OFFENSE-DEFENSE DUEL

If what we have been experiencing over the past 35 years can be described as an arms race, it is not so much quantitative — although that is how it is often depicted in terms of increasing numbers of warheads — as qualitative. A qualitative arms race is one driven by fears of a decisive technological advance that could tip the strategic balance. Each side innovates, in order to counter the anticipated innovations of the other. In doing so it spurs the other on to greater efforts to protect its position. And so on. Some have even argued that the laboratories race each other, in that it needs no more than evidence of progress from one group of scientists working on some project for another group to set to work to counter it, just in case the enemy's scientists have made the same discovery.

As an explanation for the deployment of weapons over the last 30 years this is inadequate: there have been many other factors at work. However, one underlying theme of this period has been an offense–defense duel. If one side could achieve a true first-strike capability by developing the ability either to destroy the enemy's forces on the ground or to intercept them before they could reach their targets, then this would constitute a real superiority. This prospect has exercised a notable influence on the superpowers.

After World War II the main interest was in the development of short-range missiles with proximity fuses, able to intercept incoming aircraft. Were it not for the advent of nuclear weapons, improvements in air defenses might have tilted the balance. In order to avoid the defenses, aircraft would have had to fly either at much higher altitudes, with a consequent loss

of accuracy, or at much lower altitudes, with a greatly increased fuel consumption and thus a reduced range as well as reduced safety. As more aircraft became able to carry nuclear weapons, the demands on the defense increased dramatically. Before, it would have been well satisfied with 10 percent attrition, a level which, if sustained over a series of raids, would cripple the attacker. Now with nuclear weapons it only needed a couple to get through for the defense to have completely failed.

In the end it was not the air defenses that caused the move away from bombers as the main means of nuclear delivery, but a recognition of vulnerability on the ground to

The improvement in the quality of weapons over the past three decades has been even more remarkable than that in their quantity. This diagram illustrates the pace of change as both sides introduce new missiles and bombers. Note the Soviet preference for a number of different types of missiles. The Americans decide on a preferred model prior to development.

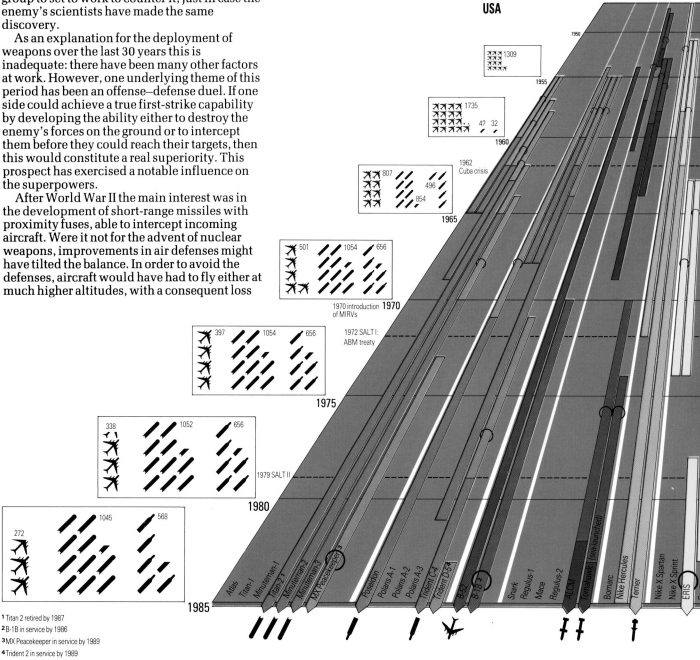

USA

1 Titan 2 retired by 1987
2 B-1B in service by 1986
3 MX Peacekeeper in service by 1989
4 Trident 2 in service by 1989

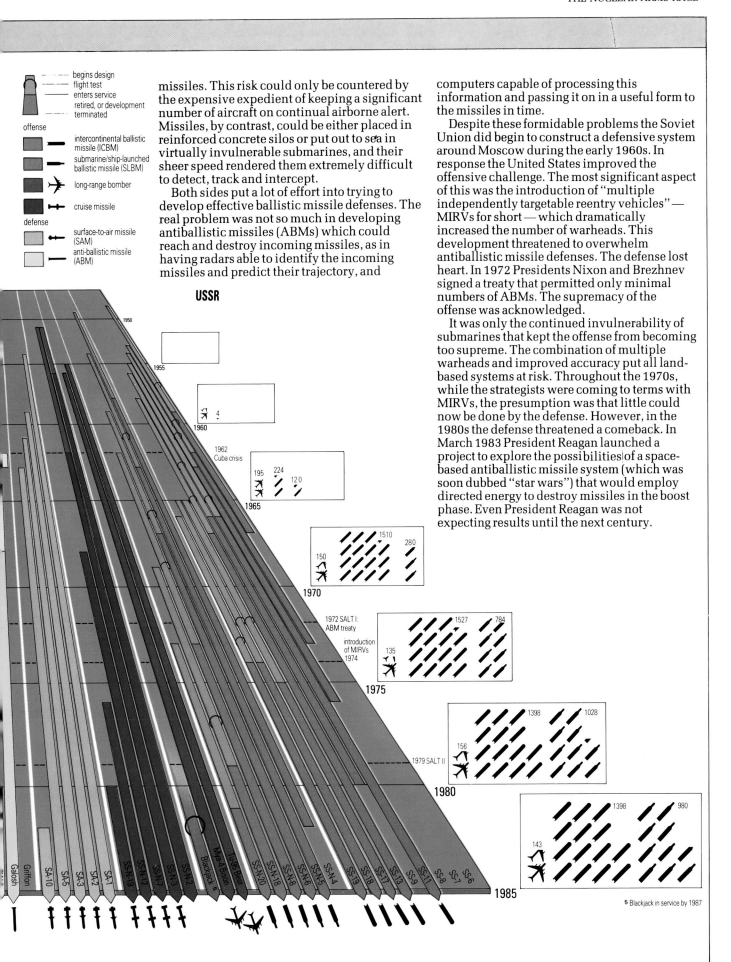

offense

intercontinental ballistic missile (ICBM)

submarine/ship-launched ballistic missile (SLBM)

long-range bomber

cruise missile

defense

surface-to-air missile (SAM)

anti-ballistic missile (ABM)

begins design
flight test
enters service
retired, or development terminated

USSR

1950
1955
1960
1962 Cuba crisis
1965
1970
1972 SALT I: ABM treaty
introduction of MIRVs 1974
1975
1979 SALT II
1980
1985

4
195 224 120
150 1510 280
135 1527 784
156 1398 1028
143 1398 980

Galosh Griffon SA-10 SA-5 SA-3 SA-2 SA-1 SS-N-19 SS-N-12 SS-N-7 SS-N-3 SS-N-2 Blackjack 6 Mya-4 Bison Tu-95 Bear SS-N-20 SS-N-18 SS-N-8 SS-N-6 SS-N-5 SS-N-4 SS-19 SS-18 SS-17 SS-13 SS-9 SS-11 SS-8 SS-7 SS-6

5 Blackjack in service by 1987

missiles. This risk could only be countered by the expensive expedient of keeping a significant number of aircraft on continual airborne alert. Missiles, by contrast, could be either placed in reinforced concrete silos or put out to sea in virtually invulnerable submarines, and their sheer speed rendered them extremely difficult to detect, track and intercept.

Both sides put a lot of effort into trying to develop effective ballistic missile defenses. The real problem was not so much in developing antiballistic missiles (ABMs) which could reach and destroy incoming missiles, as in having radars able to identify the incoming missiles and predict their trajectory, and

computers capable of processing this information and passing it on in a useful form to the missiles in time.

Despite these formidable problems the Soviet Union did begin to construct a defensive system around Moscow during the early 1960s. In response the United States improved the offensive challenge. The most significant aspect of this was the introduction of "multiple independently targetable reentry vehicles" — MIRVs for short — which dramatically increased the number of warheads. This development threatened to overwhelm antiballistic missile defenses. The defense lost heart. In 1972 Presidents Nixon and Brezhnev signed a treaty that permitted only minimal numbers of ABMs. The supremacy of the offense was acknowledged.

It was only the continued invulnerability of submarines that kept the offense from becoming too supreme. The combination of multiple warheads and improved accuracy put all land-based systems at risk. Throughout the 1970s, while the strategists were coming to terms with MIRVs, the presumption was that little could now be done by the defense. However, in the 1980s the defense threatened a comeback. In March 1983 President Reagan launched a project to explore the possibilities of a space-based antiballistic missile system (which was soon dubbed "star wars") that would employ directed energy to destroy missiles in the boost phase. Even President Reagan was not expecting results until the next century.

Submarine-launched ballistic missiles stabilize the strategic balance

breakthroughs in defense, then it would have to involve a successful surprise attack. In the 1950s there was particular concern about the possibility of the Soviet Union developing long-range ballistic missiles before the Americans. This would allow them to attack the bombers of the American Strategic Air Command while they were still on the ground at base, unable to be warned in time. In practice, it was the Americans who won the "missile race" and the Russians who had to worry about the vulnerability of their forces to a first strike. This was one reason why they attempted to increase their striking power against the United States by moving missiles to Cuba in late 1962. The resultant crisis is dealt with below (pp. 108-09).

Missile vulnerability
As both sides introduced intercontinental ballistic missiles (ICBMs) during the 1960s, first-strike fears eased. These weapons were not considered to be very good at attacking each other. Land-based, they could be placed in underground silos, protected by reinforced concrete against anything but the most direct hit — and the missiles at that time could not boast the necessary accuracy. Even less vulnerable were submarine-launched ballistic missiles (SLBMs). These became the most important source of stability in the strategic balance for they have effectively ruled out first strikes. The ability to move around the oceans undetected is the greatest asset of submarines, even though up to now this mobility has come at the expense of accuracy.

Although techniques in antisubmarine warfare (ASW) are improving, there is still a long way to go before all enemy submarines could be found, tracked and destroyed simultaneously. Countermeasures are also improving. Modern submarines are much quieter than their predecessors and, with missiles of increasing range, they can patrol wide areas. So for the foreseeable future submarines are going to be the mainstay of second-strike capabilities. It is of note that Britain and France, facing much stiffer constraints on their resources than the two superpowers, but still seeking ways to stay in the nuclear business, have decided to concentrate on a submarine-based force.

One reason why they — and the superpowers — have been forced to rely on submarines is the growing vulnerability of all land-based forces. Most attention has focused on land-based ICBMs. When they were first introduced in any numbers in the early 1960s they were felt to be reasonably invulnerable

because of their widespread dispersion around the countryside and their installation in underground silos, surrounded by reinforced concrete. If the enemy wanted to destroy all the ICBMs in a surprise attack, then it would be necessary to use up far more in the attack than he could expect to destroy because it would take at least two ICBMs to be sure of destroying one in its silo. This ratio was not changed with the steadily improving accuracy of the ICBM because the reliability of individual weapons would always be in doubt. What made the difference was the development of MIRVing — multiple warheads on individual launchers, each capable of independent targeting. This development not only completely undermined the effort to develop antiballistic missiles — in that it required many more interceptors for each missile — but it also meant that it was now possible to contemplate the load of a single missile destroying more than one missile on the ground. This dramatically changed the basic ratio. An accurate ICBM force could destroy a much larger force so long as it could catch it in a surprise attack.

This development dominated American strategic policy during the 1970s. The United States held the numbers of its ICBMs at just over 1000 (a number frozen at arms-control talks) and the Soviet Union developed a larger force of over 1400 missiles that were individually much bigger. Although the United States introduced MIRVed missiles first, the Soviet advantages in size and numbers meant that they were eventually able to exploit this new technology much more effec-

Whatever the eventual possibilities for breakthroughs in antisubmarine warfare, for the moment all of the nuclear powers are coming to rely increasingly on submarines to carry their deterrent forces. Above, the launching of the French submarine the *Tonnant* at Brest in 1980, carrying 16 M-20 missiles. Below, the test launch of an American *Trident* missile, each of which contains eight separately targetable warheads.

ANTISUBMARINE WARFARE

With the proliferation of highly accurate warheads, any fixed targets on land have become increasingly vulnerable to a surprise attack. This has led to increased reliance on relatively invulnerable submarines which can carry ballistic or cruise missiles. Submarines are also critical in anti-shipping operations during non-nuclear wars and in hunting and attacking the submarines of the other side. A great deal of effort has therefore been put into antisubmarine warfare (ASW). Although the West is ahead in this area, neither side is as yet close to the sort of capability that would allow all the enemy's missile-carrying submarines to be picked off at will. This diagram illustrates the great variety of methods employed to detect, track and deploy enemy submarines. Because the oceans are not transparent, the main method of detecting is sonar. The main methods of attack are depth charges or torpedoes. Both in the Falklands conflict of 1982 and in regular reports of Soviet submarines using Swedish territorial waters at will, the evidence suggests that the advantage still lies with the hunted rather than the hunter.

1 ASROC launch: acoustic-homing torpedo or depth charge

2 sonobuoy location by helicopter (e.g. *Sea King*)

3 sound surveillance system (SOSUS)

4 satellite observation of bases

5 radar or sonar detection by other attack submarines

6 ASW aircraft (e.g. *Orion*) with sonobuoy **(6a)**, radar and magnetic anomaly detection

7 antisubmarine captor minefield with acoustic-homing torpedoes

8 towed-array radar

tively. American planners became obsessed with the thought that a Soviet first strike using only its ICBMs would destroy the American ability to retaliate in kind and still leave it with an intimidating reserve force. The Americans could still retaliate, but only by turning the war into a much more murderous affair. Only ICBMs had the accuracy for precision attacks on military targets; remove them and the less accurate submarine-launched missiles could only attack cities. The presumption was that an American president would be so intimidated by this prospect that he would be forced to surrender after this partial first strike.

This scenario was always far-fetched. The Kremlin might not share American confidence in the reliability and effectiveness of Soviet missile technology; it could not be sure that the Americans would not simply launch their missiles at the first warning of an impending attack (although it is against American declaratory policy to do so), leaving only empty holes for the Soviet missiles to destroy; it would have to reckon that even such an ostensibly "surgical" attack, directed against military sites, would still leave millions dead, making it difficult to rely on a submissive American response.

Whatever the flaws, the scenario still exercised an enormous influence on American policy, and the responses to it have shaped the current state of the strategic balance. Three responses can be identified, of which only one has been successful. The successful side of the policy has been to build up comparable American capabilities. The development of highly accurate cruise missiles to be fitted on the old B-52 bombers has given these old aircraft a new lease of life. More important still, the coming generation of submarine-launched missiles — *Trident-II* — will be the first of their kind exhibiting the sort of high accuracies common in ICBMs. As a result, the loss of ICBMs would not prevent the United States from executing a comparable counter-force attack of its own.

The less successful side of American policy has been the search for a way to reduce the vulnerability of its land-based forces. The arms-control route failed because the Russians were not prepared to bargain away their advantage in large heavy ICBMs. The Americans have argued consistently in strategic arms-control talks that both sides should reduce the numbers of their land-based forces and put more out to sea. Certainly the American position was often presented in a rather one-sided manner (for example the proposed

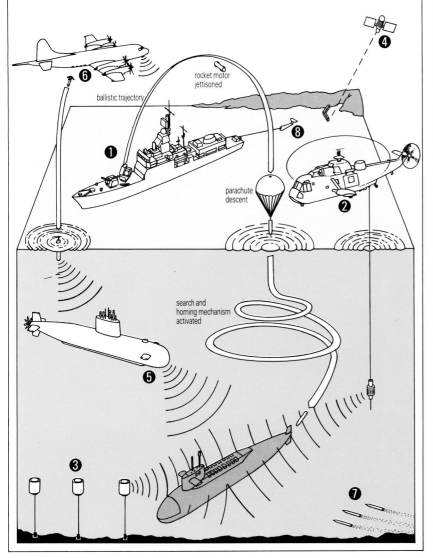

rocket motor jettisoned
ballistic trajectory
parachute descent
search and homing mechanism activated

The question of surviving a surprise attack prompts the great M-X saga

limit for MIRVed ICBMs was put conveniently close to the existing inventory). It is also the case that the Soviet Union, as a continental power, still appears far less comfortable at sea than does the more maritime-minded United States. Although there are more Soviet than American submarines, the Soviet missiles are still less sophisticated and there seem to be problems in keeping a significant number of them out on patrol at any time. So the Soviet Union feels much more dependent on its ICBMs, which make up some three-quarters of its strategic capability. At any rate, a succession of American proposals, designed to secure reductions in the most formidable component of the Soviet ICBM force, produced little — and it was this failure that was the basis of much of the ferocious criticism of the second Strategic Arms Limitation Treaty (SALT II) in the United States Senate after it had been signed in June 1979.

Although arms control was criticized for failing to reduce the vulnerability of land-based ICBMs, the force improvement route — the third strand of US policy — was no more successful. For more than 10 years the Americans discussed a variety of schemes for making it possible for their next generation of ICBMs — known as M-X for "Missile Experimental" — to survive a surprise attack. Over 200 schemes were examined. They ranged from launching the missile from aircraft, moving it along underground trenches so that the Russians would not know where it was at any particular moment, moving it around a "racetrack" with a large number of shelters available to confuse Soviet targeting, to a concept known as "dense pack" which involved putting the individual missiles so close together that the electromagnetic pulse released by the first explosions of the attacking missiles would have the fratricidal effect of disabling the warheads of the following missiles. When this idea was mooted by the Reagan administration in late 1982 it was seen more as an indication of the exhaustion of ideas on the subject than a serious suggestion. All the other proposals had been ruled out on a variety of environmental, financial and practical grounds. Eventually the president agreed to a bipartisan commission which reported that the basic problem of ICBM vulnerability was probably insoluble, but that maybe it did not matter as much as everybody had been making out. The commission argued that a number of M-X missiles should be deployed in existing fixed silos and that work should begin to develop a much

INTERCONTINENTAL DEPLOYMENT: USA

The United States' strategic deterrent was at first dependent on long-range bombers, many of which are still in service, before a ballistic missile force was built up in the 1960s. Because of concern with the vulnerability of land-based ICBMs there has been an increasing emphasis on submarine-based missiles. The latest development is the introduction of thousands of cruise missiles on board aircraft and submarines.

nuclear-capable offensive positions

- Titan ICBM base
- Minuteman ICBM base
- submarine base
- naval base
- long-range bomber base
- possible missile trajectory, selected base and target

targeted positions

- ⊕ nuclear base
- ⊕ other naval base
- ⟲ ABM radar
- ■ city with population over 1 million

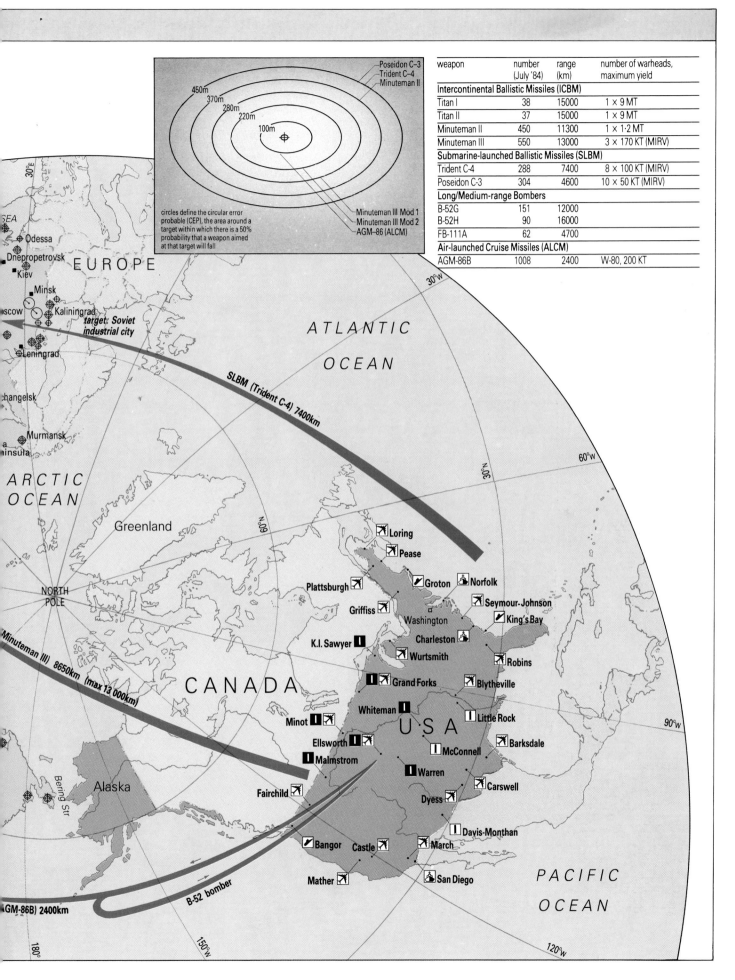

circles define the circular error probable (CEP), the area around a target within which there is a 50% probability that a weapon aimed at that target will fall

Poseidon C–3
Trident C–4
Minuteman II

450m
370m
280m
220m
100m

Minuteman III Mod 1
Minuteman III Mod 2
AGM–86 (ALCM)

weapon	number (July '84)	range (km)	number of warheads, maximum yield
Intercontinental Ballistic Missiles (ICBM)			
Titan I	38	15000	1 × 9 MT
Titan II	37	15000	1 × 9 MT
Minuteman II	450	11300	1 × 1·2 MT
Minuteman III	550	13000	3 × 170 KT (MIRV)
Submarine-launched Ballistic Missiles (SLBM)			
Trident C-4	288	7400	8 × 100 KT (MIRV)
Poseidon C-3	304	4600	10 × 50 KT (MIRV)
Long/Medium-range Bombers			
B-52G	151	12000	
B-52H	90	16000	
FB-111A	62	4700	
Air-launched Cruise Missiles (ALCM)			
AGM-86B	1008	2400	W-80, 200 KT

SEA
Odessa
Dnepropetrovsk
Kiev
EUROPE
Minsk
Kaliningrad
scow
target: Soviet industrial city
Leningrad
changelsk
Murmansk
insula
a

ARCTIC OCEAN

ATLANTIC OCEAN

SLBM (Trident C-4) 7400km

30°W

30°N

60°W

60°N

Greenland

NORTH POLE

Minuteman III) 8650km (max 13 000km)

CANADA

Loring
Pease
Groton
Norfolk
Plattsburgh
Seymour-Johnson
Griffiss
King's Bay
Washington
K.I. Sawyer
Charleston
Wurtsmith
Robins
Grand Forks
Blytheville
Whiteman
USA
Little Rock
Minot
McConnell
Barksdale
Ellsworth
Malmstrom
Warren
Carswell
Fairchild
Dyess
Alaska
Davis-Monthan
Bering Str
Bangor
Castle
March
Mather
San Diego

90°W

B-52 bomber

GM-86B) 2400km

PACIFIC OCEAN

180°
150°W
120°W

95

A SOVIET ICBM ATTACK SCENARIO

Ballistic missilses are launched by powerful boosters and their flight path is then affected by the earth's gravitational speed. Many Soviet missiles are still propelled by storable liquid fuels which can be dangerous and difficult to handle. They have been trying for some time to develop dependable solid fuels which are easier to handle and allow for a quicker launch. An intercontinental missile (ICBM), with a range of 6500 to 16 000 kilometers (4000 to 10 000 miles), passes out of the atmosphere before descending to its target. The journey will take around 30 minutes. Missiles can be launched from submerged submarines. Gas pressure forces the missile through the water and the

rocket ignites on reaching the surface. Most, but not all, modern missiles contain a number of warheads which are carried on a "bus" in the nose cone. Before the last stage of the missile reenters the atmosphere, these are dispensed from the bus and then guided by a computer to their individual targets. They will also be programmed to maneuver to confuse any defenses. Chaff and decoys may be released with the same objective. Both sides have elaborate radar networks to warn them of any incoming attack, but there is little that they can do to stop it. The Soviet Union maintains a limited antiballistic-missile capability around Moscow.

1 *00.00* boost phase

2 *00.01* ballistic missile launched from submarine at close quarters

3 *00.02* flare detected by satellite on launching

4 *00.05* bus dispenses warheads prior to reentry into atmosphere

5 *00.07* SLBM silences communications and impedes launch of retaliatory missiles

6 *00.10* midcourse phase: reentry vehicles follow ballistic trajectory c.1000 km above earth

7 *00.12* early warning radar detects attack

8 *00.24* reentry phase begins

9 *00.25* retaliatory ICBMs launched

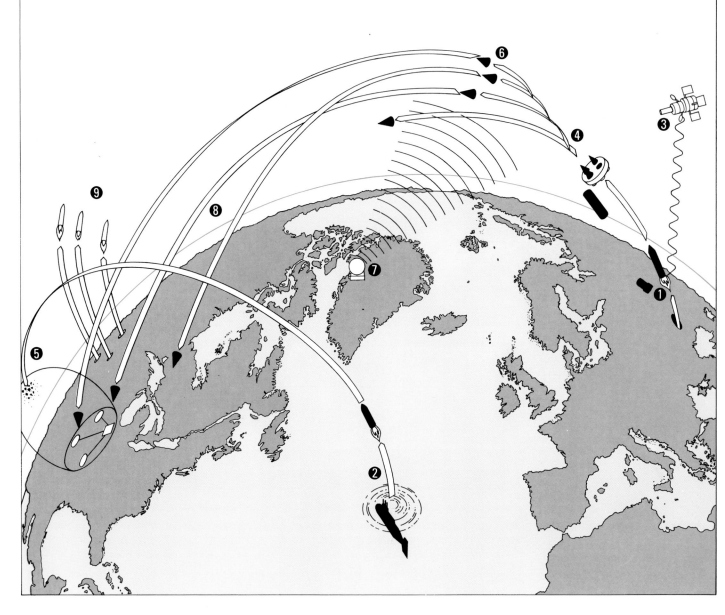

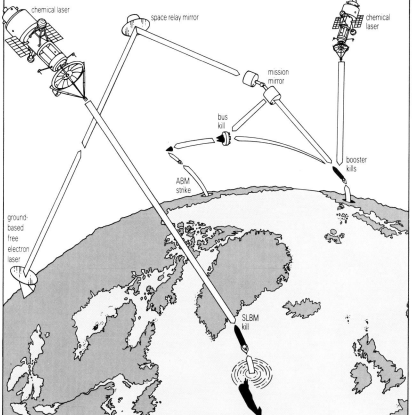

*The US commitment to Europe
— will it hold?*

the tremendous problems with sustaining command, control and communications in a nuclear environment.

This picture of relative stability is not the one communicated in the superpower argument. Neither side seems willing to acknowledge that the relationship is in balance. One reason for this is that it is very difficult for them to feel sure that disparities in numbers do not matter. We shall be looking at arms control in a later chapter. For the moment we may note that one of the perverse effects of the close comparisons between the two sides' force structures encouraged by the negotiations is the importance of relatively modest disparities in missile numbers. But these numbers are at any rate sufficiently close for there not to be any real worries even for those who are concerned to maintain an exact numerical balance between the two powers (see pp. 90-91).

Nuclear weapons in Europe

A robust balance is not without awkward consequences, not least for the doctrine of the North Atlantic Treaty Organization (NATO). In the 1950s the Americans made a series of commitments to their allies — in the Pacific as well as in Europe — to provide them with nuclear protection against attack by the Soviet Union or its allies. Nuclear weapons were to be used to deter not only nuclear attacks but also those involving conventional weapons. These commitments were taken on at a time of a substantial American superiority. Inevitably, as the Soviet Union caught up in nuclear strength, the quality of this commitment came into question. Would an American president risk the loss of Chicago or New York in an attempt to save Paris or Bonn? Despite what might seem to be the obvious answer to that question, the Americans have never reneged on their commitment and the Europeans have by and large clung to it as an act of faith — because the alternatives raise so many difficult problems. However nobody pretends that a nuclear guarantee with such suicidal implications is wholly credible. Much of NATO nuclear policy over the past three decades has been bound up with trying to remedy this defect. American nuclear weapons based in Europe have played a crucial role.

The first American weapons arrived in the early 1950s and were located in England. Aircraft able to deliver them had first arrived in 1948 during the Berlin crisis of that year. These weapons were very much part of the American threat to the Soviet homeland, but

The so-called "star wars" project, initiated by President Reagan in March 1983. Current defensive concepts emphasize a series of complementary layers starting with space-based systems attacking missiles as launched. Current plans do not envisage deployment of any new systems before the turn of the century and some estimates put the cost at a trillion dollars. Costs apart, many oppose the project as being likely to stimulate a new round in the arms race, with efforts to develop offensive countermeasures, as well as constituting a challenge to the 1972 ABM treaty, which will have to be abandoned if the new systems are to be developed. Although President Reagan describes his strategic defense initiative as a "vision" by which offensive nuclear weapons could be rendered "impotent and obsolete," other proponents have more modest objectives. These include denying the Soviet Union any opportunity to execute a first strike or just ensuring that the United States is not left behind in this area should the Soviet Union decide to put a new emphasis on defensive technologies.

smaller, non-MIRVed ICBM known as *Midgetman.*

The long-term significance of this saga may be to reorient American planning away from multiple warheads. In an associated development largely in response to Congressional pressure, the Reagan administration added to existing ideas for arms-control negotiations the concept of "build-down," which argues for the removal of more than one old warhead for every new one that is introduced. Perhaps because of the confused way in which it was proposed and the fact that in late 1983 superpower relations were in a rather parlous state, the Russians did not respond very positively. Nevertheless this might provide an interesting way forward to remove some of the remaining elements of instability from the strategic balance.

Explorations continue for new ways of deploying nuclear weapons in order to secure some strategic advantage. All come back to the same problem: there is no way of using nuclear weapons first without accepting a severe risk of retaliation. Moreover the various ideas for fighting "prolonged nuclear wars," involving a succession of relatively modest exchanges that have been canvassed by the Reagan administration, all seem to founder on the difficulties of controlling nuclear warfare once it has been set in motion. A number of studies have demonstrated

Battlefield nuclear weapons — why NATO still has them

they were later supplemented by a large number of much smaller weapons with shorter ranges intended for use in and around the battlefield. These were then known as "tactical" and are now known as "battlefield" nuclear weapons.

It was at first assumed that they could be used almost as if they were conventional weapons. In particular they might support the defense by demolishing the large concentrations of armor massed for the offensive. It soon became clear that this was wishful thinking. Not only might there be effective ways to use these weapons to knock holes in the defense but also, and much more serious, the consequences of use for any notional military purposes for civilian life in the surrounding areas would be dire. Those being defended would be destroyed by their own defense.

By the early 1960s NATO had recognized that it would be impossible to use these weapons as if they were just superefficient conventional munitions and that special — and rather cumbersome — consultative procedures would be necessary to govern their use. Unless these battlefield nuclear weapons could be used in the first stages of their campaign, the enemy tanks would be dispersed far into friendly territory and would therefore be even more difficult to attack without the most appalling consequences for civilian life. All this meant that, whatever NATO might say in theory, in practice there was a clear firebreak between the use of conventional and nuclear weapons.

Why then did these weapons stay? There were two related reasons. First, once the initial capital investment has been made, nuclear weapons are much cheaper than their conventional counterparts. They provide, as an American Secretary of Defense once put it, "a bigger bang for a buck." Once these weapons had been introduced into the NATO arsenals during the 1950s, the implications of replacing them with equivalent amounts of conventional firepower were expensive to say the least. This financial consideration has been influential from NATO's early days in encouraging an excessive dependence on nuclear forces.

But it was not just the money. Here we need to understand the fears that were developing among the European governments as the result of a stalemate at the strategic nuclear level. The Kennedy administration, which came to power in January 1961, was anxious to increase dependence on conventional forces because it felt that its nuclear guarantee had lost much of its credibility. It would have

INTERCONTINENTAL DEPLOYMENT: USSR

The Soviet Union did not develop a large bomber force in the 1950s. It concentrated its efforts on ICBMs. After a false start in the early 1960s large numbers were introduced, many much bigger than the American equivalents. ICBMs came to account for 75 percent of Soviet strategic strength. It has never been confident with its submarines, though these are now getting better, and a new long-range bomber is in development.

nuclear-capable offensive positions

⬜	ICBM base
◣	IRBM base
✒	submarine base
🛉	naval base
✈	long-range bomber base
➤	possible missile trajectory, selected base and target

targeted positions

⊕	nuclear base
⊕	other
⊘	ABM radar
▪	city with population over 1 million

weapon	number (July '84)	range (km)	number of warheads, maximum yield
Intercontinental Ballistic Missiles (ICBM)			
SS-11	520	10000	1 × 1 MT
SS-13	60	10000	1 × 750 KT
SS-17	150	10000	4 × 20 KT (MIRV)
SS-18	308	12000	1 × 20 MT
SS-19	360	10000	6 × 550 KT (MIRV)

Submarine-launched Ballistic Missiles (SLBM)			
SS-N-5	45	1400	1 × 1 MT
SS-N-6	368	3000	1 × 1 MT
SS-N-8	292	8000	1 × 1MT
SS-N-17	12	3900	1 × 1 MT
SS-N-18	224	7000	1 × 450 KT
SS-N-20	40	8300	9 × 200 KT (MIRV)
Long-range Bombers			
Tu-95 Bear	100	12800	
Mya-4 Bison	43	11200	
Air-launched Cruise Missiles (ALCM)			
AS-2 Kipper	90	200	1 × KT range
AS-3 Kangaroo	100	650	1 × 800 KT
AS-4 Kitchen	830	500	1 × 200 KT
AS-6 Kingfish	820	250	1 × 350 KT

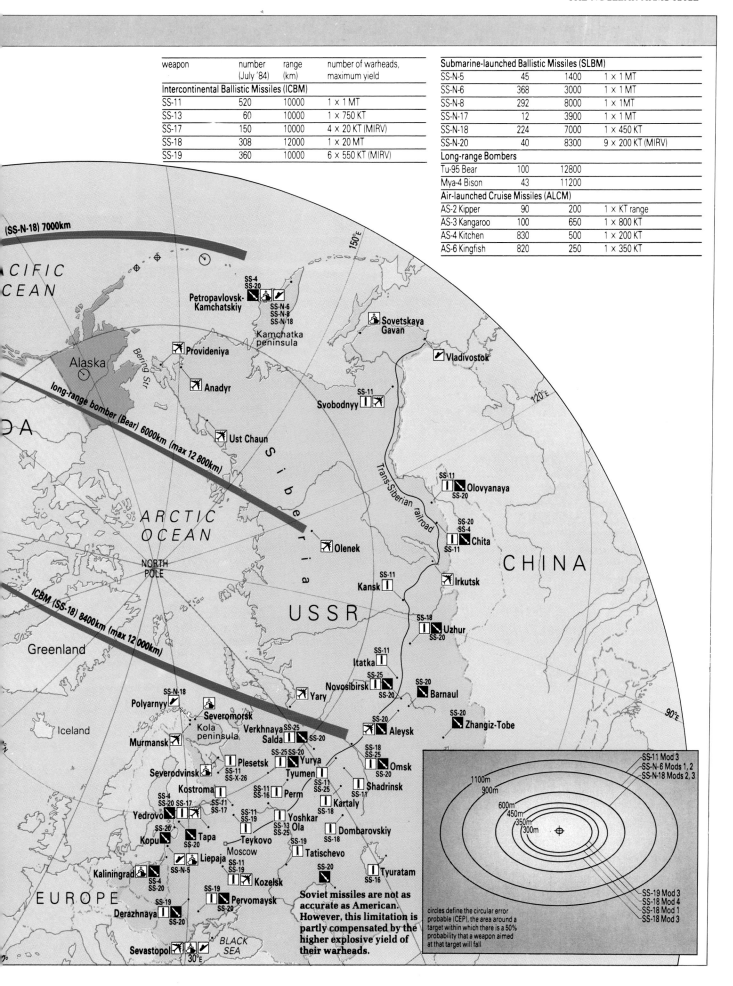

Soviet missiles are not as accurate as American. However, this limitation is partly compensated by the higher explosive yield of their warheads.

circles define the circular error probable (CEP), the area around a target within which there is a 50% probability that a weapon aimed at that target will fall

The NATO doctrine of "flexible response" and the limited nuclear war debate

preferred to remove the battlefield nuclear weapons: rather than be used to reinforce conventional forces, they were more likely to set in motion a process of uncontrollable nuclear escalation.

The European governments interpreted this as an American acceptance of increased conventional risks to their European allies if that meant reducing the nuclear risks to themselves. If it was clear that there was to be no nuclear escalation, might not the Soviet Union consider that the risks of aggression had been lowered to an acceptable level? Even if a conventional invasion failed, Soviet territory would not be threatened. For the unfortunate West Europeans, however, a "conventional war" would not appear as such a limited affair. It would devastate the central regions of the continent and possibly the flanks as well. All war, and not just nuclear war, had to be deterred. This required making it clear to the Soviet leadership that it could not assume that its territory would remain sacrosanct and that the most awful, and therefore inevitably nuclear, effects of modern war would be visited upon it. From this perspective, American nuclear weapons in Europe were valuable precisely because of the uncontrollable escalation that they threatened. They made it more likely that a conventional land war in Europe would turn into an all-out nuclear war between the two superpowers. This prospect strengthened deterrence.

This view was embodied in the NATO doctrine of "flexible response" which was adopted in 1967. This doctrine involved something of a compromise. The Europeans recognized the need to prepare for a substantial conventional phase so as to be less dependent on an incredible threat of early nuclear retaliation (although they did very little to meet this need). In return, the Americans recognized the need to sustain a serious risk of nuclear escalation. For the next decade nobody felt inclined to disrupt this compromise.

The difficulty with this view was that it assigned to the battlefield nuclear weapons an essentially symbolic role. Yet these weapons were designed to perform a number of military functions, suggesting that if they were performed adequately there would in fact be no need to escalate to higher nuclear levels. This implied the possibility of a limited nuclear war in Europe which for those living on the continent would be even worse than conventional war. This problem came to the fore in the mid-1970s as the question

of replacing the existing nuclear stockpile — which was now getting rather old — was confronted. The new nuclear weapons that the US Army wanted to introduce were much more capable than their predecessors and much more clearly designed for military uses.

The American designers had concluded that these weapons could have a credible military role if the host populations could be convinced that they would not suffer unduly from controlled nuclear explosions in their midst. They therefore attempted to design weapons with effects tailored to particular military requirements and with a minimum of collateral damage to the surroundings. One such weapon would, for example, "enhance radiation" at the expense of blast and fallout, and was to be directed against tank crews. It became known as the "neutron bomb." When news of this weapon leaked out, far from reassuring civilians, it triggered mass protest. It was castigated as a capitalist bomb for its assumed capacity to kill people while leaving property intact. In practice it would have severely damaged buildings, but anyway this charge missed the point of the new weapon. It was to be used on the battlefield and not against cities. The real criticism was that if large numbers of these weapons were used, as they would have to be against a substantial tank offensive, then the consequences for the local population were unlikely to be much happier than they would have been with the older "dirtier" bombs. Moreover there was still the risk that their use would trigger a substantial Soviet nuclear response. The net result would be premature escalation to the nuclear level. In the event, the mixture of objections caused President Carter to defer production in April 1978. Although President Reagan later authorized production, the West Europeans made it clear that they would not accept this weapon on the continent.

The next major issue concerned longer-range weapons. The problem here was different. The Americans have never been very happy about keeping missiles in Europe capable of attacking Soviet territory. After the Cuban missile crisis (see pp. 108-09) the last of the *Thor* and *Jupiter* missiles that had been brought in during the late 1950s were removed. During much of the 1960s there was in fact a cruise missile (known as *Mace*), based in Germany and capable of hitting Soviet territory, but this too was removed. During the 1970s planners began to worry that the long-range nuclear-capable aircraft — mainly the F-111s based in England — would be needed for other con-

▲ Under orders: two Soviet platoon commanders are assigned to their positions by the commander of a battlefield missile battery.

▶ A *Tomahawk* cruise missile in flight. Though far from speedy, this weapon is able to fly low enough to avoid current Soviet air defenses. However, new defenses are being developed.

Why Western Europe pressed for cruise and Pershing

ventional roles and would have difficulty penetrating Soviet air defenses, and that the *Poseidon* submarine-launched missiles that the Americans had assigned to NATO did not provide a sufficient symbol of commitment. After all, submarines are more easily removed from a combat zone than any other vehicle.

Two other factors worried NATO planners. First, the Soviet Union was exhibiting a renewed interest in weapons designed primarily for use against Western Europe. In fact Soviet interest had never waned, but there had been problems in developing reliable replacements for the weapons that had been facing Western Europe since the 1950s and early 1960s. Now a new aircraft (*Backfire*)

and a new missile (*SS-20*) were introduced and this sent alarm bells ringing around Europe. Secondly, and more worrying for the Europeans, the American preoccupation in the strategic arms-limitation talks was with weapons that could hit the continental United States. In their efforts to consolidate parity in intercontinental weapons the Americans seemed unconcerned by major disparities lower down the line, of which the most notable was in intermediate nuclear forces.

In December 1979, largely at European prompting, NATO agreed to introduce new intermediate missiles — 464 *Tomahawk* cruise missiles and 108 *Pershing-II* ballistic missiles — from late 1983 on to deal with these various problems. Britain, Germany, Italy, Belgium and Holland (the last two only tentatively) agreed to host these new missiles. It was also agreed to enter into negotiations with the Soviet Union on the possibility of reducing the actual and planned numbers of the missiles of both sides. This became known as the "dual-track" decision.

It was always going to be very difficult to reach any agreement with the Soviet Union on nuclear weapons in Europe (see pp. 102-03). The two force structures were simply not comparable. In the event, when the first missiles were installed in late 1983, it was clear that, as a method of securing restraints on Soviet forces, the dual-track decision had failed. However, NATO officials were not particularly despondent about that because they felt that the vital role of such missiles — linking the American nuclear arsenal to the defense of Europe — would still exist whatever the numbers of comparable Soviet missiles. After four years of intense political activity, during which all the relevant European governments had been put under immense pressure, there was some relief that the whole program had not been abandoned.

The debate — which was the most extensive ever to have taken place in the Western world — raised a number of issues of major importance. One of these concerned the role of American nuclear weapons in Europe. The critics argued that these weapons were being introduced into Europe as a result of American pressure in order to support a new strategy of limited nuclear war. In fact the origins of the program were much closer to Europe than to the United States. The reason why many Americans were unhappy about the new missiles was precisely that they were not suitable for limited nuclear war. The Russians have made it clear that, whatever the possibilities for limiting nuclear

101

EUROPEAN DEPLOYMENT: NATO

Since the 1950s NATO has had many battlefield nuclear weapons and medium-range aircraft, but the policy on systems that can hit Soviet territory has been uneven. In 1979 it was decided to introduce cruise and *Pershing* missiles.

weapon	number (July '84)	range (km)	number of warheads, maximum yield
Submarine-launched Ballistic Missiles (SLBM)			
Polaris A-3 (UK)	64	4600	3 × 200 KT (MRV)
MSBS M-20 (Fr)	80	3000	1 × 1MT

Intermediate/Medium-range Ballistic Missiles (I/MRBM)			
Pershing-II (US)	48	1800	1 × 5-50 KT
SSBS S-3 (Fr)	18	3500	1 × 1 MT
Submarine-launched Cruise Missiles (SLCM)			
Tomahawk (US)	48	2500	
Ground-launched Cruise Missiles (GLCM)			
Tomahawk (US)	32	2250	
Medium-range Bombers/Strike Aircraft (US)			
F-4E (US)	96	2200	
F-111 E/F (US)	150	4700	
F-16 (US)	72	3800	
A-7/F-18	48	2800	
F-104 (Allies)	281	2400	
F-4 E/F (Allies)	131	2200	
F-16 (Allies)	178	3800	
Buccaneer (UK)	25	3700	
Mirage IVA (Fr)	28	3200	
Mirage IIIE (Fr)	30	2400	
Jaguar (Fr)	45	1600	
Tornado (Allies)	223	2800	
Super Etendard (Fr)	36	1500	

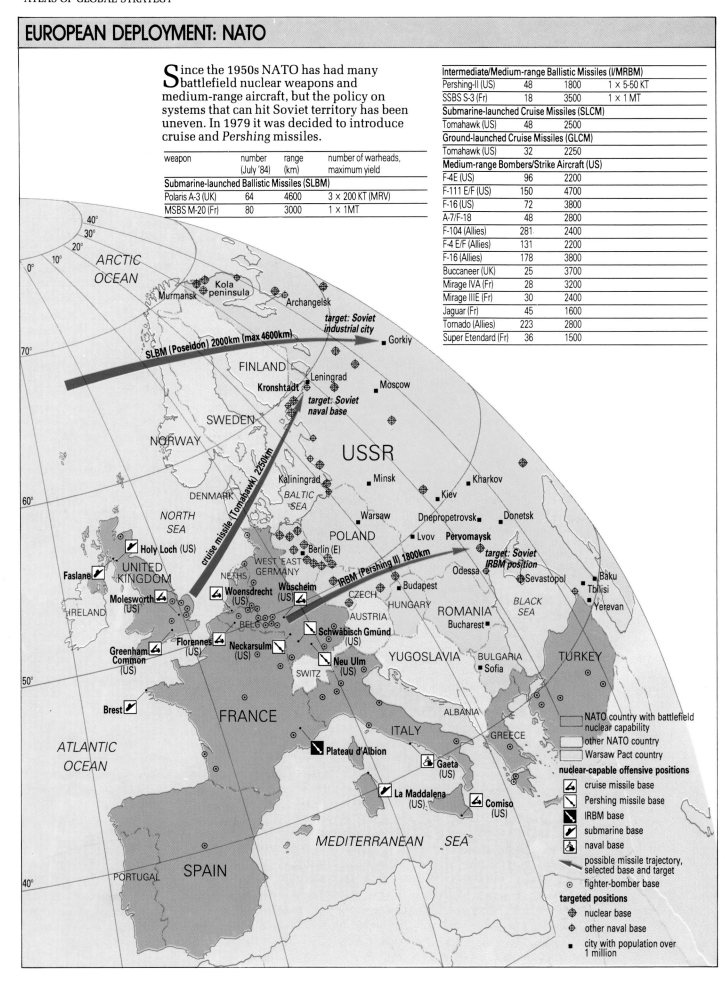

ARCTIC OCEAN

Murmansk · Kola peninsula · Archangelsk

SLBM (Poseidon) 2000km (max 4600km)

target: Soviet industrial city

Gorkiy

FINLAND

Leningrad · Moscow

Kronstadt

target: Soviet naval base

SWEDEN

NORWAY

USSR

cruise missile (Tomahawk) 2250km

Minsk · Kharkov

DENMARK

Kaliningrad · Kiev

BALTIC SEA

NORTH SEA

Warsaw · Dnepropetrovsk · Donetsk

POLAND

Lvov · Pervomaysk

target: Soviet IRBM position

Holy Loch (US)

Berlin (E)

IRBM (Pershing II) 1800km

Odessa · Sevastopol · Baku

UNITED KINGDOM

Faslane

WEST EAST GERMANY

Wüscheim (US)

Tbilisi · Yerevan

Molesworth (US)

NETHS

Woensdrecht (US)

CZECH

Budapest

BLACK SEA

IRELAND

AUSTRIA

HUNGARY

ROMANIA

BELG

Schwäbisch Gmünd (US)

Bucharest

Florennes (US)

Neckarsulm (US)

Neu Ulm (US)

YUGOSLAVIA

BULGARIA

TURKEY

Greenham Common (US)

SWITZ

Sofia

Brest

FRANCE

ITALY

GREECE

ALBANIA

ATLANTIC OCEAN

Plateau d'Albion

Gaeta (US)

La Maddalena (US)

Comiso (US)

MEDITERRANEAN SEA

SPAIN

PORTUGAL

Legend:

NATO country with battlefield nuclear capability
other NATO country
Warsaw Pact country

nuclear-capable offensive positions
- cruise missile base
- Pershing missile base
- IRBM base
- submarine base
- naval base
- possible missile trajectory, selected base and target
- fighter-bomber base

targeted positions
- nuclear base
- other naval base
- city with population over 1 million

EUROPEAN DEPLOYMENT: WARSAW PACT

The Soviet Union has consistently given the development of a comprehensive nuclear capability facing Western Europe as high a priority as that facing the United States. During the 1970s it began to introduce the *Backfire* bomber and the *SS-20* missile.

Medium-range Bombers/Strike Aircraft		
Tu-16 Badger	410	4800
Tu-22 Blinder	160	4000
Tu-26 Backfire	235	8000
Su-7 Fitter A	130	1400
MiG-21 Fishbed L	160	1100
MiG-27 Flogger D/J	730	1400
Su-17 Fitter D/H	850	1800
Su-24 Fencer	630	4000
see also Long-range Bombers		

weapon	number (July '84)	range (km)	number of warheads, maximum yield
SLBM see Soviet intercontinental deployment			
Intermediate/Medium-range Ballistic Missiles (I/MRBM)			
SS-4	224	2000	1 × 1 MT
SS-20	243	5000	3 × 150 KT (MIRV)
Submarine-launched Cruise Missiles (SLCM)			
SS-N-3	240	450	1 × 350 KT
SS-N-7	88	45	1 × 200 KT
SS-N-9	140	280	1 × 200 KT
SS-N-12	80	1000	1 × 350 KT
GLCM none			

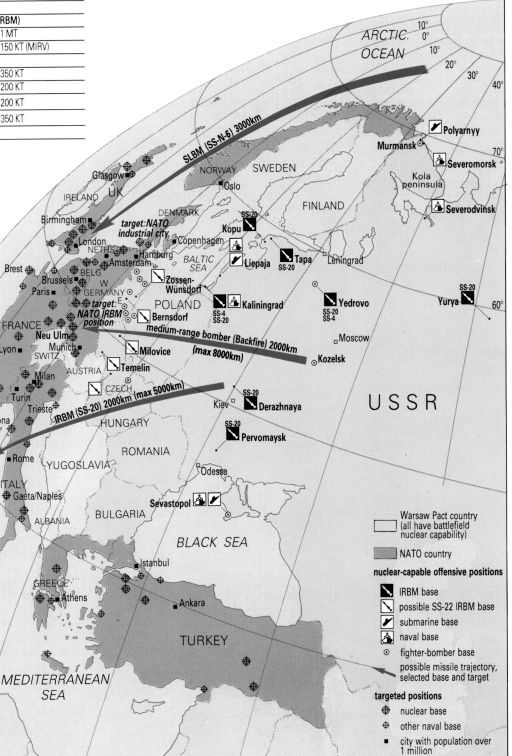

Warsaw Pact country (all have battlefield nuclear capability)

NATO country

nuclear-capable offensive positions

IRBM base

possible SS-22 IRBM base

submarine base

naval base

fighter-bomber base

possible missile trajectory, selected base and target

targeted positions

nuclear base

other naval base

city with population over 1 million

Can we trust the superpowers to behave?

hostilities when the detonations were on allied soil, as soon as any weapons exploded on Soviet territory the war would not be limited. It was precisely because the new missiles could reach Soviet soil that the Soviet Union was complaining so bitterly, and it was because the Americans understood the sort of response any use would trigger that they would have preferred to keep their European arsenal to the short-range systems. For those concerned about limited nuclear war the real villains were the battlefield nuclear weapons.

One of the more interesting but least noticed results of the debate of recent years has been a slow but steady decline in the number of battlefield nuclear warheads, at least in NATO. This has occurred partly as compensation for the introduction of the new long-range missiles but also because the rationales for the battlefield systems have been shown during the debate to be defective.

Although the argument has raged over the wisdom of introducing particular weapons into Europe and the precise state of the European nuclear "balance," the issue for much of the time was whether or not the leaders of the world's major powers could be trusted not to misuse the nuclear arsenals under their command. In Western Europe, for example, there was clear distrust of President Reagan in the United States — leading to suggestions that he might risk a nuclear conflagration in Europe in pursuit of policies of global confrontation with the Soviet Union. The history of the post-1945 period would suggest that the arms competition has as often as not followed the trend in political relations rather than reshaped those trends. The question then becomes not so much whether the nuclear balance is itself so stable that it can guarantee no slide into war but whether the risks of war have impressed themselves sufficiently on the minds of those responsible for maintaining the international order. To investigate this further we need to look at the actual behavior of the superpowers in past crises and the extent to which they have drawn upon their nuclear strength as a source of leverage in these crises.

Nuclear power and political influence

"And one of the questions which we have to ask ourselves as a country is what in the name of God is strategic superiority? What is the significance of it, politically, militarily, operationally, at these levels of numbers? What do you do with it?" This much-quoted and

FLIGHT PATH OF CRUISE

Cruise missiles have been around since the German "doodlebugs" of 1944. Developments in propulsion, guidance and warhead miniaturization have turned them into formidable alternatives to ballistic missiles for the 1980s. They can be launched from submarines, ships, aircraft or ground transporters and can deliver conventional or nuclear warheads. They fly low to avoid air defenses, but their slow speed still makes them vulnerable to interception.

TERCOM guidance: at predetermined times during flight, an onboard computer compares the terrain over which the missile is flying with a map derived from reconnaissance and stored in digitized form, giving the preprogrammed path. The computer assesses any deviation and issues course corrections (see pp.16–17).

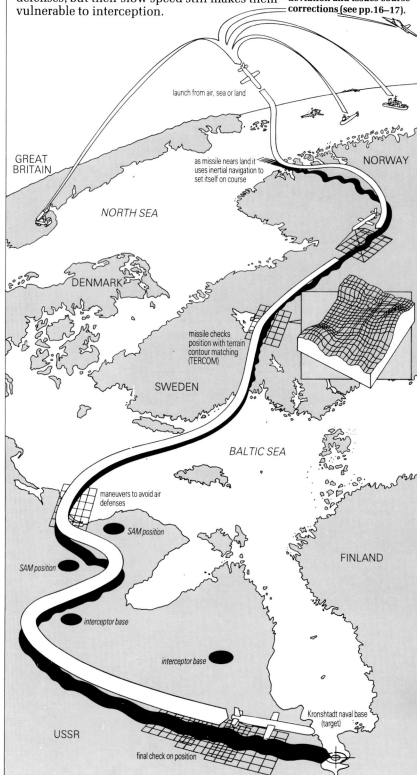

launch from air, sea or land

as missile nears land it uses inertial navigation to set itself on course

GREAT BRITAIN

NORTH SEA

NORWAY

DENMARK

missile checks position with terrain contour matching (TERCOM)

SWEDEN

BALTIC SEA

FINLAND

maneuvers to avoid air defenses

SAM position

SAM position

interceptor base

interceptor base

Kronshtadt naval base (target)

USSR

final check on position

What is superiority?

Nuclear and political symbols at President Brezhnev's last November parade in 1982.

exasperated remark by Dr Henry Kissinger comes from a period when, as US Secretary of State in 1974, he was under pressure from domestic opponents of his efforts to achieve an arms-control agreement. Kissinger was arguing that the sort of numerical disparities that might be left over after an agreement would make slight difference in the real political world.

In 1974 the consensus view in the United States was that the sort of nuclear superiority now available to either superpower was unlikely to be of much political value. The only superiority that really mattered was the ability to prevail in a war. With both sides enjoying an assured second-strike capability neither could really contemplate victory. Thus except in the most extreme and dire circumstances the two nuclear arsenals effectively canceled each other out and the threat to wage nuclear war did not constitute a realistic source of pressure in international politics.

As East–West relations deteriorated during the second half of the 1970s, it came to be argued increasingly in the West that one important cause was the Soviet ability to take advantage of American naivety on this matter. The United States had not realized how well off it had been when it enjoyed superiority up to the late 1960s because it had not appreciated the Soviet respect for raw military power. Now that Soviet aspirations and resources were at last converging, the Kremlin was flexing its muscles. Soviet foreign-policy adventures in the third world were seen as evidence that the Soviet leaders did not treat this question of superiority so lightly.

The critics argued that it may be that a crude numerical superiority, however lacking in real military substance, might still impress important if less sophisticated observers. Alternatively the capacity to launch a

partial first strike that would remove the land-based component of the enemy's retaliatory forces (which was discussed earlier) might turn out to be a source of genuine strategic advantage. Even Kissinger himself, when safely out of office in 1979, suggested that a Soviet lead in counter-force capabilities would for as long as it lasted in the 1980s create a window of opportunity for the Soviet Union which it might exploit mercilessly in pursuit of its foreign-policy objectives.

A more telling objection to the sanguine view was that, because of the nuclear guarantee that it had issued to its allies, the United States needed superiority more than the Soviet Union. The Russians, it was claimed, could draw on political and military means of promoting their objectives that could only be fully countered by the prospect of a crisis escalating into a nuclear conflict. Now that the United States had lost its nuclear advantage the Kremlin could act without restraint.

As a result of arguments such as these, by the time that the Reagan administration came to power in January 1981, a common view was that it was not enough to ensure that there was a visible and settled parity. The United States might now need something more to redress the military balance. This "something more" was never called superiority; nor was it ever made clear exactly how it would translate into political muscle. In fact, as we have already seen, it is extremely difficult to develop the sort of nuclear advantage that might actually turn the tide in war and on which one could confidently rely in peace-time. As we have also seen, the loss of nuclear superiority did cause the Americans problems in sustaining their guarantees to their allies, but NATO did manage to prevent these problems from becoming too overwhelming. As for the less predictable and less regulated political conflict outside the NATO area, the most appropriate means for assessing the validity of the claims on the relevance of superiority is not to indulge in abstract theorizing of how certain capabilities might make all the difference in some hypothetical crisis, but to look at the rich experience we now have of such crises in the nuclear age.

The United States began our period exploiting its nuclear superiority vis-à-vis Japan. It has been suggested since that the decision to bomb Hiroshima would not have been taken had Japan had a capacity to respond in kind. This may well be true, but it still leaves unanswered the question of the attitude that the Americans would have taken had the Japanese had the capacity to make any response.

Is nuclear superiority overrated?

They had no military offensive capability of any kind left. That is the sort of superiority that only comes at the end of a war. It tells us little about what might happen with a less absolute superiority prior to war.

For the rest of the 1940s the Americans did enjoy an atomic monopoly, but the weapons themselves were scarce and far less powerful individually than the thermonuclear weapons that were yet to be developed. The American leaders sought to extract what political advantage they could from this monopoly, but they recognized that they were handicapped by the lack of troops on the ground in Europe in critical areas of controversy. At any rate the American monopoly did not prevent the early Soviet gains in the cold war — and it was economic strength that was probably critical in setting limits on any future expansion (through the Marshall Plan for postwar European economic recovery).

The large number of non-nuclear states surviving in close proximity to nuclear states despite independent foreign policies is often cited as additional support for the proposition that nuclear superiority is much overrated. The European neutrals — Sweden, Austria, Switzerland — are countries which seem to survive perfectly happily without the benefit of either a nuclear alliance or their own nuclear arsenals. However, the foreign policies of nations such as these are based on the existence of a generally stable nuclear relationship between the two great alliances. Few would pretend that their life would be so comfortable beside just one all-powerful nuclear alliance. The efforts of Yugoslavia to reinforce its NATO connections at the time of the death of President Tito illustrate the desire not to be too dependent on the good sense of a moderately antagonistic superpower during periods of potential vulnerability.

Another good example of this point is China. The People's Republic has been closer to nuclear attack than any other country since 1945. It faced nuclear threats from the United States during the Korean War, the 1954 Indochina crisis, the 1958 Offshore Islands crisis and the early stages of the Vietnam War, and then from the Soviet Union in the period leading up to and just after the border skirmishes of 1969 — which took place just at the time that China's first nuclear weapons were becoming operational. While it was putting together the rudiments of a nuclear capability, it felt vulnerable to a Soviet preemptive strike and allowed a note of caution to enter its policy towards its former Communist ally.

CRISIS POINT: BERLIN

DIARY OF A CRISIS: 1961

22 February President Kennedy, on taking office, suggests a meeting with Soviet leader Nikita Khrushchev.

3-4 June The two meet in Vienna. Khrushchev creates a new crisis by arguing that Berlin should become a free city under East German control and that, if the two Germanies were unable to agree on reunification within six months, the USSR would sign a separate peace treaty with East Germany.

17 July President Kennedy reasserts Western rights over Berlin in a formal note.

12-13 August The Berlin Wall is constructed.

17 August The Western powers protest at the sealing off of West Berlin.

19 August Vice-President Johnson and General Lucius Clay sent to Berlin by Kennedy to symbolize US support.

23 August Soviet note threatening to cut off air access to West Berlin.

17 October Khrushchev lifts deadline.

26 October Tank confrontation at Checkpoint Charlie.

▲ President Kennedy with Herr Willy Brandt, mayor of West Berlin, near the Brandenburg Gate in June 1963.

▶ Border guards patrol both sides of the wall as masons on the East side repair a hole in May 1962.

to Hamburg

Spandau prison

Staaken ● *Soviet checkpoint*
Haerstrasse *FRG checkpoint*

TV and Ra

BRITISH S

Gatow airfield

rail link to W Germany

Dreilinden ○ *FRG checkpoint*

Neubabelsburg ● *Soviet checkpoint*

to Hanover, Frankfurt and Munich

road link to W Germany

Until the 1960s Berlin was a continual source of tension between East and West. At the end of World War II the occupying powers — Britain, France, the United States and the Soviet Union — divided up the German capital rather than let it just become part of the Soviet sector. As the cold war intensified, West Berlin came to be a Western outpost in the Eastern bloc. The isolation of Berlin has made it vulnerable to Soviet pressure whenever East–West relations were low. However, for the Soviet Union and its allies this Western pressure has also been something of an irritant, presenting an image of a Western way of life to the citizens of the Soviet bloc. The first Berlin crisis came in 1948 when the USSR cut off the road and rail links from West Berlin to the West. The blockade was defeated by a massive airlift of essential supplies. The net result of this was a clear American commitment to the integrity of West Berlin. A decade later this was challenged by Soviet proposals that would have put West Berlin substantially under East German control, but little was done to push these proposals in the face of Western opposition. The idea was revived in 1961, but this time the situation was made much more volatile by the increasing stream of refugees using the easy route across East and West Berlin as a means of escaping to the West. This hemorrhage of skilled manpower was finally stanched in August 1961 by the building of the Berlin Wall. Although this was an affront to human rights and provided a striking symbol of failure in the Soviet system, it also defused the crisis. The threat posed by West Berlin to East Germany was removed, especially when the Western powers indicated that they had no interest in using the crisis to reunify Germany. After that the pressure on West Berlin was eased and, in 1969, a new agreement among the occupying powers regularized its position.

CRISIS POINT: CUBA

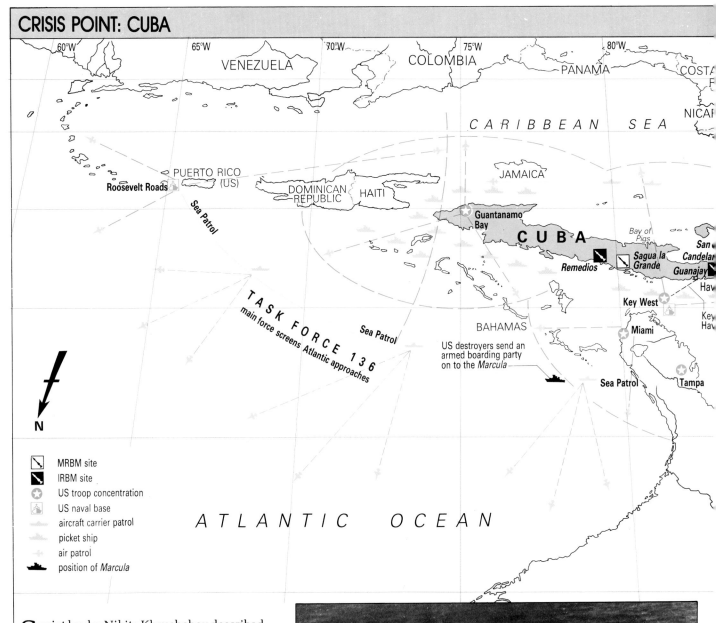

MRBM site
IRBM site
US troop concentration
US naval base
aircraft carrier patrol
picket ship
air patrol
position of *Marcula*

Soviet leader Nikita Khrushchev described the October 1962 Cuban missile crisis as "the first direct nuclear confrontation, unlike any in the history of our planet." The "smell of burning" hung in the air. Khrushchev's attempt to insinuate missiles into Cuba triggered the crisis. When President Kennedy was shown photographs of the missile bases, he determined to get them removed. His advisers reviewed a range of options from pure diplomacy to invasion. It was decided to impose a naval quarantine. After a few tense days Khrushchev backed down, with an understanding that the Americans would move comparable missiles from Turkey (which had already been scheduled for removal). The crisis is now taken to demonstrate the importance of good intelligence and diplomatic subtlety, of being firm without being provocative, and of recognizing the need for the adversary to save "face." However, it was also atypical. It was of short duration, with a clear-cut issue and no third parties to confuse matters. The strategic advantages were overwhelmingly with the United States. It was on home ground and

enjoyed conventional and nuclear superiority. Indeed it was because of their inferiority that the Russians sought to introduce the missiles — to deter attacks on Cuba and increase their nuclear threat to the US.

Departure of the missiles. The Soviet freighter *Ival Polzunov*, with crates of missiles clearly visible on deck, is intercepted by the US destroyer, *Vesole*.

Nuclear threats: how serious are they?

Once it had constructed a modest retaliatory force (very modest by the exacting standards of the West), it showed few signs of inhibition in its foreign policy.

There are other examples of states lacking a developed nuclear capability being threatened by nuclear states. Most are from the 1950s, before the nuclear relationship had settled down. Secretary of State John Foster Dulles was convinced that his nuclear hints of 1953 helped break the logjam in the Korean armistice talks. More recent scholarship suggests that he may have exaggerated this influence — though it was certainly not absent. Dulles's attempt to repeat the trick as part of his efforts to hold back the Communist advance in Indochina was less successful, and indeed probably added to the reluctance of Britain and France to get too closely associated with American policy in this area. A couple of years later Britain and France were themselves at the receiving end of a Soviet nuclear threat. Once it had become evident that the United States was not going to intervene on their behalf in the Suez crisis, they received a letter from Soviet Premier Bulganin warning that they were vulnerable to "rocket weapons." This threat was probably made only when there was absolutely no risk of implementation.

Prior to the second half of the 1960s there were a number of cases when assessments of who was ahead in the arms race seemed to matter. Khrushchev's boldness over Berlin increased in the late 1950s after the Soviet success with the first test of an ICBM and the first artificial earth satellite (*Sputnik 1*). He was helped by the bonus of the Americans being overly pessimistic about their own position. Once it became apparent in 1961 that it was the Americans that were surging ahead in the missile race, Khrushchev's confidence soon waned.

It was partly in response to this developing American advantage that the Soviet leader triggered the greatest crisis of the nuclear age. In October 1962 American intelligence rather belatedly discovered a surreptitious Soviet attempt to insert medium-range missiles into Cuba. After a forceful display of American strength Khrushchev was forced to back down. At the time the Americans enjoyed a striking superiority. However, the American homeland was by no means safe from a Soviet nuclear attack and of course America's allies were extremely vulnerable. At any rate, those responsible for the crisis management in Washington have asserted that American nuclear superiority was largely irrelevant;

DIARY OF A CRISIS: 1962

4 September President Kennedy states that US would not tolerate Cuba being turned into "an offensive military base."

14 October Presence of ballistic missiles in Cuba reported to President Kennedy.

22 October Kennedy announces imposition of naval quarantine.

23 October Quarantine sanctioned by Organization of American States.

24 October Two Soviet ships stop en route to Cuba.

26 October US search ship heads for Cuba (not carrying nuclear contraband).

27 October U-2 spy plane shot down over Cuba.

28 October Khrushchev informs Kennedy that work on "weapons construction sites" will be halted.

20 November Quarantine lifted.

▲ Limited-range missiles placed in Cuba would be the equivalent of intercontinental missiles and so, the Russians hoped, would redress American superiority.

Superpower influence is not unlimited — as both sides have discovered

local conventional superiority in the Caribbean did the trick. This was hardly the most propitious part of the world to pick a fight with the United States.

There is evidence to suggest that the Soviet leaders were inhibited during the crisis by their sense of nuclear inferiority, even if their American counterparts were less impressed by their own superiority. At the very least they must have been unnerved by the thought that, if it came to a military confrontation anywhere else, the Soviet position was weak right down the line, with substantial strengths to be found only in Europe. After Cuba, the Kremlin vowed never to be so humiliated again. This determination was fortified by the experience of 1965 when it appeared that the US interventions in Vietnam and the Dominican Republic had been facilitated by a sense of strategic superiority.

So the Soviet Union began a dramatic build-up of all its military capabilities. It was able to redress the balance because the Americans were not sure what would be lost by allowing the Soviet Union to achieve parity and were anyway too bogged down in Vietnam to mount much of a challenge. In 1972 nuclear parity was acknowledged and consolidated in the US–Soviet Interim Agreement on Offensive Strategic Arms. Since then only one international crisis — the last days of the October 1973 Arab–Israeli War — has had a nuclear component. What was notable about this episode was that the American advance of the alert status of all its forces, including the Strategic Air Command, seemed more designed to warn the USSR off a dangerous process of superpower escalation, should it intervene in the war, rather than a straightforward nuclear threat. The only other possible example of an attempt to draw on nuclear strength is that of President Carter in early 1980 when his officials made clear nuclear threats on at least three occasions to put a real sanction behind the president's post-Afghanistan attempt to emphasize an American commitment to defend the Persian Gulf.

There have been no direct superpower crises over the past decade, although indirect conflict over Angola, Ethiopia, Indochina, Poland and, most of all, Afghanistan has soured relations. It might be that a sense of equivalence in nuclear strength added to Soviet self-confidence. Certainly most commentators on Soviet foreign policy argue that superpower status matters a great deal in Moscow and that a key objective of the overall foreign and military policy has been to ensure that the USSR is seen to be second to none

and enjoys the international respect and consideration appropriate to its rank. However, the main change in Soviet military capabilities, that made possible its various interventions of the 1970s, was in the ability to project its power through airlift and sealift; and the rather mixed results obtained by its intervention may have demonstrated to the Soviet Union a lesson already learned by the United States: that super military power does not necessarily compensate for an inadequate appreciation of the political dynamics in the regions where the intervention is taking place or for weaknesses in other forms of power such as economics or for the inappropriateness of established military techniques for the local conditions. Equally, the American reticence, when it came to intervening in the third world during the 1970s, may well have

The most recent international crisis with a nuclear aspect followed the Soviet invasion of Afghanistan. In 1980 President Carter warned the USSR not to push further into the Gulf. However, most of the nuclear crises took place more than two decades ago, and in only a few cases have nuclear weapons been invoked as much more than a background warning of the dangers involved if the crisis were allowed to escalate. The incidents connected with Uruguay (1947) and Guatemala (1954) involved no more than shows of strength using strategic bombers.

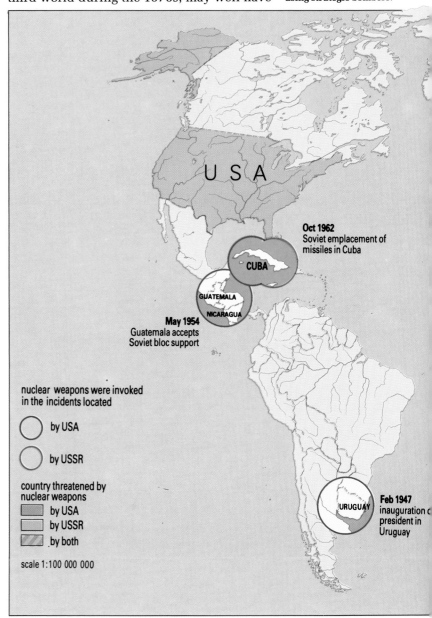

Oct 1962
Soviet emplacement of missiles in Cuba

May 1954
Guatemala accepts Soviet bloc support

nuclear weapons were invoked in the incidents located

◯ by USA

◯ by USSR

country threatened by nuclear weapons

▨ by USA
▢ by USSR
▨ by both

scale 1:100 000 000

Feb 1947
inauguration of president in Uruguay

The evidence is that the strategic relationship is essentially stable

been a result of having had these lessons brought home to it during the Vietnam War rather than a sense of a developing strategic inferiority.

In fact this analysis suggests that the two superpowers have shown full awareness of the risks of nuclear war in their foreign policies. Increasingly nuclear weapons act as a drag on rather than a spur to superpower assertiveness in international affairs. Whatever may be said about how the "spiral" of the arms race is propelling us towards an inevitable war, the evidence is that the strategic relationship is essentially stable and that, though some commentators have asserted that marginal forms of nuclear superiority can make a difference, it is very hard to find instances where this has been the case.

The United States did make use of its

nuclear muscle (although after the defeat of Japan not for decisive effect) while it enjoyed a monopoly or a substantial superiority. A Brookings Institution study in 1978 identified 15 incidents since 1945 in which the United States had used nuclear and major components of conventional armed forces together. Eleven of these were prior to 1960. The United States did not issue nuclear threats during its long and frustrating Vietnam involvement, nor in response to sundry crises in Africa and Asia during the 1970s and 1980s, and there is little to suggest that it would have done so even with a much more favorable strategic balance. Nor has the Soviet Union been given to making rash nuclear threats. Over time both superpowers have become more aware of nuclear risks and less prepared to move towards the brink.

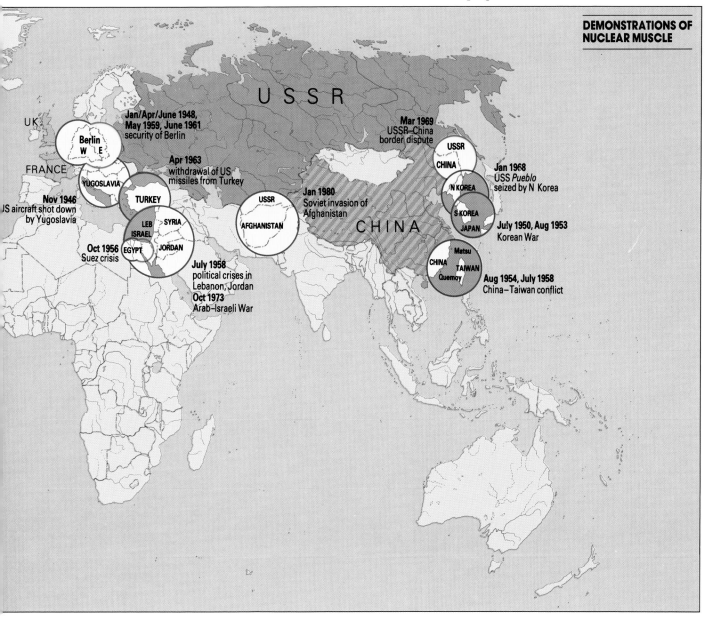

DEMONSTRATIONS OF NUCLEAR MUSCLE

USSR

UK

FRANCE

Berlin
W   E

Jan/Apr/June 1948,
May 1959, June 1961
security of Berlin

YUGOSLAVIA

Nov 1946
US aircraft shot down
by Yugoslavia

TURKEY

Apr 1963
withdrawal of US
missiles from Turkey

LEB
ISRAEL   SYRIA
EGYPT   JORDAN

Oct 1956
Suez crisis

USSR
AFGHANISTAN

Jan 1980
Soviet invasion of
Afghanistan

July 1958
political crises in
Lebanon, Jordan
Oct 1973
Arab–Israeli War

CHINA

Mar 1969
USSR–China
border dispute

USSR
CHINA

N KOREA
S KOREA
JAPAN

Jan 1968
USS *Pueblo*
seized by N Korea

July 1950, Aug 1953
Korean War

CHINA   Matsu
TAIWAN
Quemoy

Aug 1954, July 1958
China–Taiwan conflict

THE KOREAN AIRLINER

On the evening of 5 September 1983 a Boeing 747 of Korean Airlines (flight KAL 007) was just about to leave the Soviet airspace which it had inadvertently entered two hours earlier. Before it could do so, it was shot down by an Su-15 fighter with the loss of 269 lives. The shooting set back US–Soviet relations just as they were beginning to show signs of improvement after an unusally frosty period. There has been speculation about the impact such an unforeseen incident would have had on relations if the superpowers had been in the midst of a serious crisis.

Washington accused Moscow of knowingly shooting down a civilian aircraft that had wandered off course. Moscow accused Washington of using the aircraft for espionage. As the airliner had been flying near some highly secret installations and US intelligence was coincidentally active in connection with an imminent Soviet missile test, the Russians may have mistaken KAL 007 for a spy plane. Their defenses were shown to be jumpy and incompetent. The actual reason why the airliner strayed into Soviet airspace remains a mystery: it could have been pilot or computer error.

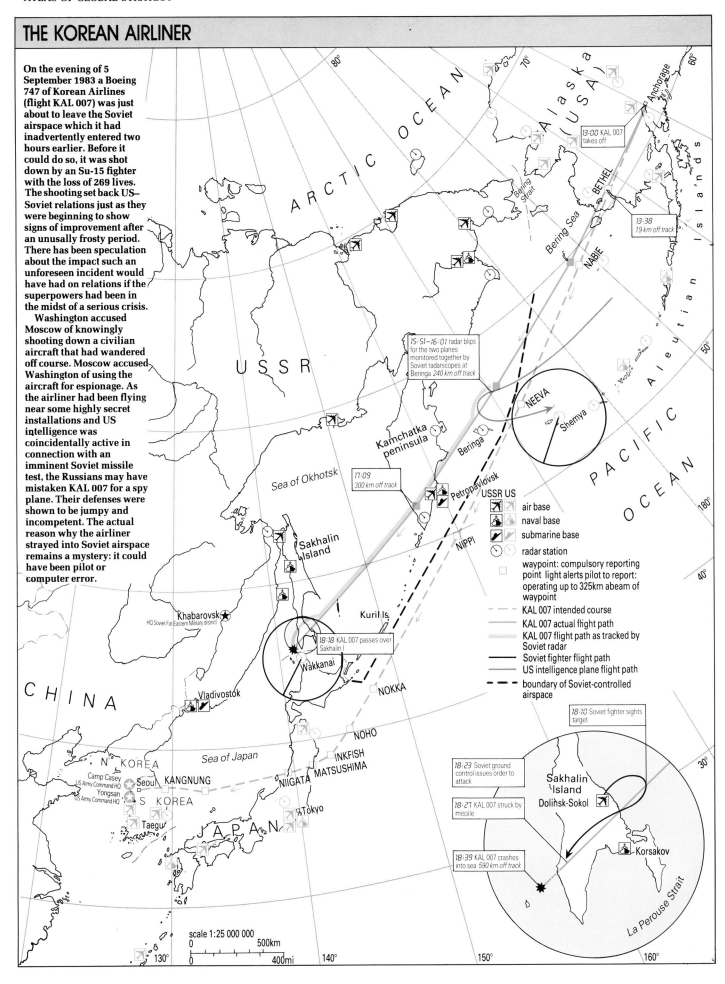

13:00 KAL 007 takes off

13:38 19 km off track

15:51–16:01 radar blips for the two planes monitored together by Soviet radarscopes at Beringa 240 km off track

NEEVA

Shemya

17:09 300 km off track

Kamchatka peninsula

Beringa

Petropavlovsk

NIPPI

Sea of Okhotsk

Sakhalin Island

Khabarovsk
HQ Soviet Far Eastern Military district

Kuril Is.

18:18 KAL 007 passes over Sakhalin I

Wakkanai

NOKKA

Vladivostok

NOHO

Sea of Japan

NIIGATA MATSUSHIMA

INKFISH

N KOREA

Camp Casey
US Army Command HQ
Yongsan
US Army Command HQ

Seoul KANGNUNG

S KOREA

Taegu

Tokyo

JAPAN

	USSR	US
air base		
naval base		
submarine base		
radar station		

waypoint: compulsory reporting point light alerts pilot to report: operating up to 325km abeam of waypoint

– – – KAL 007 intended course

——— KAL 007 actual flight path

KAL 007 flight path as tracked by Soviet radar

——— Soviet fighter flight path

US intelligence plane flight path

– – – boundary of Soviet-controlled airspace

18:10 Soviet fighter sights target

18:23 Soviet ground control issues order to attack

18:27 KAL 007 struck by missile

18:39 KAL 007 crashes into sea 590 km off track

Sakhalin Island
Dolinsk-Sokol

Korsakov

La Perouse Strait

scale 1:25 000 000
0   500km
0   400mi

CONVENTIONAL WAR

The success of a military operation depends on a wide range of variables which cannot be captured as a "military balance." The importance of new technology applied to conventional armaments can be overstated. While it may not unambiguously favor the defense over the offense, it is changing the character of war by rendering it even more frightening, exhausting and confusing. Guerrilla warfare can only prosper in favorable political conditions. Fears of a global insurrection in the 1960s drew a substantial response from the USA.

Rapier air defense missiles occupying the high ground during NATO's military maneuvers of September 1984. **Rapier** played an important role with British forces during the Falklands conflict, and was officially credited with shooting down 14 Argentine aircraft and possibly six more.

The success of nuclear weapons in creating a state of military paralysis between East and West has not stopped other sorts of conflict. Indeed, by increasing the constraints on the great powers, it may even have encouraged lesser wars to flourish. We noted earlier the changing patterns of contemporary warfare, in which regional powers take the initiative and the major powers find it difficult to intervene. The arms trade was identified as an important cause of the diffusion of power, making it possible for small countries to act on their own initiative, being less dependent on supplies or even more direct forms of aid from the major powers, and in some cases even able to take on the major powers. It is now time to review the military aspects of the conflicts that have taken place since 1945, taking care to relate them to their political context.

Non-nuclear weapons tend to be described as "conventional." The same adjective is applied to any war in which nuclear weapons are not used. "Conventional" has a rather comfortable sound to it, something well understood and familiar, fought according to well-established rules — conventions — in ways that avoid the barbarity of nuclear weapons. It might therefore be useful to establish at the outset that our experience of conventional war is limited and inconclusive; that it provides far fewer clues than might be imagined to the likely character of the sort of conventional war with which most analysts are preoccupied — a confrontation in Central Europe; and that while deaths from conventional weapons cannot reach the scale that would result from nuclear detonations, they can be even more unpleasant for those at the receiving end and can accumulate over time to remarkably high levels. Some estimates put the casualties resulting from the Iran–Iraq war since 1980 at around one million.

NATO and the Warsaw Pact face each other in Central Europe

One definition of conventional war might be a contest between professional armed forces employing non-nuclear armaments. However, in many wars, for example Vietnam, one side might have preferred to fight in this manner while the other relied on the techniques of guerrilla warfare. A better approach might therefore be to take account of the purposes for which military action is undertaken and the relationship with political action.

A spectrum of conflicts can be identified. At the high end we find a "pure" conventional war, in which the desired outcome is achieved through a decisive military victory, and any political activity is geared to creating the conditions for this victory. The sort of political action involved would be establishing alliances and gaining access to bases. At the low end, in the more unconventional war, military action is not decisive in itself but is linked to a political campaign designed to make the position of government untenable.

▶ A mainstay of the American air force, navy and marine corps: the F-4 *Phantom* fighter-bomber. First in service in 1961, this two-seat, twin-engine, all-weather, supersonic aircraft can carry both conventional and nuclear weapons.

▼ German civilians close to the iron curtain have become accustomed to regular NATO maneuvers around their homes and the considerable disruption that this involves.

It is the high end which receives the greatest attention in most analyses of conventional war. Over the past three decades NATO and the Warsaw Pact have faced each other in the center of Europe. Plans have been made, then regularly revised and updated, for the conduct of a major war. This is the conflict for which the bulk of modern weaponry is designed and tactical concepts are developed.

Because the battle lines and the battle plans for Central Europe are so well established, analysis tends to focus on the few remaining variables in the equation, and especially the

▶ The realities of war. Iranian bodies piled on top of each other in the aftermath of a battle with the Iraqis in 1982.

introduction of new equipment. This distorts the analysis of the prospective conflict because it means that little attention is paid to those matters which appear fixed (such as the composition of the two alliances) but could rapidly become unfixed in a time of tension, or to the great many factors other than the quality and quantity of equipment which determine an army's performance in war yet are extremely difficult to assess until the relevant forces can be observed in actual combat.

The focus on what would admittedly be the most substantial of all possible wars does not necessarily provide a useful guide to the generality of modern wars. The concentration on advanced weaponry means that when a war happens anywhere in the globe in which similar weapons are in use, the interest tends to be in the performance of these weapons rather than in other aspects which might actually be of greater benefit in coming to terms with the character of modern warfare, and might also alert us to factors that could be more important than is commonly recognized in a European war.

Difficulties in constructing an accurate balance

Balancing acts

This oversimplification of the military equation is exemplified by the concept of a "military balance." Such balances are examined by commentators whenever a war might be imminent somewhere in the world, or when it is considered timely to assess the state of East–West military relations. Typically, the balance will tabulate the numbers of troops, tanks, combat aircraft and warships held by the two opposing sides. As sources of basic information these balances can be useful; as guides to the outcome of any conflict they are invariably misleading.

For a start, unless it is very detailed, a balance will fail to break down the broad categories into the specific types of weapons and to draw attention to their relative age and qualities. It will be of slight consolation to know that you have twice as many aircraft as the enemy when his aircraft fly faster over longer ranges, carry more modern armaments and are much easier to maintain than yours. For example, both the Royal Navy and the Soviet Navy have developed vertical/short-takeoff aircraft which can operate from smaller carriers than those required for more orthodox naval aircraft. The British *Sea Harrier* and the Soviet *Forger Yak-36* are much the same size with similar aerodynamic performance. But because the *Sea Harrier* has one versatile engine as against the *Forger's* three, it can carry a much larger load and so is equipped with much more formidable radar and armaments.

These balances also tend to fail to include notionally civilian assets which can be put to good use in time of war. We noted earlier (p. 69) the invaluable role played by merchant ships in supporting the Falklands operation. When necessary, anything which moves and can carry men and material can be turned into a fighting vehicle.

Then we need to know the disposition of the forces. Again it is not very useful to have vastly superior forces if most, and perhaps the best-equipped and combat-ready, are located far away from the likely combat zone and can only reach the front after a long, arduous and hazardous journey. Lastly, without sufficient stocks and spares, a large force of notionally well-equipped men might find itself in a hopeless position because it has run out of ammunition or its tanks have become unserviceable.

In attempting to construct an accurate balance it is also necessary to assess not only the quantity and quality of equipment but the skill with which it can be used, including the

capacity for improvisation, and the training and morale of the forces. Napoleon observed long ago that in battle the ratio of the moral to the material is as three to one, and similar observations have been made by great generals ever since. Regular soldiers fight better than conscripts. Units which have trained together fight better than those put together at the last minute. They fight better still if they have trained for the type of combat in which they find themselves engaged. Soldiers who believe in the cause for which they are fighting or see a direct link between their performance and the fate of their families will be more determined than those who believe themselves to be the victims of a futile political gesture. Those with confidence in their commanders are likely to fight better than those badly led.

An inept commander can soon waste all the benefits of an excellent force. So might one who is simply ill-informed. Modern means of gathering information on enemy dispositions

Two superficially similar vertical/short-takeoff aircraft able to operate from small carriers. Above, the Royal Navy's *Sea Harrier*, seen here during the 1980 Farnborough Air Show, demonstrating the value of a simple "ski jump" construction in giving it an easier lift-off. Below, an American photo of the Soviet *Forger Yak-36* on the flight deck of the aircraft carrier *Kiev*.

When it comes to war, the lines between the civilian and the military soon become blurred, especially in matters relating to to transportation. Here we see British troops embarking on the luxury liner the *QE2*, which had been converted into a troop ship for the Falklands War.

have moved a long way from the traditional spy (although there have been enough *causes célèbres* in recent years to demonstrate that this method has not been totally discarded). The history of World War II had to be rewritten as more was found out about the successful cracking of German codes and the impact of this intelligence on a number of critical engagements. If the enemy can follow your every movement, then the advantage of surprise will be lost.

Even if a balance could account for all these factors, it would still be inadequate. This method of comparison tends to suggest that warships only fight other warships, tanks other tanks, missiles other missiles, aircraft other aircraft. In practice aircraft attack ships and tanks, missiles are fired at aircraft and tanks, and so on. Furthermore, terrain and climate determine the opportunities that both sides will have to exploit their best weapons. When fighting a landlocked opponent an excellent navy will be of slight value. When

movement is only possible on foot, portability becomes the sole criterion by which weapons will be judged. High-performance aircraft may have to be grounded in bad weather. We still have very little idea of the effects that modern urban sprawl is likely to have on the land battle, or for that matter the large-scale movement of refugees attempting to escape from the fighting and possibly blocking up the road network. The great battles of recent years have tended not to be fought in and around major cities.

Lastly and as always, there is the political factor. The advantages gained by those extra divisions and superior equipment can soon be lost if a vital ally defects, or a hitherto neutral country feels moved to join the opposition, or the enemy finds a ready source of new supplies. The quality of political leadership is going to be tested in forging alliances and conducting coalition warfare, in gaining agreement on bases and overflying rights, in sustaining popular support, in arguing a case

THE CENTRAL FRONT: THE SOVIET ROUTE TO WESTERN EUROPE

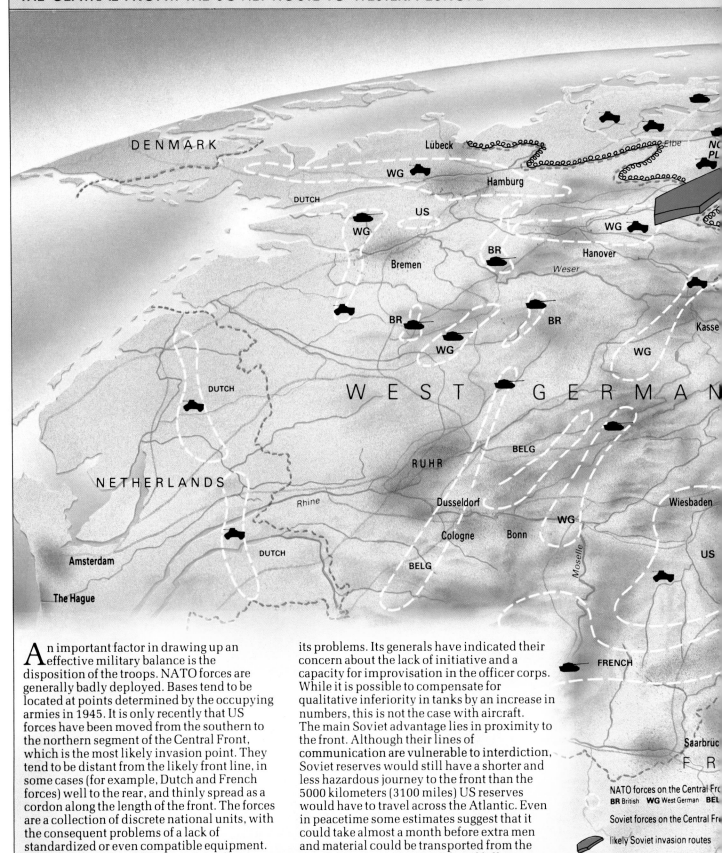

An important factor in drawing up an effective military balance is the disposition of the troops. NATO forces are generally badly deployed. Bases tend to be located at points determined by the occupying armies in 1945. It is only recently that US forces have been moved from the southern to the northern segment of the Central Front, which is the most likely invasion point. They tend to be distant from the likely front line, in some cases (for example, Dutch and French forces) well to the rear, and thinly spread as a cordon along the length of the front. The forces are a collection of discrete national units, with the consequent problems of a lack of standardized or even compatible equipment. The communications between the different national forces are inadequate, and too often run along north–south lines and are thus vulnerable to being cut in a well-judged attack.

Of course the Soviet Union would also have

its problems. Its generals have indicated their concern about the lack of initiative and a capacity for improvisation in the officer corps. While it is possible to compensate for qualitative inferiority in tanks by an increase in numbers, this is not the case with aircraft. The main Soviet advantage lies in proximity to the front. Although their lines of communication are vulnerable to interdiction, Soviet reserves would still have a shorter and less hazardous journey to the front than the 5000 kilometers (3100 miles) US reserves would have to travel across the Atlantic. Even in peacetime some estimates suggest that it could take almost a month before extra men and material could be transported from the North American continent; but if full mobilization were possible the position would be much better than if the reserves had to be brought over after the start of combat and in the face of Soviet submarine attack.

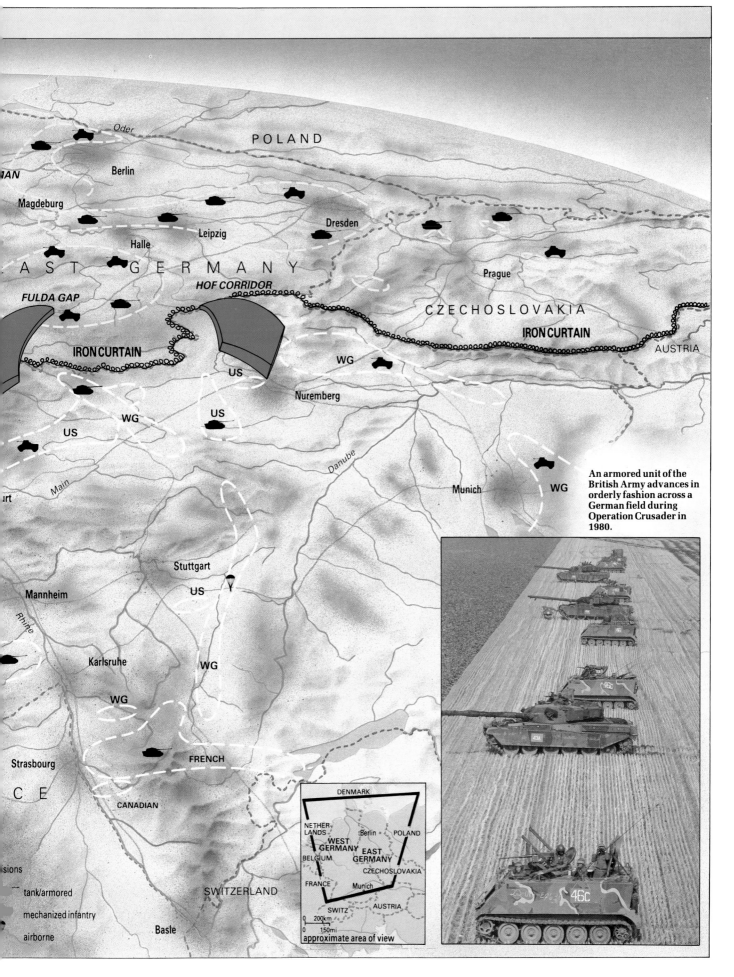

POLAND

Oder

Berlin

Magdeburg

Leipzig

Dresden

Halle

AST GERMANY

Prague

HOF CORRIDOR

CZECHOSLOVAKIA

FULDA GAP

IRON CURTAIN

IRON CURTAIN

AUSTRIA

US

WG

IRON CURTAIN

US

WG

Nuremberg

US

WG

Main

rt

WG

Munich

WG

An armored unit of the British Army advances in orderly fashion across a German field during Operation Crusader in 1980.

Stuttgart

US

Mannheim

Rhine

WG

Karlsruhe

WG

Strasbourg

FRENCH

C E

CANADIAN

isions

tank/armored

mechanized infantry

airborne

SWITZERLAND

DENMARK

NETHER-
LANDS   Berlin   POLAND

WEST
GERMANY   EAST
GERMANY

BELGIUM

CZECHOSLOVAKIA

FRANCE   Munich

Basle

SWITZ   AUSTRIA

0   200km
0   150mi

approximate area of view

CHEMICAL WARFARE

In World War I at least 800 000 casualties were reported on all sides as a result of gas. International concern at this led to the adoption in 1925 of a protocol banning gas and bacteriological methods of warfare. This has now been signed by 123 states, including all members of NATO and the Warsaw Pact, though not without qualifications. It is a no-first-use provision with states maintaining the right to retaliate and therefore to hold stockpiles. In 1972 a convention was signed banning biological and toxic weapons. This provided for the destruction of existing stocks and followed unilateral action by the Americans in destroying their own. Efforts to ban chemical weapons, which have more serious military uses, have continued, so far in vain. The main problems are definition and verification.

One of the most difficult questions concerns the role that chemical weapons could play in war. Interest in the West has reflected not so much a desire to use them offensively as a concern with Soviet intentions. Although intelligence is unreliable in respect of Soviet stocks, the Warsaw Pact seems more actively prepared to fight in a chemical weapons environment. But while as always the main focus is on the major powers, there is evidence that the countries most likely to be tempted to use chemical weapons will be in the third world.

▼ After allegations that chemical weapons had been used against Iranian troops in 1984, a United Nations delegation was sent to investigate. Here a member of the delegation kneels to photograph a chemical device that has failed to explode.

► American soldiers operating the nuclear-capable *Lance* missile have donned their protective suits which are designed to shield them from contamination by nuclear radiation and chemical weapons.

Wars are exercises in public relations as much as armed combat

at the United Nations. It is the political leader who will have to decide whether or not to mobilize and begin the movement of forces, an expensive exercise and one that can easily be deemed unnecessary or provocative, but yet if left too late can almost lose the war before it has begun.

Possibly as significant are the effects of different political structures on the spirit in which nations go to and conduct their wars. Each nation has its traditions in fighting wars, reflecting its geography, social makeup, culture and past experience. It is often assumed that totalitarian societies have inherent advantages in fighting wars because they are more secretive, are unlikely to be challenged by any domestic opponents and can enforce exceptional sacrifices. This assumption may underestimate the advantages enjoyed by open and democratic societies. It does no good at all for foolish policies and strategies to be left unchallenged; totalitarian leaders also often have little feel for the loyalty and morale of their people.

One feature of modern warfare that touches democratic societies more than others is the intrusive role played by the media. The intensive coverage of the Vietnam War by the American media helped to convince many in the military that the war was "lost" at home through the effect on the public of nightly pictures of the more gruesome aspects of war. Later research suggested that it was not so much television which lowered morale but the continuing failure to achieve results as the human, social and economic costs grew. The conviction that the media were to blame ran deep and could be seen in the rather clumsy handling of the media by the British

in the Falklands and by the Americans in their 1983 operation against Grenada. But the military and their political masters dare not ignore the media, however much they may fear that vital secrets will be compromised. If they fail to provide the hard news, it will be provided from other, less favorable, sources and the enemy may gain a propaganda coup. When the course of a war may hinge on third parties, anything that might encourage a positive attitude cannot be ignored. Modern wars are exercises in public relations as well as armed combat. The need to accommodate and service correspondents and television crews is an unavoidable feature of contemporary military operations.

The conduct of modern war

The discussion thus far has highlighted the great variety of factors that must be taken into account to make a full assessment of the likely outcome of any given conflict, and the consequent danger of an excessive preoccupation with equipment as the key to a conflict. Despite the attention devoted to the latest advanced military technology, it is worth bearing in mind that, even with the most modern armed forces, the bulk of the equipment will be somewhat long in the tooth and there may not be the opportunities to use some of the most advanced items.

These points can be illustrated by looking at some recent wars. In the Iran–Iraq War, for example, the two sides have both acquired large quantities of advanced military equipment on the arms market. Yet the difficulties of keeping aircraft serviceable, especially when there are problems with spare parts, and the thought that it would be

▶ June 1979: white flag in hand, a journalist crosses a road ravaged by fighting towards the end of the Sandinista revolution in Nicaragua. While some war correspondents are known to prefer to report wars from the safety of their hotels, the best attempt to get close to the fighting and often suffer casualties as a result. They are able to convey a sense of the tensions and dramas of combat, although, because of local censorship and the limitations on what can be understood from the front line, they are not necessarily so effective in presenting the "big picture."

unwise to waste these expensive items when they might be sorely needed at a later stage have meant that both have been reticent about exploiting them to the full. Advanced aircraft have therefore been less in evidence than might have been expected. On the ground there have been tank battles, but the most striking feature of the conflict has been the adoption of human-wave tactics by the Iranians, relying on ill-trained youngsters apparently convinced that death in battle is a sure route to paradise. Battles have often been more reminiscent of World War I than World War II, with waves of exposed troops being mowed down by machine-gun fire as they go "over the top." The Iraqis have added

to the impression by resorting to crude forms of chemical warfare.

The Falklands campaign was also in some ways more reminiscent of World War I. In the land battle, air power played a limited role and, with few roads, conditions were hardly conducive to armored warfare. In order to dislodge the enemy from entrenched positions the British relied on artillery bombardments combined with determined infantry assaults. These were somewhat more subtle in their execution than sending thousands of men over the top. Many achieved surprise by being undertaken at night. In an encounter in which the physical elements such as terrain and climate loomed as large

Each new generation of equipment can cost five times what it replaces

▼ By the start of 1984 the American attempt to maintain the Gemayel government in power in Beirut and sustain an agreement between Lebanon and Israel began to collapse in the face of Muslim and Syrian pressure. In the process Beirut once again suffered the ravages of civil war.

World War II-vintage torpedo, admittedly fired from an altogether modern British nuclear-powered submarine, HMS *Conqueror.*

Even at the highest end of our spectrum of conventional war — an East–West clash in the center of Europe — much of the equipment in use will be quite venerable. In taking decisions on whether to order the new advanced systems on offer, those responsible will have to be aware of priorities, for this extra sophistication comes at a price. It has been calculated that each new generation of equipment can be up to five times the cost, in real terms, of the equipment it replaces. After a while there is an inevitable trade of quality for quantity. In 1944 at the peak of wartime production the United States produced some 100 000 aircraft in total. By the mid-1950s some 3000 fighters were being purchased (as well as some other types). By the late 1970s the annual production rate was down to 400

▲ These Palestinian fighters at Camp Beddaoui in Lebanon were temporarily engaged not so much in a war against the Israelis or the Lebanese Christians but against each other, as a Syrian-backed faction sought to depose Yasser Arafat and his supporters from the leadership of the Palestine Liberation Organization.

as the technical, the traditional military virtues of training, morale, stamina and leadership could prove decisive. To be sure the war at sea involved more high technology. It was anticipated with some interest as the first major test of naval weaponry since the last world war. The sea-skimming *Exocet* anti-ship missile and the *Sea-Wolf* air-defense systems showed what they cound do. Yet while it was *Exocet* that achieved notoriety with its "kills," most of the damage to British ships was achieved by old-fashioned gravity bombs. The single most costly engagement in terms of human life involved a World War II-vintage warship, the Argentine cruiser, the *General Belgrano*, being sunk by a

and it dropped below 300 in the early 1980s. One American aerospace executive, after noting that from the days of the Wright brothers to the modern F-18 fighter aircraft costs had increased by a factor of four every 10 years, observed that, if this trend continued, by the year 2054 the entire defense budget would purchase just one fighter! There has also been concern that the increasing sophistication of the new weapons means that they take an excessively long time in development, are too complex to be wholly reliable and are difficult to maintain. It may not be very useful to have the most advanced equipment in the world if too few individual units can be purchased to make an impact, or if they come

at the expense of proper training and adequate stocks of fuel and ammunition.

If both sides have equipped their forces with comparable equipment, then that is another reason for doubting that technology will play the sort of pivotal role that is often supposed. It will certainly give the conflicts in which it is employed a distinctive flavor and create new challenges for the armed forces, but it will not necessarily determine the outcome. The two sides' innovations are likely to cancel each other out. The only way in which one side could benefit more would

be if it could be shown that technological trends decisively favor the defender or the attacker.

The new technologies: defensive or offensive?

This old question was raised again in the 1970s when it seemed that a revolution was under way in conventional weapons technologies. For much of the postwar period conventional weapon improvements had been largely incremental, with the major breakthroughs being achieved with nuclear

▲ An impressive parade is arguably designed as much to boost the prestige of a state as to ward off enemies. Here the Algerians put on a display during the 1984 celebrations to mark the start of the Algerian Revolution. But when contests are evenly balanced a technological advantage can make a difference. The *Exocet* anti-ship missile (here shown being fired from a coastal battery) was used to

great effect by Argentina during the Falklands War, and Iraq has acquired some for use against Iran.

▲ Helicopters came into their own during the Vietnam War, serving both as a means of moving troops from one area of operations to another and also, when armed, as a means of attacking enemy positions (or what were suspected to be enemy positions).

weapons. However, a lot of the new technologies of data processing and miniaturization could be applied to the conventional sphere. With the Vietnam War under way the military and the defense industry had an incentive to improve the quality of conventional arms.

Towards the end of the war the results of this effort began to show. The most remarkable example was the bombing of the Thanh Hoa bridge complex, an important "choke" point on the Ho Chi Minh Trail by which supplies were taken from the North to South Vietnam. From 1965 to 1968, when bombing

was halted, the bridge withstood 600 sorties by American aircraft using "dumb" gravity bombs. Some 30 aircraft were lost. When bombing resumed in 1972, the bridge was destroyed after two raids of four aircraft carrying "smart" laser-guided bombs. If it had not been for heavy clouds, one raid would have sufficed.

The term "precision-guided munition" was coined to refer to weapons whose probability of making a direct hit on a target (be it a tank, ship, airplane, bridge or any high-value asset) when fired at full range is more than half (if

RULING THE WAVES

W hatever disagreements there may be about other aspects of the military balance, there is no doubt that the United States Navy is the most powerful in the world. The Soviet Union has been catching up by moving from a coastal to an ocean-going navy and particularly by expanding its submarine force. However, the Americans retain a qualitative edge, and under the Reagan administration have embarked on a massive shipbuilding program intended to raise the inventory from just under 500 to well over 600 ships.

This diagram illustrates the range of weapons associated with the US 2nd Fleet which is deployed in the Atlantic. It carries weapons that enable it to attack targets on land as well as at sea, in the air and under water as well as on the surface. With seven aircraft carriers, 105 escort ships, 77 nuclear submarines and 720 combat aircraft this is the most powerful naval force on patrol anywhere in the world.

1. The fleet has 31 ballistic-missile-carrying submarines (SSBNs) with *Poseidon* ballistic missiles, able to deliver 10 warheads of 50 kilotons each over 4600 kilometers and the new *Trident* missiles which can deliver eight warheads of 100 kilotons each over 7400 kilometers.

2. Its 46 attack submarines, also known as hunter-killers, can attack ships with *Sub-Harpoon*, which has a high explosive warhead and a 110-kilometer range, and can attack other submarines with the nuclear-armed *Subroc*, which has a 46-kilometer range.

3. The escort vessels are made up of the heavy-tonnage cruisers, with an average displacement of 9000 to 10 000 tons, and the lighter destroyers and frigates at 3000 to 4000 tons displacement. The escorts carry a mix of weapons, including the *Harpoon* anti-ship missile and the short-range ASROC antisubmarine weapon. This is in addition to torpedoes and guns. The cruisers also carry *Standard* and *Sea Sparrow* air-defense missiles.

4. The five attack aircraft carriers are the heart of the fleet. Each carries 24 F-4 *Phantom* or F-14 *Tomcat*, with ranges of 765 and 935 kilometers respectively, equipped with AIM–7/9 air-to-surface missiles; up to 36 A-6 *Intruder* or A-7 *Corsair*, with ranges of 1205 and 885 kilometers respectively, armed with nuclear bombs; 10 torpedo-carrying S-2 *Tracker* and S-3 *Viking* aircraft, the latter with a range of over 1900 kilometers; plus 10 reconnaissance aircraft.

5. The two helicopter carriers each carry 20 helicopters, coming in a variety of types including the heavy-lift *Chinooks*, the lighter UH-1 and AH-1, and the RH-53 adapted for antisubmarine warfare.

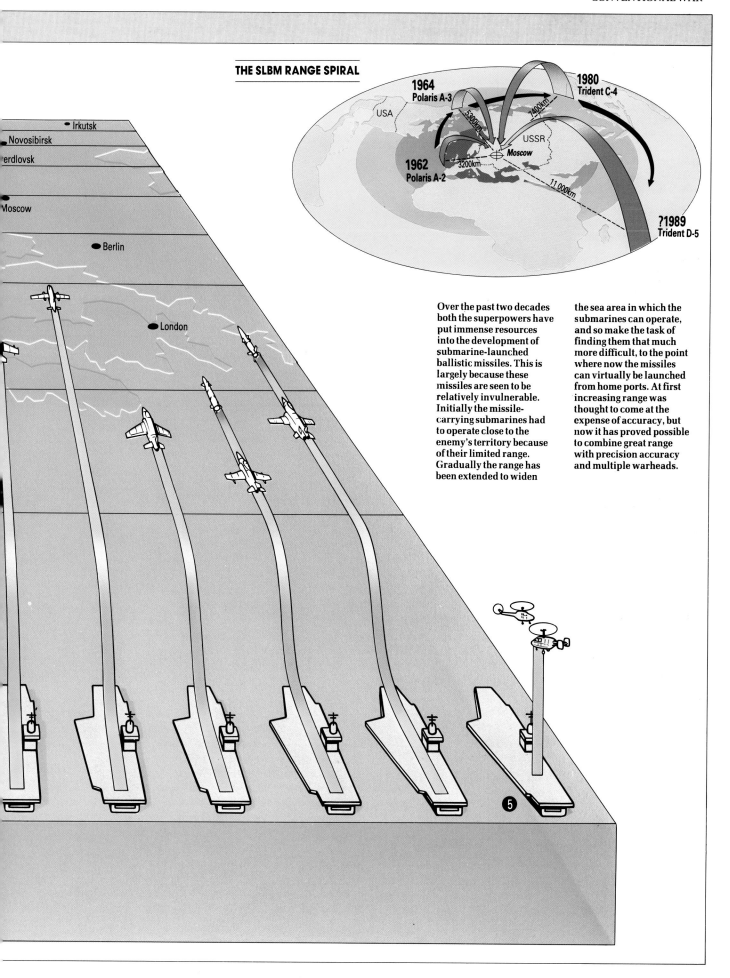

THE SLBM RANGE SPIRAL

1964
Polaris A-3

1980
Trident C-4

USA

5300km

7400km

USSR

Moscow

1962
Polaris A-2

3200km

11,000km

?1989
Trident D-5

Irkutsk

Novosibirsk

erdlovsk

Moscow

Berlin

London

Over the past two decades both the superpowers have put immense resources into the development of submarine-launched ballistic missiles. This is largely because these missiles are seen to be relatively invulnerable. Initially the missile-carrying submarines had to operate close to the enemy's territory because of their limited range. Gradually the range has been extended to widen

the sea area in which the submarines can operate, and so make the task of finding them that much more difficult, to the point where now the missiles can virtually be launched from home ports. At first increasing range was thought to come at the expense of accuracy, but now it has proved possible to combine great range with precision accuracy and multiple warheads.

⑤

The unpredictability of war

unopposed). Such a performance is only likely to be achieved by most PGMs in ideal conditions. Nevertheless, their potential was revealed during the October 1973 Arab–Israel War. Some spectacular successes were chalked up by relatively simple and comparatively inexpensive anti-tank and anti-air guided weapons. Arguably the previous encounter between the two sides in 1967 had demonstrated the potential of anti-ship missiles when the Israeli frigate, the *Eilat*, was sunk by an Egyptian missile.

Soon it came to be argued that these new weapons would revolutionize warfare: the days of the large and sophisticated tanks, combat aircraft and warships were now numbered, and without them it would be impossible to mount a serious offensive. They were now just too vulnerable. Defense could be constructed on the cheap by drawing almost entirely on the lethality of these small and accurate weapons. Just as the offense was dominant at the nuclear level, the defense would be supreme at the conventional.

This optimistic picture soon had to be qualified. First it became clear that the lessons of the October War were far more ambiguous than had at first been appreciated. Some 40 percent of the total Israeli aircraft losses had occurred in the first two days of the war. Instead of following the normal practice of suppressing air defenses, the Israelis had been obliged to provide close support for ground troops desperate to hold their lines, particularly against the Syrians on the Golan Heights. Once the line had been held, the Israelis got the measure of the air defenses and losses went down accordingly. The next time that the Israelis took on Syrian air defenses — in the Bekaa valley during the 1982 invasion of Lebanon — these were knocked out straight away. Analysis of the tank battles of 1973 revealed that a large number of those tanks destroyed had been the victims of other tanks, and again that after the initial shocks the Israelis had developed tactics designed to minimize the effects of anti-tank weapons.

The basic flaw in the optimists' argument was that they were so impressed by the ease with which one man and a missile might bring down a $20-million aircraft that they had failed to consider how this man had got to the right spot, found and tracked his target and made sure that the target was an enemy aircraft rather than one from his own side. The really impressive results could only be achieved in highly favorable and contrived conditions.

Syrian SAM-6 air defense missile batteries looking relatively safe and secure in the Bekaa valley in Lebanon.

Warfare does not take the form of a series of standard encounters in which the same result is repeated all along the front line. Each side takes account of what is known about the other's capabilities and develops countermeasures and tactics designed to exploit his weaknesses and avoid his strengths. Most important of all, it is rare that battle takes the form of a fixed defender fighting off a mobile attacker. At times the defense will need to move, to fill a gap that has opened on a flank or to engage some vulnerable enemy unit, while the attacker may want to dig in at a particular spot, for example, some valuable high ground or a captured piece of territory which will soon become the subject of a counterattack. No army can move forward continuously. It dares not stray too far away from its supply lines. Equally, no army dares stay put for too long. If its position is known, and with modern means of surveillance it is likely that it will be, then it is going to be highly vulnerable to enemy firepower, which is becoming increasingly concentrated, accurate and able to make itself felt over long ranges. Rather than warships aiming at enemy ships alongside or even at shadows on the horizon, they will be firing at blips on the radar. Modern artillery can achieve ranges of well over 16 kilometers (10 miles). There is now discussion of fitting conventional warheads onto the ballistic missiles that normally carry nuclear warheads, with ranges of hundreds of kilometers, to enable them to attack critical targets such as air bases or even troop concentrations well to the enemy's rear that would otherwise require nuclear weapons.

Even if the fronts are relatively static, both sides will need to be supplied, and supply lines, as we have discussed already, can be very long. Another feature of modern warfare is the high rate of attrition. Rapid-fire

DEFENSE AND COUNTERDEFENSE

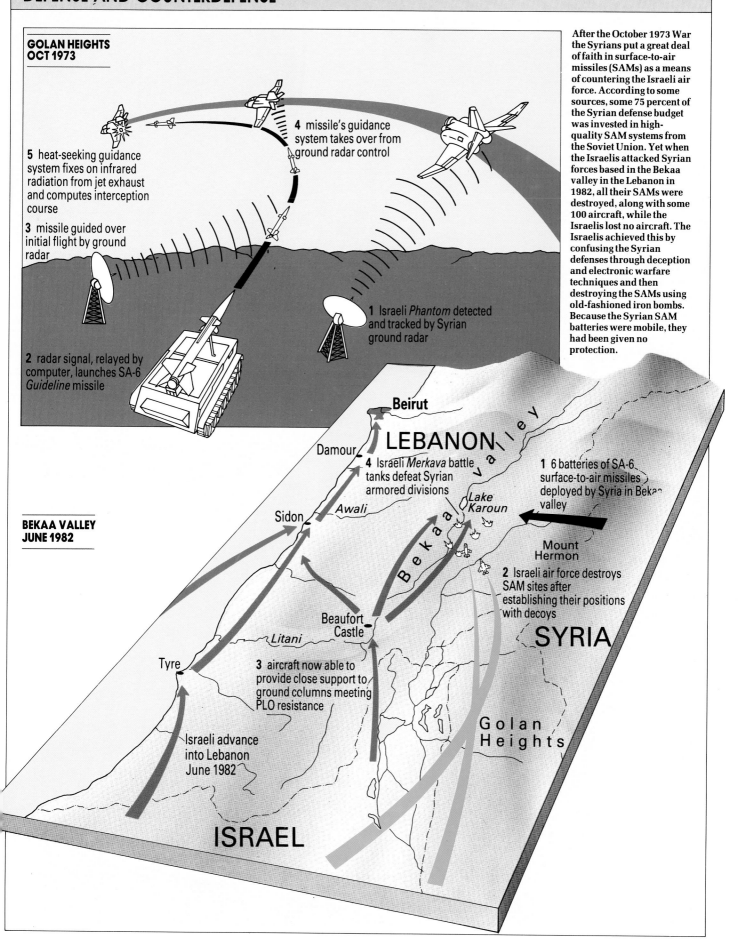

GOLAN HEIGHTS OCT 1973

5 heat-seeking guidance system fixes on infrared radiation from jet exhaust and computes interception course

4 missile's guidance system takes over from ground radar control

3 missile guided over initial flight by ground radar

2 radar signal, relayed by computer, launches SA-6 *Guideline* missile

1 Israeli *Phantom* detected and tracked by Syrian ground radar

After the October 1973 War the Syrians put a great deal of faith in surface-to-air missiles (SAMs) as a means of countering the Israeli air force. According to some sources, some 75 percent of the Syrian defense budget was invested in high-quality SAM systems from the Soviet Union. Yet when the Israelis attacked Syrian forces based in the Bekaa valley in the Lebanon in 1982, all their SAMs were destroyed, along with some 100 aircraft, while the Israelis lost no aircraft. The Israelis achieved this by confusing the Syrian defenses through deception and electronic warfare techniques and then destroying the SAMs using old-fashioned iron bombs. Because the Syrian SAM batteries were mobile, they had been given no protection.

BEKAA VALLEY JUNE 1982

Beirut

LEBANON

Damour

4 Israeli *Merkava* battle tanks defeat Syrian armored divisions

Sidon

Awali

Lake Karoun

1 6 batteries of SA-6 surface-to-air missiles deployed by Syria in Bekaa valley

Mount Hermon

2 Israeli air force destroys SAM sites after establishing their positions with decoys

SYRIA

Beaufort Castle

Litani

3 aircraft now able to provide close support to ground columns meeting PLO resistance

Tyre

Israeli advance into Lebanon June 1982

Golan Heights

ISRAEL

Bekaa valley

The high-technology environment

weapons use up ammunition at astonishing speed. If there is reliance on precision-guided munitions, then their individual cost may preclude the sort of stocks that would have been deemed necessary in earlier wars. Furthermore, complex weapons and supporting equipment put demands on maintenance in the field and require plenty of spares.

It is the unavoidable need to move forces and supplies that undermines the simpler notions of defense through relatively cheap anti-air, -ship and -tank missiles. For forces to move they need transport. As the transporters will be vulnerable, they need either armor, their own defensive weapons or at least protection from other forces with such weapons. Vehicles, ships and aircraft capable of movement and self-protection tend to look remarkably similar to the tanks, warships and combat aircraft that were supposedly becoming hopelessly vulnerable.

It may well be that it is becoming increasingly hazardous to sail in a warship in time of war. It will be necessary continually to survey the sky for attacking aircraft and scan the seas for lethal submarines. To be truly protected, naval task forces will need to be built around aircraft carriers with other escorts bristling with anti-air and antisubmarine weapons, as well as the anti-ship weapons required for their own protection. But we have also seen that, if it is desired to move large amounts of men and material long distances, this can only really be done by sea. Airlift is quicker but impractical for large amounts. If sea lines of communication are important, then they will need to be protected and so patrolled by surface task forces. The corollary of this is that, if sea lines are not so important, a modern navy may be a luxury item. It has been observed that, if NATO's navies take more than a couple of weeks to clear the lines across the Atlantic to bring over supplies (and most estimates would put the time in months rather than weeks), then by the time sufficient reserves are available to make an impact the land war will have been lost! This leads to the argument that the money might be better spent building up the prepositioned stores in Europe.

The picture that emerges at the end is not one of confident defenses lining up their small but sophisticated missiles to see off any aggressor. Rather it is one of increasing complexity. Whether or not one side or the other will be triumphant may be as much a function of the ability of those doing the fighting to cope with a high-technology environment as of the nature of the available equipment. To

SPIES IN THE SKY

Satellites provide steady surveillance of military activities anywhere that is of interest. At any sign of crisis — in the Middle East, south Atlantic or Indian subcontinent — both superpowers will direct satellites to pass overhead to keep themselves fully informed. A new American satellite, the KH-11, is able to send back instantaneous images. Overhead reconnaissance is used to check on the disposition of the other's forces. During the late 1950s there was a great scare in the United States that the Soviet Union was surging ahead in missile production. When the first reconnaissance satellites began to bring back hard information in the early 1960s, it soon became clear that it was the Soviet Union that was lagging behind. The resolutions that can now be achieved reveal quite intricate details. "Image enhancement" can highlight otherwise submerged detail by compensating for distortions or intensifying particular features. "Optical subtraction" can ensure that new features, such as the start of a missile site, are rapidly detected by electronically comparing new photographs with others of the same scene taken earlier. However, it remains the case that satellite photography can still be defeated by night and cloud cover.

It is only the superpowers that have this sort of intelligence available to them, although a few other countries are beginning to develop a limited satellite reconnaissance capability. The sort of intelligence provided by these satellites is one of the most prized gifts that they can hand over to an ally or a client engaged in a conflict, and they do so sparingly. Otherwise most countries engaged in warfare still have to make do with less sophisticated maps and intelligence information on the nature and disposition of the forces arrayed before them.

Photography from space is available from commercial satellites (LANDSAT), and pictures are also taken on manned space flights. This view of the Kennedy Space Center was taken by *Skylab 4*.

A rare published example of the quality of US satellite technology. This computer-enhanced photograph, taken by a military satellite in July 1984, shows a nuclear aircraft carrier under construction in the dry docks at the Soviet Nikolayev 444 shipyard on the Black Sea.

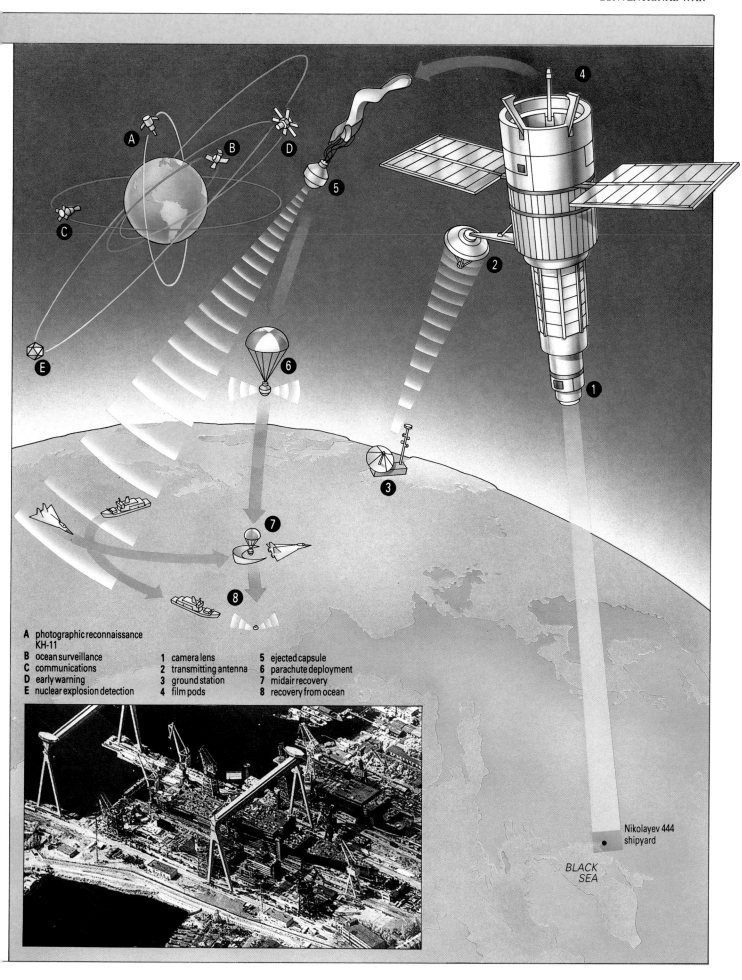

A photographic reconnaissance
KH-11
B ocean surveillance
C communications
D early warning
E nuclear explosion detection

1 camera lens
2 transmitting antenna
3 ground station
4 film pods

5 ejected capsule
6 parachute deployment
7 midair recovery
8 recovery from ocean

Nikolayev 444
shipyard

BLACK
SEA

SOS

The importance of planning, timing and luck, as well as a clearly defined task, can be seen from these two contrasting rescue missions. The Israeli rescue of passengers from a hijacked airliner being held at Entebbe airport with the connivance of the then Ugandan leader, Idi Amin, achieved and fully exploited surprise. The more difficult American attempt in 1980 to rescue diplomatic hostages held at the American embassy in Tehran failed at an early stage becase of faults with the aircraft being used to transport the rescuers. It remains unclear how well the rescue mission would have fared, even if it had reached Tehran.

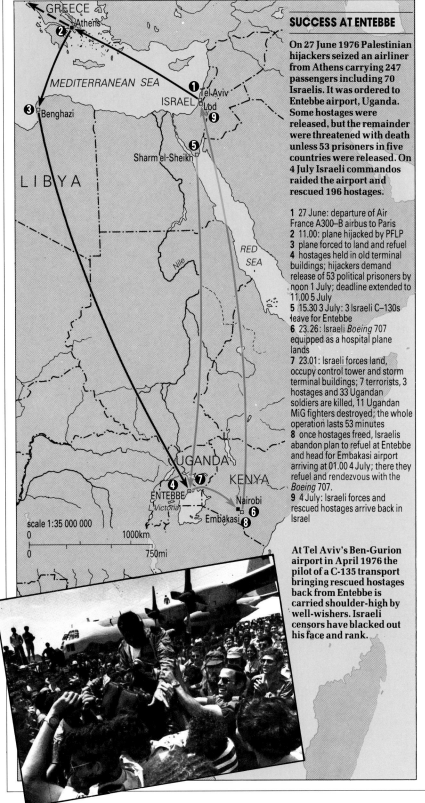

SUCCESS AT ENTEBBE

On 27 June 1976 Palestinian hijackers seized an airliner from Athens carrying 247 passengers including 70 Israelis. It was ordered to Entebbe airport, Uganda. Some hostages were released, but the remainder were threatened with death unless 53 prisoners in five countries were released. On 4 July Israeli commandos raided the airport and rescued 196 hostages.

1 27 June: departure of Air France A300–B airbus to Paris
2 11.00: plane hijacked by PFLP
3 plane forced to land and refuel
4 hostages held in old terminal buildings; hijackers demand release of 53 political prisoners by noon 1 July; deadline extended to 11.00 5 July
5 15.30 3 July: 3 Israeli C–130s leave for Entebbe
6 23.26: Israeli *Boeing* 707 equipped as a hospital plane lands
7 23.01: Israeli forces land, occupy control tower and storm terminal buildings; 7 terrorists, 3 hostages and 33 Ugandan soldiers are killed, 11 Ugandan MiG fighters destroyed; the whole operation lasts 53 minutes
8 once hostages freed, Israelis abandon plan to refuel at Entebbe and head for Embakasi airport arriving at 01.00 4 July; there they refuel and rendezvous with the *Boeing* 707.
9 4 July: Israeli forces and rescued hostages arrive back in Israel

At Tel Aviv's Ben-Gurion airport in April 1976 the pilot of a C-135 transport bringing rescued hostages back from Entebbe is carried shoulder-high by well-wishers. Israeli censors have blacked out his face and rank.

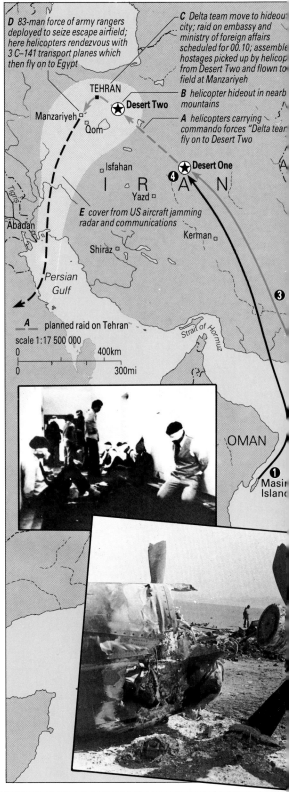

D 83-man force of army rangers deployed to seize escape airfield; here helicopters rendezvous with 3 C-141 transport planes which then fly on to Egypt

C Delta team move to hideout city; raid on embassy and ministry of foreign affairs scheduled for 00.10; assemble hostages picked up by helicop from Desert Two and flown to field at Manzariyeh

B helicopter hideout in nearb mountains

A helicopters carrying commando forces "Delta tear fly on to Desert Two

E cover from US aircraft jamming radar and communications

A   planned raid on Tehran
scale 1:17 500 000
0   400km
0   300mi

Stresses and strains of the battlefield

A US marine mourns the loss of a colleague during a 1967 assault on a hill in Vietnam.

illustrate this point, we may note three features of warfare at the high end of our spectrum which will make it increasingly stressful for those doing the fighting.

First, there will be a steady stream of high-quality information. Field commanders will be in regular touch with their superiors, being kept informed of developments elsewhere and the location and movements of the enemy. In these circumstances there is a risk of utter paralysis in decision-making, with commanders suffering from information overload, unable to digest the information they have, yet waiting for more in the hope that it will clarify the position and make the choices for them.

Moreover, the information can be passed to the highest levels. There will be all sorts of temptations to senior commanders well away from the combat zone or even to political leaders to intervene. For example, in April 1980, when an American attempt to rescue diplomatic hostages held in Tehran was aborted, President Carter and his key aides were in constant touch with the field commander and agonized with him over key decisions.

The second feature of a contemporary battlefield will be the lack of a chance to rest or hide. The accuracy of the weapons means that any unit which becomes exposed will be very vulnerable. Intensive surveillance makes it more likely that it will become so.

There will be a need for large formations to split up and disperse and move constantly. In the past it would have been possible to get some respite at night or when the weather was bad. Weapons systems are now being designed to see through cloud and operate at night. There will be litle time to rest.

Third, because both sides will be making use of electronic systems, they will also both be employing countermeasures designed to interfere with or disrupt the other's systems and in turn employing counter-counter-measures to protect their own. These various measures will involve attemps to jam communications, confuse radars, deflect incoming missiles. The men in the field will find themselves heavily dependent on the performance of all these systems, adding to the general sense of strain. In a Central Europe battle a further source of stress will be the possibility of chemical or nuclear weapons being used.

For those taking part, warfare under these conditions would be frightening, exhausting and confusing. The rate of attrition would be high, movement continuous and the demands on both the men and their equipment intense. Opportunities for sleep, replenishment and repair would be rare. One moment they could be in regular touch with headquarters and the next moment cut off. The malfunction of a vital weapon, the disruption

"War of the flea"

of supply lines, a sudden enemy break-through could all render a unit helpless. Of course, for those involved, war in the past has always been confusing and frightening, but experience of previous campaigns could provide reasonable expectations of how the different elements of an army would knit together and perform in combat. It may just be that the uncertainties facing a military planner concerning attrition rates, outcomes of individual exchanges, durability of equipment, security and efficiency of logistics, the physical and mental capacity of the troops on the ground, are such as to deter him from embarking on any military adventure without considerable superiority in men and equipment.

Guerrilla warfare

At the low end of our spectrum we find guerrilla warfare. In the previous section we looked at how regular armies attempt to do the sort of things that they have always done — gather information, move about, defend and attack — in modern conditions. For the commander his assets are tangible: men and equipment, and the supplies necessary to keep them operational. His goal is clear: a decisive military victory.

Guerrilla warfare is practiced by those who lack much by way of tangible military assets and must therefore avoid pitched battles with well-equipped armies in open conditions. They cannot measure their success in terms of the territory held. Rather they must concentrate on survival and growth. They must trade space for time and then use time to gather support. Their objective is to wear down the enemy, to harass and frustrate him, and in avoiding defeat demonstrate the limits to the power of the state. Over time, the guerrillas hope to gather more recruits and so put more pressure on the enemy forces. As enemy morale begins to crack, and there are desertions and defections, the insurgent force may eventually be able to challenge the regular army openly. Robert Taber called this the "war of the flea": "The flea bites, hops, and bites again, nimbly avoiding the foot that would crush him. He does not seek to kill his enemy at a blow, but to bleed him and to feed upon him, to plague and bedevil him, to keep him from resting and to destroy his nerve and morale."

Survival depends only partly on military skills. Like any other army the guerrilla force needs good intelligence, supplies of weapons and ammunition, and opportunities to train. It must learn the techniques of deception and surprise and hope to get its supplies by taking

GUERRILLA ACTIONS

Guerrilla warfare is a strategy adopted by the militarily disadvantaged in order to survive until they can meet head-on the forces of the state. The latter at the start of a campaign can expect to enjoy the benefits of larger numbers, better equipment and all the other resources of a government. The success of the guerrilla campaign depends on building up political support which in turn should ease operations against government forces. As the government forces become demoralized, and lose men and equipment to the insurgents, then the fight becomes more equal and may eventually be decided on conventional terms.

The methods of guerrilla warfare vary enormously. Some seek to organize alternative forms of government and institute programs of land reform to win over the sympathy of the people. Others concentrate on selective assassination to demonstrate their power and challenge the authority of the state. Nor are their objectives the same. Guerrilla campaigns have been launched from the left and the right. In practice, as the individual campaigns illustrated on this page demonstrate, the sources of support are not so much ideology as national or ethnic loyalties.

A decade after independence Angola is still at war and the government in Luanda subject to a variety of challenges. The two most substantial come from South Africa, which has entered Angolan territory to deal with the bases of the SWAPO guerrillas operating in Namibia, and the UNITA led by Dr Jonas Savimbi and supported by South Africa, which controls large parts of southern Angola and threatens central control. The Cubans, brought over in 1976, remain in place.

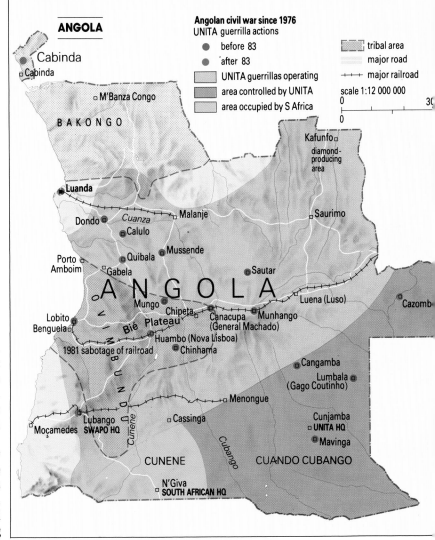

ANGOLA

Angolan civil war since 1976
UNITA guerrilla actions
- before 83
- after 83

UNITA guerrillas operating
area controlled by UNITA
area occupied by S Africa

tribal area
major road
+++ major railroad

scale 1:12 000 000

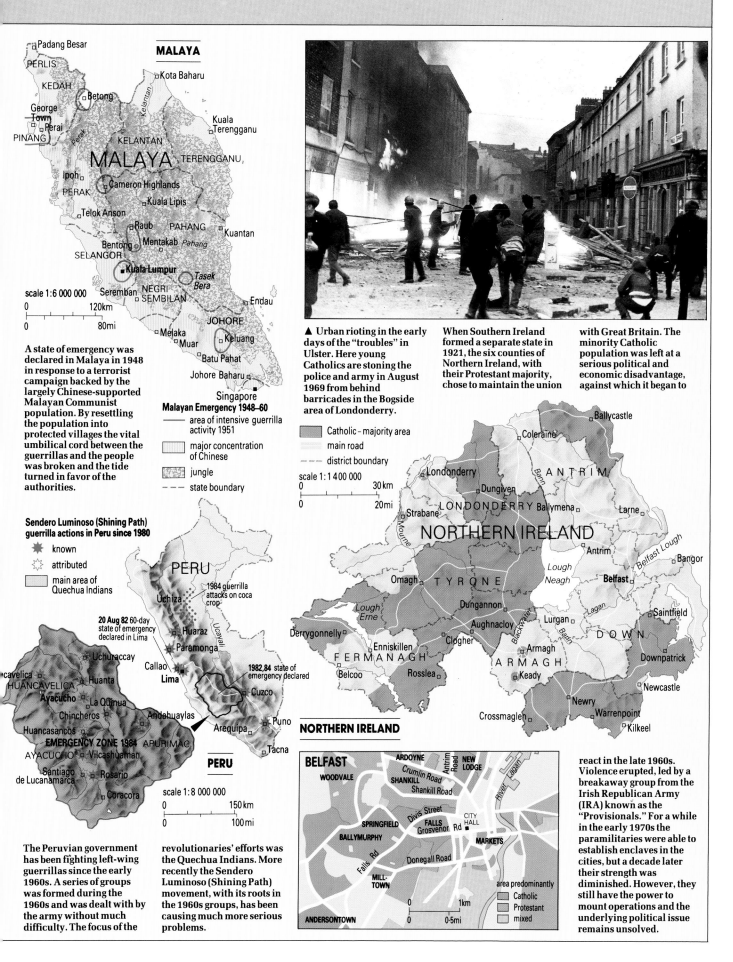

MALAYA

Padang Besar
PERLIS
KEDAH
Betong
George Town
Perai
PINANG
Kota Baharu
KELANTAN
Kuala Terengganu
MALAYA
TERENGGANU
Ipoh
PERAK
Cameron Highlands
Kuala Lipis
Telok Anson
Raub
PAHANG
Kuantan
Bentong
Mentakab
Pahang
SELANGOR
Kuala Lumpur
Tasek Bera
Seremban
NEGRI SEMBILAN
Endau
Melaka
JOHORE
Muar
Keluang
Batu Pahat
Johore Baharu
Singapore

scale 1:6 000 000
0   120km
0   80mi

A state of emergency was declared in Malaya in 1948 in response to a terrorist campaign backed by the largely Chinese-supported Malayan Communist population. By resettling the population into protected villages the vital umbilical cord between the guerrillas and the people was broken and the tide turned in favor of the authorities.

Malayan Emergency 1948–60
— area of intensive guerrilla activity 1951
▨ major concentration of Chinese
▨ jungle
--- state boundary

Sendero Luminoso (Shining Path) guerrilla actions in Peru since 1980
✹ known
✩ attributed
▨ main area of Quechua Indians

PERU
Uchiza
1984 guerrilla attacks on coca crop
Ucayali
Huaraz
20 Aug 82 60-day state of emergency declared in Lima
Paramonga
Callao
Lima
1982,84 state of emergency declared
Uchuraccay
Cuzco
cavelica
HUANCAVELICA
Huanta
Ayacucho
La Quinua
Puno
Chincheros
Andahuaylas
Arequipa
Huancasancos
EMERGENCY ZONE 1984
APURIMAC
AYACUCHO
Vilcashuaman
Tacna
Santiago de Lucanamarca
Rosario
Coracora

PERU
scale 1:8 000 000
0   150km
0   100mi

The Peruvian government has been fighting left-wing guerrillas since the early 1960s. A series of groups was formed during the 1960s and was dealt with by the army without much difficulty. The focus of the

revolutionaries' efforts was the Quechua Indians. More recently the Sendero Luminoso (Shining Path) movement, with its roots in the 1960s groups, has been causing much more serious problems.

▲ Urban rioting in the early days of the "troubles" in Ulster. Here young Catholics are stoning the police and army in August 1969 from behind barricades in the Bogside area of Londonderry.

▨ Catholic - majority area
main road
--- district boundary

scale 1:1 400 000
0   30km
0   20mi

When Southern Ireland formed a separate state in 1921, the six counties of Northern Ireland, with their Protestant majority, chose to maintain the union

with Great Britain. The minority Catholic population was left at a serious political and economic disadvantage, against which it began to

NORTHERN IRELAND

Ballycastle
Coleraine
Londonderry
ANTRIM
Dungiven
Bann
Strabane
LONDONDERRY
Ballymena
Larne
Mourne
NORTHERN IRELAND
Antrim
Belfast Lough
Bangor
Omagh
TYRONE
Lough Neagh
Belfast
Lough Erne
Dungannon
Lagan
Saintfield
Derrygonnelly
Aughnacloy
Lurgan
DOWN
Enniskillen
Clogher
Blackwater
Armagh
Downpatrick
FERMANAGH
Belcoo
Rossea
ARMAGH
Keady
Newcastle
Crossmaglen
Newry
Warrenpoint
Kilkeel

BELFAST
WOODVALE
ARDOYNE
Crumlin Road
SHANKILL
Shankill Road
Antrim Road
NEW LODGE
River Lagan
SPRINGFIELD
Divis Street
CITY HALL
BALLYMURPHY
FALLS
Grosvenor Rd
MARKETS
Falls Rd
Donegall Road
MILL-TOWN
ANDERSONTOWN

0   1km
0   0.5mi

area predominantly
▨ Catholic
▨ Protestant
▨ mixed

react in the late 1960s. Violence erupted, led by a breakaway group from the Irish Republican Army (IRA) known as the "Provisionals." For a while in the early 1970s the paramilitaries were able to establish enclaves in the cities, but a decade later their strength was diminished. However, they still have the power to mount operations and the underlying political issue remains unsolved.

them from the enemy. But all this is highly dependent on support from the local population to ensure the provision of food and shelter. Guerrilla warfare is likely to prosper only in highly favorable political conditions.

During the 1960s there was something of a cult of the guerrilla, the result of the Americans being pinned down by these sort of tactics in Vietnam and, possibly, because one of the most celebrated practitioners, Che Guevara, was photogenic. Guevara, who had fought with Fidel Castro in the Cuban revolution of the late 1950s, was an inspiration to other insurrectionary groups in Latin America and took part himself in two other campaigns. The first in the Congo in Africa

▲ Some rather uncertain new recruits to the anti-Communist UNITA guerrillas training with Chinese weapons in a camp near the Zambian border during the post-independence civil war in Angola.

Guerrillas ignore politics at their peril

was a fiasco and was soon aborted. The second in Bolivia not only failed but cost him his life in 1967. The reasons why he failed illustrate the close connection between political and military action in guerrilla warfare.

Guevara's theory was based on the *foco*, a small group of armed and dedicated men, operating in the hills, hopefully as the vanguard of a revolutionary army. By conducting small-scale operations, the *foco* will undermine the legitimacy of the government and generate increasing popular support until the revolutionaries can form an army capable of taking on the regular forces of the state.

The great weakness of Guevara's theory was, as with many other more orthodox strategic theories, that he took the politics of the matter too much for granted. He assumed that the poor and oppressed peasantry would naturally come over to the revolution once they had shown themselves capable of mounting a serious military challenge to the state. Part of the difficulty was that, although Fidel Castro, once safely in power, declared himself to be a Marxist-Leninist in 1961, when he was actually challenging the government of General Batista there were no Marxist trappings. Castro presented himself as a liberal constitutionalist and became, almost by default, leader of all the opposition forces, largely because he and his guerrilla band were able to survive while others were suppressed. The sheer unpopularity of the Batista regime did the rest. There was very little actual fighting — the guerrillas did not number more than 2000 at their peak and suffered fewer than 100 casualties during the whole of the campaign.

In Bolivia Guevara was hampered by bad luck and military and political ineptitude. Here was a white Argentinian leading a group of guerrillas, almost half of whom were also foreigners, propounding a form of socialism, in an attempt to win over a suspicious Indian peasantry. His diaries reveal the problem: "The inhabitants of this region are as impenetrable as rocks. You speak to them, but in the deepness of their eyes you note they do not believe you."

Guevara's failure (and it was mirrored in a number of other Latin American countries during the 1960s) can be contrasted with the success of the Chinese and Vietnamese operating with a quite different approach. According to the leader of the Chinese revolution, Mao Zedong, guerrilla warfare could only flourish as part of a broad political movement. It was necessary to engage the people's sympathy and cooperation and from there

move on to increase political consciousness about the nature of the struggle. In a much-quoted phrase, Mao said: "The people are to the army what water is to the fish."

Mao's doctrine of "people's war" developed out of his long experience in the Chinese Communist Party and the wars fought against the Japanese and then the Nationalists under Jiang Jieshi. Mao's success was based on indentifying himself with the nationalist and anti-imperialist sentiments of the peasantry. In this effort he had been helped by the Japanese who had provided an excellent target. A foreign invader provides many more

political opportunities than a home-grown dictator.

This point was illustrated by the Vietnamese Communist leaders, Ho Chi Minh and Vo Nguyen Giap, who also had the Japanese, then the French and finally the Americans as an imperialist presence. They were less dependent upon slowly building up

▶ Above, Fidel Castro at his moment of triumph on New Year's Day 1959. Below, the glamor of the Cuban revolution lives on. A famous picture of one of its heroes, Che Guevara, is displayed by Iranian radicals demonstrating in early 1979 against the shah.

137

popular support in the country and more able to draw upon external sources of support. Not only did they have the backing of the Chinese and the Russians, but they also recognized the psychological value of inflicting dramatic military shocks on the enemy.

Thus, in March 1954, Giap, leading the Vietminh against French colonial rule in what was then Indochina, laid siege to a reinforced French garrison at Dien Bien Phu. Eventually in May he broke through the French defenses and overran the garrison. The defeat in itself need not have been militarily decisive for the French. Giap had many more casualties (20 000 as against 7000). But the defeat came as a humiliating blow to France just as a peace conference was opening at Geneva, called to wind up

both the Korean and Indochina conflicts. The country was divided into North and South Vietnam. Later, operating from the North against the South, he used the same techniques against the United States. In the presidential election years of 1968 and 1972 massive offensives were launched in which at an enormous cost American claims that matters were firmly under control were mocked in such a way as to impress the American public. The 1968 Tet Offensive was a military defeat, although a political victory. Afterwards Giap and his colleagues all but abandoned guerrilla warfare. The local insurgents (the Vietcong) had been decimated and much of the fighting was carried out by the North Vietnamese army.

In the early 1960s the United States became

A somewhat idealized picture of Mao Zedong, leading the Long March in 1935. The march covered 9500 kilometers (5900 miles) in 13 months and cost the lives of half the 200 000 Communists involved as they retreated across southwest China from Nationalist forces. It enabled the Communists to develop their guerrilla warfare skills and Mao to consolidate his leadership.

The doctrine of people's war

▶ When the Americans embraced the concept of counterinsurgency warfare in the early 1960s, Fort Gulick in Panama was established as one of the main centers of instruction in the relevant techniques for both US forces and those of friendly governments.

obsessed by the notion that revolutionary insurgencies in the third world represented one of the most substantial strategic challenges for the future. The arrival of a Marxist government in Cuba, the increasing fervor of Chinese pronouncements on the revolutionary struggle as well as the challenges being mounted in Latin America and Southeast Asia could be seen as the disadvantaged of the south waging war against the privileged and exploiting north. In 1965 the American Secretary of Defense even appended to his annual report to Congress a copy of a tract by Mao's lieutenant, Lin Piao, entitled *Long Live the Victory of People's War*. In this Lin wrote: "In a sense, the contemporary world revolution ... presents a picture of the encirclement of the cities by the rural areas. In the final analysis, the whole course of world revolution hinges on the revolutionary struggle of the Asian, African, and Latin American peoples."

Many in the West took this sort of rhetoric more seriously than it deserved. It was seen as a logical extension of the anticolonial struggles then under way in circumstances when straightforward military clashes between East and West were becoming too dangerous. The Americans took it especially seriously. They decided that a response must involve both the adoption of new military techniques (known as counterinsurgency operations) and a sensitivity to the political circumstances from which the insurgents drew their inspiration and popular support. In Latin America, where the revolutionary challenge was in practice weak and American economic and military strength overbearing, the problem was quite manageable. In Vietnam, where the challenge was strong and the pro-Western government weak, the Americans failed miserably. The military proved themselves unable to adapt to local conditions.

More seriously, they failed to get the local politicians to reform themselves, and their own efforts at counterinsurgency often alienated rather than won over the population.

As we have noted, the North Vietnamese concluded their victory over the South using regular forces. They then went on to use these forces to establish their dominion over Laos and Kampuchea (formerly Cambodia), facing guerrilla opposition of their own in the latter case. The Chinese, having turned their doctrine of "people's war" into a general formula for defeating any enemy through guerrilla-style operations by lightly armed militias, grew nervous about its general validity and began to modernize their regular forces.

While the global insurrection envisaged during the heady days of the 1960s failed to materialize, guerrilla actions continued to chalk up successes. In 1974 the guerrilla movements in the Portuguese African colonies of Angola and Mozambique gained a classic victory. There was even, in Nicaragua in 1979, a victory by one of the revolutionary groups spawned by the Cuban revolution in the early 1960s — the Sandinistas. The Somoza regime was unpopular and repressive. After two years of bloody fighting, political action and confusing signals from the United States, which had backed Somoza in the past, the regime collapsed in July 1979. As part of the aftermath, neighboring El Salvador slid into a bloody civil war.

All this might seem to confirm the impression developed in the 1960s that guerrilla warfare was essentially an instrument of the political left leading the poor and disadvantaged. However, the political support required for successful guerrilla action appears to be less ideological than a reflection of national, ethnic or tribal loyalties. This provides the basis for a challenge not only to imperialists but also to regimes of the left.

Motivation stems more often from nationalism than from ideology

In fact, as often as not, guerrilla wars in the 1980s have been mounted against left-wing regimes. In Angola UNITA, reputedly backed by South Africa, has steadily gained ground against the MPLA faction which won control in the post-independence civil war in 1975. In Afghanistan Islamic rebels fought first against a Marxist regime which seized power in 1978 and then took up arms against the Soviet Union when it moved in December 1979 to shore up the tottering regime. Even in Central America the Nicaraguans have been challenged by the American-backed Contras.

The voluntary and highly political aspects of guerrilla warfare mean that the question of motivation is more important than in regular armies where the ordinary soldiers may feel that they have little choice but to obey orders (although the more effective armies will draw on much more than formal discipline). What would seem to be the case for both regular and guerrilla armies is that the motivation is more likely to be found in nationalism than in ideology.

19 July 1979. Crowds gather in the Square of the Republic in Managua, the capital of Nicaragua, to greet the first Sandinista guerrillas, whose column had entered the city that afternoon. Two days earlier the dictator Somoza had resigned and fled to Miami.

WARFARE SINCE 1945

Specific conflicts illustrate the general themes. Europe, where the cold war began, remains the focus of superpower attention. The Far East has experienced every brand of conflict since 1945, from America's struggles against Communist expansion to internecine struggles among the successful Communist regimes. In South Asia India and Pakistan have been uneasy neighbors, the former developing ties with the Soviet Union, the latter with the USA and China. The Middle East is of strategic significance not only because of its oil reserves but also as the meeting point of Europe, Asia and Africa: Israel is at the heart of most conflicts in the region. Civil wars have proliferated in Africa since decolonization. The sources of instability in Latin America and the Caribbean are largely domestic.

One of the more successful Sandinista commanders during the war against the Somoza regime in Nicaragua was Commander Cero, Eden Pastora. Here his troops put on a display of morale before a push into the hinterland in November 1978.

We have found reason to question the common assumptions that the causes of modern warfare are solely linked to the attitudes and behavior of the superpowers, and that its character reflects the increasing sophistication of modern weaponry. We have suggested that the capacity of the superpowers to shape international affairs, by economic and political as well as military means, has declined and a much more chaotic and confusing global politics is developing in consequence. This has been explained by reference to the profound disincentives facing the great powers in any contemplation of war in the presence of nuclear weapons, the difficulties of extending even conventional military power over long distances, and the aftermath of decolonization which has introduced numerous new independent actors into the international arena.

Many countries have now acquired advanced military capabilities, making possible a resurgence of old-fashioned war whereby regular armies are charged with the task of settling disputes through the medium of battle. However, while a number of states that once played only a subordinate role in the international system are now able to be much more assertive, many others of the more recently independent are congenitally weak. They are vulnerable to coups, rebellions, secession and incursion by stronger neighbors. The sort of conflicts that result from this weakness are by far the most common. They are fought with the whole gamut of weaponry, excluding the nuclear, with a tendency towards reliance on the cruder, low-technology types. Even in those wars where the higher-technology systems are employed, the less modern are always very much in evidence and, while not necessarily as decisive in impact, are often responsible for a large proportion of the casualties.

In this chapter the objective is to illustrate these general themes by reference to the specific conflicts that have taken place since 1945. The treatment cannot be truly comprehensive and for reasons of space is synoptic. Nevertheless it should enable us to observe the diversity of contemporary warfare, in its causes, participants, methods, forms and outcomes.

EUROPE

■ Although this book has emphasized the significance of the lack of a third major European war this century, this does not mean that the continent has been free of conflict. It was in Europe that the cold war began, dominated at first by the nature of the Soviet hold over Eastern Europe and then over the division of Germany. The East–West conflict spilled over into full-blooded violence only in Greece. It was the ferocity of the Greek civil war which helped to convince the United States that it had no choice but to intervene actively in the politics of postwar Europe.

The Soviet Union has mounted two large-scale military operations to crush dissident Communist regimes, first in Hungary in 1956 and then in Czechoslovakia in 1968. On the Western side Cyprus has been a continuing source of tension. Meanwhile there have been niggling but damaging guerrilla campaigns under way for some time both in the Basque region of Spain, mounted by a separatist organization, and in Northern Ireland, where the long-standing feud between the majority Protestant and the minority Catholic population has led some of the latter to lend support to the Provisional Irish Revolutionary Army in its campaign against "British rule."

Greece

At the end of World War II the major guerrilla organization which had been fighting the Germans — the Communist-controlled ELAS — sought to take over the country. Even while the war was still under way, it had launched attacks against other non-Communist guerrilla groups. In 1944, as the Germans left, ELAS was able to take over some 90 percent of the country, but it was opposed by British troops and by early 1945 had been defeated. A full-blooded purge against the Communists was instigated which saw many executed and imprisoned. The remnants took to the hills while the Greek army regrouped under the monarchy. Supported by neighboring Communist states (Albania, Bulgaria and Yugoslavia), the Communists returned to the fight, taking on the new Greek army in a three-year civil war concentrated around the Mount Grammos area, which left some 150 000 casualties (some two-thirds of which were Communists) and led to a million refugees. The war began to turn in favor of the government in 1947 after President Truman promised aid, taking over from Britain which was being forced to withdraw because of its own economic problems.

Cyprus 1974

Cyprus was administered as a British colony from 1878 to 1960 when it gained independence. Prior to independence some 10 000 British troops were tied down by Greek-Cypriot guerrillas known as EOKA. They wished for union with Greece — or *Enosis*. Greek-Cypriot leader Archbishop Makarios eventually accepted a plan for independence without *Enosis* and with guarantees for the Turkish Cypriots. In late 1963 an ugly civil war

broke out after Makarios attempted to remove the safeguards on Turkish rights which he saw as blocking effective government. The communal violence was brought to a close with the arrival of United Nations forces in March 1964. The Turks were excluded from power and the issue proved to be a constant source of tension between Greece and Turkey, almost leading to war in 1967. Among the Greeks the issue was whether the time was now ripe for *Enosis*, an idea that Makarios continued to reject on the grounds, which turned out to be correct, that it would lead to a Turkish invasion.

In early July 1974 Makarios accused the Greek Junta of supporting EOKA and using Greek officers attached to the National Guard to promote subversion. On 15 July the National Guard under Greek officers seized control, and installed former EOKA terrorist Nikos Sampson as president. Makarios escaped to Britain.

On 20 July Turkey invaded Cyprus, landing forces by sea at Kyrenia, with paratroopers landing in the Turkish-Cypriot village of Geunyeli. The Turkish operation was not particularly efficient and failed to follow through its initial advantages by taking Nicosia. In two days a cease-fire was agreed. Having failed in this adventure, the Greek Junta recognized that its days were numbered and recalled civilians to government. On 24 July Sampson resigned.

Peace talks opened in Geneva involving Britain, Greece and Turkey, but by the middle of August they had collapsed. Turkish forces had by this time increased to 40 000 men with 200 tanks. On 14 August they attacked Greek-Cypriot positions. Once Turkey had split Cyprus in two, it called for a cease-fire.

There was no more fighting after this point. Greeks north of the line and Turks south of it moved across to be with their respective communities. Although there has been no formal settlement, the position now is one of de facto partition.

**Budapest: November 1956.
A woman patriot keeps the crowds back from the body of a member of the hated Hungarian secret police — the AVO.**

DIARY: HUNGARY 1956

23 October Revolt begins against unpopular Communist regime headed by Party Secretary General Erno Gero.

25 October Hungarian and Soviet troops (who fired on demonstrators) forced to withdraw. Imre Nagy becomes prime minister of popular government.

26 October Gero requests Soviet troops. Renewed fighting.

28 October Temporary cease-fire.

1 November 200 000 Soviet troops and 2500 tanks surround Budapest.

3 November Military leaders of the provisional government are arrested while negotiating with Russians.

4 November Soviet troops move in to crush revolt. Nagy arrested.

Resistance was crushed in a few days. About 27 000 Hungarian and 7000 Soviet casualties resulted.

capital city

scale 1 : 22 000 000

0 — 400km
0 — 300mi

Northern Ireland
Protestant/Catholic conflict 68-

Germany
W German policy of eventual reunification

pre-1945 Germany-Poland border

Oder-Neisse line

Berlin
East-West crises 48-49, 58, 61

Czechoslovakia
Soviet invasion 68

Hungary
Soviet invasion 56

Brittany
separatist movement

Basque region
separatist movement 59-

Corsica
separatist movement

Kosovo
Albanian separatist movement 68-

Macedonia
Bulgarian territorial claim

Gibraltar
Spanish territorial claim

Mt Grammos
communist stronghold 1945-49

Greece
civil war 45-49

Aegean Sea
Graeco-Turkish border dispute 74-

Cyprus
intercommunal conflict; independence movement 55-59; Turkish invasion 74

▼ The Cyprus crisis of 1974 was prompted by a pro-*Enosis* military junta in Greece, and exacerbated by weak diplomacy by the United States, which initially appeared to support the Greek junta, and by Britain, which failed to act according to its obligations under the 1960 settlement as coguarantor of the independence of Cyprus. After the coup of 15 July, Turkey waited to see whether Britain would take action; when this failed to materialize, it acted itself.

➤ Turkish advance, 1974
Turkish front line
········ 22 July
‑ ‑ ‑ ‑ 30 July
———— 16 August cease-fire line
▨▨ British sovereign base area
▨ Greek-Cypriot area pre-1974

DIARY: CZECHOSLOVAKIA 1968

January Antonin Novotny replaced as First Party Secretary by reformist Alexander Dubcek. Program of reform set in motion.

March Novotny replaced as president by rehabilitated General Ludvik Svoboda.

May Military mission headed by Soviet Defense Minister Marshal Grechko visits Czechoslovakia, giving rise to rumors of imminent intervention.

July Warsaw Pact military maneuvers close to Czechoslovakia add to concerns.

3 August Bratislava Declaration, agreed after meeting between Soviet Politburo and Czech Praesidium, appears to defuse crisis.

20 August 40 000 invasion troops from Soviet Union, East Germany, Poland, Bulgaria and Hungary occupy Prague.

USSR

MONGOLIA

Ulan Baator

CHINA

Beijing

Pyongyang · Seoul

YELLOW SEA

Huang

Nanjing

Shanghai

EAST

Chongqing

Yangzi

Hong Kong

Canton

TAIW

Taipei

bombardment
Quemoy and M
1954–62

border clash
1969

N K

1949

1964

NUCLEAR WEAPON CAPABILITY

border clash
1969

occupation
1979

Kabul
Islamabad

AFGHANI-
STAN

?

border clash
1962

Tibet

Lhasa

invasion of Tibet
1950

border clash
1962

PAKISTAN

border clash
1949, 1971

Delhi

NEPAL

BHUTAN

invasion
1971

Dacca

BANGLA-
DESH

Calcutta

1974

border clash
1965

Karachi

INDIA

invasion
1975

BURMA

intervention
1979

Hanoi

Bombay

BAY OF BENGAL

Rangoon

LAOS

VIETNAM

SOUTH CHINA
SEA

invasion
1961
Goa

Vientiane

Manila

PHILIPPI

Madras

THAILAND

Bangkok

invasion
1978

intervention
1965

KAMPUCHEA

Phnom Penh · Ho Chi Minh City

SRI LANKA

Colombo

BRUNEI

MALAYSIA

SARAWAK

"confrontation"
1962–66

military action

Kuala Lumpur

"confrontation"
1962–66

USA

Pakistan

UK

intervention
1957, 1963

SINGAPORE

BORNEO

SULAWES
(CELEBES

USSR

Vietnam

France

Equator

SUMATRA

China

South Korea

Indonesia

INDONESI

India

Australia

capital city

Jakarta

JAVA

scale 1:32 000 000

0   1000km

0   750mi

invasion of E Timo
1975–76

THE FAR EAST

▶ A South Korean on patrol in the streets of Inchon in September 1950 after the invasion and capture of this key port by American forces.

◀ After the French found themselves unable to hold on to Indochina and with the British anxious not to extend themselves in the area, it seemed likely that the great contest for influence in the Far East would be between the superpowers. While the Americans and the Russians continue to make themselves felt in the politics of the region, the major contest at least is between China and Vietnam, with the Soviet Union having fallen out with the former and exercising less control than it might have expected over the latter. As can be seen from the map, China has used military force in one guise or another against most of its neighbors, while Vietnam, after expelling the American-backed non-Communist forces from the South, has moved on to take over Laos and attempted to do the same to Kampuchea.

■ Asia has seen most modern types of conflict imaginable, from guerrilla warfare to full-scale conventional warfare, and there is still the memory of the only nuclear weapons yet used in anger. The conflicts have taken the form of colonial struggles, challenges to the post-independence regimes, East–West confrontations and internecine warfare among the Communist countries of the area which have grown in number and strength but not cohesion. One cause of this turbulence was the decision by the victors at the end of the Pacific War to hand back those colonies that had been occupied by Japan to their former masters. The United States, despite its anticolonialist past, was anxious to maintain the British and French positions so that they could help to contain the spread of Communism. The French performance in this role was not distinguished. The Dutch fought doggedly at the end of the war, at the cost of some 25 000 casualties, to hold on to Indonesia, which eventually achieved independence in 1949.

Britain, by contrast, eased itself out of its colonial position with some credit in this area, especially in its successful handling of the Malayan "emergency" prior to that country's independence in 1957. Some 45 000 troops (Malay and Commonwealth) fought up to 10 000 guerrillas which, although notionally Communist, were largely recruited from the Chinese population. The majority population was unsympathetic to the insurgents and this was used skillfully by the authorities in a classic "hearts and minds" campaign. A similar number of troops were involved and similar factors were in play in the "confrontation" between the Federation of Malaysia, when it was formed in 1963, and the Indonesians, whose leader Ahmad Sukarno had his own

ambitions for the territory. The guerrillas infiltrated into Malaysia, mostly over the 1600-kilometer (1000-mile) jungle border between Malaysian Borneo and Indonesian Borneo, but failed to achieve any popular support. The confrontation came to an end after Sukarno was deposed following an abortive Communist coup which was ruthlessly suppressed by the Indonesian military. A decade later in 1976 Indonesia had more success in taking over the former Portuguese colony of East Timor after a vicious post-independence civil war.

The anti-Communist inspiration to American policy led the United States to support the beleaguered Nationalists on the offshore island of Formosa (Taiwan) after their defeat in the civil war, the South Koreans when invaded from the Communist North, and the South Vietnamese, also against a Communist North. In the first two endeavors the United States helped to achieve a stalemate; in the last a defeat. The collapse of the South Vietnamese government in 1975 reverberated throughout the area, with Laos and Cambodia (Kampuchea) also falling to leftist forces.

Thereafter conflict in the area became dominated by disagreements among the various Communist nations. The two giants — the Soviet Union and China — had never been as close as their 1950 Treaty of Friendship suggested, and by 1963 the split had became quite open. In 1969 there were clashes along the Amur and Ussuri rivers, and for much of the 1970s relations between the two were extremely tense, although recently there has been a slight improvement. China has taken on Russia's close ally Vietnam. A month after the latter had invaded Kampuchea in December 1978 China launched a punitive invasion of Vietnam.

THE FAR EAST (continued)

◄ Preparing an assault. Troops of the 187th Airborne Regiment make a practice jump at Taegu on 7 March 1951.

▼ Aftermath of assault. A street in the port of Inchon after the US bombardment and invasion of the town in 1950.

The Korean War: 1950-1954

The Korean War was not an outgrowth of a colonial struggle, but a result of the character of the surrender of Japanese troops in 1945. Those north of the 38th parallel surrendered to the Russians; those to the south to the Americans. The politics of the country thereafter reflected this division. Unification talks failed. The Southern Republic of Korea was established in 1947, followed by the Northern Democratic People's Republic. The Russians began to build up the North Korean Army while the Americans seemed uncertain about the degree of commitment they wished to make to the South. After a period of border skirmishes, on 25 June 1950 the North launched a surprise attack on the South, using its much more formidable army, and making rapid advances took the Southern capital of Seoul.

Taking advantage of a Soviet boycott of the UN Security Council, the Americans were able to gain United Nations support for an effort to expel the North's troops. Eventually 15 nations provided troops. By 30 June the first American forces had arrived from Japan, but they were unable to contain the North Korean advance. At the end of August American and South Korean troops were pinned down in a tiny bridgehead around the southeastern port of Pusan. The position was then retrieved in a brilliant gamble by the UN Commander, General MacArthur.

On 15 September American marines landed at Inchon to the west of Seoul, supported by a massive naval and air bombardment, established a bridgehead and were able to bring in infantry. At the same time the UN forces, now including a British detachment, began to move out from Pusan. Forces breaking out from Inchon and Pusan met on 26 September and then went on to liberate Seoul. The North Korean army was split in half and decimated. Only 30 000 of the 130 000 who had crossed the 38th parallel made it back across.

The momentum of the UN troops took them right into the North, two-thirds of which had been occupied by 24 November, when Hyesanjin close to the Yalu river was reached. As this marks the Korea–China border, the UN forces were now too close for comfort for the Chinese. China launched a massive counter-offensive on 25 November. The UN forces were ill-prepared to meet this assault and were forced back to the 38th parallel. MacArthur felt that, had he been able to take a more aggressive stance vis-à-vis China, he would have been able to anticipate the Chinese offensive or at least limit its impact. But his political masters did not want to risk a general war with the Chinese and Russians at this time and they overruled him. His task was now to organize a successful resistance. On 1 January 1951 the North with Chinese help launched a renewed invasion which, after early successes, was forced back. MacArthur wished to respond by taking the war to China, with the help of the Nationalist Chinese. He was dismissed in April for expressing this view publicly.

In July, when the Communist forces had been pushed back beyond the 38th parallel, they accepted Truman's proposals for cease-fire talks which had first been offered in March. The talks began on 12 November 1951 at Panmunjon. One of the issues that held up agreement was the refusal of the South to return to the North prisoners who had no wish to go home. Little progress was made until the Eisenhower administration entered office in 1953 and indicated that it would have no hesitation in widening the conflict if there was no progress at the talks. A cease-fire was eventually signed on 27 July 1953. The position has remained static for 30 years. Modern forces face each other across the cease-fire line and, while the South could now probably cope with a Northern invasion by itself, a substantial American garrison remains on hand, just in case.

When the Korean War broke out in 1950, many in the West believed that its true significance was a diversionary action, and that a more powerful and direct Soviet push would soon be felt in Europe. The demonstration that Soviet-backed regimes were prepared to extend their dominion by force of arms encouraged rearmament in the West and gave the cold war many of its military trappings. The actual experience of conventional warfare in Korea and the frustration felt by some senior commanders at not being allowed either to use nuclear weapons or to attack Communist air bases in China was one reason for the emphasis on nuclear deterrence that soon became a feature of Western strategy.

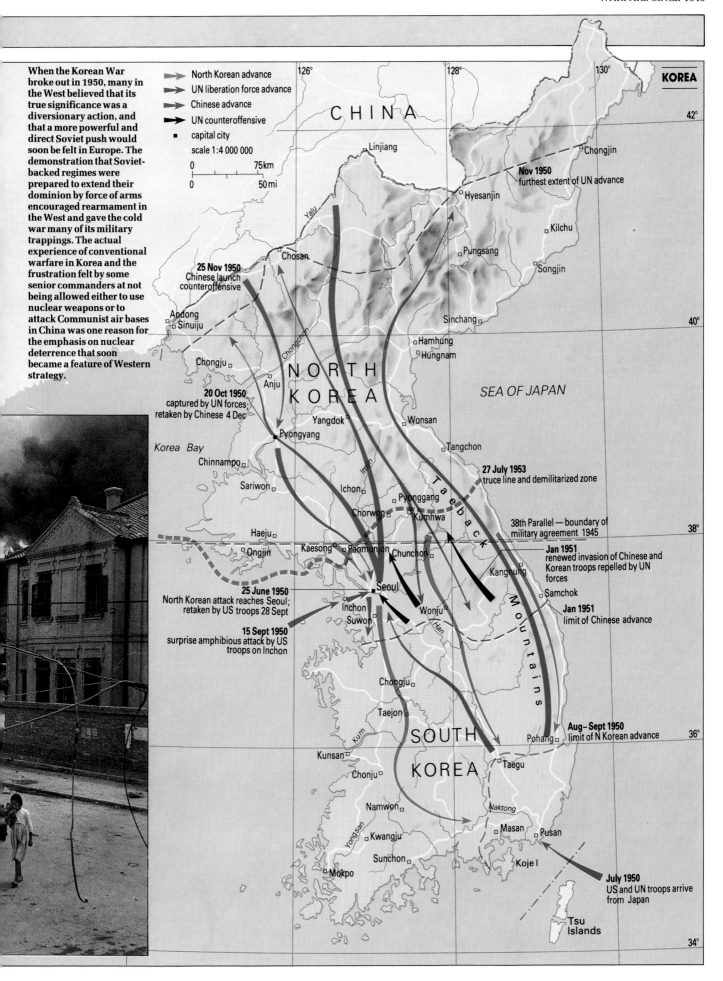

KOREA

→ North Korean advance
→ UN liberation force advance
→ Chinese advance
→ UN counteroffensive
■ capital city
scale 1:4 000 000

0   75km
0   50mi

CHINA

Nov 1950
furthest extent of UN advance

25 Nov 1950
Chinese launch counteroffensive

20 Oct 1950
captured by UN forces; retaken by Chinese 4 Dec

NORTH KOREA

SEA OF JAPAN

27 July 1953
truce line and demilitarized zone

38th Parallel — boundary of military agreement 1945

Jan 1951
renewed invasion of Chinese and Korean troops repelled by UN forces

Jan 1951
limit of Chinese advance

25 June 1950
North Korean attack reaches Seoul; retaken by US troops 28 Sept

15 Sept 1950
surprise amphibious attack by US troops on Inchon

Korea Bay

Aug–Sept 1950
limit of N Korean advance

SOUTH KOREA

July 1950
US and UN troops arrive from Japan

Tsu Islands

147

THE FAR EAST (continued)

Indochina

Against the French

The Vietnamese army can trace its roots to the Communist-backed Vietminh, founded in 1941 to challenge French colonial rule in Indochina, then comprising Laos and Cambodia as well as Vietnam. The anticolonial struggle was interrupted by Japanese occupation but resumed at the end of the Pacific War. The Vietminh, under Ho Chi Minh, sought to establish control over the whole of Vietnam on the Japanese departure. However, their position was strong only in the north. The French, who had been handed their colony back, pushed the Vietminh out of their northern strongholds by early 1946, including the northern capital of Hanoi.

The Vietminh retired to the northeast, leaving behind the rudiments of a guerrilla organization. In a series of pincer movements, French forces unsuccessfully sought to dislodge the Vietminh from their redoubt. Meanwhile guerrilla strength grew. The Vietminh received a boost in 1949 from the Communist victory in China. They now felt able to launch a guerrilla offensive which succeeded in forcing the French into a fortified line around the Red River delta. Then, somewhat incautiously, the Vietminh forces, led by General Giap, launched conventional offensives designed to penetrate the French lines. In three battles in 1951 (Vinh Yen, Mao Khe, Ninh-Binh) they failed and in consequence were obliged to return to guerrilla operations.

The French failed to grapple effectively with this new guerrilla campaign because they wanted to engage the enemy in yet more conventional battles. By the time battle was joined at Dien Bien Phu in late 1953 the Communist forces were better prepared both politically and materially. The French garrison at Dien Bien Phu fell in May 1954 (see p. 138). Later that year a settlement was agreed at the Geneva Conference by which Vietnam was divided into two independent states at the 17th parallel, with the Vietminh gaining control of the North and a non-Communist government installed in the South.

Against the Americans

The idea was to reunify under democratic elections, but neither side demonstrated great interest in such a method. The Communists were certainly anxious to control the whole country and so lent their support to a Southern-based insurgency which challenged the government of Ngo Dinh Diem. There has been some debate as to whether this insurgency was indigenous or whether it was a creature of the North. It was a combination of the two, but as the conflict dragged on, the autonomy of the Southern leaders declined.

Diem certainly believed that the North presented the main threat. His army, now under American guidance, assumed that the greatest danger came from a conventional invasion from the North and organized itself accordingly. This allowed the guerrillas to establish themselves and to challenge governmental authority (often by murdering its local representatives). By 1960 they were confident enough to proclaim a National Liberation Front (which became known to its enemies as the Vietcong). The incompetent and increasingly repressive Diem government found itself in difficulties and came to rely much more on American aid and advisers (some 4000 by 1962).

The politics of the South became characterized increasingly by civil unrest and instability at the top. Diem himself was assassinated in 1963. Such an unstable government was unable to cope with the insurgency, yet the political instability could only be resolved if the insurgency was contained. The situation could only be retrieved by a greater American involvement. In August 1964 President Johnson used an ambiguous incident in the Gulf of Tonkin, when it was alleged that North Vietnamese patrol boats had attacked US destroyers, to obtain Congressional authorization for greater intervention. In the summer of 1965 US troops were formally committed to combat. Total US troop strength reached 215 000 by February 1966 (it eventually reached 525 000). Australia and South Korea also agreed to send troops. The next month a bombing campaign was launched against the North.

The bombing campaign was based on the presumption that this sort of punishment would force the enemy to desist from its aggression. This view turned out to be no more valid in this instance than it had been in the bombing campaigns of World War II. It also turned out to be a crude and inadequate means of interrupting the North's supply lines to the South. Guerrilla operations continued mainly in the Central Highlands around Pleiku and in the Mekong delta district. They achieved mixed success, but they were helped by the clumsiness of the Southern and American response which was caught between the two slogans of "hearts and minds" and "search and destroy" and often left the local population feeling more vulnerable then before. Governmental authority continued to erode. When American and South Vietnamese forces were able to engage in conventional operations they had much more success.

By the start of 1968 it appeared that the war was beginning to swing against the Communists. The Tet Offensive, which began on 30 January 1968, in military terms reinforced that trend, but politically it had the opposite effect (see p. 138). After some optimistic assessments of the course of the war, the American public, which was already becoming frustrated at the cost and length of the war, was suddenly treated to pictures of ferocious fighting in many Vietnamese cities, including the national capital of Saigon and the old imperial capital of Hue where fighting was especially fierce. The insurgents achieved none

▲ The ubiquitous helicopter in Vietnam, here delivering supplies to South Vietnamese soldiers.

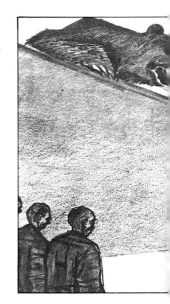

political concessions. There were, for example, major raids against Hanoi in December 1972 in a final push for a more favorable settlement.

On 27 January 1973 an agreement was reached in Paris between the United States, the North and South Vietnamese governments and the National Liberation Front. The results were a cease-fire, which did not last for long, an International Commission for Control and Supervision, withdrawal of foreign troops, repatriation of prisoners and eventual reunification. The last provision was soon achieved, solely on North Vietnamese terms. The North had been left in control of many of the key strategic areas in the South. A Communist offensive in late 1974 led to a decision by the South Vietnamese government in March 1975 to abandon the northern provinces. This resulted in a severe drop in morale of its armed forces which on paper still ought to have been a match for those of the Communists. The whole country was soon under Communist control, Saigon falling on 30 April.

The Communists had paid a high price — over 900 000 dead as opposed to fewer than 200 000 of the South Vietnamese. Some 46 000 Americans had been killed and 300 000 wounded. The United States had spent some $112 billion trying to save South Vietnam.

Against the Chinese
When South Vietnam fell to the Communists, so did Laos and Cambodia. Laos had been part of French Indochina. It was granted independence in 1949 and its neutrality had been recognized at the 1954 Geneva Conference. However a local Communist insurgency, known as the Pathet Lao, had soon after begun to conduct operations against the Royal Laotian Army. With American support a government composed of the major non-Communist factions managed to hold off the Pathet Lao challenge during the 1960s. Eventually with North Vietnamese help they gained control of the Plaine des Jarres area in the north. When the government forces were eventually defeated in 1975, the price of victory for the Pathet Lao was a permanent North Vietnamese garrison.

Cambodia had achieved its independence in 1953 and also had its neutrality guaranteed at Geneva in 1954. The head of state, Prince Norodom Sihanouk, was inclined towards the Communists and even came to accept a large number of North Vietnamese in his country which they used as a sanctuary for conducting operations against South Vietnam. This upset the internal political balance and eventually Sihanouk was overthrown in an anti-Communist coup, led by General Lon Nol. Lon Nol was soon fighting a Communist "Khmer Rouge" insurgency, but the country's main problems resulted from being an extension of the Vietnamese battleground. In February 1973 a major Khmer Rouge offensive against the capital Phnom Penh was launched and by April it was close to success. There were no American troops available to support Lon Nol, and in August Congress, annoyed about

▼ **The Sino–Soviet dispute. While China is divided by the Cultural Revolution, the Russian bear growls menacingly over the Great Wall.**

of their immediate objectives and suffered massive casualties, but they did succeed in denting American confidence.

In April 1968 President Johnson proposed cease-fire talks. The invitation was accepted by the North and the talks were convened in Paris in May 1968. In October a bombing halt was ordered to help improve the atmosphere. The Nixon administration, which came to power at the start of 1969, sought to extract the United States from the war in the least humiliating way possible. It was made clear to the South Vietnamese that they were expected to take on the bulk of the fighting. American troops were to be gradually withdrawn. By August 1972 the last American combat troops had been removed.

However, the administration was not averse to other forms of escalation, for example by invading Cambodia and Laos (in May 1970 and February 1971 respectively) in an effort to interrupt the Communist supply lines. The main result was further to destabilize these two countries. Air raids were also used spasmodically both to achieve military objectives and to prod the North into more

THE FAR EAST (continued)

past deception on the degree of American activity in Cambodia, refused to authorize any more bombing on Lon Nol's behalf. He hung on until April 1975. Then, isolated and with the Communists on the offensive everywhere, resistance collapsed.

The resultant Khmer Rouge regime under Pol Pot was unusually vicious and unattractive, even by local standards. It was not, however, dependent upon the Vietnamese and, whatever the ideological similarities, it was highly resistant to any suggestion that the old French Indochina should be recreated under Vietnamese control. Somewhat reckless and sensitive to Vietnamese encroachments upon its territory, it encroached itself against Vietnam. Vietnam prepared the ground for its response by signing a treaty in November 1978 with the Soviet Union, designed to deter Chinese intervention on behalf of the Khmer Rouge. In the last week of 1978 it launched a massive attack using 12 divisions and had soon cut through all of Cambodia (now known as Kampuchea). By 7 January it was in control of Phnom Penh and was soon in charge of most of the major cities. However, the ease of this victory was qualified by the fact that the enemy had not resisted but — some 60 000 strong — had melted away into the countryside from where it now began to conduct guerrilla operations.

China was also anxious to prevent the establishment of a Greater Vietnam and had also had its own border squabbles with Vietnam. It was aware of the risks of trying to defeat Vietnam decisively in battle but felt that it ought at least to be taught a lesson. Following the invasion of Kampuchea, China launched its own invasion, employing some 33 divisions, on 17 March 1979. By 3 March it had captured the provincial capital of Lang Son. On 16 March it announced that its punitive aims had been met and it was to withdraw to its own boundaries. The Chinese forces did not cover themselves with glory in the invasion. The Vietnamese were well equipped and fighting on excellent defensive terrain. The Chinese were using obsolete equipment and supply lines that soon became stretched; they often resorted to human-wave tactics and suffered severe casualties.

It is not altogether clear that the invasion embarrassed Vietnam and it certainly did not prevent further incidents on the border. However, it did tie down Vietnamese forces in the border area. Vietnam also failed to achieve a decisive victory in Kampuchea. The Khmer Rouge joined up with non-Communist forces and used Thailand (which, if invaded, could well have brought a firm Western response) as a sanctuary. They reclaimed some territory and denied Vietnam a complete victory. This left Vietnam overextended. It is one of the poorest nations and yet its 1 220 000-strong army is the world's fourth largest.

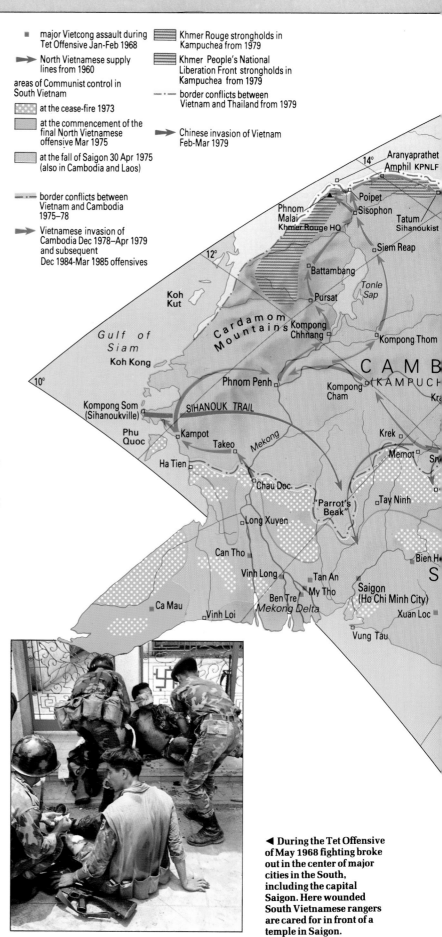

- ■ major Vietcong assault during Tet Offensive Jan-Feb 1968
- ➤ North Vietnamese supply lines from 1960

areas of Communist control in South Vietnam

- ▦ at the cease-fire 1973
- ▦ at the commencement of the final North Vietnamese offensive Mar 1975
- ▦ at the fall of Saigon 30 Apr 1975 (also in Cambodia and Laos)

- —·— border conflicts between Vietnam and Cambodia 1975–78
- ➤ Vietnamese invasion of Cambodia Dec 1978–Apr 1979 and subsequent Dec 1984-Mar 1985 offensives

- ▤ Khmer Rouge strongholds in Kampuchea from 1979
- ▤ Khmer People's National Liberation Front strongholds in Kampuchea from 1979
- —·— border conflicts between Vietnam and Thailand from 1979
- ➤ Chinese invasion of Vietnam Feb-Mar 1979

◄ During the Tet Offensive of May 1968 fighting broke out in the center of major cities in the South, including the capital Saigon. Here wounded South Vietnamese rangers are cared for in front of a temple in Saigon.

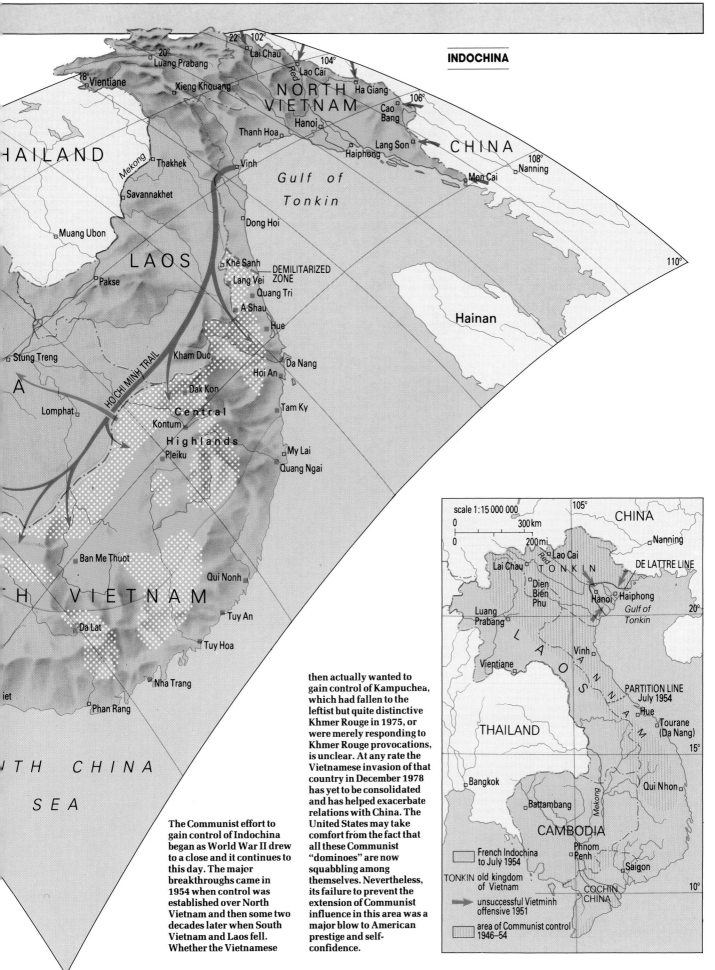

INDOCHINA

The Communist effort to gain control of Indochina began as World War II drew to a close and it continues to this day. The major breakthroughs came in 1954 when control was established over North Vietnam and then some two decades later when South Vietnam and Laos fell. Whether the Vietnamese then actually wanted to gain control of Kampuchea, which had fallen to the leftist but quite distinctive Khmer Rouge in 1975, or were merely responding to Khmer Rouge provocations, is unclear. At any rate the Vietnamese invasion of that country in December 1978 has yet to be consolidated and has helped exacerbate relations with China. The United States may take comfort from the fact that all these Communist "dominoes" are now squabbling among themselves. Nevertheless, its failure to prevent the extension of Communist influence in this area was a major blow to American prestige and self-confidence.

scale 1:15 000 000

| French Indochina to July 1954 |
| TONKIN old kingdom of Vietnam |
| unsuccessful Vietminh offensive 1951 |
| area of Communist control 1946–54 |

151

SOUTH ASIA

■ Since the end of the British Raj in 1947 India and Pakistan have been uneasy neighbors. The differences between the two sides remain but the dismemberment of Pakistan in 1971, with the eastern part forming Bangladesh, swung the regional power balance decisively in India's favor. Pakistan has become more dependent on its relations with the United States and China, while India has hedged its bets by developing close, though by no means intimate, relations with the Soviet Union. The major change in the Soviet position has been the role that it now plays in the old thorn in the side of the Raj — Afghanistan.

The Indo–Pakistan wars

Prior to independence in 1947 relations between India's two largest communities — the Hindus and the Muslims — were so bad that the new state had to be partitioned with the Muslim areas becoming Pakistan. On independence there was a confrontation over the predominantly Islamic Kashmir whose ruler was a Hindu. By the time that a cease-fire had been arranged in January 1949, the bulk of Kashmir was under Indian control. In 1957 it annexed this part of Kashmir.

India's relative position then began to worsen. Pakistan, ostensibly to help keep watch on its Soviet neighbor but with more than an eye on India, went into alliance with the United States. This introduced an awkward superpower dimension into the politics of the region which might otherwise have been absent. Also India's neglect of its armed forces was shown up in October 1962 when Chinese forces overran Indian positions on a disputed border and then, having made their point, unilaterally announced a cease-fire and withdrew.

This emboldened Pakistan which began to assert itself along the disputed border area of Karachi and also the virtually uninhabited Rann of Kutch. Sporadic fighting began in March 1965, but it took off in earnest in August before concluding the next month with a draw.

Indian forces had acquitted themselves well and were beginning to show the benefits of the reforms and expenditure that had been set in motion after the 1962 humiliation. By the time of the next clash in 1971, the Indian army was in even better shape. The cause this time was the tension between the dominant West and the subordinate East of Pakistan. The Bengali East wanted more autonomy and a more conciliatory relationship with India. A repressive response to unrest in the East resulted in immense hardship leading to a flood of refugees into India — over one million from March to December 1970. This gave rise to border tension and serious fighting. The Indian army with the aid of local militias soon defeated West Pakistani forces in the East, thereby creating the new state of Bangladesh, while holding off Pakistani offensives in the West. A longer war might have allowed the Americans to help Pakistan, but the Indian victory was too rapid.

Pakistan was severely weakened as a result.

Its inferiority was confirmed in March 1974 by the test of an Indian "peaceful" nuclear device, which has served as a spur to its own nuclear program. A poor record on human rights led the United States to cut back its military assistance. However, in 1980 Pakistan found itself on the frontline of an East–West confrontation over the Soviet invasion of Afghanistan, which had led to refugees streaming over the border, often to establish bases to mount guerrilla operations against the occupying forces. Pakistan then found the United States more receptive to its requests.

Afghanistan

In April 1978 Communist officers overthrew Afghan President Daud in a bloody coup. He was replaced by Ahmad Taraki. The new regime instituted a program of reform but found it difficult to consolidate its position. In September 1979 President Taraki was replaced by President Amin, but the government was still

▲ Members of the Mukti Bahini, the Bengali resistance, hold prisoner collaborators with the

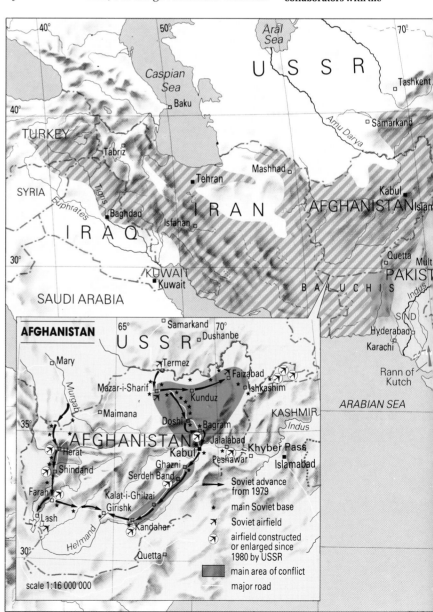

AFGHANISTAN

Soviet advance from 1979

★ main Soviet base

✈ Soviet airfield

✈ airfield constructed or enlarged since 1980 by USSR

main area of conflict

major road

scale 1:16 000 000

unable to cope with guerrilla warfare from Muslim rebels (Mujaheddin) appalled by the arrival of a Communistic government.

The Soviet Union was disturbed by the instability on its border and the possibility of a Marxist regime being toppled by Islamic rebels. On 27 December 1979 it stepped in to take control of the situation. Amin was removed and replaced by the more congenial Babrak Kamal. Some 85 000 Soviet troops moved in with the initial intention of supporting Afghan troops in their anti-guerrilla operations. They soon found themselves taking the brunt of the fighting as the Afghan army melted away. From a strength of 80 000 at the end of 1979 defections and desertions reduced it to some 30 000 by 1983. The Russians became reluctant to arm the Afghan soldiers properly as this was turning into a method of supplying the rebels. They soon contented themselves with maintaining central government and holding on to major towns and the important north–south highway.

The Mujaheddin were kept at bay through search-and-destroy missions.

Soviet troop numbers grew modestly to just over 105 000 by late 1983, by which time losses had risen to some 17 000-20 000 killed or wounded. At the start of 1984 they were increased to 135 000 and Soviet tactics hardened. Increased pressure was put on the civilian population by both direct bombardment and indirect starvation. With equipment limited in quality and quantity the rebel campaign could only be one of patient harassment; they could not muster superior force to dislodge the Russians. The main weaknesses of the Mujaheddin were their own internal dissensions and the gradual depopulation of the countryside. Some three million fled to Pakistan and two million to the cities. It is difficult to see how the Russians are likely to be able to extricate themselves from Afghanistan, as a congenial government could only be sustained by a Soviet garrison.

Pakistan government during the Indian push into East Pakistan in December 1971.

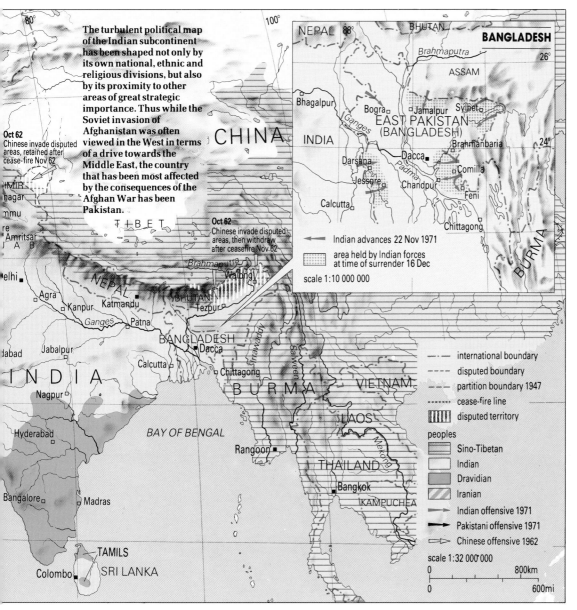

The turbulent political map of the Indian subcontinent has been shaped not only by its own national, ethnic and religious divisions, but also by its proximity to other areas of great strategic importance. Thus while the Soviet invasion of Afghanistan was often viewed in the West in terms of a drive towards the Middle East, the country that has been most affected by the consequences of the Afghan War has been Pakistan.

Oct 62
Chinese invade disputed areas, retained after cease-fire Nov 62

Oct 62
Chinese invade disputed areas, then withdraw after ceasefire Nov 62

Indian advances 22 Nov 1971

area held by Indian forces at time of surrender 16 Dec

scale 1:10 000 000

international boundary
disputed boundary
partition boundary 1947
cease-fire line
disputed territory

peoples
Sino-Tibetan
Indian
Dravidian
Iranian

Indian offensive 1971
Pakistani offensive 1971
Chinese offensive 1962

scale 1:32 000 000
0   800km
0   600mi

DIARY: INDO–PAKISTAN WAR OF 1971

3 December Ineffective Pakistani air strike against Jammu and Kashmir, followed by ground offensive.

4 December India invades East Pakistan with 160 000 troops. Moves forward on more than 20 salients avoiding direct confrontation with 73 000 Pakistani troops and disrupting their communications. Air superiority achieved at outset by destroying Pakistani air force's only jet runway. Indian navy blockades sea exits. Pakistani counterattack in west. Stalemate develops despite fierce fighting.

6 December India recognizes independence of Bangladesh.

10 December India crosses Meghna river. Dacca under siege.

16 December Pakistan commander surrenders at Dacca.

17 December President Yahya Khan of Pakistan agrees to cease-fire. Later resigns.

THE MIDDLE EAST

■ We noted earlier the assumption of many in the West that the Soviet Union entered Afghanistan for reasons more to do with the Gulf than Afghanistan itself (p. 36). This assumption said more about a Western sense of vulnerability than Soviet aspirations. The strategic importance to the West of the Middle East is a consequence not only of its oil reserves but also of its position as a meeting point of the European, Asian and African continents. It also contains holy places for three of the world's great religions — Judaism, Christianity and Islam. Many of these are concentrated in what was once called Palestine and is now known as Israel — "the much-too-promised land."

The state of Israel has been at the center of most, but not all, of the major wars that have rocked the region over the past decade. Another feature has been the decline of British influence in the area. Apart from Israel itself the only country which actually battled for its independence from Britain was Aden (now South Yemen). A guerrilla campaign began in 1963 building up to a peak in 1967 when Britain granted independence. Britain's influence was largely based on a series of protectorates. Association with Britain became a severe disadvantage for the conservative forces in the area after the Suez debacle of 1956. In the end the cost of maintaining military bases undermined Britain's will to continue. The final withdrawal from "East of Suez" was completed in 1971. However, the British still maintained good connections with a number of states. For example, informal help was provided to the sultan of Oman (as it was also by Jordan and Iran) in his fight against left-wing rebels in the province of Dhofar. The rebels were defeated by 1975.

Radical forces took advantage of the British decline — in Egypt, Libya and Iraq in particular — and this helped draw the Soviet Union into the area. It forged links with a number of Arab countries, in the process generating considerable anxiety in the West. Despite providing a great amount of practical and diplomatic support to the Arab side in the later wars against Israel, it never succeeded in consolidating its position. The most dramatic break came with Egypt. After investing substantial resources in the country since the early 1950s, the Russians were expelled in the early 1970s. Even though they still maintain strong links with the radical elements in the Middle East, their influence has remained limited, particularly when the radicals start arguing among themselves.

In more recent times the major source of radicalism has been not leftist Arab nationalism but Islamic fundamentalism. This made itself felt most dramatically in 1979 when the shah of Iran was overthrown and the Ayatollah Khomeini took over. Islamic fundamentalism tends to be hostile to the West and Western ways, and this has forced other Arab countries vulnerable to this movement to reassess their pattern of economic development. However, the Soviet Union has failed to benefit from this

► Lebanon has become the major victim of the Arab–Israeli conflict. Its delicate internal balance between Muslims and Christians was disrupted by the influx of Palestinians after they had been expelled from Jordan in 1970. Lebanon was too weak to resist this influx or to respond decisively when Israel began to bomb targets in Lebanon in retaliation against attacks launched on its territory by the Palestine Liberation Organization (PLO). Eventually the strain became too much and the country turned in on itself in a bitter civil war and provided an opportunity for its more powerful neighbors — Syria and Israel — to meddle directly.

Both Iran, in 1954, and Egypt, in 1956, alarmed Britain by nationalizing vital assets — the oil and Suez Canal companies respectively. With American help Britain successfully and covertly ensured a more congenial regime in Iran; with France, it failed overtly to achieve the same result in Egypt. Thereafter Iran was recognized as a friend to the West while Egypt was troublesome. Now Egypt has mended its fences while Iran has become a source of instability. The other Gulf states have supported Iraq in the war since 1980.

LEBANON UNDER OCCUPATION FEB 1984

Druze and Shia Muslim militias

Lebanese army and Phalangist militia

Syrian

Israeli

religious areas

Shia Muslim

Sunni Muslim

Druze

Maronite Christian

road

Sidon

AWALI LINE

ISRAELI WITHDRAWAL PHASE 1 (FEB 85)

Jez

ISRAELI-OC

Khalde

Damour

Baa

MEDITERRANEAN SEA

Nabatea

Marjayoun

Zrariye

Litani

Beaufort C

Tyre

ISRAELI WITHDRAWAL PHASE 3 (SEPT 85)

UNIFIL (UN forces)

Qiryat Shemona

HADDAD CHRISTIAN MILITIA

B

Sabra and Cha refugee camps

US warships offshore

►US

AIRPORT

ISRAEL

multinational peacekeeping force

Chouefat

Khalde

Souk el

40°

Ankara

TURKEY

GREEKS

Caspian Sea

CYPRUS

SYRIA

Euphrates

KURDS

Tehran

Nicosia

LEBANON

Baghdad

IRAN

AFGHANI-STAN

MEDITERRANEAN SEA

Beirut

Damascus

Tigris

Suez Canal

Alexandria

ISRAEL

Amman

IRAQ

Isfahan

Benghazi

Jerusalem

Sinai

JORDAN

KUWAIT

Cairo

see p159

Kuwait

Persian Gulf

Bandar Abbas

Str of Hormuz

LIBYA

EGYPT

SAUDI ARABIA

Riyadh

BAHRAIN

QATAR

to Oman

Gulf of Oman

UNITED ARAB EMIRATES

Abu Dhabi

Muscat

RED

Mecca

OMAN

ARABIAN SEA

20°

Jedda

Nile

SEA

60°

SUDAN

YEMEN

SOUTH YEMEN

Khartoum

Sana

peoples of the Middle East

Djibouti

Aden

Gulf of Aden

Semitic and Hamitic

scale 1:48 000 000

ETHIOPIA

SOMALIA

Iranian

0   800km

0   500mi

Addis Abeba

40°

50°

Turco-Tatar

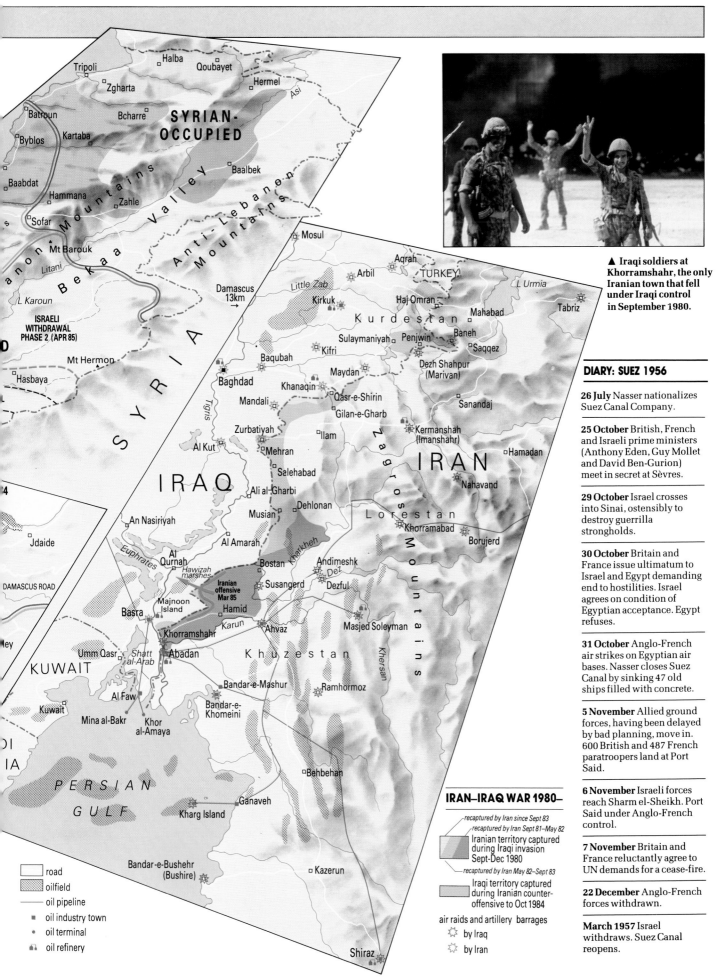

Tripoli
Halba
Qoubayet
Zgharta
Hermel
Batroun
Bcharre
SYRIAN-
OCCUPIED
Byblos
Kartaba
Baabdat
Baalbek
Hammana
Zahle
Sofar
Mt Barouk
Litani
L Karoun
Damascus
13km
→
ISRAELI
WITHDRAWAL
PHASE 2 (APR 85)
Mt Hermon
Hasbaya

Mosul
Aqrah
Arbil
TURKEY
L Urmia
Little Zab
Kirkuk
Haj-Omran
Mahabad
Tabriz
Kurdestan
Sulaymaniyah
Penjwin
Baneh
Saqqez
Kifri
Dezh Shahpur
(Marivan)
Baqubah
Maydan
Sanandaj
Baghdad
Khanaqin
Qasr-e-Shirin
Mandali
Gilan-e-Gharb
Kermanshah
(Imanshahr)
Zurbatiyah
Ilam
Hamadan
Al Kut
Mehran
IRAQ
Salehabad
Nahavand
Ali al-Gharbi
Dehlonan
Lorestan
Musian
Khorramabad
An Nasiriyah
Al Amarah
Borujerd
Jdaide
Al
Qurnah
Euphrates
Hawizah
marshes
Bostan
Andimeshk
Dez
Kharkheh
Iranian
offensive
Mar 85
Susangerd
Dezful
DAMASCUS ROAD
Majnoon
Island
Hamid
Masjed Soleyman
Basra
Karun
Ahvaz
Khorramshahr
Khuzestan
Umm Qasr
Shatt
al-Arab
Abadan
KUWAIT
Bandar-e-Mashur
Ramhormoz
Kuwait
Al Faw
Bandar-e-
Khomeini
Mina al-Bakr
Khor
al-Amaya
PERSIAN
Behbehan
GULF
Ganaveh
Kharg Island
Bandar-e-Bushehr
(Bushire)
Kazerun
Shiraz

IRAN
Zagros Mountains
SYRIA
Tigris
Kersan

▲ Iraqi soldiers at
Khorramshahr, the only
Iranian town that fell
under Iraqi control
in September 1980.

DIARY: SUEZ 1956

26 July Nasser nationalizes
Suez Canal Company.

25 October British, French
and Israeli prime ministers
(Anthony Eden, Guy Mollet
and David Ben-Gurion)
meet in secret at Sèvres.

29 October Israel crosses
into Sinai, ostensibly to
destroy guerrilla
strongholds.

30 October Britain and
France issue ultimatum to
Israel and Egypt demanding
end to hostilities. Israel
agrees on condition of
Egyptian acceptance. Egypt
refuses.

31 October Anglo-French
air strikes on Egyptian air
bases. Nasser closes Suez
Canal by sinking 47 old
ships filled with concrete.

5 November Allied ground
forces, having been delayed
by bad planning, move in.
600 British and 487 French
paratroopers land at Port
Said.

6 November Israeli forces
reach Sharm el-Sheikh. Port
Said under Anglo-French
control.

7 November Britain and
France reluctantly agree to
UN demands for a cease-fire.

22 December Anglo-French
forces withdrawn.

March 1957 Israel
withdraws. Suez Canal
reopens.

IRAN–IRAQ WAR 1980–

recaptured by Iran since Sept 83
recaptured by Iran Sept 81–May 82
Iranian territory captured
during Iraqi invasion
Sept–Dec 1980
recaptured by Iran May 82–Sept 83
Iraqi territory captured
during Iranian counter-
offensive to Oct 1984
air raids and artillery barrages
✿ by Iraq
✿ by Iran

road
oilfield
oil pipeline
■ oil industry town
● oil terminal
🏭 oil refinery

THE MIDDLE EAST (continued)

change. Iran, appalled by the treatment of fellow Muslims in Afghanistan, has been as hostile to the Soviet Union as to the United States.

The Arab–Israeli wars

1948–49

Palestine was one of the territories Britain controlled under first a League of Nations, and then a United Nations, mandate after the collapse of the Ottoman empire at the end of World War I. Since the Balfour Declaration of 1916 there had been a presumption by Jews that Palestine would become their homeland, and the experience of Nazi persecution added to the desire to return to Zion. However, the Arabs who already lived in the area resented the Jewish immigration and resisted the establishment of a Jewish state. After a fierce guerrilla campaign Britain decided to withdraw. Israel became the first and only country to be created by a decision of the United Nations. The decision called for partition with Jewish and Arab areas designated.

Fighting had broken out between Jewish and Arab partisans prior to the ending of the mandate. When the new state of Israel finally came into being on 13 May 1948, over 30 000 Arab troops from five different countries attacked at once. The 15 000-strong Israeli defense force had to fight on three fronts and was ill-equipped, but it made up for this with improvisation and skillful tactics, depending a lot on mobility and surprise. Setting the pattern for the future wars, this one was fought under pressure from the UN for a cease-fire. Armistice agreements were reached in July 1949. Also setting a pattern for the future, Israel not only managed to avoid elimination but used the war to expand.

1956

The hostility felt by the Arab world to the Jewish state meant that Israel could not feel secure. It came to depend on the quality and vigilance of its armed forces. In 1956 it saw an opportunity to draw on outside support to assert its position vis-à-vis its neighbors as a result of the dispute that Egypt was having with Britain and France. France was annoyed by the Egyptian leader Nasser's support for the rebels in Algeria (see p. 160). Britain was angry at Nasser's nationalization of the Suez Canal Company upon which both European countries depended. British troops had only left the Suez Canal Zone in June 1956 after 74 years in occupation as a result of an agreement reached with Nasser in 1954 when he had come to power after a coup.

The nationalization of the Suez Canal Company in July 1956, which Britain and France considered illegal, was followed by intense diplomatic efforts to resolve the crisis before the two aggrieved parties decided secretly to solve the matter by force of arms. The intention was to use an Egyptian–Israeli war as a pretext for regaining control of the canal.

However, the eventual military operation was mismanaged and allowed time for international pressure, especially from the United States, to force the European countries to withdraw. Israeli forces were successful but also had to withdraw, only gaining in return a UN Emergency Force to watch over the border with Egypt and to supervise the Strait of Tiran which led to Israel's Red Sea port of Eilat. The main victor was Nasser who had lost the military battle but, with the colonialists humiliated, had won the political war.

1967

There was an uneasy peace for a decade as both sides built up their forces. Within the Arab world there was a desire to renew the pressure on Israel and, while Nasser might not have actually wanted a war, the actions he took in May 1967 eventually gave Israel little choice but to go on to the offensive. Although, as it turned out, discretion in this case would have been the better part of valor, the sense of strength in the Arab world led Jordan, Syria and Iraq to join with Egypt. Largely as a result of the decimation of Arab air power on the first day of the war, the

▲ British personnel inspect the *Exodus 1947* after it had reached Haifa with 4500 immigrants aboard.

▼ Israeli troops watching
and waiting in the Sinai
desert during the October
1973 Arab–Israeli War.

Israeli forces moved rapidly to occupy the
Sinai, then forced the Jordanians off their
territory on the West Bank of the river Jordan,
putting all of Jerusalem into Israeli hands, and
finally, successfully beating the UN cease-fire,
they took the Golan Heights from Syria. Israeli
settlements had been shelled from the Heights
prior to hostilities. Israel had lost 800 dead,
compared with Egypt's losses of some 10 000.
This time the Israelis did not hand over any of
the territory seized during the campaigns. This
offered more secure borders but also a major
headache in the control of the large Arab
population of the West Bank. The completeness
of the Israeli triumph increased the frustration
and bitterness in the Arab world.

1973
The major powers started making demands for a
permanent settlement of the dispute, largely
based then, as they still are now, on Israeli
withdrawal from the territories occupied in
1967 in return for Arab recognition of the state
of Israel. Neither side was prepared to make the
requisite concessions. The Palestinian Arabs,
many still languishing in the refugee camps
established in the late 1940s, and represented
by the Palestine Liberation Organization (PLO),
turned increasingly to guerrilla warfare and also
to international terrorism to draw attention to
their cause. This campaign, and the Israeli
reprisals that tended to follow individual
operations, led to tensions within the Arab
world. Jordan especially became annoyed with
the increasing PLO presence and King Hussein
grew nervous about their influence. In
September 1970 he took action against the PLO
which was expelled from Jordan.

There was some military action from 1969 to
1970 which became known as the war of
attrition. Israel began to construct a defensive
line (known as the Bar-Lev line) along the Suez
Canal. Egypt attempted to impede the
construction by means of commando raids and
artillery bombardments which in turn led to
Israeli air raids against targets such as air bases
and anti-air-missile complexes.

In September 1970 Nasser died and was
succeeded by Anwar Sadat who saw the only
possibility of retrieving the lost territory to be in
administering at least a military shock to Israel
and improving Arab links with the United
States, which was the only country that could
act as a mediator. Arab planning this time was
much more meticulous and cautious than it had
been in the previous wars. Although Israel
noticed Syrian and Egyptian preparations, it
took time before it accepted that these were
serious. The Israeli government, nervous of
international reaction and the cost of regular
mobilizations, did not respond in time and for
once the Arabs achieved the advantage of
surprise.

Some of the most ferocious initial fighting
was on the Golan Heights, with Israel only just
managing to push back a determined Syrian
offensive. Eventually they managed to move to
within 32 kilometers (20 miles) of the Syrian

capital of Damascus. In the Sinai the Egyptians,
after a well-executed crossing of the canal and
penetration of the Bar-Lev line, were too
respectful of Israeli air power to move far ahead
of the cover provided by defensive missiles and
so failed to exploit their advantage. By the time
they were ready to do so, the Israelis had sorted
themselves out, the American resupply effort
was getting under way (see p. 63), and they were
able to counterattack. A small Israeli tank unit
managed to cross the canal to prepare the way
for a full army brigade which eventually
surrounded the Egyptian 3rd Army.

Israel lost 2500 men; Syria and Egypt about
8000 each. Both sides lost half their tanks. Egypt
and Syria lost 250 aircraft out of about 800;
Israel 115 out of 500. Unlike the previous wars,
this one did at least loosen up the diplomatic
situation. The "shuttle diplomacy" of US
Secretary of State Henry Kissinger resulted in
modest withdrawals by both sides and a
renewed linkage between the Arab world and
the West, encouraged by an awareness of the
"oil weapon" that was now a prominent part of
the Arab armory.

1982
In the aftermath of the Yom Kippur War the
politics of the Middle East began to change
dramatically. President Sadat moved to break
the diplomatic deadlock. In 1975 he entered
into a formal agreement with Israel to regain
control of the useful parts of the Sinai and to
enable the Suez Canal to be reopened. In 1977 in
a dramatic gesture he invited himself to Israel
and set in motion a peace process which
concluded with the 1978 "Camp David"
agreements. This led to diplomatic relations
between Egypt and Israel but, because the latter
had been unyielding on the question of the West
Bank, other Arabs considered it a sellout and
Egypt was left isolated.

The guerrilla campaign against Israel
continued, causing more disruption to the
PLO's hosts than to Israel. This was particularly
true in Lebanon which was already a deeply
divided country. The two dominant groups —
the Christians and Muslims — were themselves
split into a bewildering array of factions.
Lebanon had attempted to survive by staying
out of trouble (participating only in the 1948–49
war) and keeping good relations with the West.
Some of the Maronite Christians developed
close relations with Israel.

When the PLO moved into Lebanon in 1970,
after it had been pushed out of Jordan, the
Lebanese were unable to resist, though they
then suffered from Israeli reprisals after PLO
operations. In 1975 a civil war began which
only in 1984 began to draw to a close. Syria used
the conflict to establish a stronghold in Lebanon
and was not above deserting the Muslims in
order to prevent Lebanon turning into a PLO
state. As the civil war continued in the south,
the Israelis lent their support to the Christian
Phalangists. In March 1978 the Israelis mounted
an invasion of Lebanon using some 20 000
troops. The somewhat indiscriminate character

THE MIDDLE EAST (continued)

of the Israeli attack put it under severe international pressure. Eventually it withdrew in return for a UN peacekeeping force to act as a buffer between it and Lebanon.

The UN force was not completely successful in preventing PLO infiltrators from attacking Israeli settlements in Galilee. On 5 June 1982, using the pretext of the attempted assassination of the Israeli ambassador in London, Israeli forces moved into Lebanon, pushing the UN forces aside. Although the initial aim was to establish a limited security zone, the temptation to smash the PLO as a military entity became too great.

Syrian air defenses in the Bekaa valley were destroyed and Syrian aircraft proved no match for those of Israel in dogfights. This enabled the air force to provide close support to ground forces which moved up the Lebanese coast against PLO resistance. Syrian armor was defeated in a tank battle around Lake Karoun on 11 June. By that day Israeli forces had encircled Beirut, where 7000 PLO fighters and some from Syrian and other Lebanese Muslim factions were trapped. After intensive diplomacy in August the PLO agreed to be evacuated from Beirut to outside Lebanon and they eventually left in September. A multinational force was to be established to keep the peace until the Lebanese army could be reconstituted. Crucial to the success of any deal was the relaxation of civil conflict and the Islamic population feeling assured that they would not be victimized in the absence of the PLO.

The murder of President-elect Basir Gemayel made that impossible. The Christian reprisal was a massacre of Palestinians in the refugee camps at Sabra and Chatilah which the Israelis failed to prevent or indeed to stop — leading to an international outcry and a political crisis in Israel. A US-sponsored agreement of May 1983 envisaged Israeli withdrawal from Lebanon in return for "normalization" of relations between the two countries, but that depended on Syrian and Muslim compliance which was not forthcoming. This made national reconciliation impossible and the civil war broke out again, with the multinational force (US, France, Italy and Britain) caught in the middle. The government began to collapse and in early February, after the American and French had suffered severe casualties, the multinational force was withdrawn. President Amin Gemayel (Basir's brother) could only maintain his position by abandoning the May 1983 agreement. This helped to calm the situation, though it meant that Israel's gains from the enterprise were very limited. Israel's forces continued to occupy Lebanese territory south of the Awali and still suffered at the hands of local terrorists. As they began to withdraw in 1985, they left behind a much more hostile and divided population than they had found on arrival, with President Gemayel now dependent on the Syrians.

Iran–Iraq War
Tensions between Iraq and Iran are of long

standing. From 1961 to 1975 the conservative shah of Iran sought to make life difficult for radical Iraq by supporting Kurds who were seeking to achieve self-determination. In 1975 the two signed the Treaty of Baghdad, by which, in return for Iran abandoning the Kurds, Iraq abandoned its claims to the Shatt al-Arab waterways and the Abu Musa and Tamb islands which lie close to the Strait of Hormuz.

In 1980, with the shah gone and Iran in tumult, Iraqi leader Saddam Hussain saw the opportunity to abandon the Treaty of Baghdad and also prevent any attempts to export the Shia revolution from Iran to Iraq. On 17 September he renounced the treaty. There then followed four days of artillery bombardment, concluding with air attacks against 10 Iranian airfields. Iraqi forces crossed into Iran where they soon occupied large areas of land. However, the Iraqis had underestimated the residual strength of the Iranian army and overestimated the disaffection of the local population from Tehran. They also allowed themselves to be distracted by laying siege to the cities of Khorramshahr and Abadan (critical to Iranian oil production) instead of pressing forward further into Iran. By the time the autumn rains came the offensive had run out of steam. Hussein offered a cease-fire which Iran rejected.

With three times the population and twice as many men under arms (though with inferior equipment) Iran began to move onto the offensive with its own declared aim of toppling Hussein. The first counterattack in January 1981 failed, but by September the siege at Abadan had been lifted. In March 1982 an Iranian offensive with some 100 000 men at the Dezful sector broke through and pushed the Iraqis back with heavy casualties. By September Khorramshahr had been recaptured, but as the offensive was carried into Iraqi territory the advantages of defending home terrain started to tell. The Iranians put pressure on Basra.

Early in 1984 the Iranians mustered some half-million men, many young, improperly trained and badly equipped, for a "death blow" to Iraq. Iraqi forces held off the first "human-wave" assaults, employing at one point chemical weapons. As the year went on, it appeared that the Iranians had recognized their weaknesses and were adopting more cautious tactics. Up to this point it seemed that Iraq's only hope was in attacking Iran's oil exports. Iraq's own exports had been severely disrupted by Syria's action of cutting one of the two oil pipelines out of Iraq. The possibility was raised on delivery of some French *Super-Etendard* aircraft in October 1983 of mounting an attack on the oil installations at Kharg Island. The likely Iranian response was to attempt to cut off the Strait of Hormuz to all oil traffic. Apart from some attacks on shipping, neither side took such a drastic step. In 1985, after the failure of yet another Iranian offensive, Iraq, now enjoying greater success in obtaining arms supplies, was more secure in its position but unable to obtain a satisfactory settlement. In frustration it began to hit civilian targets.

The Arab–Israeli wars have been distinctive for their speed and decisiveness. With its armed strength dependent on the mobilization of a large proportion of its civilian population, Israel would find a long war a great economic and social strain (as has been shown to a limited extent by its intervention in Lebanon). Given time, Israel's enemies could mobilize superior strength and force Israel on to the defensive on two or more fronts. Hence the need for quick knockout blows and the reluctance to wait to discover the enemy's true intentions. Thus in May 1967, when Egypt moved 100 000 troops close to Israel, demanded and received the removal of the UN Emergency Force and blockaded the Gulf of Aqaba, Israel felt obliged to act. The 1967 war demonstrated the strategic benefits of preemption; the 1973 war the potential strategic costs of allowing the enemy to seize the initiative.

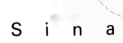

S i n a

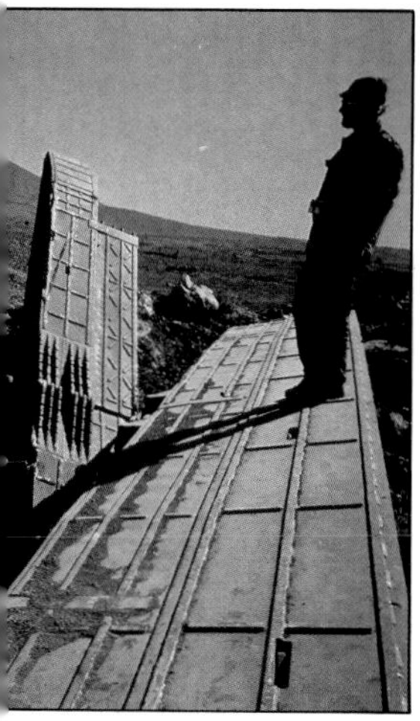

▲ **The aftermath of war. A soldier surveys the wreckage of destroyed tanks in the Sinai in October 1973.**

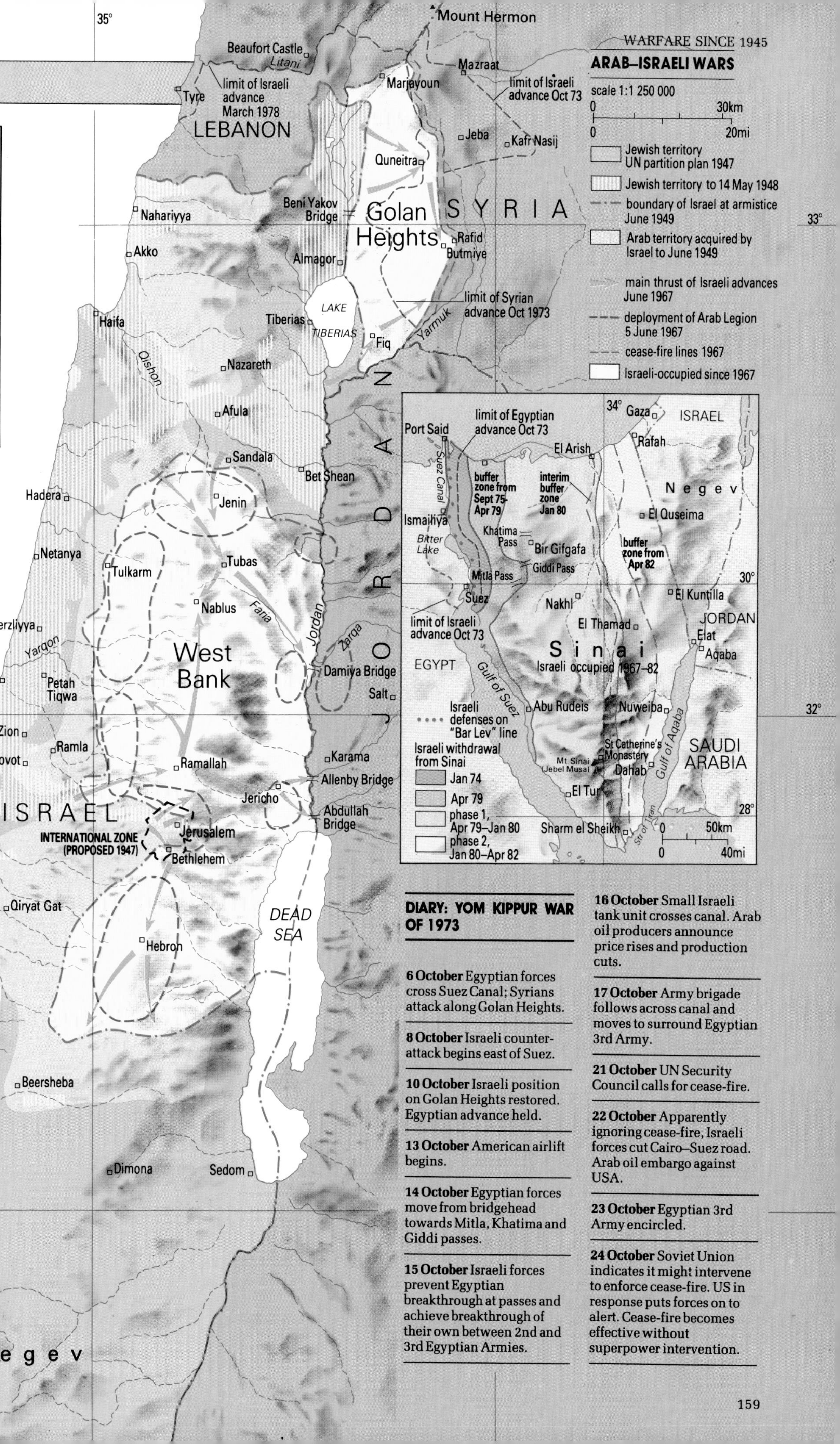

ARAB–ISRAELI WARS
scale 1:1 250 000
0 30km
0 20mi
Jewish territory UN partition plan 1947
Jewish territory to 14 May 1948
boundary of Israel at armistice June 1949
Arab territory acquired by Israel to June 1949
main thrust of Israeli advances June 1967
deployment of Arab Legion 5 June 1967
cease-fire lines 1967
Israeli-occupied since 1967
35°
33°
32°
Mount Hermon
Beaufort Castle
Litani
limit of Israeli advance March 1978
Tyre
LEBANON
Mazraat
Marjayoun
limit of Israeli advance Oct 73
Jeba
Kafr Nasij
Quneitra
SYRIA
Nahariyya
Beni Yakov Bridge
Golan Heights
Rafid
Butmiye
Akko
Almagor
Haifa
Tiberias
LAKE TIBERIAS
Fiq
Yarmuk
limit of Syrian advance Oct 1973
Qishon
Nazareth
Afula
Sandala
Bet Shean
Hadera
Jenin
MEDITERRANEAN SEA
Netanya
Tulkarm
Tubas
Nablus
Faria
Jordan
Herzliyya
Yarqon
Zarqa
West Bank
Tel Aviv
Petah Tiqwa
Damiya Bridge
Salt
JORDAN
Rishon le Zion
Ramla
Rehovot
Ramallah
Karama
Allenby Bridge
Jericho
Abdullah Bridge
Ashdod
ISRAEL
INTERNATIONAL ZONE (PROPOSED 1947)
Jerusalem
Bethlehem
Qiryat Malakhi
Ashqelon
Qiryat Gat
DEAD SEA
Hebron
Gaza
Gaza Strip
Khan Yunis
Besor
Beersheba
Dimona
Sedom
Negev
34°
Gaza
ISRAEL
Port Said
limit of Egyptian advance Oct 73
El Arish
Rafah
Suez Canal
buffer zone from Sept 75–Apr 79
interim buffer zone Jan 80
Negev
Ismailiya
El Quseima
Bitter Lake
Khatima Pass
Bir Gifgafa
buffer zone from Apr 82
Giddi Pass
Mitla Pass
30°
Suez
Nakhl
El Kuntilla
limit of Israeli advance Oct 73
El Thamad
JORDAN
Elat
Aqaba
EGYPT
Sinai
Israeli occupied 1967–82
Gulf of Suez
Israeli defenses on "Bar Lev" line
Abu Rudeis
Nuweiba
Gulf of Aqaba
Israeli withdrawal from Sinai
Jan 74
Apr 79
phase 1, Apr 79–Jan 80
phase 2, Jan 80–Apr 82
St Catherine's Monastery
Mt Sinai (Jebel Musa)
Dahab
SAUDI ARABIA
El Tur
28°
Sharm el Sheikh
Str of Tiran
0 50km
0 40mi

DIARY: YOM KIPPUR WAR OF 1973

6 October Egyptian forces cross Suez Canal; Syrians attack along Golan Heights.

8 October Israeli counter-attack begins east of Suez.

10 October Israeli position on Golan Heights restored. Egyptian advance held.

13 October American airlift begins.

14 October Egyptian forces move from bridgehead towards Mitla, Khatima and Giddi passes.

15 October Israeli forces prevent Egyptian breakthrough at passes and achieve breakthrough of their own between 2nd and 3rd Egyptian Armies.

16 October Small Israeli tank unit crosses canal. Arab oil producers announce price rises and production cuts.

17 October Army brigade follows across canal and moves to surround Egyptian 3rd Army.

21 October UN Security Council calls for cease-fire.

22 October Apparently ignoring cease-fire, Israeli forces cut Cairo–Suez road. Arab oil embargo against USA.

23 October Egyptian 3rd Army encircled.

24 October Soviet Union indicates it might intervene to enforce cease-fire. US in response puts forces on to alert. Cease-fire becomes effective without superpower intervention.

AFRICA

■ Africa was the most colonized continent and the least prepared for independence, with arbitrary boundaries that had been designed for colonial convenience and often took little account of ethnic differences or economic viability. As Britain, France, Belgium and finally Portugal dispensed with their empires, the continent entered into a tumultuous period. With some exceptions, most notably in Algeria, the achievement of independence was less bloody than the civil wars which followed.

The anticolonial wars

Algeria
The campaign for Algerian independence had begun in the 1940s but only took a serious military turn in 1954 when the Front de Libération Nationale (FLN) began a guerrilla

campaign. French troops were moved in to quell the revolutionary forces, receiving the firm backing of the European settlers, some million and a half in number, who preferred the official policy of integration with France. Using Tunisia as a base, the guerrillas presented a formidable challenge. Some 425 000 French troops were eventually garrisoned in the country and it proved necessary to adopt some drastic measures, including the "Morice Line" along the Tunisian border, designed to keep out insurgents by means of electric fencing, barbed wire and minefields. The conduct of both sides left much to be desired and there were many atrocities. The ruthlessness of the settlers and the French army in Algeria led to tensions with the mainland. In 1958 a revolt by officers in Algeria led to the collapse of the French government and Charles de Gaulle's rise to

power as the first president of the Fifth Republic. This mollified the settlers until they realized that de Gaulle was prepared to negotiate a settlement with the FLN. This led to the formation of a terrorist organization, OAS, and an army mutiny in April 1961 headed by General Salan. Eventually a cease-fire came in July 1962 with the promise of an independent state. As Algeria became independent, some 1 380 000 Europeans left the country and only 30 000 stayed behind. Some 17 500 French soldiers had lost their lives in the struggle along with over 3000 European civilians. Estimates of the number of Algerian Muslims who lost their lives range from 300 000 to one million.

Kenya
The only serious military problem that faced Britain during the decolonization was with Kenya. As tension mounted between the European settlers and the Kenya African Union, led by Jomo Kenyatta, members of the Kikuyu tribe formed the Mau Mau secret society. In 1952 the Mau Mau began a campaign of riots and murders. A declaration of a state of emergency in October 1952 was followed by imprisonment of a number of known and suspected Mau Mau leaders including Kenyatta. Once the security forces had got themselves organized, most of the Kikuyu tribe were screened and tough measures were taken against the terrorists (of whom some 10 000 were killed). By the end of 1955 the tide was turning and in 1956 the rebellion was all but over. The main victims of Mau Mau violence had been other Africans, of whom almost 2000 were killed compared with 32 Europeans. Without any outside support and confined to one tribe, the Mau Mau never had much chance of success. Nevertheless, it took 10 000 British and African troops, 21 000 police and 25 000 home guard four years to defeat them, so warning the British government of the costs of resisting the "winds of change" in Africa. Kenyatta was not released from prison until 1961 and he led his country to independence two years later.

Rhodesia
In 1965 the British might have used force to quell another rebellion when the white settlers of Southern Rhodesia, under pressure to accept black-majority rule, declared independence. Military action was ruled out because of logistical problems and because of a concern that the forces might not take on European rebels with the necessary sense of commitment. Economic sanctions were used instead which proved to be ineffective. In the end it was the development of guerrilla warfare within Rhodesia, which towards the end became quite vicious, which led to the collapse of white-

minority rule and the creation of the new state of Zimbabwe in 1980.

The Portuguese colonies
It was the Portuguese who resisted the winds of change most doggedly. Fighting broke out in Angola in 1961, in Portuguese Guinea in 1963 and in Mozambique in 1965. By the time the wars were brought to a close by the overthrow of the Caetano government in a coup in Lisbon, estimates suggest that Portugal had some 33 000 troops in Guinea, 70 000 in Angola and 65 000 in Mozambique. Of this total of 168 000 just less than half were white. Estimates also suggest that the colonial wars were responsible for 13 000 Portuguese dead and 65 000 wounded.

South Africa
South Africa is now the remaining symbol of European rule of the continent. The white regime in Pretoria has had to face guerrilla and terrorist campaigns but has so far been able to cope. More difficult have been the activities of the South West African People's Organization (SWAPO) which has caused problems in Namibia, a territory administered by South Africa and about which independence negotiations have been under way for some time. When Angola became independent, SWAPO was able to use it as a base. This, as we shall see below, led South Africa to begin asserting its superior military strength around the region with a subtle blend of economic and military sticks and carrots.

The civil wars
A number of African states settled down after independence to tackle the problems of economic development in reasonably stable political conditions. Many did not. Often the instability took the form of one faction replacing another by means of a coup d'état with only slight consequences for the everyday life of the people. For example, in the two decades from 1960 Benin had six coups and 10 heads of state. In a number of states, especially those with an unstable tribal balance, civil wars resulted, some of them leading to immense loss of life. In Burundi in the early 1970s up to 100 000 members of the Hutu were estimated to have been killed by members of the ruling Tutsi after a Hutu revolt. The generally low level of military development of those fighting often means that external intervention, sometimes on quite a small scale, can make a significant difference.

Congo/Zaïre
One of the first post-independence civil wars was in the former Belgian Congo. The United Nations became heavily involved in this to the tune of 200 000 troops. The first post-independence leader, Patrice Lumumba, was murdered after a 1960 coup led by Colonel Joseph Mobutu, Army Chief of Staff. He took until 1965 to defeat the Katanga-based rebels and then changed the country's name to Zaïre, signifying a fresh start. However, the problems

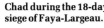

▲ A French DC-4 shot down in March 1978 in Chad during the 18-day siege of Faya-Largeau.

◀ Two French soldiers in Algeria with the bodies of FLN guerrillas shot during a major push by the French army in 1956.

AFRICA (continued)

of Katanga (now renamed Shaba province) remained. In 1977 and 1978 Mobutu had to cope with two insurgencies by Shaba dissidents aided by neighboring Angola. In 1977 they advanced on the town of Kolwezi. The response of the Zaïre army was somewhat feeble. It required the arrival of 1500 Moroccan troops to put the rebels to flight. In 1978 a rebel force of some 3000 claiming to be the Congolese National Liberation Front succeeded in capturing Kolwezi and massacred some 200 Europeans and 500 Africans. This time it was the French Foreign Legion which came to help, followed a few days later by Belgian paratroopers. They helped to eject the rebels. The European forces were replaced by contingents of sympathetic African troops, largely from other Francophone states.

Nigeria
In May 1967 the Ibo tribe of Nigeria's Eastern region declared a Republic of Biafra under the leadership of Colonel Odumegwu Ojukwu. This followed the murder of 10 000 to 30 000 Easterners in the north and reflected a lack of confidence in the ability of the new Nigerian leader General Yakubu Gowon to restore national unity. The federal government immediately blockaded Port Harcourt and claimed to have defeated the Biafrans in an early battle at Nsukka. However, the Biafrans fought back skillfully and made gains in the mid-west of the country. Britain and the Soviet Union supported the federal government, with a number of Francophone states supporting Biafra.

In May 1968 Port Harcourt was seized and the federal forces were able to capture the whole coastline. Biafran-held territory shrank. The headquarters were moved to Owerri. Having already been lost and recaptured, Owerri finally fell on 11 January 1970. A few days later Biafran forces surrendered, defeated by lack of food as much as by military capability.

Chad
One of the most confusing and complex of all civil wars is that which has been under way in Chad since that country gained independence from France in 1968. Almost immediately there was a revolt by the Muslim north organized by FROLINAT and supported by Libya against the ruling Christian south and west supported by France. France kept on trying to reduce its involvement but was forced to reenter the fray in 1975 when the situation deteriorated. FROLINAT held most of the north, and the new leader of the government, General Malloum, who had recently come to power after a coup, was just holding a line in the middle of the country.

FROLINAT split into a moderate faction under Hissène Habbré and a militant one under Goukouni Oueddi. In July 1978 an agreement was made between Malloum and Habbré to forge a government of national unity, which was opposed by Goukouni. When Habbré fell out with Malloum, there was a move to bring him

together again with Goukouni. This was opposed not only by Malloum but also by Colonel Gaddafi of Libya who somewhat cynically even supported Malloum before launching an invasion of his own with 2500 regular troops.

Goukouni eventually split with Habbré claiming an attempt to overthrow him with French support. He returned to the Libyan fold, and the two leaders began to fight it out for control of the country. The war hotted up in February 1983 when the forces of President Habbré began a campaign to wrest the Aozou strip, bordering Libya, from Libyan forces. They were forced back to the center of the country and Goukouni forces made advances to take Abéché in July. Habbré then counterattacked forcing Goukouni back to Faya-Largeau, which he also soon lost. He returned in August, fortified by Libyan troops, to retake Faya-Largeau. Concern that Libya would push further led France to send 1000 paratroopers, supported by 2700 soldiers from Zaïre, to help stabilize the situation. This was achieved. In September 1984 France and Libya agreed to mutual withdrawals from Chad, although it seems too much to hope that the country will find longterm stability.

Western Sahara
When Spain relinquished control of the Western Sahara in 1976, the territory was to be jointly run by Morocco and Mauritania, who both had long-standing claims. However, this arrangement was opposed by the Polisario independence movement, backed by Algeria, which proclaimed the Saharan Arab Democratic Republic and launched a guerrilla war. After a number of reverses Mauritania agreed a cease-fire in July 1978 and withdrew. Morocco declared the whole territory to be a Moroccan province. There were then many clashes between Moroccan and Polisario forces. Since 1980 Moroccan strategy has been based on the development of a string of fortifications, known as the "Hassan Wall" after the king of Morocco, surrounding the more densely populated and economically useful parts of the Sahara. Within this wall there are now some 10 000 troops. This has succeeded in frustrating the Polisario whose active strength appears to have declined from about 12 000 in 1981 to around 4000. The Organization of African Unity recognized the Polisario claim in 1982, leading Morocco to walk out of its summit conference of that year with 18 other states, leaving it without a quorum and virtually paralyzed. The OAU then encouraged negotiations between the two parties which Morocco has thus far refused to entertain.

The Horn of Africa
Another area of complex rivalries and shifting allegiances, complicated further by external intervention, is the Horn of Africa. Ethiopia can boast 2000 years of independence, punctuated only by five years of Italian occupation from

The boundaries of Africa were determined largely to suit the convenience of the colonial administrators, and often bore only slight relation to geographical or ethnic realities. When the colonialists left, the leaders of Africa decided that they had little choice but to retain these often artificial boundaries. The decision was understandable, if questionable. New states, unsure of their status, foresaw only greater weakness as a result of dismemberment. But large groups of people were left living under regimes in which they had little confidence. When they attempted to secede, the consequences for all concerned were usually bloody and disastrous, even though by and large the countries concerned remained intact.

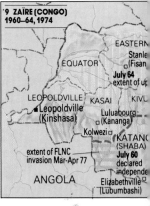

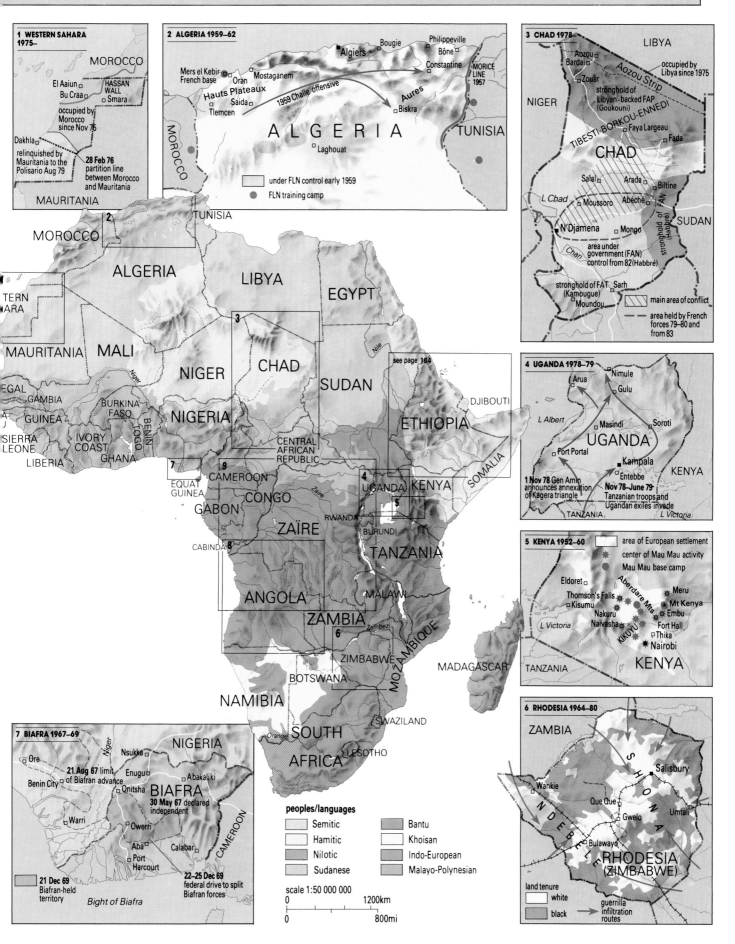

1 WESTERN SAHARA 1975–

MOROCCO
El Aaiun
Bu Craa
HASSAN WALL
Smara
occupied by Morocco since Nov 76
Dakhla
relinquished by Mauritania to the Polisario Aug 79
28 Feb 76 partition line between Morocco and Mauritania
MAURITANIA

2 ALGERIA 1959–62

Mers el Kebir French base
Oran
Mostaganem
Bougie
Algiers
Philippeville
Bône
Constantine
MORICE LINE 1957
Hauts Plateaux
Saïda
Tlemcen
1959 Challe offensive
Aurès
Biskra
ALGERIA
Laghouat
MOROCCO
TUNISIA
under FLN control early 1959
FLN training camp

3 CHAD 1978–

LIBYA
Aozou
Bardaï
Zouar
occupied by Libya since 1975
Aozou Strip
stronghold of Libyan-backed FAP (Goukouni)
NIGER
TIBESTI-BORKOU-ENNEDI
Faya Largeau
Fada
CHAD
Salal
Arada
Biltine
L Chad
Moussoro
Abéché
stronghold of FAN (Habbré)
SUDAN
N'Djamena
Mongo
Chari
area under government (FAN) control from 82 (Habbré)
stronghold of FAT (Kamougue)
Sarh
Moundou
main area of conflict
area held by French forces 79–80 and from 83

4 UGANDA 1978–79

Nimule
Arua
Gulu
L Albert
Masindi
Soroti
Port Portal
UGANDA
Kampala
KENYA
1 Nov 78 Gen Amin announces annexation of Kagera triangle
Entebbe
Nov 78–June 79 Tanzanian troops and Ugandan exiles invade
TANZANIA
L Victoria

5 KENYA 1952–60

area of European settlement
center of Mau Mau activity
Mau Mau base camp
Eldoret
Aberdare Mts
Meru
Thomson's Falls
Mt Kenya
Kisumu
Embu
Nakuru
Naivasha
Fort Hall
KIKUYU
Thika
L Victoria
Nairobi
TANZANIA
KENYA

6 RHODESIA 1964–80

ZAMBIA
SHONA
Salisbury
Wankie
Que Que
Gwelo
Umtali
NDEBELE
Bulawayo
RHODESIA (ZIMBABWE)
land tenure
white
black
guerrilla infiltration routes

7 BIAFRA 1967–69

Niger
NIGERIA
Ore
Nsukka
21 Aug 67 limit of Biafran advance
Enugu
Benin City
Abakaliki
Onitsha
BIAFRA
30 May 67 declared independent
Warri
Owerri
CAMEROON
Aba
Calabar
Port Harcourt
21 Dec 69 Biafran-held territory
22–25 Dec 69 federal drive to split Biafran forces
Bight of Biafra

Main map labels:
MOROCCO, ALGERIA, LIBYA, EGYPT, TUNISIA, WESTERN SAHARA, MAURITANIA, MALI, NIGER, CHAD, SUDAN, SENEGAL, GAMBIA, GUINEA, SIERRA LEONE, LIBERIA, IVORY COAST, GHANA, BURKINA FASO, TOGO, BENIN, NIGERIA, CAMEROON, CENTRAL AFRICAN REPUBLIC, ETHIOPIA, DJIBOUTI, SOMALIA, EQUAT GUINEA, GABON, CONGO, ZAÏRE, RWANDA, BURUNDI, UGANDA, KENYA, TANZANIA, MALAWI, ANGOLA, CABINDA, ZAMBIA, ZIMBABWE, MOZAMBIQUE, BOTSWANA, NAMIBIA, SOUTH AFRICA, SWAZILAND, LESOTHO, MADAGASCAR
Nile, Niger, Zaïre, Zambezi, Orange
see page 164

peoples/languages

Semitic	Bantu
Hamitic	Khoisan
Nilotic	Indo-European
Sudanese	Malayo-Polynesian

scale 1:50 000 000
0 — 1200km
0 — 800mi

AFRICA (continued)

1936 to 1941. The ruling group from the Christian Amhara have found it difficult to forge national unity. A particular source of difficulty has been the province of Eritrea which was incorporated into Ethiopia as late as 1962. Prior to this an Eritrean Liberation Front (ELF) had been founded to campaign for independence and has been conducting a guerrilla campaign. There is also a secessionist movement in Tigre. To add to Ethiopia's problems, neighboring Somalia laid claim to the desert region of the Ogaden.

The frustration engendered by the failure to suppress the Eritrean rebels was one factor behind the military coup which overthrew Emperor Haile Selassie in 1974 and led eventually to the rule of Colonel Mengistu. After falling out with the Americans, who had backed the emperor in the past, the new rulers looked increasingly to the Soviet Union for help.

This was awkward for the Soviet Union which had developed a close relationship with Somalia, including building up the port of Berbera. There had been a pro-Somali guerrilla group operating in the Ogaden since 1964. In 1976 the West Somali Liberation Front embarked on a new campaign with great vigor as well as support from Somali troops and weapons. By November 1977 it was virtually in control of the whole of the Ogaden with the exception of the cities of Harer and Diredawa. At its height the fighting involved some 80 000 Somalis against 120 000 Ethiopians, of which only one third were regulars.

The Soviet leaders had been trying to bring the two sides together, but when Somali actions made that impossible, they swung behind Ethiopia. The Somali government expelled Soviet advisers and abrogated the 1974 friendship treaty with the Soviet Union. It opened up contacts with the United States, and by 1980 had agreed to let the Americans have access to Berbera. However, the Americans were not willing to help Somalia hold on to its gains in the Ogaden. The arrival of Soviet and Cuban military "advisers" and large quantities of hardware turned the tide. A counteroffensive launched in 1978 pushed the Somalis back. On 9 March Somalia announced withdrawal of its troops from the region. Limited guerrilla warfare continued. In July 1982 3000 Ethiopian troops did cross into Somalia; they did not get very far, but nor did they withdraw.

Meanwhile things had been going badly for the Ethiopians in Eritrea. By October 1977 most of the major towns in the region were in rebel hands. Agordat had fallen in a bloody battle in September. By December the provincial capital of Asmera was under threat when its sea port of Massawa was captured. However, with the aid of Soviet equipment and Cuban troops (estimates suggest up to 15 000 Cubans in Ethiopia) as well as some from South Yemen and possibly East Germany, the tide turned on this front as well. By September 1978 the siege of Asmera had been lifted, and Massawa and many other towns recaptured. In November the

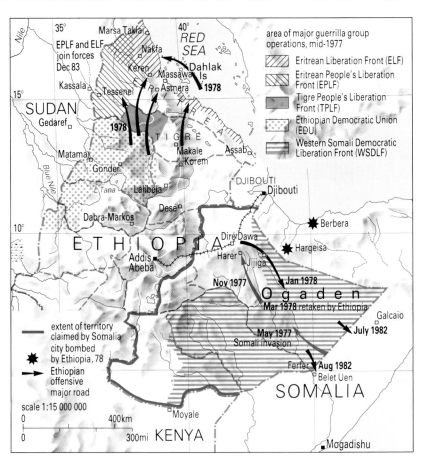

rebels' stronghold in Keren was taken. Some 30 000 Eritreans are said to have been killed during this offensive and 900 000 displaced, leading to a massive refugee problem which has since got worse and, combined with drought, has resulted in a catastrophic famine (see p. 174).

The Eritreans fought on and government efforts to defeat them failed. In the spring of 1982 a major offensive failed with heavy losses. Meanwhile guerrilla activities were stepped up in the neighboring Tigre province, adding to the difficulties of getting fresh troops and supplies to Eritrea.

Angola

When Angola gained its independence from Portugal in 1975, there were three liberation movements which turned their attentions from Portugal to each other. Two non-Marxist groups, UNITA and the FNLA, joined forces against the Marxist MPLA. The arrival of 14 000 Cuban troops plus Soviet equipment swung the war between these factions decisively in favor of the MPLA. The South Africans entered the conflict briefly on behalf of UNITA (it is not clear that this was a response to the entry of the Cubans or that the Cubans entered because of the South Africans). Zaïre had supported the FNLA but desisted in return for a promise by Angola not to encourage further insurgencies into its own Shaba province.

The regime has been less successful in consolidating its position in the south against UNITA. Backed by South Africa, UNITA has

THE HORN OF AFRICA

▲ Few parts of the world better illustrate the fickleness of countries preoccupied with local conflicts when it comes to sorting out their East–West allegiances than the Horn of Africa. A region so close to a vital sea route inevitably attracts great-power attention. In the early 1970s the United States enjoyed good relations with independent Ethiopia, led by Emperor Haile Selassie, while the Soviet Union was cementing its ties with neighboring Somalia. By the end of the decade, Somalia had turned to the West after the Soviet Union had moved to support revolutionary Ethiopia. Soviet support — in the form of Cubans — helped Ethiopia fight off the Somalis but could only stabilize the battle with secessionist movements (also ostensibly Socialist). Nor could it help when domestic upheavals combined with bad harvests in the 1980s to produce famine on a terrible scale.

been able to exercise control over the southeast of the country and its units are engaged in operations in the central regions. This causes maximum inconvenience to the MPLA government and has put its forces on to the defensive. UNITA leader, Jonas Savimbi, has said that his ambition is to force the MPLA into peace talks rather than take the country over.

South African forces have mounted operations in retaliation for Angolan support of SWAPO guerrillas in Namibia. By late 1983 they occupied much of Cunene province in the southwest. In December 1983 South Africa offered to withdraw its forces if Angola promised not to let SWAPO exploit the withdrawal. Angola refused and there was yet another South African incursion, this one reaching as far as Cassinga, 200 kilometers (125 miles) north of the Namibian border. Meanwhile, South Africa was pursuing a similar strategy against Mozambique. It supported a rebel force in Mozambique which had caused immense economic disruption, and was partly responsible for a famine which left 40 000 dead. In late December, recognizing where the power lay in southern Africa, Marxist Mozambique was forced into talks with South Africa. For the sake of its economic survival it was forced to abandon support of African National Congress guerrillas which had been using its territory as a base. Eventually in February 1984 Angola too entered into talks with South Africa on the removal of all foreign troops (including Cubans) from Angolan territory and removal of support for SWAPO. So far agreement has not been reached, but for the moment at least South Africa still has the upper hand.

▼ A mortar attack being prepared by members of a commando group of the Cuban-backed MPLA in the "Barra do Dande" region during the Angolan civil war in August 1975.

Uganda
Uganda achieved its independence from Britain in 1962. In 1966 the first head of state, Sir Edward Mutesa, was overthrown in a military coup. The prime minister, Milton Obote, became president. In 1971 Obote was overthrown in turn by the commander of the army, Idi Amin. Amin's rule was marked by a combination of eccentricity and terror. His victims were the Asian community, southerners, professionals and eventually anyone who could be portrayed as a threat to Amin's rule.

In 1978, with unrest developing in his own power base of the army, Amin mounted military operations against neighboring Tanzania, ostensibly to seize the disputed northwestern border area. It has been suggested that some 10 000 people were killed in the attack which caught the Tanzanians by surprise. In November a Tanzanian counteroffensive forced Amin to withdraw.

In March 1979 a force of 10 000 Tanzanians moved into Uganda, accompanied by 1000 Ugandan exiles, in a two-pronged attack. They moved forward on foot, which allowed them to make steady if slow progress and outmaneuver Ugandan forces who were inhibited by their dependence on wheeled armored troop carriers. The Ugandan resistance was not great and much of the little serious opposition came from Libyans (as many as 400 Libyans may have been killed in the campaign). By mid-April Kampala had been taken and the rest of Amin's forces were in full flight. Amin himself escaped into exile. After elections in 1980 Obote returned to power but has thus far failed to bring order and unity to this troubled country.

LATIN AMERICA

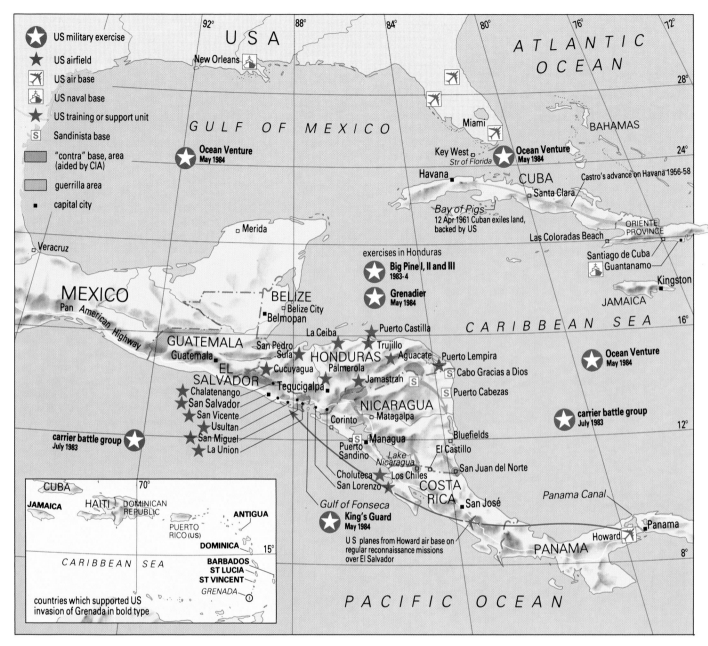

Legend:
- US military exercise
- US airfield
- US air base
- US naval base
- US training or support unit
- Sandinista base
- "contra" base, area (aided by CIA)
- guerrilla area
- ▪ capital city

USA
New Orleans
GULF OF MEXICO
Ocean Venture May 1984
Merida
Veracruz
MEXICO
Pan American Highway
GUATEMALA
Guatemala
EL SALVADOR
Chalatenango
San Salvador
San Vicente
Usultan
San Miguel
La Union
carrier battle group July 1983

BELIZE
Belize City
Belmopan
San Pedro Sula
La Ceiba
Puerto Castilla
Trujillo
HONDURAS
Aguacate
Puerto Lempira
Palmerola
Cucuyagua
Jamastran
Cabo Gracias a Dios
Tegucigalpa
Puerto Cabezas
NICARAGUA
Corinto
Matagalpa
Managua
Bluefields
Puerto Sandino
El Castillo
Lake Nicaragua
San Juan del Norte
Choluteca
Los Chiles
San Lorenzo
San José
COSTA RICA
Gulf of Fonseca
King's Guard May 1984
US planes from Howard air base on regular reconnaissance missions over El Salvador
PANAMA
Howard
Panama
Panama Canal

exercises in Honduras
Big Pine I, II and III 1983-4
Grenadier May 1984

ATLANTIC OCEAN
BAHAMAS
Miami
Key West
Str of Florida
Ocean Venture May 1984
Havana
CUBA
Castro's advance on Havana 1956-58
Santa Clara
Bay of Pigs 12 Apr 1961 Cuban exiles land, backed by US
Las Coloradas Beach
ORIENTE PROVINCE
Santiago de Cuba
Guantanamo
Kingston
JAMAICA
CARIBBEAN SEA
Ocean Venture May 1984
carrier battle group July 1983

PACIFIC OCEAN

Inset map:
CUBA
JAMAICA
HAITI
DOMINICAN REPUBLIC
PUERTO RICO (US)
ANTIGUA
DOMINICA
BARBADOS
ST LUCIA
ST VINCENT
GRENADA
CARIBBEAN SEA
countries which supported US invasion of Grenada in bold type

■ South American armed forces have a reputation for close involvement in their countries' internal affairs but they have not been actively involved against each other. There are a number of long-standing disputes that occasionally seem likely to spill over into war — for example, between Argentina and Chile over the Beagle Channel, and between Guatemala and the former British colony of Belize, in which some British forces are still based. There have been a number of border skirmishes. In 1981 Peru and Ecuador almost went to war over some disputed territory. Some of the civil wars have been quite substantial. For example, from 1948 to 1953 a civil war in Colombia claimed the lives of an estimated 200 000 people. Many of the anti-guerrilla campaigns have led to rather indiscriminate killing of people suspected of opposing the existing regimes.

The United States takes a close interest in Latin America and has been accused at times of getting too much involved, either overtly or covertly, through the Central Intelligence Agency. Three interventions in particular have been important in regional politics: the weak support for the anti-Castro forces in the Bay of Pigs in 1961, and the more successful interventions in the Dominican Republic in 1965, and in Grenada in 1983. More recently it has been closely involved in the turmoil in Central America, which involves directly El Salvador, Nicaragua and Honduras, and less directly Costa Rica, Guatemala and a number of other countries with an interest in the outcome of the various disputes in the area. The most direct intervention by an external power in the region was by Britain in 1982 when it reoccupied the Falkland Islands after they had been taken by Argentina.

▲ The keen interest taken by the United States in this area reflects not only its economic involvement but also three strategic concerns: that radical regimes would subvert their neighbors so that the area would never settle down; that they could serve, along with Cuba, as forward bases for the Soviet Union; that the vital waterway of the Panama Canal which links the Pacific to the Atlantic could be closed. The 1983 invasion of Grenada involved 12 ships and eventually as many as 6000 marines and rangers. Resistance, which included 700 Cuban construction engineers, was greater than expected.

The American interventions

Cuba

The campaign against President Batista that led to his overthrow at the start of January 1959 had begun in late 1956 when Fidel Castro set up a guerrilla base in Oriente province. As Batista's political support crumbled, the guerrillas became progressively bolder until eventually his army collapsed without ever having put up much of a fight. The United States did little to defend Batista, recognizing his unpopularity, because Castro appeared to be the leader of a broadly based movement. Once in power, he annoyed the Eisenhower administration by nationalizing US-owned oil refineries and questioning the status of the US naval base at Guatanamo. The American response of economic sanctions pushed him towards the Soviet bloc. By the time that the Kennedy administration came to power in January 1961, Castro had been indentified as a threat to US regional interests and a possible Soviet outpost.

Kennedy had inherited a CIA-sponsored plan to mount an invasion of Cuban exiles. On 12 April 1961 some 1200 anti-Castro Cubans equipped by the United States landed at the Bay of Pigs. The plan was ill-thought-out and depended on optimistic assumptions about the degree of anti-Castro sentiment. As the invasion faltered, Kennedy decided against backing it up with US air power. Within days most of the exiles had been either killed or captured. On 1 May 1961 Cuba was proclaimed a Socialist state.

Dominican Republic

Following the assassination of the dictator Rafael Leonidas Trujillo in 1961, internal disorders increased, with Cuba encouraging the rebels. In a popular revolution, sparked off by a coup led by junior officers on 24 April 1965, the right-wing regime was overthrown. However, the bulk of the armed forces were against the coup and began to take action against the rebels. At first the armed forces looked like retaking the capital, Santo Domingo, but after tough fighting

against the city's population who had been armed by the coup leaders, they ground to a halt and began to disintegrate.

The United States became nervous about the leftist elements supporting the new government and on 30 April landed a force of 23 000 troops close to Santo Domingo. This was presented as a peacekeeping exercise, and eventually some 2000 troops from other Latin American countries arrived to give the exercise a veneer of respectability. The intervention did ensure that the fighting was concluded and a cease-fire was signed on 6 May. All the various factions of the army were reunited and a provisional government was established until elections were organized. These were held in June 1966 and were won by Joaquin Balaguer. The intervention force was then withdrawn.

Grenada

Grenada achieved independence from Britain in 1974. In March 1979 the first prime minister, Eric Gairy, who was becoming increasingly unpopular, was overthrown in a coup led by Maurice Bishop of the radical New Jewel Movement. A People's Revolutionary Government was formed. It gained some support from Cuba, which included help with the construction of a new international airport at Salines. The Americans were concerned that this would be suitable for Cuban/Soviet military operations. Grenada joined the Non-Aligned Movement but edged towards the Soviet bloc. However, faced with mounting economic difficulty, Bishop moved to repair the deteriorating relations with the United States (a move that was not reciprocated by Washington), and this created tensions within the ruling group. The instability resulting from Bishop's murder in October 1983 provided the United States with an excuse to invade the island and help establish a more congenial government.

Central America

The small states of Central America have a history of instability and quarreling. In 1948 and 1955 Costa Rica had to drive off insurgents from Nicaragua. In 1969 resentment in Honduras against some 300 000 immigrants from overcrowded (but richer) El Salvador led to what became known as the "Football War." This was because it was triggered by riots against a Honduras football team visiting San Salvador for a world-cup play-off and counter-riots against Salvadoran immigrants in Honduras. Salvadoran troops moved across the border on 14 July and advanced steadily against rather weak Honduran forces. There were a number of air strikes, of which one of the more effective was by the Hondurans against El Salvador's main oil refinery. The fighting lasted about a week. Together with the riots it cost up to 4000 lives. It slowed down after the acceptance of an OAS cease-fire call. El Salvador only agreed to withdraw after guarantees for the safety of its nationals in Honduras. It took the threat of OAS sanctions

▲ Below, Eden Pastora's forces encounter heavy fighting against the National Guard in Nicaragua. Pastora eventually broke with the Sandinistas and now leads rebel guerrillas against the new regime from bases in Costa Rica.

▲ Above, the leaders of the Nicaraguan junta celebrate Army Day in September 1984, proud of their success in the guerrilla war against the old regime but anxious about the prospect of a new right-wing guerrilla campaign being waged against them.

LATIN AMERICA (continued)

before it finally agreed to withdraw on 30 July, under the supervision of OAS observers.

We have already noted (p. 139) how in June 1979 the Nicaraguan dictator General Somoza was forced to flee after a fierce civil war. This was the first successful leftist insurrection since Batista had been overthrown in Cuba almost exactly two decades earlier. The new revolutionary Sandinista government provided a sanctuary for guerrillas operating in neighboring states and an opportunity for Cuba and the Soviet Union to gain a foothold on the mainland. One country where guerrilla activity was stepped up was Guatemala. This led to a repressive response by the military government which accounted for some 13 000 dead by early 1982. The severe tactics meant that the guerillas were contained.

El Salvador was less successful. A November 1979 coup had overthrown the repressive General Humberto Romero. The new leaders were in turn overthrown by conservative officers and the regime moved steadily rightwards, until the election of the more moderate Napoleon Duarte as president in May 1984. The war against the guerrillas was prosecuted with great ruthlessness and a lack of discrimination. By 1982 the victims of the right-wing "death squads," often composed of off-duty soldiers, were running at 10 000 a year. Under pressure from the United States this was reduced, although by no means to zero. The US Congress made progress on human rights a condition of military assistance to the Salvadoran government. Despite a lackluster performance by the Salvadoran army, the guerrillas have not been able to make much headway, although they do control much of the east and north. In October 1984 Duarte met with some of the guerrilla leaders to explore the possibilities of a negotiated settlement.

The United States has been concerned about the development of a collection of leftist states with close links to the Soviet Union in its "backyard." Conscious of popular concern over the risks of getting involved in a protracted counterinsurgency operation, it has restricted its assistance to the provision of equipment, training and "advice." It has encouraged the Honduran government to take steps against guerrillas using its territory as a supply route into El Salvador. Furthermore, Honduras has allowed itself to be used as a base by the anti-Sandinista "Contras" in their own insurgency against Nicaragua. This insurgency has put the Nicaraguan government in some difficulty, although it is still in control. Some of the larger Latin American states in the region, including Venezuela and Mexico, known as the Contadora group, have developed a peace formula. The United States has yet to make clear whether its objections are to the activities of the Sandinista regime or the regime itself.

The anti-Sandinista forces are not united, with more moderate elements using Costa Rica as a base. Their prominent role in the region has put Honduras under some strain. It is not itself immune to the radical forces in the area. Also,

its old feud with El Salvador has resurfaced and this may limit the cooperation between the two in their anti-guerrilla efforts.

One method by which the United States had demonstrated its interest in developments in the area has been by conducting large-scale military exercises. In July 1983 two carrier-battle groups were deployed off the Central American coast. In September of that year 4000 American troops took part in the "Big Pine" exercises with the Honduran armed forces.

The War of the Falkland Islands

The British possession of the remote and sparsely populated Falkland Islands has been contested by Argentina (where they are known as the Malvinas) since the middle of the last century. Negotiations for a settlement of the sovereignty issue had been under way since the 1960s, but Argentina was becoming increasingly frustrated by British prevarication. A dispute in March 1982 concerning the status of some Argentine scrap-metal dealers on the related island of South Georgia gave Argentina a pretext for an invasion of the main islands which was carried out successfully on 2 April against a British garrison of 60 marines.

Argentina may have invaded under the misapprehension that the lack of interest in the welfare of the islands hitherto demonstrated by Britain would continue. Nevertheless, Britain at once sought to bring economic, military and diplomatic pressure to bear, and the United States stepped in as a mediator. Britain sent off to the south Atlantic a substantial task force involving a major logistical effort (see p. 68). Argentina remained intransigent. By the end of April the United States had tilted decisively to Britain's side.

Military operations began in earnest at the start of May, including the most dramatic and costly incident of the war — the sinking of the Argentine cruiser, the *General Belgrano*, torpedoed by a British nuclear submarine. Two days later a British destroyer, HMS *Sheffield*, was sunk by an *Exocet* sea-skimming missile. On 21 May British forces landed at Port San Carlos in a remarkably successful amphibious operation. As the bridgehead was consolidated, British ships were subjected to continuous air raids and a number were sunk or badly damaged, with the Argentine air forces suffering heavy losses. After a slow move out of the bridgehead British troops captured Goose Green and Darwin in a fierce battle with Argentine troops on 28 May. Within a couple of weeks the Argentine garrison at the capital of Port Stanley was surrounded and eventually succumbed to a sustained bombardment and the superior professionalism of the British troops. The Argentine forces on the islands surrendered on 14 June. Britain lost 250 killed and Argentina up to 1000. The war did not settle the dispute. Britain became even more reluctant to relinquish sovereignty and felt obliged to maintain a substantial and extremely expensive garrison, outnumbering the civilian population of around 1500.

WHAT IS TO BE DONE?

Does disarmament assist the cause of peace? Contemporary arms control begins with the Partial Test Ban Treaty of 1963. The Non-Proliferation Treaty of 1970 effectively freezes the status quo. Attempts to control offensive nuclear arms have got sidetracked into a preoccupation with formal parity. The diffusion of power means that even the most substantial countries often lack leverage over others. Hope lies in the fact that warfare is rarely an easy or attractive option.

As is suggested by this 19th-century lithograph by Daumier, with the caption "After you!", there has never been a lack of enthusiasm for the general idea of laying down weapons of war, only a certain reluctance to take the first step.

Few parts of the globe escape from the ravages of war. The human costs are high, and they extend well beyond the immediate casualties of the fighting. War disrupts economic and social development; it destroys the work of centuries; it creates bitter legacies that divide communities for decades; it drives people from their homes. Nor is it just the combatants who suffer. Supplies of key commodities can be disrupted; world markets are turned upside down; innocent third parties get caught in the crossfire; innocent countries find their resources stretched by a sudden inflow of refugees.

The institutions and symbols of war stress mankind's differences and rivalries rather than its shared heritage and common interests. The cost of preparing for war uses up scarce resources. Scientists devote their talents to devising instruments of death and destruction; energies are expended training people to kill. Meanwhile other, more genuine, needs are unmet. Few comparisons seem more potent than those between the world's expenditure on arms and that on disarmament. The 1982 Report of the Independent Commission on Disarmament and Security Issues, chaired by the Swedish statesman Olaf Palme, provided some choice examples: "Total military spending in 1982 will amount to over 650 000 million US dollars. This is more than the entire income of 1500 million people living in the 50 poorest countries. The price of a single modern fighter plane would be sufficient to innoculate three million children against major childhood diseases. The price of one nuclear submarine with its missiles would provide a hundred thousand years of nursing care for old people."

Yet, it is argued, this great expenditure has not led to improved security. Far from this being the case, the high incidence of war and the constant tension in which many states exist suggest that, if anything, the net security of the world's states has declined.

Fewer arms does not mean more peace

Often the only result of extra spending on defense is the stimulation of comparable expenditure by the adversary. The result is an arms race, with an exacerbation of mutual suspicions and at best the same level of security as before, except at a higher level of expenditure. The wastefulness and destructiveness of armaments encourage calls for disarmament, for reducing force levels to the minimum required for security.

Calls for disarmament and the transfer of resources away from the military strike a responsive chord throughout the globe. However, attempts to turn the sentiment into practical policies have not been resounding successes. Before examining the various solutions that have been proposed over the years, it might be useful first to consider whether the problem that they seek to address has been properly understood.

Arms and peace

It is unfortunately not the case that fewer arms mean more peace. The relationship between the incidence of wars and the amount of weaponry available for fighting them is tenuous. Disarmament as a method of removing war as an option for the settlement of disputes can only work at all if absolute in its effect. If only partial, then sufficient means will exist for starting wars, and there will still be the potential for rapid rearmament once hostilities have begun. With conventional war disarmament can at least make the initial killing more restricted than it might otherwise have been (though possibly not that restricted unless inroads have been made into stocks of small arms). In the nuclear era partial disarmament makes very little difference, given the destructive power of just a few weapons.

So disarmament is unlikely to stop wars altogether: can it still make them less likely? The evidence gives as much support to those who believe that a high density of armaments makes war less likely as to those who believe the opposite. The millions of people killed in wars since 1945 have not, with a few notable exceptions, been the victims of the world's larger military powers; they have not been killed by hyperexpensive and supersophisticated weapons but rather by mundane, small arms of the sort that could have been used in previous generations and even centuries; and they have resided in the poorer regions of the world. We have stressed the extent to which in recent years the most modern military equipment has been distributed around the globe via the arms trade, and how this might be blamed for a flurry of

regular interstate wars, but it remains the case (almost by definition) that the bloodiest wars are labor- rather than capital-intensive.

Where the arms race has been at its most intense, and where there is the greatest concentration of advanced weaponry — Central Europe — there has been relative peace, stability and prosperity. Along the Sino–Soviet border deep antagonism and large military deployments coexist. When countries have relaxed their guard, they some-

▼ Western leaders commemorate the 1944 D-Day landings in Normandy which began the liberation of France, perhaps reflecting that this war at least both removed an evil force from European politics and has been followed by an extended period of peace.

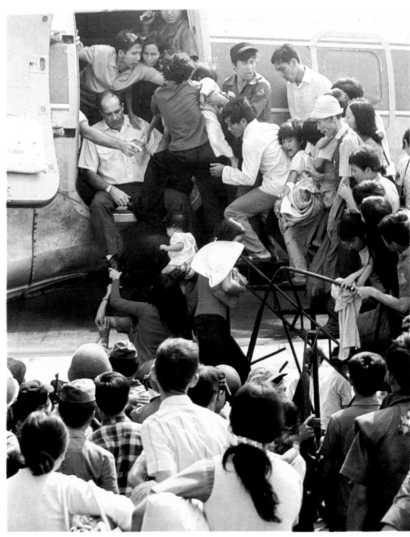

The political climate governs the success of arms control

times do find themselves in trouble. For example, the military in post-shah Iran was for a while in a shambles. Perhaps because this partial disarmament was not combined with a disarmament in rhetoric, it was seen in Iraq as a chance to redress grievances.

This is not to argue that somehow arms races invariably have peaceful consequences, so that we disrupt them at our peril; just that our focus should be on the cause of war rather than on its instruments. These causes are to be found in long-standing differences over territory and sovereignty, or in religious, ideological, ethnic and tribal tensions, memories of past injustices and bitterness over current oppression, desire for aggrandizement and fear of eradication. Given so many potential causes, there is a need for a more political response than that suggested simply by the regulation of the levels of arms. To see what can be achieved by regulating the level and types of armaments we must now turn attention to the postwar negotiations designed to achieve progress in this area.

The ideal of disarmament was not as powerful in the international community at the start of World War II as it had been after World War I. Explanations for the 1914–18 war pointed to Anglo–German naval competition and then the general staffs imposing their own timetables on the crises and forcing the hands of their political masters. The interwar disarmament negotiations, designed to prevent a repetition, were characterized by cynical machinations and deadlocks. What was agreed had a minimal effect on the course of the 1939–45 war, with the possible exception of the 1925 protocol prohibiting the use of poisoned gas (although even here military prudence was as important). The explanations for the outbreak of the second war pointed, if anything, to a failure to engage in an arms race with the Germans.

It was only the new atom bomb that ensured disarmament a high place on the postwar international agenda. The United States did propose in 1946 that atomic energy should be internationalized and put to use for

◀ **The human costs of war.** The scramble to get out of the South Vietnamese capital in 1975 as the North Vietnamese close on the city.

▼ **Victims of the terrible famine in Ethiopia** which was brought to the world's attention late in 1984, the scale of which can be partly attributed to the prolonged war against the Eritrean and Tigrean secessionist movements.

THE GEOGRAPHICAL DIMENSION OF ARMS CONTROL

▲ The signing in Moscow of the Partial Test Ban Treaty in August 1963 by three foreign ministers, Dean Rusk of the United States, Andrei Gromyko of the Soviet Union and Lord Home of Great Britain. This was the first major postwar arms-control agreement. It was intended to make this treaty, which banned only atmospheric tests, comprehensive by taking in underground tests. Despite some negotiations in the late 1970s this has yet to be achieved.

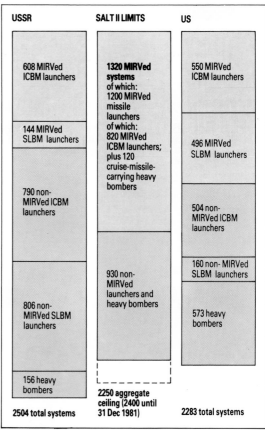

USSR	SALT II LIMITS	US
608 MIRVed ICBM launchers	1320 MIRVed systems of which: 1200 MIRVed missile launchers of which: 820 MIRVed ICBM launchers; plus 120 cruise-missile-carrying heavy bombers	550 MIRVed ICBM launchers
144 MIRVed SLBM launchers		496 MIRVed SLBM launchers
790 non-MIRVed ICBM launchers		504 non-MIRVed ICBM launchers
	930 non-MIRVed launchers and heavy bombers	160 non-MIRVed SLBM launchers
806 non-MIRVed SLBM launchers		573 heavy bombers
156 heavy bombers	2250 aggregate ceiling (2400 until 31 Dec 1981)	
2504 total systems		2283 total systems

When it comes to setting the boundaries for arms-control negotiations both sides are very conscious of the way in which relevant forces can be excluded by drawing a line in a particular way. For example, with conventional forces the Western nations have been anxious to ensure that all the western military districts of the Soviet Union are included in the Stockholm talks on confidence-building measures. With the negotiations on intermediate nuclear forces, NATO would argue that the Urals made an unsatisfactory boundary because of the extent to which missiles based outside of the European USSR can attack Western Europe.

peaceful purposes with military exploitation prohibited (the Baruch Plan). Unfortunately it was possible for the Soviet Union to read the plan as being designed to deprive them of a chance to match the American nuclear capability without guaranteeing that the Americans would give up their weapons. The initiative was lost in the onset of the cold war.

A variety of negotiations were conducted under the aegis of the United Nations but they were soon bogged down. The less serious they became, the more utopian and far-reaching the proposals on the table. The West argued that it could not make concessions on nuclear arms unless the Soviet Union relinquished its conventional superiority, and that there could be no progress at all unless Soviet society was opened up for Western inspection in order to ensure that there was full compliance with any agreement. To the Kremlin these arguments appeared designed to produce Western superiority and increase the Soviet vulnerability to espionage.

In the early 1960s, when disarmament negotiations had become a byword for futility, the conditions changed to make possible a form of progress. First, having gone so close to the brink during the Cuban missile crisis, the superpowers entered into a modest détente. Second, the development of reconnaissance satellites meant that each side could watch the other's military developments without having to send in observers. These satellites, which were still largely used for the purposes of espionage, eventually came to be known as "national technical means of verification."

Third, there was a conceptual change towards more modest but realistic objectives for diplomatic activity in this area. Rather than pretend that either East–West antagonism or nuclear weapons could be removed from the international scene, this new approach stressed the need to come to terms with these facts of life in order to render them less dangerous. Rather than attempt to eliminate armaments, better to ensure that those that did exist were so configured that they were unlikely to be used. No war must be allowed to start because of some military imperative forcing the pace before all diplomatic options had been exhausted. It had to be possible to hold back on military action without fear of being caught in a surprise attack or losing an opportunity to gain a quick victory. The new approach was known as "arms control." Its focus was on the stability of military relationships.

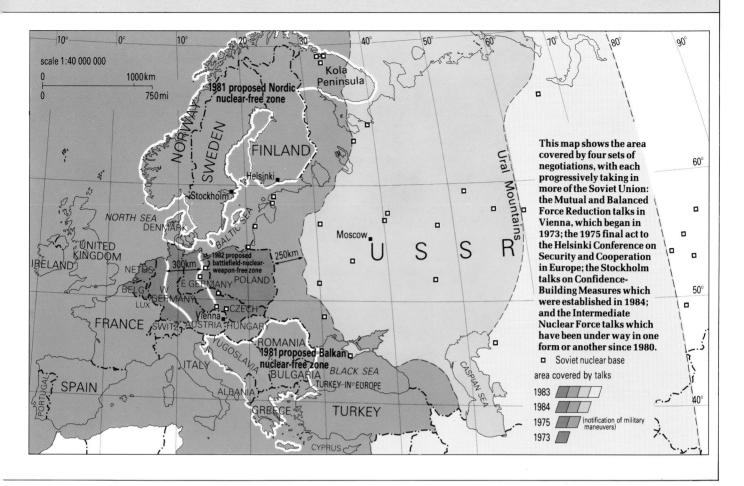

This map shows the area covered by four sets of negotiations, with each progressively taking in more of the Soviet Union: the Mutual and Balanced Force Reduction talks in Vienna, which began in 1973; the 1975 final act to the Helsinki Conference on Security and Cooperation in Europe; the Stockholm talks on Confidence-Building Measures which were established in 1984; and the Intermediate Nuclear Force talks which have been under way in one form or another since 1980.

□ Soviet nuclear base

area covered by talks

1983
1984
1975 (notification of military maneuvers)
1973

Arms control

The first fruit of the post-Cuba détente was the 1963 Partial Test Ban Treaty. Negotiations to ban nuclear weapons tests had been under way since 1958 but they had faltered on the verification problem. If it had been possible to agree on a comprehensive ban, then the development of nuclear weapons would have been at least slowed down and we might have been spared some of the unsettling technological advances of the next two decades. As it was, all that could be achieved was the banning of atmospheric tests, so sparing us the radioactive fallout that had been responsible for so much popular alarm. Testing was allowed to continue underground.

Other agreements were more successful. In 1960 it had already been agreed in the first postwar arms-limitation treaty to ban nuclear weapons, and indeed any other military activity, from Antarctica. The 1966 Outer-Space Treaty kept weapons of mass destruction out of space; the 1970 Seabed Treaty kept such weapons off the ocean floor (not that anybody had displayed much interest in putting any weapons there). The Non-Proliferation Treaty, which also came into force that year, effectively limited the number of declared nuclear powers to five.

Having contained the nuclear arsenals, the second objective was to ensure that the superpower strategic relationship was as stable as possible. A start was made on this in the post-Cuba détente with the 1963 hot-line agreement to establish an emergency communications link between Moscow and Washington. There were also other measures adopted by both sides, though without the benefit of a formal agreement, to improve command and control mechanisms to reduce the risk of accidental launches. A 1971 superpower agreement on "Measures to Reduce the Risk of Outbreak of Nuclear War" involved pledges to maintain and improve the organizational and technical safeguards against accidental or unauthorized use of nuclear weapons, to arrange for instant notification, should a risk of nuclear war arise from such incidents, and to notify in advance any planned missile launches beyond one side's territory and towards the other.

As we saw earlier, the basic problem of maintaining a stable nuclear balance did not turn out to be as difficult as many had suspected during the 1950s. The basic requirement was that both sides should be confident in their second-strike capabilities so that they could "ride out" any nuclear attack

THE HUMAN FALLOUT

The office of the UN High Commissioner for Refugees (UNHCR) was established in Geneva in 1951. It was at first concerned primarily with the problems of those that had been displaced by the fighting in Europe during the war. Refugee status was presumed to be temporary, with the prospect of either a return to the country of origin or resettlement elsewhere. The character of the refugee problem has now been dramatically transformed. In 1959 it was estimated that there were 1·2 million refugees receiving international assistance through the UNHCR. The figure is now 10 million and there are many other displaced people not receiving such assistance.

The growth in numbers of refugees reflects the growth in the number of third-world conflicts. For example, since 1975 some two million people are estimated to have fled from Indochina. The hundreds of thousands of "boat people" who attempted to escape from Vietnam by sea, often only to perish at the hands of pirates or the elements, captured international sympathy. Over 900 000 have been resettled in the West. The refugees from most third-world conflicts are not so lucky.

ETHIOPIA: WAR AND WANT

militarized zone
main movement of refugees, drought and famine victims
aid distribution center
refugee camp
airstrip

OPERATION MOSES JAN 85
journey taken by Falasha Jews *en route* to Israel

WORST AREA OF FAMINE

area held by EPLF
area held by TPLF

scale 1:12 000 000
0   200km
0   150mi

refugee intake to Jan 1984
more than 1 000 000
100 000–1 000 000
10 000–100 000
fewer than 10 000
exodus route from war zone

The political climate governs the success of arms control

▲ **Few catastrophes have generated such widespread alarm as the plight of millions of Ethiopians whose fate began to be publicized in 1984. A natural disaster of continued drought was compounded by the dislocations of civil war. The massive relief operation demonstrated that, when sufficiently provoked, humanitarianism can be a powerful force in international affairs.**

without feeling obliged to launch on warning or preempt.

The self-evident value of protecting at least one part of the deterrent from surprise attack encouraged the development of relatively invulnerable ballistic-missile-carrying submarines. These became a substantial obstacle to a successful first strike. Otherwise, only the development of effective ballistic missile defenses might still have upset stability. It was the possibility of such a development that led the Americans to suggest in 1967 the discussions that led eventually to the Strategic Arms Limitation Talks (SALT). These began in 1969 and concluded their first stage successfully in 1972 with the Antiballistic Missile Treaty, which is now considered by many to be the most important achievement of contemporary arms control.

The achievement was made somewhat easier by the fact that the relevant technology was still in its early stages of development and faltering. Comparable achievements in the area of offensive arms proved to be more elusive. Here the technology was advanced and developing all the time. Although similar in many respects, the two sides' force structures were sufficiently different to render close comparisons difficult.

It is arguable that, with missile-carrying submarines roaming the oceans with impunity and ABMs virtually prohibited, there was little that actually needed to be done to make the situation more stable. Indeed, despite the recent failure in nuclear arms control, there is no evidence that the strategic relationship has become dangerously out of kilter, even though the political relationship has been unsettled.

It is probably the deterioration in political relations that is the main reason for the lack of success in arms control over the past decade. This has increased mutual suspicions and made the two sides less willing to indulge in give and take in the bargaining. It has made it harder for the governments to argue for agreements against domestic opposition. For example, in June 1979 Presidents Carter and Brezhnev agreed on a Strategic Arms Limitation Treaty, but President Carter then failed to convince the necessary two-thirds of the US Senate to ratify the treaty, and he withdrew it himself from further consideration after the Soviet invasion of Afghanistan at the end of that year.

Two other reasons can also be suggested for the failure to achieve a durable agreement. The first is the pace of technological development. Not all new technologies are mischiev-

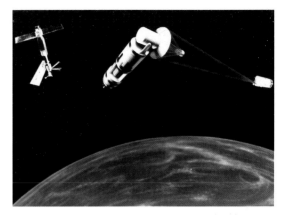

The shape of wars to come: an artist's impression of a space-borne laser weapon **able to knock out other satellites or even ballistic missiles.**

ous in their effects. Moreover, one of the problems posed by the new technologies for arms negotiators is not that their strategic effects are especially destabilizing but that they are extremely difficult to count because they vary in range, or in their ability to carry conventional or nuclear warheads, or in the sort of platforms from which they can be launched. They therefore fail to sit in one of the neat categories — conventional/nuclear, intermediate/strategic, land-/air-/sea-based — in which the negotiators like to place different weapons. The versatile modern cruise missile exemplifies this sort of problem. One big question for the future may be how controls on submarine-launched cruise missiles might be arranged when only a small but significant proportion of the thousands being deployed by the United States are designed for carrying nuclear warheads to attack targets on land, but when these cannot be readily distinguished from those designed to achieve less fundamental tasks.

Some new technologies are found to be strategically unsettling. We discussed earlier (p. 85) the impact of multiple warheads — MIRVs — on strategic calculations. Although their overall impact may not be as great as many fear, they have nevertheless confused matters considerably. The United States was the first to put MIRVs on its missiles and, while it saw this as an area of superiority, it displayed slight interest in control. It was only as the Soviet Union began to follow suit with its much larger ICBMs that the desirability of constraints became apparent. The difficulty with controls was in knowing how many warheads were carried by individual missiles without peering down the nose cones. At first it was thought possible to control only the number of missiles with MIRVs, but not the warheads themselves. Later it seemed possible to limit the number

How do you define parity?

of warheads, by assuming that each MIRVed missile carried the maximum number of warheads with which it had been tested. By the time that this had been worked out, the only constraints that could be arranged still allowed for massive multiplication of warheads.

Another reason for the failure to achieve a durable agreement lay in the tendency towards the adoption of parity as a negotiating objective (perhaps reflecting a more fundamental failure to work out an agreed definition of strategic stability). This was forced upon the negotiations in 1972. Along with the ABM treaty, the United States and the Soviet Union agreed a five-year Interim Agreement on Offensive Arms which took the form of a "freeze" on existing ICBM or SLBM launchers or those being prepared for deployment. The Soviet Union enjoyed a significant numerical superiority in both types of system, but this was supposed to be balanced by American advantages in bombers and MIRVs. However, Congress baulked at accepting Soviet superiority and added a proviso to its ratification, insisting that future agreements should be based on a strict parity. To those doing the negotiating this did not necessarily seem to be too much of an imposition. The concept of parity reflected the diplomatic profession's inclination towards notions of equity, the idea that neither side should expect an advantage out of a fair bargain. Parity allows both sides to leave the negotiating chamber claiming that they are second to none.

Nor did parity at first appear to be causing too many problems. In November 1974 Presidents Ford and Brezhnev met at the Soviet Far Eastern city of Vladivostok and agreed on a framework for a Strategic Arms Limitation Treaty. This allowed for 2400 delivery vehicles (bombers and missiles) for each side, of which 1320 could be missiles with MIRVs. Unfortunately, when the technicians were asked to fill in the details of this framework, a number of knotty problems soon emerged, including the extent to which US cruise missiles or the Soviet *Backfire* bomber (which is designed for use in Europe but could at a pinch reach the United States) should be covered. It took five years, and much playing around with the broad framework as well as the details, to reach the SALT II Treaty (see p. 172). This was not only extremely complicated, it was also permissive in that it did not stop either side doing much that they would have been planning to do anyway. As a result it failed to cap-ture the popular imagination and became a

victim of the general decline in East–West relations.

This did not deter the superpowers from further efforts to achieve agreements based on parity. The discussions were split into two, with those of the core strategic systems carrying on as the Strategic Arms Reduction Talks (START), renamed by President Reagan to reflect his more radical objectives. Meanwhile discussions on systems of a lesser range, whose impact was likely to be felt mainly in Europe or Asia, were hived off into separate Intermediate Nuclear Force (INF) talks.

The need to set up these separate talks was in itself a reflection of the difficulties with parity. The lack of clarity in the relationship between the size and composition of the nuclear arsenals and their strategic purposes may make it easier for both sides to accept the concept of parity, but it also makes it difficult to explain what parity should entail. There is no self-evident measure of nuclear capability. Do you count launchers, warheads, throw-weight (the weight of the front end of the missile deliverable over a given range), or some even more arcane measures, such as lethality, designed to reflect the ability to destroy a protected target? Are the nuclear weapons of Britain, France and China (most of which are directed at the Soviet Union) to be included? Where does one draw the line between one category of nuclear weapons and another?

The lack of an agreed measure meant that it was open to both sides to propose the particular dimension which suited its case. If, in order to achieve true parity, unequal concessions are required, these are rarely forthcoming. As a result the adoption of parity has turned out to be a recipe for a long and tedious negotiating effort. Thus the opening US bid in the INF talks — "zero option" — required the Soviet Union to dismantle hundreds of missiles already in place in return for the Americans not going forward with the introduction of missiles yet to go into production. The Soviet position was no less unrealistic. The Kremlin composed a picture of existing equality by matching against Soviet bombers and missiles many Western systems that ought to have been excluded, even according to its own definitions. The main Soviet objective was not to achieve parity but to prevent the introduction of new cruise and *Pershing* missiles into Western Europe. When the first missiles arrived in late 1983, the Russians walked out of the talks.

The same tendencies have also been at

A high point of détente. In 1975 the leaders of 33 European countries, plus those of Canada and the United States, met in Helsinki to sign the final act of the Conference on Cooperation and Security in Europe. This affirmed the postwar boundaries of Europe and set in motion cooperation in political and economic matters. The promise was never fulfilled and was overtaken by wrangles over conflict in the third world, human rights and economic debt. Here two of the architects of détente, Soviet President Leonid Brezhnev (seated) and American Secretary of State Henry Kissinger, confer.

"Build-down" — a promising idea

Apart from the fact that the lack or progress in all these areas is frustrating and demoralizing to those involved, it is doubtful that in the attemps to control parity the negotiators have even been addressing the most important problems. In asserting the importance of parity, we are asserting the danger of disparities, even when the practical significance of the differences between the two sides is marginal. Earlier we examined the value of military balances and found them to be wanting as useful indicators of military capabilities. The simple head count in the conventional force negotiations reveals little about the durability of deterrence, let alone the outcome of battle. This requires consideration of equipment, training, stamina and doctrine as well as terrain. An agreement might limit forces within an agreed area, but this leaves open the speed with which reinforcements might be introduced from outside into this area. The proximity of Soviet territory to the Guidelines Area for MFR means that this crucial area of Soviet advantage is barely touched.

New approaches

The frustrations with arms control, as it has been practiced over the past decade, have led to a variety of suggestions for how it might be improved. Those most worried about the levels of armaments have argued for a freeze in which the two sides would not be allowed to develop or test, never mind produce and deploy, new nuclear weapons. The difficulties with this proposal are that it requires a series of quite complex separate agreements, often in areas, such as a comprehensive test ban, that have proved awkward in the past, and the destabilizing types of weapons would be frozen along with the stabilizing. Both the United States and the Soviet Union have in the past proposed freezes, but this has normally been at times when they have felt themselves to be superior.

Another and possibly more promising idea for adding an extra dynamic to the negotiations is known as "build-down." This recognizes that both sides will wish to modernize their forces but seeks to ensure that this is not an excuse for an expansion. In its simplest form, build-down would require that for every new warhead introduced, two were removed. A somewhat more complicated version was incorporatated into the US position in the strategic arms talks in 1983 but was not taken seriously by the Russians. In principle, however, there is no reason for them to object to the concept and it may yet be revived.

work in the conventional sphere. As early as 1967 the NATO countries hinted at an interest in talks with the Warsaw Pact on mutual force reductions. In 1971 the Russians agreed in principle and in 1973 the talks — on Mutual Reductions in Forces and Armaments and Associated Measures in Central Europe (MFR for short) — began. They have yet to be concluded. There has been an agreement on what might constitute parity in this area: 900 000 air and ground troops with a sublimit of 700 000 for ground troops. The impact of this on the military picture in Central Europe would be tangible if not enormous. The real problem is that both sides disagree on the starting point for the Warsaw Pact. NATO data show a Warsaw Pact superiority by about 150 000 troops; Warsaw Pact data conveniently show virtual parity already.

Limiting war in space

A second sort of approach argues that arms control works best with modest objectives and that a prime aim ought to be to nip menacing new developments in the bud before they have an opportunity to complicate further the strategic scene. A favorite target in recent years has been anti-satellite weapons. Both sides have come to rely more and more on satellites for early warning, surveillance, command, control and communications and other aspects of what might be called the "strategic nervous system." In 1967 they agreed not to put weapons of mass destruction into space, but there are no prohibitions on systems designed to attack these increasingly important satellites. Since 1967 the Soviet Union has been experimenting with a crude anti-satellite device. Although it does not seriously threaten most American satellites in its current form, the Russians resisted proposals to ban such systems during some limited talks in the late 1970s (perhaps because they might be useful against the Chinese). As soon as the Americans started to develop a system of their own in the 1980s, the Russians started to become much more interested. Now it was the American turn to be difficult. Negotiations almost began in 1984, but failed to materialize as it proved difficult to separate them from the much larger questions of the general state of East–West relations and the state of other negotiations on offensive arms. There are also many links between the development of anti-satellite weapons and that of anti-ballistic missiles. President Reagan has been less attached to the 1972 ABM treaty than his predecessors. When the two superpowers met again in 1985 in an effort to revive arms control, the Russians insisted that President Reagan abandon his strategic defense initiative (see p.97) as a prerequisite for any progress on reducing arms, though it is only at the research stage.

The third approach, which may prove to be the most fruitful of all, has been to consider moving discussions away from issues of military balance and towards a concern with the actual preparations for the deployment and employment of armed forces in crisis and conflict. This would involve looking at questions relating to command and control of forces, and the effects on each other's plans of the preparatory moves for conflict. Would mobilization act as a provocation or a deterrent? What would be the effect of raising the alert status of strategic forces as a warning signal in a crisis? Might the two sides steadily raise their forces to hair-trigger readiness simply by responding to each other's move-

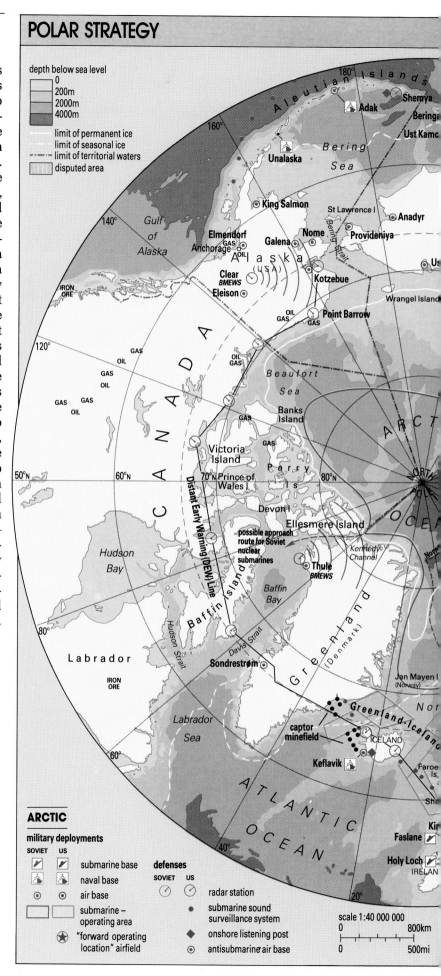

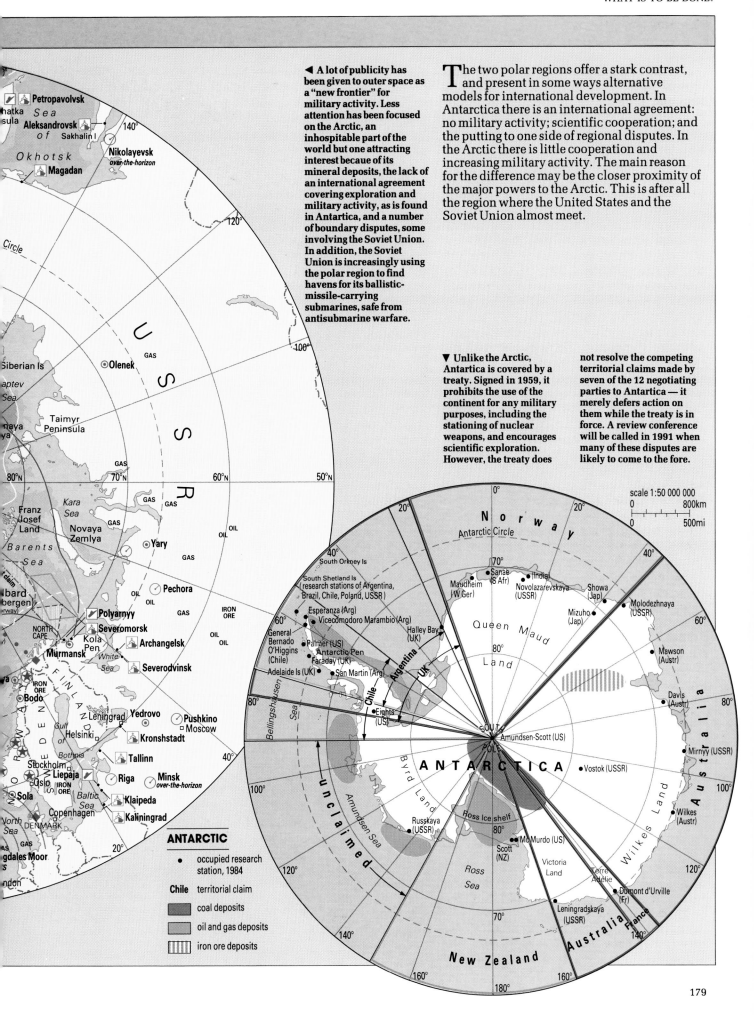

◀ A lot of publicity has been given to outer space as a "new frontier" for military activity. Less attention has been focused on the Arctic, an inhospitable part of the world but one attracting interest becaue of its mineral deposits, the lack of an international agreement covering exploration and military activity, as is found in Antartica, and a number of boundary disputes, some involving the Soviet Union. In addition, the Soviet Union is increasingly using the polar region to find havens for its ballistic-missile-carrying submarines, safe from antisubmarine warfare.

The two polar regions offer a stark contrast, and present in some ways alternative models for international development. In Antarctica there is an international agreement: no military activity; scientific cooperation; and the putting to one side of regional disputes. In the Arctic there is little cooperation and increasing military activity. The main reason for the difference may be the closer proximity of the major powers to the Arctic. This is after all the region where the United States and the Soviet Union almost meet.

▼ Unlike the Arctic, Antartica is covered by a treaty. Signed in 1959, it prohibits the use of the continent for any military purposes, including the stationing of nuclear weapons, and encourages scientific exploration. However, the treaty does not resolve the competing territorial claims made by seven of the 12 negotiating parties to Antartica — it merely defers action on them while the treaty is in force. A review conference will be called in 1991 when many of these disputes are likely to come to the fore.

ANTARCTIC

• occupied research station, 1984

Chile territorial claim

▨ coal deposits

▨ oil and gas deposits

▥ iron ore deposits

Nuclear-free is not the same as nuclear-safe

ments? What would be the effect of demilitarized zones separating potential belligerents?

Questions such as these are starting to be addressed seriously. In the conventional area, as long ago as 1975, agreement was reached at the Conference on Security and Cooperation in Europe (CSCE) which took place at Helsinki on what have become known as Confidence-Building Measures (CBMs). These are measures designed to reassure other countries that they will not be victims of suprise attacks or indeed military aggression of any kind. They could include advance notice of military exercises, naval movements and reequipment programs. Proposals often relate to ensuring that all military activity remains visible to those who fear that they could be put at risk. The problem with this, as with other CBMs, is that they can seem like an excuse for espionage, and it is by no means axiomatic that, when the full extent of another's military activities is exposed, the result will be reassuring. There is often an assumption among those seeking to reform international affairs that many of our problems result from the fact that nations fail to understand each other or harbor unwarranted suspicions. The sad truth is that often they understand each other only too well and the suspicions are quite justified!

The CBMs agreed in 1975 were modest. All 35 participating countries were expected to give prior notification of ground-force maneuvers of over 25 000 troops. Provision was also made for voluntary notification of maneuvers below that level and also for the invitation of observers. There has only been limited employment of the voluntary provisions, with the Warsaw Pact countries being particularly reticent. In successive follow-on conferences to the original Helsinki gathering ideas for more CBMs have been mooted. Eventually in 1983 agreement was reached to set up a whole new conference to examine them properly. The current proposals envisage mandatory notification of all out-of-garrison movements, so encouraging a greater familiarity with the general pattern of military movements in Europe and making it less likely that a surprise attack could be organized. The Soviet Union has also agreed that this time its European territory (up to the Urals) should be included, rather than the small amount currently involved.

This issue of the geographical coverage of particular arms-control regimes (see p. 172) is interesting because it reveals the political dimension informing many proposals that

superficially might appear to be confined to purely military matters. For much of the postwar period the main motive underlying Warsaw Pact proposals on European disarmament was to secure recognition of the territorial status quo, especially the division of Germany. Once that had been secured by more direct means, many of the relevant proposals were abandoned. Similarly with ideas for nuclear-free zones. In practical terms these are less promising than might appear, in that places within a zone can be readily targeted from outside. Nuclear-free is not the same as nuclear-safe! However, the main significance of many proposals for such zones has been political in that they signify an attempt to detach the relevant areas from superpower competition. This is especially true in Europe — and most marked with those proposals that call for a nuclear-free zone from Poland to Portugal, as if the European part of the Soviet Union were of no concern.

A hope of positive political consequences is often the main inspiration behind arms-control efforts. If only the great powers can agree on sensitive military matters, perhaps they could also agree on some of the more fundamental issues that divide them. Unfortunately the very sensitivity of the military matters makes it very difficult to reach agreements unless the political relationship is already moving in the right direction, and a failure can exacerbate negative trends. The attempt to impose on arms control the political burden of improving overall East–West relations has largely been counterproductive.

Arms control is a modest but useful tool for managing military relationships and setting limits on military activity. It cannot be much more than that because the main sources of instability are largely political. If our world is to be more peaceful, this is where the most intensive and constant activity is required. The high priority assigned to the control of arms should not detract from the more traditional forms of diplomatic activity.

The politics of peace
A simple diagnosis of the political problem stresses the anarchic nature of international society, made up of independent states and lacking the firm control of a strong central authority. If there were no sovereign states, then who could call a war? So the remedy on this diagnosis is world government. This is clearly a nonstarter. Governments are not going to cede sovereignty along with their armed forces to a supranational authority

▲ Above, NATO's decision of December 1979 to introduce US cruise and *Pershing* missiles to Britain, Germany, Italy, Holland and Belgium sparked off mass protests throughout Europe, which reached their peak in 1983 with the imminent arrival of the first missiles. Here hundreds of demonstrators stage a "die-in" in the streets of Bonn.

▲ Below, one of the most sustained protests against the missiles was the women's peace camp established at Greenham Common in Britain, where 160 cruise missiles are to be based. The picture shows a protest at the gates of the base as the first missiles arrive in November 1983.

Can we hope to manage our unruly world?

Crisis management is normally taken to refer to the conventions by which nations seek to ensure that there is no slide into general war, even while they pursue their conflicting interests in an unusually tense situation. A crisis is a period in which the contradictory pressures of conflict and co-operation are at their most severe, usually because of a sense of an impending deadline. It is a crunch point, possibly similar to a medical crisis — the point at which the patient is likely to get much better or much worse. The compressed time-scale and the issues at stake make these moments of high drama, with frantic activity and flowing adrenaline in the corridors of power, of somber but stirring presidential broadcasts, of "hot lines" buzzing, of emergency sessions of the UN Security Council, and so on.

The idea behind the United Nations was that it should provide both the locale and the institutions for the settlement of disputes or at least the management of crises. The work of its agencies would create the conditions for improved understanding among nations — through programs on education, health and poverty, as well as disarmament. The General Assembly, in which every member has one vote, would provide a means of sounding out world opinion on the pressing issues of the day. However, the real weight of the UN would reside in the smaller Security Council, dominated by the five veto-holding permanent members. The Secretary-General, if given sufficient authority by the Security Council, could serve as an international statesman offering with his staff disinterested mediation.

It is easy enough to be cynical about the UN. Nevertheless, its agencies — especially those, such as the World Health Organization, that have avoided becoming too politicized — can boast real achievements. It still serves as the main location for crisis diplomacy. The Security Council provides an opportunity for some expression of general international feelings about the rights and wrongs of a particular dispute and allows individual nations the opportunity to declare their support. When some agreement has been cobbled together, whether or not the good offices of the UN have been used, it is often in a Security Council or General Assembly resolution that the achievement is marked. On many occasions it has been through the UN that peacekeeping forces have been organized to patrol cease-fire lines.

What it has lacked is the ability to impose solutions on warring parties. This ability

unless they are convinced that the new authority will not act against their interests. No such assurances could be given. A world government would be unwieldy and remote, with such concentrated power creating a potential for corruption and evil as much as for peace and beneficence. Nor would such an authority necessarily abolish war, except that all wars would now be civil. So any remedies will need to be more modest than total disarmament or world government. The best we can hope for is to manage our unruly and dangerous world. We might prevent catastrophe, even if we cannot eradicate war itself.

The prognosis need not be wholly gloomy. The sort of wars that would do the greatest damage have so far been prevented. Postwar Europe, with the development of the European Economic Community and the close cooperation between West Germany and France, demonstrates the extent to which traditional enemies can overcome their differences. This book has been full of disputes which have spilled over into war; little has been said about those instances where some accomplished diplomacy has allowed cooler heads to prevail. There is now a substantial body of experience on how best to prevent crises getting out of hand and organize the termination of wars. In exploring this experience we may begin to get some clues as to the best hopes for peace in current conditions.

KEEPING THE PEACE

When warring neighbors arrange a cease-fire, the United Nations is often called upon to provide forces to mark the new boundaries and keep erstwhile belligerents apart. Some countries, such as Sweden and Ireland, pride themselves on their readiness to provide forces for this sort of operation. By and large the peacekeeping forces have been successful, especially in consolidating a boundary that neither side has the means or the inclination to challenge. Where such challenges have existed, the record has been less impressive. For example, the United Nations force in south Lebanon (UNIFIL) was not able to prevent either Palestinian guerrilla operations against Israel or the Israeli retaliations. Israeli forces swept past UNIFIL when invading Lebanon in 1982. When the cease-fire was arranged, the preference this time was for a multinational force, made up of sympathetic Western nations rather than neutrals. A force of this type worked well in the Sinai, separating Israel from Egypt, but less well in the highly charged atmosphere of Lebanon. By 1985 even Israelis had come to the conclusion that the answer to the weakness of the UN forces might be to strengthen rather than replace them.

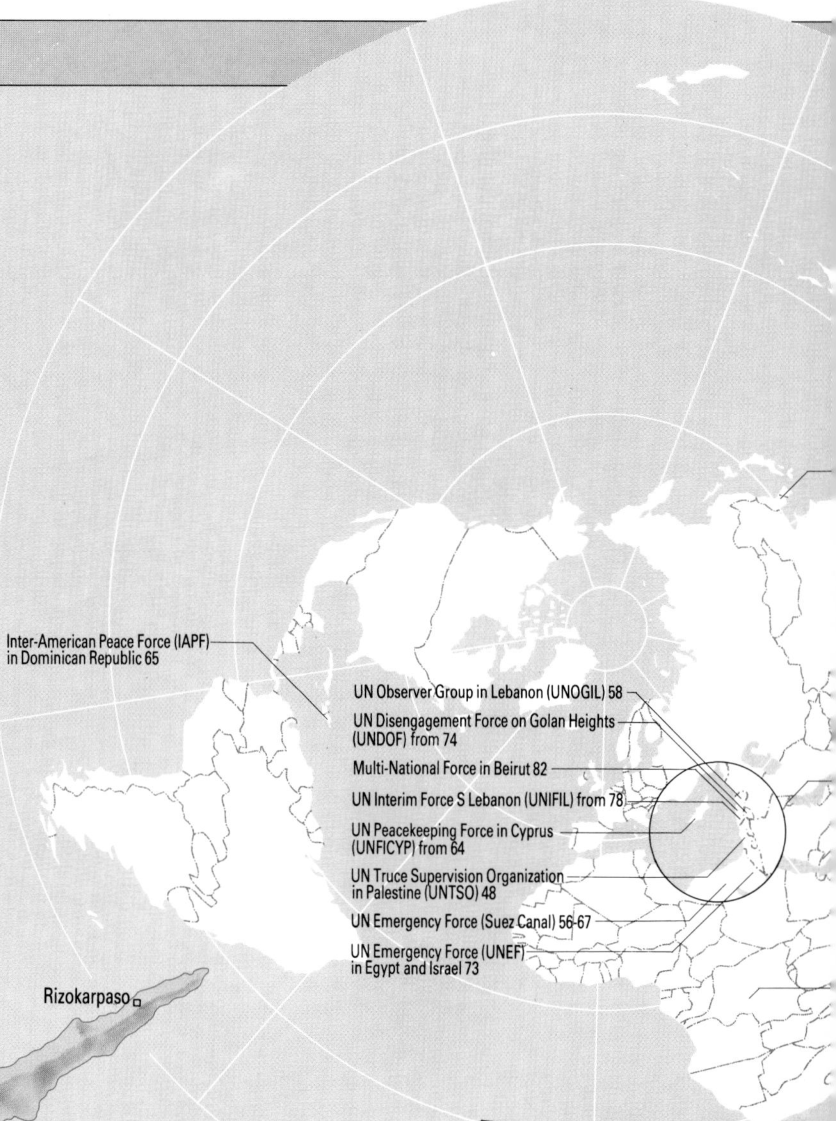

Inter-American Peace Force (IAPF) in Dominican Republic 65

UN Observer Group in Lebanon (UNOGIL) 58
UN Disengagement Force on Golan Heights (UNDOF) from 74
Multi-National Force in Beirut 82
UN Interim Force S Lebanon (UNIFIL) from 78
UN Peacekeeping Force in Cyprus (UNFICYP) from 64
UN Truce Supervision Organization in Palestine (UNTSO) 48
UN Emergency Force (Suez Canal) 56-67
UN Emergency Force (UNEF) in Egypt and Israel 73

UNFICYP CYPRUS 1964-

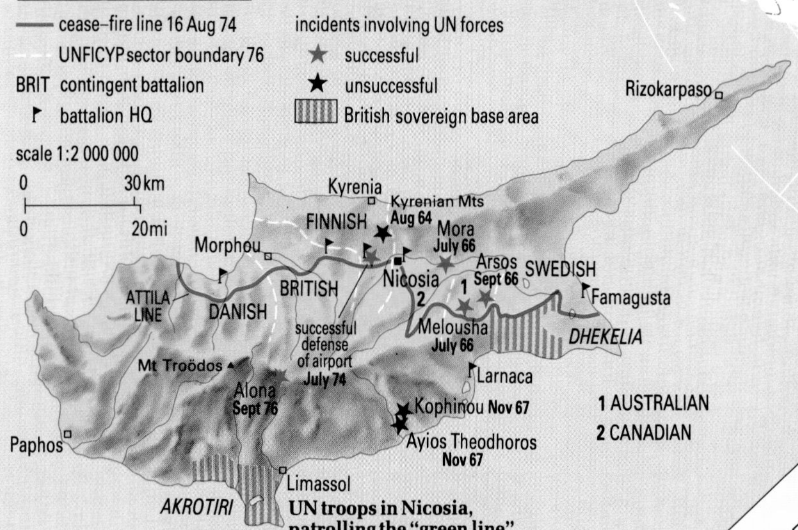

—— cease–fire line 16 Aug 74

—— UNFICYP sector boundary 76

BRIT contingent battalion

⌐ battalion HQ

incidents involving UN forces
★ successful
★ unsuccessful

||||| British sovereign base area

scale 1:2 000 000

0 ————— 30 km

0 ————— 20 mi

Rizokarpaso

Kyrenia
FINNISH
Kyrenian Mts Aug 64
Mora July 66
Morphou
Arsos Sept 66
Nicosia
SWEDISH
BRITISH
2
1
Famagusta
ATTILA LINE
DANISH
Melousha July 66
DHEKELIA
successful defense of airport July 74
Mt Troödos ▲
Larnaca
Alona Sept 76
Kophinou Nov 67
Paphos
Ayios Theodoros Nov 67
Limassol
AKROTIRI

1 AUSTRALIAN
2 CANADIAN

UN troops in Nicosia, patrolling the "green line" which separates Greek and Turkish Cypriots.

UNIFIL LEBANON 1978-

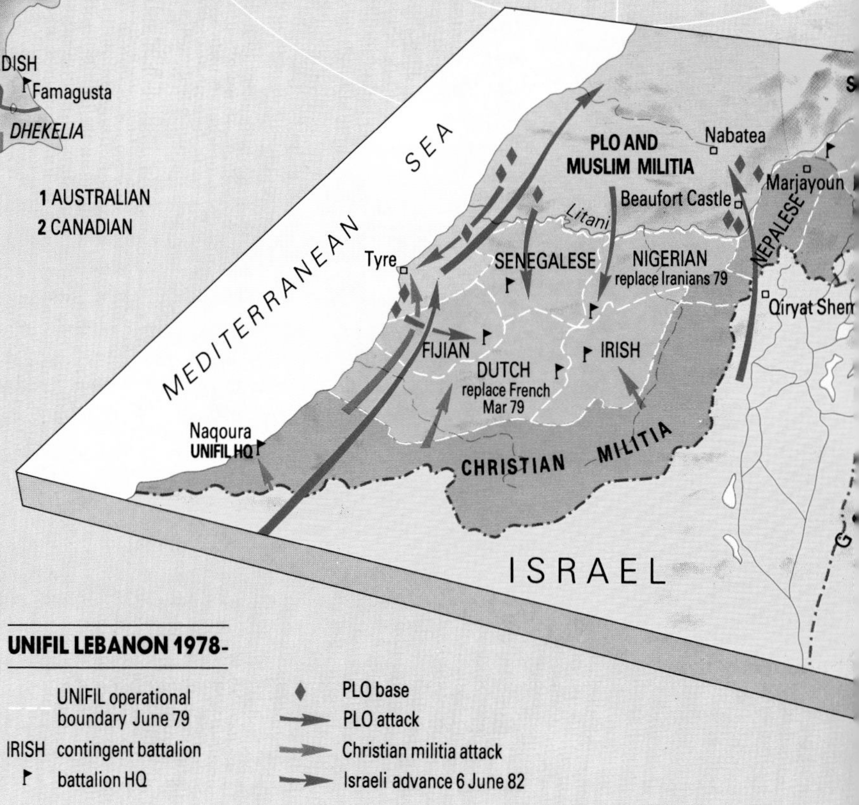

—— UNIFIL operational boundary June 79

IRISH contingent battalion

⌐ battalion HQ

◆ PLO base

→ PLO attack

→ Christian militia attack

→ Israeli advance 6 June 82

MEDITERRANEAN SEA

PLO AND MUSLIM MILITIA
Nabatea
Beaufort Castle
Marjayoun
Litani
Tyre
SENEGALESE
NIGERIAN replace Iranians 79
NEPALESE
FIJIAN
IRISH
Qiryat Shem
DUTCH replace French Mar 79
Naqoura UNIFIL HQ
CHRISTIAN MILITIA
ISRAEL

The experience of war strengthens the status quo

UN in West New Guinea (UNTEA) 62-63

UN in Korea 50–53

UN Military Observer Group in India and Pakistan (UNMOGIP) 48

UN India and Pakistan Observation Mission (UNIPOM) 65-66

Arab League Forces in Kuwait 61

UN Yemen Observation Mission (UNYOM) 63-64

UN Operation in the Congo (ONUC) 60-64

SYRIA

UNDOF ZONE

could only come through a general consensus among the permanent members and this has been noticeably lacking since the first days of the organization. The power of veto means that any solution which appeared to favor East at the expense of West or vice versa could not get far.

The weakness of the UN has meant that the superpowers have been seen as having the major responsibility for crisis management. Indeed the basic objective of crisis management has been seen to be to prevent a direct clash between the United States and the Soviet Union or a major East–West confrontation developing out of a conflict involving clients of the major powers. As we have seen in the preceding chapters, such a view no longer reflects the realities of contemporary international affairs. The superpowers have not had a real confrontation since the October 1962 Cuban missile crisis, except for the flurry at the end of the Arab–Israeli War 11 years later. However, the most exemplary crisis management during that war concerned the American attempts to use it to create the conditions for a later resolution of the Arab–Israeli dispute, the arguments the United States faced with its European allies in the organization of the support operation for Israel and the impact of the Arab appreciation of the power of the "oil weapon."

We have noted that, rather than international affairs taking the form of a continuing struggle between East and West, individual superpowers find themselves managing crises within their own "family," often able to trace only a small part of their difficulties to the activities of the opposing bloc. With many conflicts neither superpower is either able or willing to get involved and both steer clear.

Even when the superpowers are in agreement or at least indifferent on the most appropriate settlement to a conflict, working within or without the UN, they have found it increasingly difficult to impose solutions, simply because the relevant countries feel able to resist such impositions. The diffusion of power means that even the most substantial countries often lack leverage over others, or will use what leverage they have only to protect their own interests rather than to promote some general good. Regional organizations such as the Organization of African Unity or those with other ties to the parties in conflict such as the Islamic Conference are increasingly trying their hands at arranging settlements, but while they might be more sensitive to the nuances of local conditions, they still suffer the same problems as the

more international organizations in being paralyzed by any divisions among the more powerful members.

The future

On this basis it may seem that the best that can be offered for the future is more of the same. The superpowers will continue to respect each other's nuclear capabilities and avoid direct confrontations. Meanwhile, in a world beset by a series of economic and social problems, where boundaries and loyalties remain in dispute, and where there has been widespread distribution of military means, groups will continue to take up arms against unpalatable regimes and nations against hostile neigbors.

This picture is probably as realistic as any, but there are important qualifications that might be made. The propensity to go to war is in part conditioned by an awareness of its costs and the expectation of success. The American experience in Vietnam has had a lasting effect on that country's willingness to intervene with its own forces in the conflicts of others. The Soviet experience in Afghanistan may well have dampened its appetite for further overseas adventures. While neither would preclude employing military force anywhere on the globe to protect vital interests, both are sufficiently aware of the dangers of getting trapped in a military quagmire to be extremely cautious when making and implementing commitments to help others by military means. Britain recently discovered that it could not count on the easy presumption that its military forces have no role to play outside the NATO area. The Falklands campaign also demonstrated that it is not inevitable that wars drag on without a conclusion. However, the necessity of maintaining a substantial and expensive garrison on these remote islands to guard against a reinvasion is a reminder that the awkward consequences of a war can linger on long after the fighting has stopped. Once forces have been sent to an area to stabilize a situation, the fear will always be that their removal will lead to a revival of the previous instability. The preference of the major powers will still be to provide the instruments of war but not the manpower.

The largest question may be whether some of the newer military powers are coming to doubt the efficacy of war as an instrument of policy. The "quagmire" phenomenon, in which conflicts are revealed to be much easier to enter than to leave, has begun to affect them. For example, the Vietnamese

Future stability depends on prudent statesmanship

have been stuck in Kampuchea and the Iranians and Iraqis deadlocked throughout the 1980s. After wars in the previous three decades that were over within days, the Israelis found it extremely difficult to extract themselves from the Lebanon. These conflicts drain national treasuries, sacrifice youth and lose international goodwill. Governments are also aware that, while their populations may rejoice in military victory, they are unforgiving when it comes to those responsible for their defeat. Military dictatorships in Portugal, Greece and Argentina collapsed as a result of military failure.

Conclusion
Many of the more familiar tension points in the world are coming to resemble the Central European situation, with the demarcation lines between the potential belligerents well understood, with armed forces serving to mark out the boundaries and create forms of mutual deterrence, and international and regional diplomacy at a sufficient level of development to cope with any attempts to disrupt the status quo. This can be seen — in varying degrees — in the Middle East, in the Indian subcontinent and along the Sino–Soviet border. Three decades after the formal conclusion of the Korean War, North and South Korean forces, backed up in the latter case by the United States, still face each other across the cease-fire line.

This is not to say that we can anticipate a war-free future for all or any of these areas in the future. They remain tension points because of the powerful political differences at work. While it might be hoped that prolonged periods without actual fighting would allow forms of cooperation to develop and even a long-term settlement, this is not always the case. Some dramatic change in the area — for example a revolution in a hitherto moderate country or a sudden shift in the local balance of power — can destabilize the situation and lead to war.

It may be the case that the experience of war in the Middle East has not been encouraging for any of the participants. But the association of deeply felt religious differences with the occupation of particular pieces of territory is going to make it extremely difficult in the foreseeable future to envisage a lasting peace based on a genuine political settlement rather than a military standoff.

Even Europe, which has enjoyed remarkable peace and prosperity over the past four decades despite being divided and over-armed, has become very dependent not only on the prevailing sense of mutual deterrence but also on the durability of the underlying political arrangements, and in particular that of the two alliances. At various times since its formation the Warsaw Pact has been rocked by upheaval in one or other of its member states. Often by means of quite drastic measures, the Pact has managed to survive more or less intact. At some point in the future the recalcitrant might not be brought to heel so easily and the resultant shock waves could reverberate throughout the continent. Similarly, though not with the same intensity, NATO leaders have at times worried about the impact on the alliance of Communists coming to power in a country such as Italy.

It should not be thought that major political change invariably spells trouble. By removing a hostile element from the scene it can open new possibilities for reconciliation. All that is being stressed is that with warfare rarely offering itself as an easy option for those in dispute with their neighbors, it will need some substantial events to propel them into a confrontation with well-armed opponents.

Meanwhile the major causes of armed conflict in the future, as in the past, are likely to be domestic strife in countries suffering from economic or social troubles, or in those unable to command the loyalty of important sections of the community. When these break out into open conflict, external powers with an interest in the country may well get dragged in. A powerful neighbor or a superpower may feel tempted to intervene to swing a regional balance in its favor; a weak neighbor may find its territory being used by insurgents and then invaded by those seeking out the insurgents. So in many ways civil strife can take on a larger international dimension, and when it occurs in the midst of one of the critical regions such as the Middle East or Europe, then it could serve as the spark for the sort of conflagration that we all fear.

So far the international community has shown itself able to prevent wars getting completely out of hand but not to prevent them altogether. As the causes of war are to be found in the everyday life of nations and not just in high diplomacy, it would be unwise to exaggerate the impact that can be made by a constructive diplomacy and the strengthening of international institutions. Yet in the end it is prudent statesmanship upon which we must rely if the most awesome of the many engines of war that we have described are not to be set in motion, should the most severe of all the disputes that we have encountered erupt into violence.

BIBLIOGRAPHY

The issues raised in this book have generated a vast amount of literature, some of it highly specialized and some of it rather sensational. The sheer amount makes it impossible to print a comprehensive bibliography here and it has proved necessary to be extremely selective. The present bibliography attempts to give some indication both of the works that have been found useful in putting together this book and of the ones that are likely to be accessible to a reader interested in following up some of the issues raised. Articles in specialist journals have not been included, nor have more specialized books or polemics.

A number of institutes around the world now cater for those interested in security affairs. Often they are associated with a particular point of view, but the best maintain high standards of objectivity and provide a useful service in putting together high-quality information and analyses.

The most important of these is the London-based International Institute for Strategic Studies. Its annual, *Military Balance*, is the standard reference work for all facts and figures on military forces throughout the world and has been an important source for much of the information contained in this book. The Institute's other annual publication, *Strategic Survey*, reports on the major developments in defense policy, arms control, military technology and international conflict over the preceding year, and includes a useful chronology. Another standard reference work is the annual yearbook on *World Armaments and Disarmament* of the Stockholm International Peace Research Institute. SIPRI has done pioneering work on the arms trade and on chemical weapons. It has also made more effort than most institutions to popularize its findings. One example, which has been used in the preparation of this book, is *Countdown to Space War*, by Bhupendra Jasani and Christoper Lee (London, 1984).

Other institutes provide more specialized coverage. The Boston–based Institute for Defense and Disarmament Studies produces *The Arms Control Reporter*, described as a "chronicle of treaties, negotiations and proposals." The Georgetown Center for Strategic and International Studies backs the *International Security Yearbook*, edited by Barry Blechman and Edward Luttwak, two distinguished scholars normally associated with opposing positions on the political spectrum. This *Yearbook* provides an in–depth analysis of a few major issues and made a promising start in 1984. A number of organizations support an impressive individual effort by Ruth Leger Sivard on *World Military and Social Expenditures*. The Natural Resources Defense Council in the United States is sponsoring a major project to collect and publish full data on nuclear weapons. The first fruits of this project have been published as *Nuclear Weapons Databook*,

Volume 1, *US Nuclear Forces and Capabilities*, by Thomas B. Cochran, William M. Arkin and Milton M. Hoenig (Cambridge, Mass, 1984). Books like this are largely put together by sifting through the mass of information which can be found in official US publications, Congressional hearings and documents obtained through the Freedom of Information Act. The US Secretary of Defense's and the Chairman of the Joint Chiefs of Staff's annual reports to Congress contain a lot of information on US policies and plans. In recent years the Pentagon has also produced a glossy booklet on *Soviet Military Power*, which needs to be treated with care. The Arms Control and Disarmament Agency provides reference works on *Arms Control and Disarmament Agreements* and *World Military Expenditures and Arms Transfers*. The second of these is always a little out of date and suffers from the notorious problems faced even by the most impressive information–gathering machine in the world in obtaining reliable material on the arms trade.

The Soviet Union itself does not produce much information on its forces, though it has countered the Pentagon's assessment of its military power with one of its own on Western American military power, rather quaintly entitled *Whence the Threat to Peace*. Other countries, such as Britian with its annual *Statement on the Defence Estimates* and West Germany with its less regular *White Papers* on defense, are quite forthcoming.

Another substantial work of reference that does not have the advantage of being brought up to date regularly but provides full information on the history, background and composition of the armies of the world is *World Armies*, edited by John Keegan (London, 1983).

There are a number of atlases already available covering aspects of this book's subject matter. One example is *The War Atlas*, by Michael Kidron and Dan Smith (London, 1983) which uses maps to demonstrate the international distribution of military power. Tom Hartman and John Mitchell, *A World Atlas of Military History* (London, 1984), became available after this book was almost complete and covers the ground of Chapter Five. It provides some useful maps of actual campaigns. Another useful set of maps combined with a helpful text on the Middle Eastern conflicts is found in *The Middle East Conflicts from 1945 to the Present*, edited by John Pimlott (London, 1983). Also of use are *Atlas of 20th Century History* by Richard Natkiel (London, 1982) and *An Atlas of Territorial and Border Disputes* by David Downing (London, 1980).

An introduction to many of the issues raised in this book is *The Two Edged Sword: Armed Force in the Modern World* (London, 1982) by Laurence Martin, as is a book edited by the same author, *Strategic Thought in the Nuclear Age* (London, 1979). For a stimulating collection of essays on contemporary and historical questions see Michael Howard's *The Causes of Wars* (London, 1983). All the books and institutes mentioned above are relevant to a number of different sections.

Introduction

Those interested in the geographical dimensions of the subject should read *The Geography of Warfare*, by Patrick O'Sullivan and Jesse Miller (London, 1983). Two recent works drawing on traditional concepts of geopolitics and applying them to contemporary conditions are *The Geopolitics of the Nuclear Era* , by Colin Gray (New York, 1977) and *On Geopolitics: Classical and Nuclear*, edited by Ciro E. Zoppo and Charles Zorgbibe (Dordrecht, 1985).

For those interested in the history of strategic thought the best introduction remains the collection edited by Edward Meade Earle in 1943, *Makers of Modern Strategy* (Princeton, NJ). A new version of this with the same title and from the same publisher, but this time edited by Peter Paret, is expected soon. The changing character of war and its relationship to changes in society as a whole is covered in *War and Society in Europe, 1870–1970* (London, 1984) by Brian Bond.

The Changing International Order

For a readable if overstated account of the cold war see Daniel Yergin's *Shattered Peace: The Origins of the Cold War and the National Security State* (London, 1978). An excellent history of the origins of NATO is found in Sir Nicholas Henderson's *The Birth of Nato* (London, 1982), and of its later development in Alfred Grosser's *The Western Alliance: European–American Relations since 1945* (London, 1980). On the Soviet side, Thomas Wolfe's *Soviet Power and Europe, 1945–1970* (Baltimore, Md, 1970) is thorough although dated. For a more up-to-date discussion see Johnathan Steele's *World Power: Soviet Foreign Policy under Brezhnev and Andropov* (London, 1983). The full flavor of superpower diplomacy in the early 1970s, as the two edged towards détente, is found in the two volumes of memoirs of Henry Kissinger, who began as National Security Adviser to President Nixon in 1969 and concluded as President Ford's Secretary of State in 1976. The two volumes are *The White House Years* and *Years of Upheaval* (Boston, Mass, 1979 and 1982 respectively). A provocative account of the deterioration of superpower relations in the 1980s is found in Fred Halliday's *The Making of the Second Cold War* (London, 1983).

A useful reference work on non-fuel minerals is Philip Crowson's *Minerals Handbook, 1982–83* (London, 1982). A full discussion of the security issues raised by both fuel and non-fuel minerals is found in Hanns Maull's *Raw Materials, Energy and Western Security* (London, 1985).

The Changing Pattern of Warfare

There have been surprisingly few books on war since 1945. One exception is Michael Carver's *War since 1945* (London, 1980) which contains excellent short analyses of the course of some of the major conflicts and is especially strong on colonial wars. One author who has written extensively on individual wars is Edgar O'Ballance: *The Indo-China War* (1964); *Korea 1950–1953* (1969); *The Algerian Insurrection* (1967); *Malaya: The Communist Insurrection* (1966); *The Third Arab–Israel War* (1972), all published in London.

Vietnam is now attracting a considerable amount of analysis, of which one of the more controversial contributions is Harry G. Summers's *On Strategy: A Critical Analysis of the Vietnam War* (Novato, Cal, 1982). R.B. Smith has embarked on *An International History of the Vietnam War*, of which the first volume, *Revolution versus Containment, 1955–1961*, has now been published (London, 1983). Two other unusually perceptive books on individual wars are Chaim Herzog's *The War of Atonement* (London, 1975) on the 1973 Arab–Israeli War, and Max Hastings and Simon Jenkins on *The Battle for the Falklands* (London, 1983). These sources were used in Chapter Five.

The Brookings Institution has produced two volumes on the uses of armed forces as political instruments: Barry M. Blechman and Stephen S. Kaplan, *Force without War* (Washington, DC, 1978) and Stephen S. Kaplan, *Diplomacy of Power* (1981). Alexander George edited *Managing US–Soviet Rivalry* (Boulder, Colo, 1983). Michael Yahuda's *China's Role in World Affairs* (London, 1978) covers the Sino–Soviet split and China's foreign policy.

On terrorism see Paul Wilkinson's *Terrorism and the Liberal State* (London, 1977) and Walter Laqueur's *Terrorism* (London, 1977).

There is no adequate discussion of logistics in contemporary warfare, but an important study of the development of logistics up to 1945 is Martin Van Creveld's *Supplying War: Logistics from Wallenstein to Patton* (London, 1977).

The statistics on the arms trade were discussed earlier. The best attempt to make sense of the trade is Andrew Pierre's *The Global Politics of Arms Sales* (Princeton, NJ, 1982). Nuclear proliferation has also generated a large professional literature. One example of the collected essays which seem to be the normal form in which this issue is discussed is *Nuclear Proliferation: Breaking the Chain*, edited by George Quester (Madison, Wis,· 1981). A perceptive and readable discussion of the main issues is Norman Moss's *The Politics of Uranium* (London, 1981). An unusual account of the arguments that might work in favor of a particular country obtaining its own nuclear weapons is Shai Feldman's *Israeli*

Nuclear Deterrence: A Strategy for the 1980s (New York, 1982).

The Nuclear Arms Race

The best study of the consequences of nuclear war was produced by the Office of Technology Assessment of the US Congress, though *The Effects of Nuclear War* (1979) does not reflect more recent research on the "nuclear winter." The most thorough discussion of the consequences of the first two atomic bombs is found in the book compiled by the Committee for the Compilation of Materials on Damage Caused by the Atomic Bombs in Hiroshima and Nagasaki: *Hiroshima and Nagasaki: Physical, Medical and Social Effects of the Atomic Bombings* (London, 1981). A fair spread of the varying interpretations concerning the reasons why the first bombs were used is found in *The Atomic Bombs: The Critical Issues*, edited by Barbara J. Bernstein (Boston, Mass, 1976).

Lawrence Freedman's *Evolution of Nuclear Strategy* (London, 1981) provides a history of the main themes of nuclear strategy. Somewhat racier is Fred Kaplan's *The Wizards of Armageddon* (New York, 1983) which discusses the strategists themselves. Two books by Michael Mandelbaum, *The Nuclear Question* and *The Nuclear Revolution* (Cambridge, 1979 and 1981), of which the second is better than the first, discuss the impact of the advent of nuclear weapons on the international system. Robert Kennedy wrote a lively memoir of the Cuban missile crisis, *Thirteen Days* (London, 1969). On nuclear strategy as it relates to Europe see David N. Schwarz's *NATO's Nuclear Dilemmas* (Washington, DC, 1983) and also *Nuclear Weapons in Europe*, edited by Andrew Pierre (New York, 1984). The Brookings Institution in Washington has produced important collections on some of the critical issues in nuclear strategy, for example, *Cruise Missiles: Technology, Strategy, Politics*, edited by Richard Betts (1981) and *Ballistic Missile Defense*, edited by Ashton B. Carter and David Schwarz (1984).

Conventional War

There has been surprisingly little literature dealing with the theory of conventional warfare, but this may now be changing, as there is a growing interest in the subject. One example, although not wholly convincing as a general theory, is John Mearsheimer's *Conventional Deterrence* (Ithaca, NY, 1983). Less ambitious but useful surveys are Geoffrey Till's *Maritime Strategy in the Nuclear Age* (London, 1982) and M.J. Armitage and R.A. Mason's *Air Power in the Nuclear Age, 1945–1982* (London, 1983). On some of the ideas for the employment of high-technology weapons see the report of the European Security Commission, *Strengthening Conventional Deterrence in Europe* (London, 1983). General Sir John Hackett's *The Third World War: The*

Untold Story (London, 1982) gives some flavor of the possible dynamics of a European war, although it is fiction.

On guerrilla warfare see Robert Taber, *The War of the Flea: A Study of Guerrilla Warfare Theory and Practice* (London, 1965); Chalmers Johnson, *Autopsy on People's War* (Berkeley, Cal, 1983); and Douglas Blaufarb, *The Counter-Insurgency Era* (New York, 1977). Che Guevara's writings were at one time widely distributed. His *Guerrilla Warfare* and *Bolivian Diary* were published in London in 1969.

What is to be Done?

The Report of the Independent Commission on Disarmament and Security Issues was published as *Common Security: A Programme for Disarmament* (London, 1982). A collection of essays which takes this report as a starting point is Josephine O'Connor Howe's *Armed Peace: The Search for World Security* (London, 1984). An excellent introduction to a range of arms-control issues is Coit D. Blacker and Gloria Duffy's *International Arms Control Agreements* (Stanford, Cal, 1984). A fascinating view of the first Reagan administration's approach to nuclear arms control is Strobe Talbott's *Deadly Gambits: The Reagan Administration and the Stalemate in Nuclear Arms Control* (New York, 1984).

On crisis management see Phil Williams, *Crisis Management: Confrontation and Diplomacy in the Nuclear Age* (London, 1975), and Coral Bell, *The Conventions of Crisis: A Study in Diplomatic Management* (London, 1971). On the question of restraints once a war has started see *Restraints on War: Studies in the Limitation of Armed Conflict*, edited by Michael Howard (Oxford, 1979).

LIST OF ILLUSTRATIONS

INDEX